H. O. Nethercote, Charles Edmonds

The Pytchley Hunt

Past and Present. Second Edition

H. O. Nethercote, Charles Edmonds

The Pytchley Hunt
Past and Present. Second Edition

ISBN/EAN: 9783337134891

Printed in Europe, USA, Canada, Australia, Japan

Cover: Foto ©ninafisch / pixelio.de

More available books at **www.hansebooks.com**

THE
PYTCHLEY HUNT;

PAST AND PRESENT

ITS HISTORY FROM ITS FOUNDATION TO THE PRESENT DAY; WITH PERSONAL ANECDOTES, AND MEMOIRS OF THE MASTERS AND PRINCIPAL MEMBERS; INCLUDING THE WOODLANDS; ALSO UNPUBLISHED LETTERS OF SIR F. B. HEAD, Bart.,

BY THE LATE

H. O. NETHERCOTE, Esq.

FIFTY YEARS A MEMBER OF THIS FAMOUS HUNT.

WITH PORTRAITS OF EARL SPENCER, SIR CHARLES KNIGHTLEY, COL. ANSTRUTHER THOMSON, MR. GEORGE PAYNE, AND THE AUTHOR; AND A VIEW OF OLD PYTCHLEY HALL.

EDITED BY

CHARLES EDMONDS,

EDITOR OF THE "ISHAM" SHAKESPEARE; "BASILICON DORON" OF KING JAMES I.;
"THE POETRY OF THE ANTI-JACOBIN," ETC.

SECOND EDITION.

LONDON:
SAMPSON LOW, MARSTON, SEARLE, & RIVINGTON,
Limited,
St. Dunstan's House,
FETTER LANE, FLEET STREET.
1888.

In four volumes, Imperial 8vo, 31s. 6d. each,

Portraits of Celebrated Racehorses,
Past and Present, from 1702.

Containing over 400 plates, reproduced in fac-simile from the best pictures.

LONDON:
SAMPSON LOW, MARSTON, SEARLE, & RIVINGTON, LD.,
ST. DUNSTAN'S HOUSE, FETTER LANE, E.C.

Dedication.

~~~~~~~~

DEAR LORD SPENCER,

To whom could a history of the Pytchley Hunt be more fittingly dedicated than to a member of that illustrious family which has, not only from the earliest days of its institution been its main pillar and support, but which has furnished four of its most efficient and notable Masters?

Not aiming at writing a work that is likely to reach the dignity of "Criticism," I ask you to accept, for what it is worth, this effort of a "'prentice hand;" which is to give a record of hunting scenes and of hunting friends—many of the latter no longer to be found amongst us—many, happily, still remaining, to think of the past and hope for future joys. Though it would please me to think that within the pages of this work something will be found to interest those who live *outside* the "Pytchley Hunt,"—and not them only, but even the "Sporting World" generally,—it is, nevertheless, written by a "Pytchley man" for "Pytchley men;" and its biographical notices refer mainly, if not entirely, to certain of those who have, from time to time, during the last hundred years, been Masters or followers of this famous Hunt.

A fifty years' experience in the latter category enables me to speak with some authority of the persons and events alluded to in these pages; and I would fain hope that as "Naught has been set down in malice," so from "Neither fear, favour, nor affection" has anything been portrayed in any other light than that of

TRUTH.

TO THE READER.

The past and present History of the Pytchley Hunt was prepared for publication by its lamented Author, with great care and with no slight pleasure, in the hope that it might interest and amuse not the Hunting-world alone, but also a more extended circle of readers. Owing to the sad fact that the manuscript was completed only one day before his unexpected death, there was no opportunity for giving any finishing touches, or correcting any oversights.

The whole work has been superintended during its progress through the press, and the index, &c., compiled, by the Author's old friend and bookseller, Mr. Charles Edmonds, who had been previously solicited by him to perform these duties, at the appointed time.

C. F. N.

CONTENTS.

Part I.

HISTORY OF THE PYTCHLEY HUNT; TO THE DEATH OF MR. GEORGE PAYNE.

CHAPTER I.

Preliminary—John Bright and the Pytchley Hunt—Mr. B. Disraeli as a hunting-man—Sir Walter Scott, Dandie Dinmont's and the Pytchley packs—Alwin the hunter at Pytchley village, *temp.* William I.—Old Hall at Pytchley—Abbot of Peterborough a fox-hunter, *temp.* Richard II.—First pack of hounds; Lord Arundel's, 1670-1700; Hugo Meynell's, 1782; Earl Spencer's, 1750—The hounds and Club at Pytchley—"Order of the White Collar"—EARL SPENCER, *Master*, 1783-1796—Members of the Hunt in 1782—Mr. BULLER of Maidwell, *Master*, 1796—Diary of Thomas Isham, of Lamport—Mr. JOHN WARDE, *Master*, 1797-1808—Lane Family—Various dispositions of hounds—LORD ALTHORP, *Master*, 1808-1817—Letters to his father—Club at Pytchley re-established—"Rapping"—Three and four-bottle men—Jem Wood—Mr. Elwes and Mr. Small, great dandies—Mr. Davy—Mr. Nethercote of Moulton—Mr. Cook of Hothorp—Lords Jersey and Plymouth—Mr. Peter and Colonel C. Allix—Mr. Lucas—Mr. Bouverie of Delapré—Colonel Bouverie—Mr. Curwen—Mr. John Stevenson of Northampton—The Rev. John Whalley—Lord Waterford—Mr. Elmore—Mr. Andrew of Harleston—Charles King and his hunting-diary—Hunting better in old days—Sport-spoilers—Excellence of Sywell Wood—Lord Althorp resigns the Mastership 1

CHAPTER II.

Character of Lord Althorp; an Agriculturist and Breeder of Shorthorns; a boxer and supporter of pugilism; with anecdotes of Parson Ambrose; Lord Byron, and Jackson the prize-fighter; Gully, Cribb, and others—The prize-ring—FREDERICK, fourth EARL SPENCER—The Althorp District—Sandars Gorse—SIR CHARLES KNIGHTLEY, *Master*, 1817-18; a fine horseman, and breeder of Shorthorns—an ardent Horticulturist—his house at Fawsley, and secret chamber—LORD SONDES, *Master*, 1818-19—SIR BELLINGHAM GRAHAM, *Master*, 1819—Notices of some of the usual visitors to a Pytchley Meet: Dick Gurney; Squire Wood of Brixworth; Matthew Oldacre; Sir R. Murchison; Captain Blunt; Admiral Sir W. Pell; Rev. Vere Isham; Rev. John Whalley; Rev. W. Dickens; Rev. J. C. Humphrey; Rev. J. Wickes; and Rev. Loraine Smith—Henry Couch, a military deserter and felon; his singular career and extraordinary letters . . 31

CHAPTER III.

MR. JOHN CHAWORTH MUSTERS, *Master*, 1821—Opinions on his hounds—Troublesome foxes—Attachment of his hounds—His qualifications for the Mastership—MR. OSBALDESTON, *Master*, 1827—His appearance, manners and abilities—Excellence of his hounds—The best riders at Melton, 1820-30—Osbaldeston's excellence as a steeplechase rider—Race on 'Grimaldi' against 'Moonraker'—Celebrity of his bitch-pack—Run from Misterton to Laughton Mills—Match to ride 200 miles in ten hours, with the horses used—Challenges all the world for 20,000*l.*—As a shot, a cricketer, a boxer, an M.P., and a turfite—MR. WILKINS, *Master*, 1834—Jack Stevens, Huntsman, his early death—"Billy" Russell—MR. GEORGE PAYNE, *Master*, 1835—The EARL OF CHESTERFIELD, *Master*, 1838—Lords Cardigan, Maidstone, and Macdonald—Old times and manners—Perfection of Lord Chesterfield's arrangements—His resignation in 1840—The Hon. Wilbraham Tollemache—"Ginger" Stubbs, and other hunters—Dick Christian and Matty Milton—Old horses not so safe as young ones—Daniel Lambert—Mr. T. Assheton Smith—Dick Christian and Bill Wright 78

CHAPTER IV.

MR. T. "GENTLEMAN" SMITH, *Master*, 1840—SIR FRANCIS H. GOODRICKE, *Master*, 1842-44—The Brixworth Sporting-

Pauper—Mr. GEORGE PAYNE, *Master*, 1844-48—Mr. Bouverie and Mr. C. C. F. Greville, his turf-confederates—"Alarm," "Speed the Plough," and "West Australian"—Whist playing, 1836—Lord De Ros accused of cheating; and his action for slander—Mr. Payne a witness; his cross-examination—Sir W. Ingilby, a witness—Lord Alvanley's bon-mot—Mr. Payne's avidity for speculation—One in tallow—"Dirty Dick"—Fatal accidents in the hunting-field to Mr. Sawbridge and Lord Inverurie—Mr. Payne, a good host—His iron constitution—Warm affection for his sisters and brother—Letter to Mr. Nethercote on the latter's death—A regular church-attendant—A good "whip"—Sam Daniel, J. Harris, J. Meecher, Davis, and Jim Pearson, popular coachmen, till ruined by railways—An inebriated horse—Mr. Payne and his brother, bad cricketers—Excellence of the Northamptonshire Cricket Club—Mr. Payne a skilful pugilist, and a patron of the P.R.—Presentation of a silver Epergne—Resigns the Mastership, 1848, and retires from the hunting-field—His death—Song in his honour by a Northamptonshire farmer 112

Part II.

MEMOIRS OF THE FOLLOWING MASTERS
(Continuing the History to the Present Time).

Lord Alford, the Earl of Hopetoun, the Hon. F. Villiers, the Hon. C. Cust, Col. Anstruther Thomson, Mr. J. A. Craven, Earl Spencer, Mr. Herbert Langham (the present Master) . 149

Part III.

MEMOIRS OF MEMBERS.

Mr. A. A. Young, Capt. G. Ashby Ashby, Mr. Ambrose Isted, Mr. R. Lee Bevan, Mr. W. Angerstein, Capt. "Bay" Middleton, Capt. Mildmay Clerk, Major Whyte Melville, Hon. H. Liddell (Lord Ravensworth), Rev. H. Rokeby, Mr. W. H. Foster, Mr. and Mrs. Simson, the late Capt. Gist, Mr. Pender,

Contents.

PAGE

Mr. Jameson, Mr. Hazelhurst, Mr. Daniel, Mr. P. A. Muntz, Lord Braye, the late Rev. J. T. Drake, Lord Erskine, Mr. C. Wroughton, Mr. F. and Miss Langham, Sir Rainald Knightley, Bart., Mr. Drury Wake, Mr. J. Nethercote, Major Newland, Mr. Stirling Crawfurd, Lord Henley, Mr. J. Lovell, Sir Francis Bond Head, Bart., Capt. Riddell, Miss Alderson, Sir Charles Isham, Bart., Mr. J. Gilbert, Mr. John Bennett, Mr. Mills, Mr. J. Entwisle, Mr. J. Gough 233

MEMOIRS OF THE NORTHAMPTON BRIGADE . 330
MEMOIRS OF FARMER MEMBERS . . 333

MEMOIRS OF WOODLAND MEMBERS.

The Duke of Buccleuch, the Earl of Cardigan, Mr. Tryon, Lord Lilford, Lord Lyveden, Mr. Clarke Thornhill . . . 348

Appendix.

"THE PYTCHLEY:" A HUNTING-POEM 358
LETTER OF A YOUNG LADY-NATURALIST 360
UNPUBLISHED LETTERS OF SIR FRANCIS BOND HEAD, BART., on Hunting Subjects (including his last) 362

LIST OF PLATES.

	PAGE
VIEW OF OLD PYTCHLEY HALL	*Frontispiece*
PORTRAIT OF EARL SPENCER	188

    For the use of this portrait (on a reduced scale), the publishers are indebted to the courtesy of the proprietors of the "County Gentleman" *Sporting Gazette*.

PORTRAIT OF SIR CHARLES KNIGHTLEY, BART.	45
PORTRAIT OF MR. GEORGE PAYNE	99
PORTRAIT OF COLONEL ANSTRUTHER THOMSON	166

THE PYTCHLEY HUNT,
PAST AND PRESENT.

CHAPTER I.

Preliminary—John Bright and the Pytchley Hunt—Mr. B. Disraeli as a hunting-man—Sir Walter Scott, Dandie Dinmont's and the Pytchley packs—Alwin the hunter at Pytchley village, *temp.* William I.—Old Hall at Pytchley—Abbot of Peterborough a fox-hunter, *temp.* Richard II.—First pack of hounds; Lord Arundel's, 1670-1700; Hugo Meynell's, 1782; Earl Spencer's, 1750.—The hounds and Club at Pytchley—" Order of the White Collar"—EARL SPENCER, *Master*, 1783-1796—Members of the Hunt in 1782.—Mr. BULLER of Maidwell, *Master*, 1796—Diary of Thomas Isham, of Lamport—Mr. JOHN WARDE, *Master*, 1797-1808—Lane Family—Various dispositions of hounds—LORD ALTHORP, *Master*, 1808-1817—Letters to his father—Club at Pytchley re-established—" Rapping "—Three and four-bottle men—Jem Wood—Mr. Elwes and Mr. Small, great dandies—Mr. Davy—Mr. Nethercote of Moulton—Mr. Cook of Hothorp—Lords Jersey and Plymouth—Mr. Peter and Colonel C. Allix—Mr. Lucas—Mr. Bouverie of Delapré—Colonel Bouverie—Mr. Curwen—Mr. John Stevenson of Northampton—The Rev. John Whalley—Lord Waterford—Mr. Elmore—Mr. Andrew of Harleston—Charles King and his hunting-diary—Hunting better in old days—Sport-spoilers—Excellence of Sywell Wood—Lord Althorp resigns the Mastership.

IT may be safe to assert that no institution, sporting or otherwise, ever received a more unintentional and marked tribute to its popularity, than in the laughter which greeted the ears of Mr. John Bright when one night in the House of Commons he called "the Pytchley Hunt" "the Pitchley." Honourable Members seemed

B

astonished that one of their number, and that so distinguished a one as the senior member for Birmingham, should be ignorant of the proper mode of pronouncing the name of this well-known hunt, and received the "lapsus linguæ" with shouts of amusement. Often before had the great orator moved the august occupants of the benches around him to laughter, but on no previous occasion, perhaps, had he so fairly "brought down the House" as on this. Unlike his great political opponent, Lord Beaconsfield, who, at least on one occasion, seems to have distinguished himself on the "Pigskin," Mr. Bright had probably never seen a pack of hounds in the field. To him "the Quorn," "the Pytchley," and "the Cottesmore," are institutions unworthy the notice of any rightly thinking man, and great must have been his surprise at finding that so small an error had raised so great a laugh. His illustrious rival, on the occasion just referred to, seems, by his own account, to have accomplished a feat in the saddle quite equal to any that he performed on the floor of the "House." Writing to his sister in 1834, he says, "I hunted the other day with Sir Henry Smith's hounds, and, although not in pink, was the best-mounted man in the field; riding an Arabian mare, which I nearly killed, a run of thirty miles; and I stopped at nothing." A run of thirty miles on an Arabian mare, and stopping at nothing! The reader of such a performance may well borrow the exclamation of Dominie Sampson, and exclaim "Prodigious." "Of all pleasure cometh satiety at last," says the moralist; and whatever the sensations of the rider may have been during the last three or four of the thirty miles, it is clear that the Arabian mare had had enough of it. But as the "Dizzy" of old could, according to this statement, have given the great demagogue any amount of weight across a country, so he, on his part, would have been "lost" by his opponent across the waters of a salmon river. Had the unpretentious stream dividing the Lordships of Pytchley and Isham been a rapid torrent, the home of speckled trout or lordly salmon, instead of only that of the pugnacious minnow and lowly "miller's thumb," a residence in the village for fishing purposes might have taught the great piscator the correct pronunciation of its name. Even in this respect Mr. Bright was in good company, as Sir Walter Scott, in describing the fox-hunting with Dandie Dinmont's heterogeneous pack, says that a member of the "Pychley" (leaving out the "t") Hunt might have cast a supercilious look both on the equipment of the horsemen, and the queer admixture of the hounds! It is somewhat singular that in the records of the village from whence the Pytchley Hunt derives its title there is to be found, in the times prior to those of William the Conqueror the name of one "Alwin the huntsman;" evidently a personage of some importance, whose duty it was to destroy the wild animals frequenting the adjacent forests. Those who are fortunate enough to possess the clever pen-and-ink sketch of the "Old Hall at Pytchley,"[1] done by the late George Clark, schoolmaster of Scaldwell, will see that it was built in the reign of Queen Elizabeth by Sir Euseby Isham, and that the ancient Lords of the Manor held it of the King on the condition

[1] A reduced copy of this sketch forms one of the illustrations to the present volume.—ED.

"to furnish dogs at their own cost to destroy the wolves, foxes, polecats, and other vermin in the counties of Northampton, Rutland, Oxford, Essex, and Buckingham." The house and estate passed successively through the families of Isham, Lane, Washbourne, and Knightley. It then became the property of Mr. George Payne, who pulled the house down in 1829, and afterwards sold the estate to Mr. Jones Loyd, father to the late Lord Overstone, who left it to his daughter and her husband, Lord and Lady Wantage, whose property it now is (1886). The conditions upon which the Lords of the Manor of Pytchley held their possessions seem to have been sufficiently onerous; but it must not be forgotten that hunting in those days and hunting in the present differ from each other in a far greater degree than hunting with the Quorn or Pytchley, and hunting with trencher-fed packs on the Cumberland Hills, do now.

At the period when wolves and other beasts of prey inhabited the forests which covered the greater surface of the island, the one object of the hunter was to kill and destroy in the interest of the occupant of the land. The wolf of that day had not been educated up to lying down with the lamb, unless he was inside him; and the ravages among flocks and herds by wild animals greatly added to the difficulties of the agriculturist. He who now kills a fox, otherwise than by the aid of hounds (unless indeed by accident), earns for himself the opprobrious name of "Vulpicide," and is likely to become a "Pariah" in society and a "Boycottee." In the far-off days of which we are speaking, the Lupicide and the fox-killer were looked upon as public benefactors, and worthy of all commendation. An "unsportsmanlike"

PYTCHLEY HALL.

action could not, at that period, be committed, as the meaning now attached to the word "sport" was then unknown. "Crossbow" and "net" first, and "gun" afterwards, were the legitimate allies of hounds and terrier, nor was it easy, even with this assistance, to keep down the number of the destroyers. In the days of Alwin, the Pytchley huntsman, who has been referred to above, the fox was not even included in the list of animals of the chase. The stag and hare are constantly mentioned as being hunted by the Anglo-Norman sportsmen, but the first notice we have of the fox occurs in the reign of Richard the Second, when the Abbot of Peterborough becomes entitled by charter to pursue that wily animal.

It is not easy to say when the first regularly appointed pack of hounds was established, but this could not have been until the beginning of the last century at soonest. So long as the country remained disafforested, the hart, the wolf, the wild boar, and the hare were the principal objects of the chase: and the harrier long had the precedence of the foxhound. At first the neighbouring farmers kept a hound or two each (as is still the custom in Cumberland and some of the neighbouring counties), and joined together occasionally to kill a fox that had waxed fat upon their lambs and poultry. Next a few couples were kept by small Squires who could afford the expense; and they joined packs: and so by slow degrees, as riding in "the open" became more feasible, the present system was elaborated. It is known, however, that Lord Arundel kept a pack of foxhounds between the years 1670 and 1700, which hunted in Wiltshire and Hampshire; and it is from the descendants of those hounds that the famous Hugo Meynell formed his pack at Quornden in 1782.

About thirty years before this, John George, Earl Spencer, the first of the four Masters furnished by this noble house, formed a club at the old Hall in the little village of Pytchley, and removed the hounds from Althorp to kennels erected at that place. Lord Spencer now introduced the system of dividing the country into two, and hunting the woodlands and that part of the open lying east of the Northampton and Market Harbro' road, during certain months of the season; the part lying west of the dividing-line being reserved for the remaining months. The system of not drawing any covert over the allotted boundary was so rigidly adhered to, that, even in the event of a kill, the hounds were always taken back to the side on which the fox was found. This so circumscribed the country that the same coverts were being constantly disturbed, with the result that blank days were of frequent occurrence; an event unknown in the present time.

The county gentlemen and strangers who were members of the Club made the old Hall their residence for just as long as suited their convenience; the apartments, as they became vacant, being eagerly taken up by candidates for the "Order of the White Collar." It is somewhat singular that it is uncertain to what cause this badge of distinction owes its origin; nor is any allusion to it to be found in any of the records of the hunt kept at Althorp.

Lord Spencer, the founder of the Pytchley Club, died in 1783; and his son, also named "John George," who took a prominent part in politics, and became First Lord of the Admiralty, assumed the Mastership of the country, and held it thirteen years. He was a very fine horseman, and his stud was formed of animals of the highest class only. So different were the customs of that time from what they happily are now, that it was held to be contrary to etiquette for any one to pass his lordship in the field, except the huntsman. During these years, the Pytchley Hunt attained a high degree of popularity, many of the magnates of the land being desirous of becoming members of it. To what an extent this was the case may be learned from the subjoined list of the names on the books at the Club in 1782 :—

Earl Spencer.
Earl of Jersey.
Earl of Westmoreland.
Marquis of Graham.
Viscount Althorp.
Duke of Devonshire.
Viscount Torrington.
Earl of Winchelsea.
Lord R. Cavendish.
Earl of Aylesford.
Earl of Powis.
Hon. G. St. John.
Mr. Knightley.
Mr. Scawen.

Mr. Powis.
Mr. Conyers.
Mr. C. Finch.
Mr. Raynsford.
Earl of Lincoln.
Viscount Fairoord.
Sir Horace Mann.
Hon. F. Granville.
Mr. Bouverie.
Mr. Poyntz.
Mr. Fleming.
Mr. Hatton.
Mr. Doughty.
Mr. Assheton Smith.

To the great regret of all connected with the Pytchley Hunt, political duties necessitated Lord Spencer, in 1796, to relinquish the post he had filled with so much distinction for thirteen years; and for one season, Mr. BULLER, of Maidwell Hall, undertook the management of affairs. Lord Spencer's celebrated huntsman, "Dick Knight," has left a name which will ever be remembered in the records of not only the Pytchley Hunt, but also of the huntsmen-heroes of the past. Born at Courteenhall, of parents in whose eyes there was "nothing like leather," he was brought up to make rather than wear a top-boot; but a natural love for all things pertaining to sport soon got him among hounds and horses; and advancing step by step he succeeded in attaining the pinnacle of his ambition by becoming Huntsman to the famous Pytchley Hounds. In the well-known picture by Mr. Loraine Smith, of Enderby Hall, Knight is portrayed as finishing a run on a cart-horse taken out of a plough team, his own animal being completely knocked up. In a second picture by the same skilful hand, he is depicted jumping a fence beneath the overhanging bough of a tree, with head bowed downwards and both legs over his horse's neck. The reason of his appearing in this somewhat unusual attitude was, that one day at the Meet a stranger said to him, " Knight, I've heard a good deal of your riding, but if you beat me to-day, I will give you the horse I am on." " All right, sir," said Knight, " we shall see." During the run they came to a fence, the only jumpable place in which was under a tree, the branches of which overhung, and scarcely left space sufficient for a man and horse to get through. Bending his head and throwing his legs over his animal's neck, Dick went through the opening like a clown through a drum. This was too much for the stranger, who preferred losing his horse to risking his neck by following, and honourably carried out what he had undertaken to do, by sending his steed to the more plucky horseman on the following morning. Knight was famous for possessing a voice so powerful that a well-known sportsman used to declare that from his house at Wellingborough he could on a clear frosty morning hear Dick's "holloa" in Sywell Wood, a distance of, at least, three miles as the crow flies. This speaks well for the acoustic properties of the atmosphere between the respective points spoken of, as well as for the strength of Dick's lungs. But a still more remarkable instance of the far-reaching power of sound is given in the interesting diary, written in Latin in the seventeenth century (admirably translated by the Rev. Robert Isham), of Mr. Thomas Isham of Lamport Hall. It is there stated that during the naval engagement between the English and French combined fleets on the one hand, and the Dutch on the other, in 1672, the report of the guns was distinctly heard at Brixworth. It was in this action that Lord Sandwich, the admiral, was blown up in his ship, with eight hundred of his men, though the Dutch were defeated, and were pursued to the coast of Holland by the English fleet. If this story be correct, and some may be tempted to say "Credat Judæus," the voice of the cannon must have travelled a distance of over 120 miles, Southwold being at the mouth of the Blythe, twenty-eight miles north-east of Ipswich. In 1827, during the battle of Navarino, Mr. John Vere Isham, then quartered at Corfu, distinctly heard the firing at a distance of, at least, 200 miles; and on the naval reception of the Sultan by the Queen at Portsmouth, the sound of guns discharged on the Welsh coast was plainly distinguished at Portsmouth.

Knight was so highly esteemed by his master that the latter overlooked a freedom of speech in him which certainly would have been ventured upon by no other man, be his position what it might. It was said that on one occasion, seeing Lord Spencer taking a longish look at a fence, he called out to him "Come along, my lord, the longer you look at it, the less you will like it." The line of hills facing Marston and Theddingworth village being neutral, a good deal of jealousy arose between the "thrusters" of the respective hunts; and Mr. Assheton Smith (father of Tom A. Smith) used to try and cut down Dick Knight. Hence the *motif* of the picture, by the same talented hand as the others before spoken of, in which the Pytchley Huntsman, mounted on his famous horse "Contract," is supposed to be saying that "he would show these d—d Quornites a trick."

In the following year, 1797, the country was taken by the well-known sportsman and M.F.H., Mr. JOHN WARDE, a gentleman, who at the termination of his hunting career was able to boast that he had been a Master of Hounds for fifty-seven years. Not approving the system of dividing the country into two parts, he established himself in the old Hall at Boughton, near Northampton, built kennels there, and made that village his place of residence. During the eleven years of his Mastership, the Club at Pytchley was closed, and it seemed as if "Ichabod" were written on the portals of this fashionable seat of hunting. Another member of the Spencer family, however, as will shortly appear, restored it to all its pristine glory. For three generations, the care and management of the Club in all its domestic arrangements were in the hands of the family of Lane, a member of which, himself born in the old Hall, still survives to tell the tale of other days. Nearly fourscore years having constituted him the oldest tenant on the Wantage estate, he was called upon at the audit dinner of 1886, to propose the health of the new landlord, Lord Wantage. Few then present will forget the impressive manner in which the venerable and much respected gentleman performed this duty, the feeling of his being a link with the phase of the county history now passed away adding in no slight degree to the interest of his words and appearance. May the name that he bears long survive to uphold the high character of the Northamptonshire tenant-farmer, and remind future generations of the old Pytchley days.

Mr. Warde, who from a photograph in the possession of the writer (taken, of course, from a picture) in which he is represented mounted on a well-bred horse, with a favourite hound looking up in his face, must have been a man of enormous bulk, and in every respect one of the old-fashioned sort. He was remarkable for the bone, size, and power of the hounds he bred; which he did on the principle that you may at pleasure diminish the size and power of the animal you wish to breed, but it is not easy to increase or even maintain a standard that it has taken years to attain. It was thought that his hounds always carried too much flesh; but he defended this on the score that it was essential in a country where big woodlands had to be hunted. In this view he was supported by the celebrated Tom Rose, Huntsman to the grandfather of the present Duke of Grafton. Such hounds would hardly be suited to the present style of riding, when the "ladies" are kept for the "big" Meets, because they are smaller, more active and more capable of escaping danger from the mob of horsemen than the less wieldy "gentlemen." The former, too, have another advantage over the rival sex.

When ridden over they forget it sooner, and do not take the injury so much to heart as their " big brothers" are in the habit of doing. These will frequently resent the offence for an entire day, skulking about and doing no work; whilst one of his " little sisters" will forgive and forget a few minutes after having received an injury. In more points than people are aware of, are hounds of like passions with human beings. Like their masters, not only are they loving, grateful or industrious, but they form high opinions of their own abilities and give themselves airs so ridiculous as to be highly amusing to those who are conversant with their habits. All who are accustomed to hounds are often struck with the opposite characters of those of one and the same litter. Mr. Warde bred two puppies in 1787, Alfred and Audrey; the former was the wildest and most difficult hound to break he ever had; the latter was steady from the first and gave no trouble, and her master used to say of her, "When the rest are of no use, Audrey is my best friend." During a fair hunting-run, one day, from Sandars Covert to Holcot Bridge, a puppy was observed by one of the field to be following on the line when some of the older ones had failed to acknowledge it. "That will make a good hound, some day, Will," said the gentleman who had noticed the performance, to the Huntsman. "Yes, sir," was the reply, "if what he has just done doesn't make him too *conceited.*" At the time when hard riding first came into vogue, and Mr. Warde's big hounds began to be voted "slow," the Meltonians were in the habit of speaking of them as "Warde's jackasses;" but they never brayed without reason, and were so much better on cold-scenting days than the smaller and faster hounds, that they were in high favour with all who enjoyed hunting for hunting's sake. One of the great runs of Mr. Warde's time was from Marston Wood to Skeffington in Leicestershire. It would seem from the subjoined letter of Lord Althorp to his father, dated May 28th, 1804, that there must have been some difficulties between Mr. Warde and certain members of the hunt, on the withdrawal of the hounds from Pytchley to Boughton. In it he writes: "At the Pytchley meeting on Saturday, Doughty, Carter, Cartwright and Thornton, desired to take their names out of the list; but we agreed not to do it until they had heard what we settled about the hounds going to Pytchley. We agreed that the first meeting should begin the first Monday in November, and last four weeks: and that the second should begin the second week in February, and last six weeks. John Warde said that the hounds should hunt from the Pytchley kennels during the whole of both these meetings, though I confess that I do not think that he is pledged to it so completely as I could wish. I hope, however, that you will be able to settle the arrangement completely when you see him."

Four years afterwards, writing from Delapré Abbey to his father, Lord Althorp says: " Feb. 12th, 1808. Dear Father,—I have to tell you that I have concluded the bargain with John Warde, and am to give him a thousand pounds for the hounds, and not to have anything to do with the horses. I have done this because I should not have felt comfortable if, after all the civilities he has all along shown me, he had any excuse whatever to complain of my conduct towards him." A fortnight after this we read in a letter dated "Pytchley,

March 2nd, 1808. Dear Father,—John Warde has put the hounds entirely into my management, and never comes out himself; so that at present I am answerable for all the merit and the reverse of the pack that comes out. My luck has as yet been extreme. Monday was the first day I took them out in the open. It was a bad scent, but the old pack hunted quite perfectly, and we ran from Sywell Wood to Drayton Park, but did not kill. I took the young hounds out yesterday, who are as bad a pack as anybody ever saw; but fortunately we had a good scent, and got a tolerable run. We found a second fox in Harrington Dales and went away with him at best pace to Shortwood. We then hunted at a forward hunting-scent over Lamport earths to Maidwell, where we again set to very hard running over Harrington and Rothwell fields, through Thorpe Underwood over the brook by Gaultney Wood; got a view of him near Dob Hall, and killed him near Gaultney Wood, in an hour and twenty minutes. From Maidwell to killing was a decided burst without a check; and every horse was tired except my 'Poacher' and Felton Hervey's horse. I do not often give you an account of a run, but I think you will be pleased to hear of my beginning so well, as it will make people sanguine about my system (though it has nothing to do with it), and will keep up the subscriptions." Then follows a postscript, not without its interest: "I have gained some credit for not hunting on Ash Wednesday, when every pack in the neighbourhood did."

We have now, John, Viscount Althorp, afterwards Chancellor of the Exchequer, one of the most distinguished statesmen of the day, established as Master of the Pytchley

Hunt. The hounds were again taken back to Pytchley for a part of the season, as of old; and the Club so long left out in the cold, recovered all its former attractions. Writing of this period, "the Druid" says: "Pytchley was at that time in the zenith of its glory. The mornings afforded unmixed pleasure, and nectar crowned the night." Among the names of members of the Club at that time, those of Knightley, Elwes, Payne (father of George Payne), Nethercote, Lord Sondes, Davy, Rose, Cook, Hanbury, Isham, were all of the county—whilst among the strangers were those of Hugo Meynell, Gurney (Dick), Sir David and James Baird, Allix, Lucas, Bowen, Frank Forester, Sefton, Hervey, &c., &c. The studs were of the first order, and the riders were worthy of them. Jealousy was unknown, and sport alone was the object of all." In asserting thus much the author of "Silk and Scarlet" contemplates a state of things which probably never existed at any time or in any place where men and horses were jointly concerned; but it is likely that jealous riding was not nearly so common then as now. There were "bruisers" in those days, but they were not so frequent as they became when, wealth getting more generally diffused, the number of hunting-men increased twentyfold. A somewhat peculiar custom at the Club was, that any member after dinner, on depositing half-a-crown in a wine-glass, might name and put up to auction the horse of any other member, the owner being entitled to one bid on his own behest. This custom was called "rapping," from the raps on the table which accompanied each bid. It was on one of these occasions that Mr. Nethercote sold "Lancet" to Mr. John Cook, of Hothorp, for the then unprecedented sum of 620*l*. To judge of him from a painting at Moulton Grange, he was a chestnut horse, standing about 15.3, with good shoulders, strong quarters, a sensible head, and a hunter all over in appearance. Sir Charles Knightley, than whom there was no better judge, used to say that barring a little lack of quality, he was as nice a horse as could be seen. By the advice of his friend, the Rev. Loraine Smith, Mr. Nethercote bought him from a doctor at Leicester for 120 guineas, and so highly did he himself esteem him as a performer in the field, that his own bid for him was 400 guineas. On the following morning, the vendor, thinking it likely that his old college-friend had bid under the influences more common after dinner than at an earlier hour, proposed that the bargain should be off. Mr. Cook, however, declared his determination to retain the horse; and many years afterwards assured the writer of these lines that he only wished that at that moment he could find another "Lancet" at the same price. The incident created some sensation at the time, and is referred to in a history of Northamptonshire, by the Rev. W. James, of Theddingworth. The amount, large as it was, was exceeded soon after by Lord Plymouth giving Mr. Peter Allix of Swaffham House, near Newmarket, 700*l*. for a mare not fit to carry more than twelve stone; and this purchase was not an after-dinner one, when things are apt to be somewhat in favour of the vendor. When the wine is in, the wit is said to be elsewhere; and at a period which may be called the "three-bottle one," it must have been incumbent on every prudent man not to take part in the post-prandial "rap." In the days now spoken of, the man who could not quietly dispose of three bottles of old port was not held in much esteem as a boon companion; nor did the seasoned soaker see any necessity for drawing a line at three bottles, as we learn from an anecdote of the times, in which it is stated that a lady, hearing a gentleman say that "he had finished his third bottle" of port after dinner, asked in some surprise: "What, sir! unassisted?" "Oh, no, ma'am," was the answer, "I was assisted by a bottle of Madeira!" In these days we can scarcely believe that the greatest statesman of his own and perhaps of any time, as he entered the House of Commons one night, declared to the friend by his side that "he saw two Speakers!" and that he did this *sans peur et sans reproche!*

Never did country have a more efficient Master than John, Viscount Althorp, who, politics notwithstanding, devoted himself heart and soul to his new duties. For eight months out of the twelve he was constantly with his hounds; and he spared no expense nor trouble in the improvement of the pack, the size of which he thought it wise to reduce. A bold and determined rider, heedless of the convenient gate, and with no sort of knowledge of the whereabouts of " Shuffler's bottom," his song to his hounds ever was, " Where thou goest I will go." Posting horses at convenient distances on the road, he would frequently ride from Spencer House, St. James's, to Pytchley, for the next day's hunting. Though a courageous, he was by no means a polished, horseman; and a loose seat brought with it many a fall that might have been avoided. So frequently did he dislocate his shoulder that he sent one of his whips to the Northampton Infirmary to be instructed how to put it in. So liable did the limb become to dislocation that it would occasionally get displaced if he chanced to throw up his arm in going over a fence. In the cub-hunting season he usually took a cottage at Brigstock with Sir Charles Knightley, so that he might watch the conduct of the new entries; and he thus acquired a thorough knowledge of hunting. His stud usually consisted of about thirty horses, all of high character, and the cost of his establishment was seldom less than from 4500*l.* to 5000*l.* per annum. In the summer of 1810, writing from Ryde to his father, with his thoughts, as usual, ever full of hunting, he says: "Since you have been gone, I have been learning to draw horses and hounds, in order to increase the number of my Brigstock amusements; and for the furtherance of this purpose I have ordered George Bentley to show you some studies of horses by Stubbs and Gilpin, and bring them here with you. I was surprised and rather disappointed at putting my shoulder out in opening a window, but am somewhat comforted at finding it is a very likely thing to do; for in opening the same window with my left arm, I perceived that the whole strain came from the shoulder."

After Lord Althorp's marriage with Miss Acklom, heiress to the Wiseton estate in Nottinghamshire (who died in her confinement in the following year), he lived for one year at Dallington Hall, but Spratton being vacant he wished to move there, the position being more favourable for hunting. In the spring of 1814, he thus writes on this matter to his father: "I do not quite agree with you on the relative merits of Dallington and Spratton. I allow that the house at Dallington is the best of the two, but Spratton is quite good enough,

The neighbourhood at Spratton is better than the other; the roads better, and the country, if anything, rather prettier. The distance to ride from Althorp is nothing, and Esther (Lady Althorp) will not want to go backwards and forwards often in a carriage. When to these considerations I add that it is in nearly the best possible situation for hunting both the Pytchley and Althorp countries, I cannot help preferring it to the other." In a letter dated Spratton, March 31st, 1815, he says: "We have had the most extraordinary sport I ever saw in my life. On Tuesday, after a burst from Blueberries of forty minutes to ground beyond Brixworth, we found at three o'clock at Pursers Hills, and after a ring by Maidwell and Scotland Wood, went straight away and killed our fox beyond Little Harrowden in two hours. Yesterday we ran from Sywell Wood to Pipwell, and killed there in an hour and a half." The shoulder-trouble continued, for we find in a letter written from Ecton to his father, two years after the above: "I had a severe fall yesterday and put my shoulder out again. I was copiously blooded and am rather weak and stiff to-day." One of Lord Althorp's best runs was from Pursers Hills, by Hothorp, to Wistow in Leicestershire, where the fox was killed; the first fifty minutes being without a check. Twice in one year a fox found at Crick was killed in Badby Wood; and on another occasion, after a brilliant hour and seventeen minutes from the same covert, by Lilbourne, Hempton, Naseby and Sibbertoft, the death took place at Marston village. Besides the Master himself, amongst the many who rode well to hounds, were Sir Charles Knightley, who will be referred to later on; Mr. Elwes of Billing—light as a feather, and so great a dandy that he had his hunting-boots made by three different artists, the tops by the well-known Tom Marshall of Northampton, and the centres and feet by two separate professors. In point of dandyism, however, the Squire of Billing was not "in the hunt" with a Mr. Small, whose great object in life seems to have been to act the "Beau." He wore a round-crowned hat, fitting him like a hunting-cap; a pepper-and-salt coat; leather breeches, beautifully cleaned, buttoning high above the boot; boots like polished ebony, very short tops; and narrow leather garters with small silver buckles. He was no less particular about the appearance of his horses, his bits and stirrups being most highly polished. He had two black mares exactly alike; both had their ears cropped and he rode each in a martingale. His saddle was old-fashioned, the pommel low and back, and the panels of plush. Whenever his horses travelled, he had stuffed pads to hang on the pillar of the stall, to prevent any chafing of the hips. Sir Charles Knightley's only rival in point of horsemanship and sporting-appearance when *mounted*, was Mr. Davy, who resided alternately at Spratton, Pitsford, and Duston. Tall, slim, and exceedingly neat in his attire, he possessed the advantage of good hands and seat; and was so active that he would jump into the saddle with his horse at full gallop. Mr. Nethercote, noted for his eye to hounds, and his quiet and determined style of riding, was always in a good place when hounds were running, and made an excellent pilot for any stranger who wished to see what was going on. This gentleman is referred to by a writer in the *Sporting Magazine* of 1846, who, quoting from one who was present on the occasion, and gave a description of the day's sport, thus writes: "One day at Sywell Wood we were not able to throw off till 12.30 for the snow: at that time it had sufficiently melted, and an immediate find was followed by a very sharp burst; and in the bustle the snowballs from the horses' feet were anything but sport. We soon came upon an ox-fence—a very high flight of rails —a sort of a hedge and a deep, wet, broad ditch on the other side. The leading man, Mr. Nethercote, a determined rider, charged it on a well-known hunter, whose four legs, however, the snow took from under him on taking-off, and he went *through* into the next field; as ugly a fall as need be, where he lay, horse and all, doubled up like a hedgehog. I made use of the fallen man's clearance, and hearing from himself that, as the Irishman says, he was not kilt entirely, I made play as I was best able." The writer continues, "We had a trying sharp burst of five miles, to a drain, whence our fox was bolted in about five minutes, and thence a very severe chivy by Orlingbury and Isham to a large homestead near Barton Seagrave where King (huntsman) seeing that Pug was likely to prove tricky, gave the hounds a lift and turned up Charley in a ditch. Jem Wood, the first whip, than whom no more brilliant rider ever lived, not excepting Dick Christian himself, went extraordinarily well in this run, on a raw five-year-old of Mr. Elwes of Billing. All the time Wood seemed going at his ease, and the mare at hers apparently, and made no bones about it. I have seen him on all sorts, and once on a coach-horse, to which he was reduced by an accident; and it was all the same. They all went brilliantly, but *how* was probably as much known to Wood as to themselves. His style, in every sense of the word, was 'impressive.' He put them at anything, generally fastish. That he had them at his will in an extraordinary way, I infer, as I can safely say that I never saw a horse refuse with him. He had a fine voice, knew his business to a T, and was one of the civilest beings living."

Mr. Cook of Hothorp, the purchaser of the high-priced "Lancet," without being a great horseman, was always well in the front and did not know what it was to let another man pound him at any place. Lords Jersey and Plymouth were both first-rate men to hounds, and hunting from Market Harbro' did not want for opportunities to try and cut down either Quorn or Pytchley thrusters as occasion offered. Mr. Peter Allix, afterwards M.P. for Cambridgeshire, was one of the rough-and-ready school, who meant going, and never failed to carry out his purpose. Not at any time having the fear of a bullfinch before his eyes, be it ever so thrusty, he earned for himself the nickname of "Scratchface." He afterwards kept a pack of harriers in the neighbourhood of Newmarket, and showed a great deal of such sport as may be got out of the pursuit of "poor puss." His brother, Colonel Allix of the Grenadier Guards, who, like his brother, hunted from Brixworth, was noted for being one of the three handsomest men in London. Anxious to see as much as he could with a stud not overlarge, his maxim was, never to keep the horse out long who was expected to come out often. His return home, therefore, was usually at an earlier hour than most of the field; but should there have been a run during the time he was out, no man was more sure to have seen it. In after years, a guest at Moulton Grange for a few weeks' hunting in the old country, he was to be seen on a thorough-bred chestnut horse by "Economist" called "Rhino"—the veriest slug that ever went into a hunting-field. With the aid of a stout cutting whip and a sharp pair of spurs, the still-handsome old Guardsman was not to be denied; and many a younger man was not too proud to wait until the Colonel had made a hole in the big place through which he might find a way into the field beyond. All too soon he received his summons to "join the majority;" but his connection with the Pytchley is still kept up by his son having married a daughter of Mr. Richard Lee Bevan of Brixworth Hall. Mr. Lucas, at that time one of the wearers of the White Collar, had good reason to remember a dark evening on a cold December day, when on his return to Pytchley after a distant kill, the darkness became so intense that he lost his way in attempting to find a gate out of a grass-field. Happily he stumbled on a barn, where he and his horse passed the weary hours of a winter's night as best they could, causing no little anxiety to the more fortunate members of the Club, seated safe and sound around the dinner-table. For many years the place of shelter was known as Lucas's barn.

The Squire of Delapré, though never an enthusiastic sportsman or much of a performer in the field, was a frequent attendant at the Meets, where few excelled him in the neat and dapper appearance of himself, horse or groom. His son, Colonel Bouverie, for many years in command of the Blues, like his father, was never remarkable for his achievements across country, but on the flat had scarcely a rival as a gentleman-jockey. In the "old" *Sporting Magazine* for March, 1838, an amusing account is given of a match for 50*l.*, which came off at the Pytchley Hunt Races on March 28th of that year, between Mr. Hungerford's "Brilliant" and Mr. (Billy) Russell's "Valentine," ten stone each. Colonel Bouverie rode the former, and the latter was steered by a Mr. Curwen, an Irishman, who at that time was hunting from Abington Abbey. The betting on the race seems to have fluctuated from 25*l.* to 1*s.* to 100*l.* to 2*s.* 6*d.* on the winner: a bet which was offered by Mr. George Payne when the horses were within the distance. "Valentine," who had been last for the Tally Ho stakes, made the running, the mare hanging on his quarters and scarcely being able to go slow enough. Thus they kept to the distance-post, where all the wind seemed to have left poor "Valentine's" body. His jockey, however, appeared bent upon reaching the winning-post; but not content with flogging him for 200 yards before attaining the desired point, he gave him two or three, just for friendship's sake, after passing the chair ! Bursts of laughter greeted Mr. Curwen on his return to the winning-post, who explained his action by saying that "he was actually *obliged* to whip him to keep him moving." A postscript is added to this effect: "N.B.—Mr. Curwen would be a perfect treasure to any one in want of a portable threshing-machine."

"True Blue," a famous horse at that time as a steeple-chaser—the property of a well-known liquor-merchant of Northampton, Mr. John Stevenson—won the Farmers' Cup of fifty sovereigns on the same day; Mr. S. Harris of Wootten being second with his bay mare "Adelaide."

Familiar in many a Northamptonshire ear will be the names of the county-gentlemen who were on the small Stand on that occasion, well-nigh half a century ago. Lords Southampton, Bateman, Compton, Lilford; the Hon. P. Pierrepont, F. Villiers, H. Watson, C. Forester, R. Needham; Sir F. H. Goodricke, C. Knightley, Nethercote, Loraine Smith, Peyton, Wellesley, Curzon, Copeland, Lambs. Of these one only survives, the Rev. John Whalley, then Rector of Ecton, to call to mind the Pytchley Hunt Meeting of nearly fifty years ago. On the day following, a steeple-chase, in which many of the most celebrated horses of the day were engaged, came off at Little Houghton, over a course of such severity that the complaints of its impracticability were numerous, and Captain Phillipson—known as "handsome Jack"—withdrew his mare "Mirth" on account of the size of the fences. None of the jockeys, not even the famous Captain Beecher, quite relished the formidable aspect of either the timber or the water that had to be negotiated, except Lord Waterford, who liked everything as big as possible. His horse "Yellow Dwarf" started second favourite to Mr. Anderson's (the horsedealer) "Jerry," who carried twelve pounds extra, the prices respectively being five to two, and seven to two. Captain Childe's "Conrad" and "Yellow Dwarf" made the running, and jumped the first brook splendidly; afterwards taking the gate on the towing-path to avoid the heavy ground. Lord Waterford now forged ahead, and at the second brook was 200 yards in advance of the nearest horse. At the place where it was to be jumped an immense crowd of Northampton snobs were collected, who so closed in upon the "Yellow Dwarf" that his rider had to take it almost at a walk. He contrived, notwithstanding, to reach the opposite side, but the bank giving way he fell backwards into the water, and could not be got out until all chance was over. " Conrad" cleared the brook in fine style, and won the race easily; "Jerry" being second, and Captain Beecher third, on Mr. Fairlie's grey horse "Spicey." Captain Childe being quartered at Northampton the result of the race gave great satisfaction to the locals, though there is little doubt that Lord Waterford would have won it had he had fair play at the second brook.

From another steeple-chase, open to all England, which came off in this locality, and which was won by "Cigar," Mr. Elmore's "Lottery" was barred; the greatest compliment, probably, that ever was paid to a horse, and a striking testimony to his exceeding merit.

Some few may still remember a race on the Northampton Course, in which a worthy mercer and citizen of the town competed with H.M. King William IV. for the Gold Cup. The names of only two horses figured on the card for this race, and these were his Majesty's "Hindostan" and Mr. Whitworth's "Peon." The latter, somewhat a commoner in appearance, was troubled with the "slows," and "Hindostan" appropriately carried off the piece of plate, which may possibly still be found amongst the treasures of the Empress of India.

This was prior to the days of the new Stand, and when the little County Stand occupied a position opposite to the winning-post on the north side of the course. In the old *Sporting Magazine* of 1844 we learn that on the

29th of July of that year, the first stone of a new Stand was laid at Northampton by Mr. John Stevenson (owner of "True Blue" and "Duenna,") accompanied by the mayor of the borough and the town council, and other gentlemen favourable to racing. After the ceremony the company retired to a marquee erected on the ground, to partake of wine, the mayor presiding. After the customary toasts, the healths of the Marquis of Exeter, Earl Spencer, the Earl of Cardigan, the Hon. Captain Spencer, George Payne, Esq., and Fox-hunting were given; and there appeared on the part of all assembled a determination to use every endeavour to make the Northampton Races second to none in the kingdom.

Mr. Andrew of Harleston was a good man on a horse, and like his friends and neighbours, Messrs. Elwes and Bouverie, was short in stature and light in weight, though scarcely so particular in the shape and cut of his garments as either of these. This trio of country squires were each fond of the turf; but the owner of Harleston could not boast the prudence of either of the others, and so seriously injured his fortune by his speculations that, after a while, the property passed into the hands of Lord Spencer, and became part of the Althorp territory.

No name as a Huntsman is more familiar to old Northamptonshire, or at all events to that portion of it hunted by the Pytchley hounds, than that of Charles King. Unknown to the present generation, in the time of Lord Althorp it was to the hunting-man of that day what the names of Charles Payne and Will Goodall have been during the last thirty years. He was tall and slight, riding considerably under twelve stone, and though a good horseman he would always let an aspiring rider break the binders for him, and would rather get his horse's hind legs into a fence and make him creep through than jump it. He had a sharp eye for a gap, and could bore a hole through a big fence as well as any man. King's hands and seat were as good as could be, and his face was bright and intelligent. During a run, it lit up with singular animation, and wore a look of such extreme satisfaction as to give a beholder the feeling that he was in the full fruition of the greatest happiness to be found here below. To him, life might be a "wale" as Mrs. Gamp declared; but if it were taken in the "wale" of Cottesbrooke or that about Misterton or Crick, it was not such a very bad place after all. Having had the advantage of a good education, he could not only ride, dance, play the fiddle, and hunt a pack of hounds better than most men, but he kept a diary of each day's proceedings, which is remarkable for the minuteness and accuracy with which the different incidents were recorded. No day closed without his setting down the names of those who were out, and the list of the hounds, with observations on their behaviour, such as: "'Plunder' noisy at her fences." "'Glider' ran a hare to Byfield and back to Charwelton spinny." "The young hounds ran a cur and two greyhounds half a mile down a lane. Corn was standing (November 18th, 1816) as we went through Kilsby Field." "Young F. dug out a fox, and sold him in Kettering Market." Several volumes of these records, full of interest to any hunting-man, are to be found on a shelf of the Althorp library, and are open for the perusal of all who find pleasure in the literature known as "*Notæ Venaticæ.*" When Lord Spencer gave up the Mastership, King resigned the horn, having established for himself a reputation second to none in the kingdom as a huntsman of the highest class. He took a small farm under his old master at Brington, but even in those ante-free-trade days, he soon discovered that the "cobbler who does not stick to his last" is apt to find a new trade bad to live by.

It is seen by the journals so accurately kept by King, that the sport during the years of his huntsmanship was far better, day by day, than what is experienced at the present time. It is not likely that scent has greatly altered, the drain-pipes notwithstanding; but flocks, and herds, and shepherd-dogs, the three great antagonistic forces to sport, have increased twentyfold since those days, as have "hard riding," "spring-Captains," and foot-folk of all descriptions. Game, too, being far more plentiful than of old, and rabbits more abundant, the fox's *salle à manger* is never far distant from his *chambre de nuit*; and except when he would "a-wooing go," he has little chance of acquiring any knowledge of distant points. Even in that case, after having made arrangements with his "Vixena" to "meet him by moonlight alone," the chances are that the trysting place is only in some neighbouring wood, from whence, being roused by an unsympathetic hound, he straightway returns to a home which he is able to reach in the course of ten or fifteen minutes. Railways must not by any means be left out of the category of sport-spoilers: obstructionists with whom the huntsman of old had in no way to deal. Apart from the danger attendant on hounds running a mile or so down a line, the navvy is ever at work, and heads the fox, probably unconsciously to himself, or the animal disappears in some unexpected drain at the very moment when the acquisition of his brush seems assured. Though large coverts like Sywell Wood and Wilma Park have been shorn of much of their acreage within the last few years, plantations and small spinnies have greatly increased; and as they mostly contain a few hares and rabbits, the scent of the fox loses some of its aroma when mixed up with that of other game, and tends to stop hounds and favour the escape of the object of pursuit. No covert in the whole of the Pytchley open country is looked upon with more respect, and also with more dread, by the *habitué*, than the well-known " Sywell Wood." It has earned the first from being a sure " find " when all other places have failed, as is sometimes the case during the latter part of the season. The second arises from the adhesive nature of the circumjacent soil, and from the fact that the foxes frequenting it, when sent upon a journey by hounds, almost invariably return after a short " outing." Many a fine run has had its origin in Sywell Wood, but few take a higher rank than that which, in 1816, ended in a kill at Ashley by Welland, when Sir Justinian Isham carried his knife in his hand for the last twenty minutes, declaring, " that he and no other should cut off the brush," which he did. This must have covered a distance of, as the crow flies, about seventeen miles.

A bad fall in November, 1817, during a two hours' run from Brampton Wood, so shook Lord Althorp, that at the end of that season, to the great regret of every Pytchley man, he resigned the Mastership into the hands of his friend, Sir Charles Knightley.

CHAPTER II.

Character of Lord Althorp; becomes an Agriculturist and Breeder of Shorthorns: a boxer and supporter of pugilism; with anecdotes of Parson Ambrose, Lord Byron, and Jackson the prize-fighter; Gully, Cribb, and others—The prize-ring—Prize-fight at Achères, near Paris—FREDERICK, fourth EARL SPENCER; a breeder of racehorses; an excellent shot, and patron of cricket—The Althorp District—Sandars Gorse—SIR CHARLES KNIGHTLEY, *Master*, 1817-18; his fine horsemanship and deficient eloquence—Rivals Lord Althorp in breeding Shorthorns—An ardent Horticulturist—Resigns the Mastership—His house at Fawsley; its secret chamber: a Martin Mar-prelate Tract covertly printed there—LORD SONDES, *Master*, 1818-19—SIR BELLINGHAM GRAHAM, *Master*, 1819—Notices of some of the usual visitors to a Pytchley Meet: Dick Gurney; Squire Wood of Brixworth; Matthew Oldacre; Sir Roderick Murchison; Capt. Blunt; Admiral Sir W. Pell; The Rev. Vere Isham; The Rev. John Whalley; The Rev. W. Dickens; The Rev. J. C. Humphrey; The Rev. J. Wickes; and The Rev. Loraine Smith—Henry Couch, a military deserter and felon; his singular career and extraordinary letters—John Dunt, a worthy old soldier, and his letter.

AMONG a long list of honoured names, the Pytchley Hunt can point to none more notable than that of John Charles, Viscount Althorp. Like the great Duke himself, the polar star of his life was duty, and his most marked characteristic, "thoroughness." Whatever he undertook he did with all his might, and in the best possible manner, without much regard to cost. By sheer force of character, and a straightforwardness of conduct never equalled in the tortuous paths of political life, the position he attained in the House of Commons is almost without a parallel. Entirely wanting in the great gift of oratory, without which it is usually impossible to gain the ear of the House; his words, loosely strung together and destitute of polish or arrangement, were listened to with the deepest attention from their being the expression of a thoroughly honest man. So completely did the country, at critical times, look to him for guidance, that he was the "Atlas" who upheld the Government of Lord Grey, and his main support in passing the Reform Bill of 1832. Although Chancellor of the Exchequer, and the most important member of the Cabinet next to the Prime Minister, he never was so happy as when away from the turmoil of political life. A thorough countryman, when in London his song might have been at any time: "My heart's in the Midlands, my heart is not here;" and long after he had given up hunting he used to say that "he never should forget the beautiful music of Sywell Wood." After resigning the chase, agriculture and the breeding of shorthorns became the great passion of Lord Althorp's life. An interesting letter to his father, dated Wiseton, October 3rd, 1818, shows how thoroughly he had entered upon this new and fascinating pursuit. He writes: "My expedition to the county of Durham answered. I did not spend quite so much money as I told you I was prepared to do, and I got what I wanted, viz. three cows and a bull. When I saw 'Lancaster,' the bull for which Champion and I were to enter into a confederacy, I did not like him or his produce sufficiently well to hazard a large sum of money on him; but Simpson and Smith, who live at Bakewell's farm at Dishley, bought him for 621 guineas. I got the two best cows, and had to pay for them handsomely, giving 370 for one, and 300 for the other. I bought another cow for 73 guineas, which may turn out as valuable as either of the others; but she sold cheap because she is a very great milker, and looked uncommonly thin. A bull calf, not six months old, sold for 278 guineas." Such were some of the early plunges of Lord Althorp, which if they did not prove a mine of wealth, raised him into the first rank of shorthorns. The annual loss upon the Wiseton farm, where the high-bred shorthorns were kept, was about 3000*l*. The best year he ever experienced was one in which the balance on the wrong side was 400*l*. only. His farm in Northamptonshire was almost always profitable, the grazing being managed with a view to making it pay. Although a farmer, and dependent on land for his income, he threw himself heart and soul into the " Free Trade " movement, believing that the measure would be beneficial to the country at large. Not foreseeing the gigantic growth of the railway-system in the corn-growing countries, he did not apprehend any material fall in the price of cereals, and would have laughed had he been told that within forty years after he had passed away, wheat would be selling at 28*s*. per quarter. Always fond of shooting, as he was of all outdoor sports, in spite of great practice he never became a good shot; he amused himself by keeping an account of every shot he fired in the course of the year, whether he missed or killed, making up his book periodically.

Long after he had given up hunting, and was leader of the Opposition in the House of Commons, he went with a party to Deville, the craniologist, or "skull-reader," to test his skill in telling character by the bumps of the head. " The man knows nothing about it," he said on his return; "he entirely missed my leading passion." "What do you consider that to be?" asked a friend. "To see sporting-dogs hunt," was the reply, "nothing in the world gives me the same pleasure." Not inheriting his father's (the great bibliophile of the day, to whom the Althorp Library is indebted for its priceless possessions) love for books, he patronized all athletic exercises, and made a real study of boxing, taking lessons from the best instructors. He had many a "set-to" with his fellow-Harrovian, Lord Byron,—a very handy man with his fists,—and so hard did he hit, that it used to be commonly said of him that he was a "prize-fighter thrown away." This was the halcyon era of the prize-ring. The British public, from the Prince Regent to Jack the sweep, had imbibed the notion that a fight was an English and a manly institution, and was an antidote to the foreign practice of settling disputes with the knife. All its roguery and its attendant blackguardism were ignored, and the principal pugilists of the time, men springing from the lowest dregs of society, were treated as equals by the magnates of the land. Jackson, Gully, Spring, and Cribb, were looked upon as heroes cast in no ordinary mould; and the first was treated on the most familiar terms by Lord Byron; whilst the Regent thought it no degradation to drive about Brighton with the second by his side. Lord Althorp used to say that his conviction of the advantages of boxing was so strong that he had been seriously considering whether it was not his duty to attend every prize-fight, so as to encourage the noble science to the utmost of his power. He would tell his friends, with no little animation, how he had seen Mendoza the Jew knocked down in the first five or six rounds by Humphrey, and seeming almost beat till his brethren got their money on, when a hint being given him, he began in earnest and soon turned the tables. He loved to describe the "great mill" between Gully and "the chicken," which came off at Brickhill in Bedfordshire; how he rode down and was loitering about the inn-door when a barouche and four drove up with Lord Byron and a party of friends and Jackson the trainer; how they all dined together, and how pleasant it had been. Then the fight the next day—a scene, says the describer, "worthy of Homer." We read in the Life of Lord Althorp by Sir Denis Le Marchant, that when the party come together to witness this affair had assembled overnight at the "George Hotel," it was found that the beds were not sufficient in number; so they tossed up, and the winners turned in first. At a certain hour these were called, and the losers took their places. Among the company was the Rector of Blisworth, "Parson Ambrose," a man too well known in sporting-circles. He disgraced a profession he might have adorned, as he was clever and had a remarkably fine delivery. Macklin, the actor, left him fifty pounds, to preach his funeral sermon. Obliged at last to fly from his creditors, he died abroad in misery and want. As a proof of the intimate relations existing between Byron, the peer and poet, and Jackson, the prize-fighter, we give a letter from the former to the latter, bearing date September 18th, 1808.

"Newstead Abbey.

"DEAR JACK,—I wish you would inform me what has been done by Jekyll about the pony I returned as

unsound. £25 is a sound price for a pony; and by
heavens, I will, if it costs me £500, make an example of
Mr. J. if the money be not returned at once.
"Believe me, dear Jack,
"Yours, &c.,
"Byron."

Of John Gully, pugilist, publican, hell-keeper, betting
man, country squire, and member of parliament, we read
as follows in "Riley's Itinerant:"—

"One evening I accompanied honest Jack Emery (the
well-known actor), to a tavern in Carey Street kept by
John Gully. He unfortunately was from home, but Cribb,
the champion of England, was officiating as his *locum-
tenens*, handing about pots of porter and grog with perse-
vering industry. Mrs. Gully, a neat little woman, civil
and attentive, superintended at the bar, where we obtained
leave to sit, Emery evidently being in great favour.
Cribb, who had obtained popularity by his prowess, was
originally a coalheaver, and has several brothers in the
same employment. He is sturdy and stout-built: stands
five feet eight, and is clumsy in appearance and hard-
featured. Having detained him a few minutes in
conversation, Emery said to me: 'Well, what do you
think of him? The greatest man in his way, or perhaps
in any other, that England can boast.' In spite of
there being "nothing like leather," we here see the
actor giving precedence to the "fighting-man" over
all of his own craft, and prepared to invest him with a
greater halo of renown than he would assign to a Kean
or a Kemble a Liston, or a Mathews! The feeling
that the "P.R." as it was termed, fostered public
courage, and on the whole was a praiseworthy institu-

tion, had got so firm a hold on national sentiment, that though contrary to law, it was something more than winked at by judges and by magistrates too. On one occasion, a Cabinet Council was postponed, so that its members might be present at a much talked-of contest between two well-known pugilists; and even the clergy, it was said, could not refrain from witnessing the exhilarating spectacle. The robberies, the dishonest part taken by the principals who were always ready to sell the fight, and the scenes of violence and tumult that usually took place, gradually disgusted the patrons of the "ring," and brought about its downfall. The sporting papers, which had lavished on a fight, in a jargon peculiar to themselves, minutiæ of description similar to those now bestowed on a cricket match or boat race, did their best to restore vitality to a sinking cause; but "law" came to the aid of an improved state of feeling, and the "fisticuffian" candle guttered out. Driven from pillar to post, and finding no rest for the sole of his foot on his native soil, the puzzled pugilist, as a last resource, betook himself to the land of the Gaul. It may truly be said that wonders will never cease; for in the London morning papers of February 16, 1886, it was stated that a "fight for the Championship of England had taken place the day before, between two men, Smith and Greenfield, on ground in the neighbourhood of Paris."

"Cœlum non animum mutant qui trans mare currunt."

The change of soil and atmosphere, and the passage over the sea, in no way changed the nature of the plunder-seeking pugilist. As on this side of the Channel, the mock battle ended in a riot, the backers of the man about to suffer defeat, as soon as they saw that their money was in jeopardy, breaking into the ring and putting an end to the contest. The French journals teemed with wrath at the brutal exhibition that had been transferred from our shores to theirs; and in this igno- minious fashion, a hideous practice and national disgrace have received, it is to be hoped, their death-blow. A Paris correspondent of one of the London daily papers sent the following account of the affair. "To-day there was a real boxing-match at Achères in the forest of St. Germain, which horrified the representatives of the Paris press who were invited to attend it. The combatants were Smith and Greenfield, who, fearing police inter- ference if they fought in England, came over here with a party of about 250 amateurs of the "noble art of self- defence." They were told by a member of the horsey population at Maison-Lafitte that there was a clearing in the forest at Achères which was an ideal spot for a P.R. fight. Twenty mail-coaches took the chief members of the party out there in the afternoon; the others went by rail. Smith and his friend fought for forty minutes. There were twenty-five rounds before the bottle-holder of Greenfield threw up the sponge. Greenfield was fear- fully punished, and seemed terribly exhausted while he was being attended to. Smith was vociferously cheered by his backers. The fight was for £500. A forester, who was looking on, fainted when he saw how Greenfield was being punished. I believe the Paris press will call upon the Minister of the Interior to prevent this peculiar kind of sport being acclimatized in France." The above very inaccurate account of this example of civilization, as understood on the English side of the

Channel, shows how little the French correspondent comprehended the nature of the thing about which he was writing.

During many years of his life, Lord Spencer suffered much from his hereditary enemy, gout, which, in his person, defied all the resources of medical science. A rigid attention to diet and regular exercise, served to scotch, but could not kill the foe; and no one more than he realized the unwisdom of the lady's maid, who declared that "health, after personal appearance, is the greatest blessing as is." So severe was the abstinence practised by him in the matter of food, that it created great depression both in mind and body. He used to weigh his breakfast, and then, having eaten the small portion he allowed himself, would rush from the room to avoid any further temptation. In the autumn of 1845, he was, with Lord G. Bentinck, steward of Doncaster races. On the second day of the meeting, he was seized with sudden indisposition, but he rallied sufficiently to be able to join his guests at dinner. Gradually the attack assumed a more serious aspect, and though he was able to return to Wiseton, it was evident that his end was rapidly approaching. He prepared himself for death in the calmest possible manner, had his will read out to him by his brother, said, "Don't feel for me, I'm perfectly happy, and the happiness I have enjoyed in this life, makes me hope that it will be granted me in the next." Towards five o'clock in the morning of the first of October, 1845, he breathed his last, and Northamptonshire lost a "worthy," of whom it may well be proud for all time.

Twenty masters of the Pytchley Hunt have come and

gone since Lord Althorp resigned its management; but fondly as some of these are remembered, not one more completely realized the idea of what a master of hounds should be than John Charles, Viscount Althorp.

Sir Denis Le Marchant's "Life of Earl Spencer" has suffered the usual fate of biographies, and been pronounced "dull, feeble, and unsatisfactory." Criticism, always more ready to find faults than merits, has set its *imprimatur* on Boswell's "Life of Johnson—" "Vitarum facile Princeps"— Southey's "Nelson," Lockhart's "Scott," Stanley's "Arnold," Trevelyan's "Macaulay," Miss Marsh's "Hedley Vicars;" few, very few more. But, however tempting the subject, the intending biographer will do well to remember the commandment, "Thou shalt not scribble thy neighbour's life." The fate awaiting the neglect of this injunction may be that which overtook Copleston's "Life of Lord Dudley," of which the kindly critic says:—

> "Than the first martyr's, Dudley's fate
> Was harder must be owned;
> Stephen was only stoned to death,
> Dudley was Coplestoned!"

The Hon. Frederick Spencer, R.N., succeeded his brother in the title and estates, but not in the desire to become a master of hounds.

Having passed the early years of his life at sea, he had little opportunity for developing the sporting instincts which he shared with the other members of his family, but there was nothing connected with out-door life which had not all his sympathy. Without ever becoming a regular "hunting-man," he usually appeared at the meet when it was in the immediate neighbourhood of Althorp, and for a few years kept a pack of harriers, with which he hunted regularly. The sporting traditions of the family were adhered to with an interest which almost amounted to enthusiasm in the cause of hunting, and at no time were foxes more strictly preserved in the Althorp district. To hear of and talk over the various and varying incidents of a good day's sport, was a thing in which the noble lord greatly delighted, and he held in special esteem those of his neighbours who were known to go well with hounds. To him the "Pytchley" are indebted for the covert so well known as "Sandars Gorse." Believing that the picturesque and popular "Cank" had seen its best days, and was losing its attraction for foxes, he established in 1853 a new covert in its immediate neighbourhood. This he wished to call "Balaclava," in honour of the famous charge which had recently occurred, but the name never took root, and the place, after a while, was known as "Sandars Gorse," from the excellent sportsman upon whose farm it stood, and to whose guardianship it was committed. Owing to the unremitting care and attention of Mr. Henry Sandars and his son, there are few coverts in the country, in which a fox is more sure to be at home than this, and a handsome silver tankard, presented by gentlemen in the neighbourhood, marks their appreciation of the services he has rendered to the Hunt. Though no longer to be seen making the best of his way to the front, or cramming his horse at a woolly place, years and rheumatism are a heavier handicap than the dead weight so sorely trying to horse and rider. No sooner has

Goodall put his hounds into the well-known covert than

> "At the end of the gorse, the old farmer in brown
>   Is seen on his good little mare,
> With a grin of delight and a jolly bald crown,
>   To hold up his hat in the air.
> Though at heart he's as keen as if youth were still green,
>   Yet (a secret all sportsmen should know)
> Not a word will he say till the fox is away,
>   Then he gives you a real 'Tally Ho!'"

Many a gallant fox has had his home in Lord Spencer's substitute for the sloping sides of the prettiest covert in Northamptonshire; but it was not until long after his lordship's lamented death that "Cank the beautiful" was improved from off the face of covert-land.

A morning spent in scentless Harleston Heath and Nobottle Wood is not usually an exhilarating amusement; but so long as it is felt that "Sandars Gorse" is looming in the future, despair finds no place in the breast of the sanguine sportsman. On three separate occasions in the season of 1883, in a snug piece lying in the north-east corner of the covert, was found the "friend in need," who was a "friend indeed," and who always made his way to some undiscoverable "bourne," in the region about Naseby. Each time the gallop was a good one, and a fourth attempt to elude his pursuers would have again proved successful, had not a whip, sent ahead to look about him—to take a mean advantage, some call it—seen the nearly lost, weary one creeping alongside a distant hedge, probably hugging himself in the feeling that having saved his brush, he should now say goodbye to his old home. A judge *puts on* the black cap before sentencing his victim to death, a whip *takes off* his. Isaac's cap was seen to be raised aloft, the end of as stout-hearted a fox as ever stood before hounds was known to be near. In a few minutes little was left of an animal who had fairly earned for himself the monumental inscription, "In life respected, in death regretted."

It was in a gallop from this covert that H.R.H. the Prince of Wales seemed on the point of sharing with the roach and dace the secrets of the Spratton Brook; and from here, late on a November afternoon, few remaining to share in the gallop, a "stranger" from Sywell Wood just got home in time to save his life from Captain Austruther Thomson's hounds. For some time before the end the song of all except the fox had been :

"Shades of evening close not o'er us,
Leave us quite alone awhile."

and the way out of one field into another had been difficult to find; but it was not until the field adjoining the wood had been reached that the master gave the order to stop the hounds. It was fondly hoped that on the next "drawing" of Sywell Wood, the same fox might retrace his steps on a return journey to the covert from whence he had so lately been driven; but he was never found again.

Like others of his neighbours, Lord Spencer had a decided leaning to the turf, and availed himself of the beautiful paddocks at Harleston to make some experiments in breeding. A mare, named "Wryneck," from an accident in her stall which caused her neck to be crooked, had sufficient merit to give him hopes of success; and the famous "Cotherstone" for some time was "at home" at Althorp. Fond of shooting, and an excellent shot, the "Rocketer" might well crow with satisfaction, who had escaped the dangers of the middle passage between Harleston Heath and Brampton fox-covert. Neither height nor distance would avail him much if his line of flight took him within range of the noble lord's unerring weapon; and he might get what satisfaction he liked out of the fact that he was pretty sure to be dead before he reached *terra firma*.

A great admirer and patron of cricket, Lord Spencer was always ready, at the time when "gate-money matches" were almost unknown, to bear a portion of the expense of an important contest; and to him the public were indebted, in a great measure, for the interesting match at Leicester in 1838, between the North and South of England, when Alfred Mynn got 126 runs, and so injured his left leg in attempting to make a new hit, known then as the "Cambridge Poke," that he was laid up for many weeks.

To the great sorrow of all the county, before he had quite reached his sixtieth year, Lord Spencer succumbed to a complaint which he had long known was incurable.

Without at any time laying himself out for popularity, few men ever lived, who by his own intrinsic wholeheartedness had so won the respect and affection of those of whom he had himself formed a favourable opinion. So great indeed was the confidence he inspired in individuals, that in cases of difficulty, when the advice of a soundly-judging mind was required, he was the chosen one to whom the friend in trouble

was the first to go. His hospitality was of that genial description which, while it included friends of his own rank, did not leave out in the cold the neighbouring squire or parson—indeed, he never seemed more happy than when his guests were those of his own neighbourhood.

After the resignation of Lord Althorp in 1817, into no hands more appropriate could the mastership of the hounds have fallen than into those of his friend, Sir Charles Knightley, who by virtue of his keenness, knowledge of hunting, social position, and general popularity, was in every way suited to the position. A horseman of the highest class, Sir Charles at no time had a superior in riding to hounds, and on either of his famous thorough-breds, "Sir Mariner" or "Benvolio," he was more than a match for the "swells" from Melton or Market Harbro'. A hedge and brook between Brixworth and Cottesbrooke, just to the left of the station, still known as "Sir Charles's leap," is sufficient evidence that he was not to be stopped by a fence, however formidable, when the necessity arose for a little extra steam. Tall, thin, with aquiline nose and high cheek-bones, the appearance of the Fawsley baronet was such as to make him remarkable among a multitude—an appearance enhanced as he advanced in years by a habit he had acquired of carrying his head bent upon his chest. A consistent inflexible Tory of the old school, he represented a division of his native county in Parliament for several years, and fought many a contested election. Not greatly blessed with the gift of eloquence, and with a slight difficulty of utterance, his attempts to address the great "unwashed" in the County Hall, or from the balcony of the George Hotel at Northampton, were generally provocative of much amusement. Unable to remember what he wished to say without the assistance of notes, his thoughts seemed to be evolved from the depths of his hat rather than from his own consciousness, a mode not at all times successful; for either from not being clearly written, or from not being held at an angle suiting the vision, the "hatograph" occasionally refused to yield up its written treasures without some coaxing and manipulation. This excited the mirth of the "paid unruly" attached to the opposition, and gave rise to cries of, "Put on your hat, Charley;" "What 'a you got a-looking at inside of that hat?" and other irreverent remarks begotten of beer and bribery and electioneering manners. It was not until he had ceased, and his eloquent "Fidus Achates," the Reverend Francis Litchfield, the well-known rector of Farthinghoe, had taken up "the running," that the mob fairly settled down into quietude. To the glib and energetic utterances of this bulwark of the Tory faith, all were content to listen.

A parliamentarian of the higher class thrown away, the oratorical gifts of the Farthinghoe parson were of no common order, and an ardent social though not political reformer, his eloquent philippics, delivered before his brother magistrates at Quarter Sessions against what he termed the "drink-shops," would have sent Sir Wilfrid Lawson into a frenzy of delight. Not a member of the House of Commons possessed a more marked individuality of dress and address than Sir Charles Knightley; and though he rarely trusted himself to "give tongue" before the critical audience, his opinion was always treated with respect. With his friend and colleague, Lord Althorp, he was at one in all matters except politics; and there they were as far asunder as the poles. Their rivalry in the field of "shorthorn" breeding was of the most amicable description, though the herd of the noble lord, known to agriculturists as "Farmer Jack," never touched the same point of excellence as that of the Fawsley baronet. For many a year, the three strains of blood most eagerly sought for and commanding the highest prices were those of Bates, Booth, and Sir Charles Knightley; and though shorthorns, in sympathy with the collapse of British agriculture, have fallen from the high position which they once enjoyed, a scion from the stock of any of these magnates of the herd-book is still looked upon as a valuable possession. Wearying of the mastership all too soon, or perhaps from not meeting with a sufficiently liberal support, Sir Charles retired at the close of his first season.

The reins of office were then taken up by Lord Sondes; but he, finding that twelve months of power were as much as he cared for, resigned at the end of 1819, in favour of Sir Bellingham Graham.

At this time, hunting from so distant a point as Pytchley having been found very inconvenient, Sir Charles Knightley and certain of the county gentlemen determined to erect kennels at a more central point, and Brixworth was fixed upon as the most suitable spot for the new hunting capital. The old Pytchley Club, with all its glories, and all its old associations, was now done away with; and in a few more years the ancient building itself was pulled down by order of its owner, Mr. George Payne.

On the retirement of Lord Sondes, there seems to have been a great difficulty in finding a successor. We read in a letter of Lord Althorp's, dated Althorp, April, 1820, "I think that the hounds will be entirely given up, and that there will be no hunting at all in this county. John Warde offered himself for fifteen hundred a year; but he was refused. Hanbury, afterwards Lord Bateman, offered to take them if two thousand a year could be raised; but this could not be done. I think Knightley ought to subscribe largely; but he will not subscribe at all unless he is paid for all the expense he has been at at Brixworth. He will lose more comfort by this, if he intends to live in the county, than twice the sum he wants will procure him."

After the hounds had been finally established at Brixworth, the most prominent members of the Hunt appear, the one to have given up the chase entirely, the other to have grown comparatively indifferent to its attractions. Politics and agriculture, and the cares attendant on a large estate, engrossed all Sir Charles Knightley's attention. Towards the end of his days another love sprang up to occupy his time and thoughts, viz. horticulture. Into this new hobby he entered heart and soul; and was never satisfied until he had placed in his hothouse or greenhouse the latest production from foreign lands. For two or three summers one of his greatest pleasures was to take his friends into the garden to show them a row of a new and costly zonale geranium, known as "Mrs. Pollock." After his eightieth year, he would think nothing of driving sixteen miles to spend an hour in the garden of a brother floral fanatico, and return home afterwards. Quick of temper and kind of heart, the worthy old baronet on going into the stable-yard after breakfast was wont to be approached by sundry old women from the village, each with her separate tale of woe, and her humble prayer for pecuniary assistance. Right well did the cunning old suppliants know their man! Loud, sometimes strong words, threats and accusations of imposition, only heralded the inevitable shilling or half-crown; and the scene never seemed to weary either party by repetition.

Universal was the regret when it became known that death had summoned, in his eighty-fifth year, this unique specimen of the fine old country gentleman to join the ancestors who for upwards of five hundred years had been lords of the manor of Fawsley.

The stranger, whether attracted by a meet of the hounds or in search of the picturesque, who sees Fawsley for the first time, cannot but feel that he is looking at one of the old historic mansions of England. Situated on a lawn of gentle elevation, it commands an extensive and beautiful prospect, and is surrounded by a well-timbered park, which, inclusive of the well-known "Badby Wood," covers an area of upwards of six hundred acres. In 1416, this property was purchased by Richard Knightley, the descendant of an old Staffordshire family, deriving its name from the manor of Knightley in that county. During the Civil Wars the owner of the property was a warm adherent of the Commonwealth, and married a daughter of Hampden, thereby strengthening the tie with the anti-royalist's party. The common saying of "under the rose" is stated to have its origin from the councils which were held in a secret chamber above the oriel window in the saloon in Fawsley House, where was placed a printing-press; and the papers there printed were dropped through a rose in the ceiling * to be despatched throughout the country.

Though he had long given up appearing at the meets, Sir Charles was almost daily in the saddle to the last; his seat, dress, and appearance bearing ample testimony to the fact that in no place was he more at home than on the back of a horse. To sit with an old friend over a bottle of old port that for many a year had been mellowing in the Fawsley cellars, and to talk over old Pytchley days, was a treat in which the veteran sportsman greatly delighted. To fight his battles with Tom Assheton Smith, "Jersey," and "Plymouth" o'er again —to recall the incidents of the "Lancet" sale—to chuckle over the *mauvaises heures* of "Lucas" in the barn, or to dwell on the merits of favourite hunters, were topics of which he never wearied.

Not able to brook contradiction, nor prone to see much merit in parliamentary opponents, it was prudent for a Whig guest to keep off the tender ground of politics, and to leave delicate questions of state undiscussed. Accustomed to have his own way, that of others was not greatly respected, and if things were going " contrary-like," either in garden or farm, the passer-by might have cause to think that the language he heard issuing from the lips of Fawsley's lord was not that inculcated by his own rector, or by any of the neighbouring clergy. Be that as it may, few county magnates have left behind

* Here was secretly printed the second of the *Martin Marprelate Tracts*, called the *Epitome*, 1588.—ED.

them a more honoured name, or one that will stand out in bolder relief in a county's annals.

The following highly characteristic letter, written by Sir Charles only a few days before his death, was received by the author of this volume:—

"My dear Nethercote,—"The venison is very good, and I shall be very happy to send you a haunch whenever you like it. How have you been lately? I have been rather fishy, and I thought that the old gentleman who stalks about with a scythe and an hour-glass was going to give me a punch; but he has let me off for a time, and I am quite fresh again.

"Yours ever sincerely,

"C. Knightley."

"Sunday, 22nd August,"—four days before his death.

In less than a week after the above was penned, that "old gentleman with the scythe and the hour-glass" had repeated his "punch," and the heart, so full of hospitable thought and kindly feelings, had ceased to beat for ever.

With the transference from Pytchley to Brixworth of the hunting establishment, the modern history of the "P.H." may be said to commence. Old things passed away. The Club, for some time on the wane, ceased to exist; and even the "white collar," so long the distinctive mark of the "Pytchley man," now disappeared from sight.

Before discussing the incidents of the new era, it will be well to pass in review some of those strangers as well as natives, who from time to time had formed, and for some years continued to form, the component parts of a "Pytchley meet." *Place aux étrangers.*

Remarkable for his weight, and for his success in riding to hounds, in spite of that disadvantage was the well-known Norfolk squire, Dick Gurney. Favouring, as it suited him, either Quorn or Pytchley with his company, good nerve and a thorough knowledge of what hounds were doing, and a quick eye for the right spot in a fence, enabled him to hold at defiance the handicap of "too, too solid flesh." The fame of his leap over the Canal Bridge near Heyford, on his famous horse "Sober Robin," is still an incident of note in Pytchley history; and old Quornites love to tell how, after warning Tom Assheton Smith not to go into a canal after a hunted fox, he plunged in himself, fetched the animal out, and on reaching the sloping bank laid with his head downward and his legs upturned to allow the water to escape out of his boots! Riding nineteen stone, Mr. Gurney was fain to put up with horses that could carry the weight, without being too particular as to quality; and the best animal he ever possessed was, in his appearance, nothing less than a cart-horse,—a brown bay with a blaze down his face, with coarse vulgar quarters, and a rat-tail of a peculiarly aggravating type. He could go alongside of "Benvolio" or "Sir Mariner," with Sir Charles Knightley on them; and he greatly distinguished himself on the hardest and best day that had been seen in the country for many years. Another horse in his stud, totally lacking in quality, and nothing but a machiner to look at (a bay with black legs, and with plenty of hair about the fetlocks), helped to falsify the notion that without blood no horse could go the pace and last.

Squire Wood of Brixworth Hall, about the same time, rode a chestnut horse with white legs, who for five-and-twenty minutes could carry his eighteen stone up to any hounds in England. A brougham horse, and rather a commoner than that, so far as appearance went, he was a sufficiently good hunter for his owner to decline parting with him to Lord Jersey for five hundred pounds. In our own day we have seen the welter, Matthew Oldacre of Clipston, a rare specimen of the Northamptonshire hunting-farmer, going well ahead on horses whose fathers and mothers must have been well acquainted with the operations necessary for seed-time and harvest. The cases here mentioned are probably the exceptions that form the rule, as to the advantages of quality in horse as well as in man; but they serve to prove two things: first, that a horse can go in any shape and almost of any birth; secondly, that well-nigh everything depends upon the " man on the box."

An occasional attendant at the meets about this time was a sportsman, who, in after years attained distinction amounting to a world-wide celebrity in an arena very different from that of the hunting-field.

When Mr. Murchison rode up to the covert side, not one then present could have supposed that he was greeting one, who in a few short years would have established the reputation of being the greatest geologist of his time. Even then, however, the bacilli of earth-lore and scientific knowledge had entered into his system, and on every non-hunting day his time was passed in examining the gravel-pits and stone-quarries of the neighbourhood.

About this date a " craze " had entered the heads of the

good people of Northampton that coal was to be found at
Kingsthorpe. Asked for his opinion on this important
question, Mr. Murchison unhesitatingly affirmed that
"no coal was to be found anywhere in Northamptonshire." The stone, however, had been set rolling; the
spirit of speculation was stalking abroad, and the opinion
of a geologist who had not a coaly mind was held of
little worth. A company was formed; shares were
taken up by small tradesmen and domestic servants; a
shaft was sunk at Kingsthorpe; and loud were the
promises of the consulting engineer. For a time, all
went on merry as a marriage-bell. Hope played her
usual part and filled the air with flattering tales. The
shareholders of moderate means felt assured that the
ship they had been so long dreaming of had come in at
last, and that they were about to be as well off as other
folk, if not better! When one fine day it was noised
abroad "that coal of good quality had been found in the
pit," the excitement was uncontrollable. The bells of
the Northampton churches were set a-ringing; flags
were displayed from the windows; pedestrians in the
streets congratulated each other; and it was agreed on
all sides that the shoemakers' city was to become an improved Birmingham. The rejoicings, however, were
but short-lived. On some of the exultant shareholders
wishing to hear all about the discovery from the
engineer himself, he was nowhere to be found! But
he left a statement to the effect that the pieces of the
much desired mineral *had* been found in the pit, but—
that they were only what he had taken down himself!
He kindly added the information that "to the best of
his belief, there was no other coal within miles of where

they had been digging." Thus the bubble burst, and many an honest, hardworking man lost the savings of a lifetime. The chimney of the shaft still remains as a monument of man's folly and credulity.

Mr. Murchison's new pursuit speedily grew too engrossing, and took up too much of his time to allow of a frequent visit to Brixworth. Science had not, at that time, begun to teach that the Book of Genesis was all wrong—that the world was millions of years old—that man's first parent was a bit of jelly, which, by process of improvement called "evolution," first grew into an "ape," and then into being a "man." A body of philosophical faddists—known as "Positivists" or "Cocksureists"—had not then written books to prove that seeing is not believing without touching and handling; and the unscientific and simple-minded poet had not "chaffed" his philosophical friends with the lines:—

> "An ape there was in the days that were earlier;
> Centuries passed and its hair it grew curlier;
> Centuries more gave a thumb to its wrist,
> And then it was man and a Positivist."

After quitting Northamptonshire, Mr. Murchison (afterwards Sir Roderick) never again pursued the "wily one," unless it was to dig out its fossilized remains from the bowels of the earth, where he may have fallen a victim to a Deinotherium or some other Palæozoic monster.

Another welcome visitor at Brixworth at this time was Captain Blunt, of Crabbit Park, Sussex, father to Mr. Wilfred Scawen Blunt, so well known as the friend of Arabi, the Soudanese, the Parnellites, and all the enemies of his country, and of the opposers of legitimate authority.

Attractive in appearance and manner, the handsome ex-guardsman won for himself additional sympathy from having lost a leg at the Battle of Corunna, where his regiment greatly distinguished itself. The disadvantage of having but one available leg, however, did not seem greatly to affect his riding, for although a "monoped" himself, there was scarcely a "biped" in the field who had greatly the advantage of him in a run. A frequent and always a welcome guest wherever he went, he was always accompanied by an old and faithful servant, who was well known by his skill in playing the Jew's harp, —a musical instrument now quite unknown. Summoned into the dining-room after dinner, the modest but skilful performer used to delight the company with the effect he produced; the children of the family, permitted to sit up on purpose, being always the most appreciative portion of the audience. How the little instrument, held between the jaws, capable of only small things at the deftest hands, got its original and self-evident name of "*Jaw's* harp" converted into "*Jew's* harp," it is not easy to say. Another producer of sweet sounds in vogue at the same time, and known as the Æolian harp, like the Jew's harp, seems to have gone out of favour. Fashioned like an elongated zithern, it could lay claim to a certain weirdness from the sounds it produced being elicited without the agency of human hand. Resting in the sill of a window, the breeze passing across the strings caused it to emit tones so plaintive and soothing that for a time they were pleasant to listen to; a little of the "fairy-like music," however, went a long way, and the jaded ear a bit wearied of the monotony.

Unconsciously following in the steps of Mr. Blunt, a

late Italian minister, M. Negré, used to take into the country with him, for the amusement of his hosts, a chef, his cook, who was no less skilful in the conjuring than he was in the culinary art.

Another one-legged man who had "all his buttons on," as regarded hunting, as well as seafaring matters, was Captain, afterwards Admiral, Sir Watkin Pell, R.N., of Sywell Hall. Losing his leg when a midshipman, in an attempt to cut out an enemy's gun-boat, he got so accustomed to the ways of a cork leg, that it formed no impediment to him in his profession, or in the enjoyment of life, be he where he might. Fond of hunting, as of all wild sports, he rode boldly, though in thorough sailor-like fashion, and clinging on, "fore and aft," took the fences pretty much as they came. Having once come to grief in jumping the brook under Pytchley, the "old salt," with pardonable exaggeration, was wont to boast that he had made acquaintance with the bottom of every stream in the county. His last command, before being appointed to the snug berth of the Deputy-Governorship of Greenwich Hospital, was the fine old three-decker, *The Howe*. An excellent officer, a strict disciplinarian, and a bit of a martinet, no ship in Malta Harbour was in such trim as *The Howe*. The night before leaving the island, dining with a friend to whom he had handed over his Maltese cook, the performance of his late "chef" did not at all come up to the high recommendations he had given him. Begging that he might be sent for as soon as the ladies had left the dining-room, the Admiral informed him that "had he sent up such a dinner on board, he would have received three dozen there and then!"

> "Next came the parson,
> The parson, the parson,
> Next came the parson,
> The shortest way to seek.
>
> "And like a phantom lost to view,
> From point to point the parson flew.
> The parish at a pinch can do
> Without him for a week."

So sings Whyte-Melville, the Horace of hunting-poets, who at all times had a rhyme to spare in favour of the black coat and white tie that marked the clerical sportsman. Of the four rectors now to pass before the reader of these pages, not one was qualified to excuse himself to his bishop for his hunting-ways, "that he never was in the same field with the hounds." Long and fast must they have run before they out-stripped that Rector of Lamport, who some sixty years since, had no superior as a horseman, and who was too thankful to pick up at a reduced figure the animal that was "one too many" for some less skilful rider. The father of four sons, three of whom could find their way across Northamptonshire rather better than most men, the Rev. Vere Isham called no man master for nerve, and for keeping a good place on a rough mount. Kind, courteous, and pleasant with all, not a member of the Hunt was regarded with greater respect, and the "coarse-mouthed Squire" (Osbaldeston) on one occasion received from him a lesson in "soft answers" which he would have done well not to forget. "Where the h— are you coming to, you d—d fool, you?" exclaimed the Pytchley master, when one day the Rector of Lamport had a difficulty in stopping a hard-pulling horse. From some, an address couched in such language would have provoked a reply in corresponding terms; but the only remark of the kindly minister was: "Fool, fool, am I? I daresay that you are no judge, Squire." In no respect is the advance of refinement more marked than in the style of speech common in the "twenties" and long after, and that which prevails in the present day. Then, one of the objections raised to a clergyman's hunting was the coarse language that would be sure to meet his ears in the field: now, if every sportsman present were a parson, the tone of conversation could not be more free from anything that is objectionable.

No styles of riding could be more different from each other than those of the Rector of Lamport and of the Rev. John Whalley, Rector of the village of Ecton. Tall, slim, and of a peculiarly graceful carriage when on horseback, the latter seemed to glide rather than ride across a country, and was a worthy rival of Sir Charles Knightley and of Mr. Davy, though of a rather later date.

Always riding horses of a good stamp and with plenty of quality, the man who found himself in front of the Ecton parson might be sure that he was quite as near hounds as he ought to be.

The Rev. William Dickens of Woollaston was a "customer" of another school. Living on the Oakley side of the country, it was only occasionally that he met the Pytchley at Harrowden, Finedon, or Hardwicke village; but not a member of either hunt was more sure to be "there or thereabouts" than Woollaston's somewhat irreverent reverend. Enjoying something of a reputation for "smart sayings," as well as smart riding, he one day proved his title to the first at the expense of his brother-cleric, the Rev. Mr. Partridge. This gentleman, beginning to feel some qualms as to the propriety of a clergyman hunting, but unable to forego his favourite amusement, thought to " hedge " by appearing in trousers and shoes, intead of the usual breeches and boots. Greatly tickled at this change in his friend's attire, " Billy " Dickens forthwith proceeded to christen him " Perdrix aux choux."

For many a long year there was no more familiar figure seen at certain of the Quorn and Pytchley meets than that of the Rev. John Cave Humphrey of Laughton. The long, straight back, the " once-round " white linen scarf, and the raucous voice still dwell on the memory of many a Pytchley man; as does the form of the fair niece who was said to be the heroine of Whyte-Melville's immortal " Market Harboro'." For some time it seemed in the eyes of niece as well as uncle, that there was nothing more enjoyable in this world than the hunting-field. " It is a very solemn thing being married," said a parent to his daughter, on her announcing her acceptance of a suitor. " Yes, father, I know it," said the *fiancée*, " but it is a deal solemner thing being single ! " So thought, too, the fair huntress of Laughton. Runs with the hounds, however long, all of a sudden seemed to her nothing worth compared with a lifelong run with a husband, and the worthy old rector was left alone in his glory. He, to whom a day with the hounds had seemed for many a year to be the one great enjoyment of life, was now no longer seen with Pytchley or with Quorn; and after a while, a strange name appeared in the Clergy List as Rector of the parish of Laughton.

In this small clerical hunting-pantheon a niche must be assigned to a reverend sportsman, who, living at one time of his life at Dodford, and afterwards at Boughton, near Northampton, for many years got his twice-a-week with hounds with commendable regularity. Without any clerical duties to perform latterly, or to engage his attention, to see a fox well hunted, and to get a chat with friends at the meet, was for several seasons a legitimate source of pleasure to this true lover of the chase. Jumping, with its attendant demands upon the nervous system, and other drawbacks, was at no time a part of the pastime he greatly affected; but an accurate knowledge of the geographical position of all gates and gaps enabled him to see much of what was going on. Living in close proximity, at Boughton, to the house occupied by the author of "Digby Grand," he greatly enjoyed both his society and his abilities as a writer, and was in the habit of telling his reverend brethren that "if they would only read extracts from Whyte-Melville's novels instead of preaching sermons of their own, it would be to the advantage of their congregations as well as of themselves." The apt remarks and weather-beaten visage of this reverend sportsman will long be kindly borne in mind by those who esteemed him for his genial nature, his willingness to assist a brother cleric in time of need, and above all, perhaps, for his genuine love of hunting. The unenlightened Esquimaux hopes that his paradise will not be without plenty of whales; and probably that of the old hunter just spoken of will not suffer in his eyes by the possession of a nice sprinkling of foxes.

Sixth, and last, on the present list of clergy, whose

more or less spare time was given to hunting the fox, comes one whose costume, habits, and general lack of self-devotion to the things more immediately pertaining to his walk in life, rendered him, for full half a century a conspicuous member of society. The scion of an old Leicestershire stock, noted for its love for sport of any kind, Mr. Loraine Smith inherited a full share of the "family failing." For such a one to take "holy orders" is indeed to mistake one's profession. But *humanum est errare*; and at that time to be shovelled into the Church was a provision for a son eagerly sought for by puzzled and impecunious parents. By nature and education more of a country squire than a country parson, the Rector of Passenham, near Stony Stratford, a small parish without exacting duties, made fox-hunting his chief occupation and amusement. A brilliant horseman, strong and determined, the Grafton Hunt had no finer rider among its members, nor one whom a stranger would so speedily pick out as "the character" of the party assembled at the meet. Barely tolerating the black coat that was the index of his profession, his hunting waistcoat had a broad scarlet binding, and the colour that was forbidden to himself came out in bold relief on the riding habits of the lady members of his family. Present for once in a way at a "Visitation" held at Northampton, the rigid sombreness of his clerical attire attracted the attention of two hunting church-wardens, who had never seen his reverence in black and all black. "I'll bet you a bottle of wine there's some scarlet about him somewhere," said one. "Done with you," said the other, and lost his bet; as on closer investigation a scarlet under-waistcoat was discovered beneath the conventional "vest." Many of his intimate friends being among the gentry of Northamptonshire, a gallop with the "Pytchley" was always a red-letter day to him; and his favourite mount was kept for the occasion. To many beyond, as well as within, his own neighbourhood, he is known by an engraving in which he is portrayed charging a formidable-looking "oxer," on his famous horse "Gatto." The attitude of both horse and rider is given with much spirit and accuracy; and the resemblance to the latter merits a higher degree of praise than was accorded to the portrait of an old and esteemed coachman in the family of the writer taken in livery. The old man's wife was requested to give her opinion as to the amount of resemblance she saw in the picture to her husband. "Very like," she said, "but particular the buttons!" Devoted to flowers in general, and the growth of roses in particular, he found in his garden his greatest pleasure during the summer months; and the well-shaped pansy or picotee was to him almost an object of worship. The delights of a garden, however, did not erase from his thoughts the recollection of winter joys, and a "lick of red paint" upon pump, water-pot, and flower-prop, served to remind him of the " good time coming." A cricketer of the old school, his favourite "get-up" of nankeen knee-breeches, silk stockings, and a sock rolled over to protect the ankle, gave his appearance a "chic" which would in vain be looked for now-a-days. Dressed as described, slowly running to the wicket to bowl a ball destitute of pace, curl, twist of any sort, he looked the model of an old-fashioned, well-bred country cricketer. The details of a singular experience met with by Mr. Loraine Smith in his capacity of a magistrate, cannot fail to interest the reader of these pages.

A deserter from the 58th Regiment then stationed at Canterbury, Henry Couch, on the false pretence of being on furlough and unable to reach his home from having been robbed of his money, induced Mr. L. Smith to advance him ten shillings. Discovering the imposition, the police were speedily on the track of the rogue militant, who, ere many days had elapsed, found himself an occupant of a cell in Northampton gaol, on a charge of defrauding the Rev. Loraine Smith of the sum of ten shillings. A very short acquaintance with the new comer was sufficient to show the governor of the gaol that he had got hold of a "character," and that he was not entertaining "an angel unawares." Whilst awaiting his trial, Couch helped to pass away the time by writing letters to the Rector of Passenham for pecuniary assistance for his defence at the Quarter Sessions. These letters, being without parallel in the annals of correspondence, are here given for the amusement of the reader, who will not fail to observe that each letter is headed with a text from Scripture.

To account for a cleverness and a language that seem inexplicable coming from a common soldier, it must be stated that he had been in some way connected with the press, and so was a man of good education, as well as of unusual natural abilities.

Letter No. 2.

"Now therefore there is utterly a fault among you, because ye go to law one with another. Why do ye not rather suffer yourselves to be defrauded?"— 1 Cor. vi. 7.

"June 10th, 1851.

"Rev. Sir,—Not to my knowledge having a friend upon earth to whom I could apply for a favour in any case of emergency, I have been prevailed upon to do violence to that native modesty which has marked every action of my life to apply to you to befriend me with a copy of the depositions taken at Mr. Congreve's office on Friday last. My situation in this establishment is not a very enviable one, being incarcerated within the four walls of a small cell, with a six-inch door and sundry bars of iron between myself and liberty. Another walk from Stony Stratford to Passenham would afford an agreeable relief. I heard related at Stony Stratford the other day, by a person of most retentive memory, a part of a sermon delivered by yourself, in which you stated, 'that it often struck you how the devil must laugh when he sees so many thousands posting hourly and momentarily the downward path to perdition.' I entirely agree with you; and it has recently struck me that his mirth must have been extreme when he saw me posting down the road from Passenham to Paushanger, on the afternoon of the third ultimo: he must have enjoyed a double-barrelled laugh then, one at me, the other at your Reverence. Pray, Sir, take great care of yourself before the Sessions. I am given to understand that you are partial to the noble sport of fox-hunting. It is doubtless an invigorating amusement; but if in one of these excursions you should happen to break your neck over a gate or hurdle, though it would be consistent with my profession as a Christian to forgive that gate, I certainly should never forget it."

In the next letter he expresses his gratitude for the receipt of the required papers, and solicits assistance for his defence.

LETTER 3.

"REV. SIR,—It is with a deep sense of gratitude that I acknowledge your kindness in complying with the request contained in my last letter relative to the depositions. Depend upon it if I can render you a similar service I will not fail to do so. In order to facilitate my defence, I have consulted a legal gentleman, who will undertake it for four pounds. I shall have no difficulty in obtaining the whole of this sum, with the trifling exception of 3*l*. 19*s*. 11½*d*.; and this amount I see little prospect of getting. Would it be too much to ask you, who are a minister of that Gospel which affirms that 'it is more blessed to give than to receive;' and that 'he that hath pity upon the poor, lendeth unto the Lord,' who is a very punctual Paymaster, and wishes to oblige me? Now I want the loan of that amount, for a very short time, on my own personal security. I don't wish you to give it, merely lend it; and to place it in your ledger under the ten shillings you so obligingly lent me at Passenham. I promise very faithfully that you shall have the ten shillings again, and I refer you for the payment of the 3*l*. 19*s*. 11½*d*. to Proverbs, chapter xix. verse 17, where you will find that the money is in very safe hands. Nor are these the only terms on which I wish to negotiate this loan with you. You will remember that my regiment is stationed at Canterbury, and that the barracks are within ten minutes' walk of the palace of the Archbishop. Although I am at present in Northampton gaol, few know the extent of my influence out of it. It is just possible that may be the means one day of getting your letters addressed to the Very Rev. Loraine Smith, and of having your low-crowned gossamer superseded by a best superfine "beaver," with upturned brims. There are two other eminent ecclesiastics with whom I am intimately acquainted, and who might have it in their power to help you for my sake. Now do reflect upon this. Consider that it would be a very slight satisfaction for you to deprive a widowed mother of an only son, by getting him sent to some penal settlement.

"Mr. Loraine Smith, allow me to inquire, have you a son? an only son? a wild reckless youth? I hope not; but it is not an absurd proposition: if you have, lend me the money. Do not keep me in suspense; it is a very uncomfortable state of existence. Please to convey my warmest thanks to Mr. Congreve (Clerk to the Magistrates of the Stony Stratford bench), for sending me a copy of the depositions: also my respects through him to Mrs. Congreve, and to all the diminutive, juvenile Congreves; in short to the whole box of Congreves. Tell Mr. Congreve that in the case of the next prisoner brought to his office for examination, I trust he will not ignite on so slight a friction, as he did in my case over the warrant."

In the next letter, the last of this set, the reckless impertinence of the writer reaches its culminating point. As usual it commences with a text.

"Whoso hath this world's goods, and seeth his brother in need, and shutteth up his bowels of compassion; how dwelleth the love of God in him?"

LETTER 4.

"Rev. Sir,—Intense anxiety caused by receiving no reply to a letter I addressed to you on Friday last, makes me fear that you must be unwell, perhaps seriously unwell. This notion causes me infinite mental anguish, considering as I do, that illness alone could have prevented you answering my former letter. Let me entreat you then, if you are suffering from some attack of illness, to avail yourself immediately of the professional assistance of the most skilful medical practitioner in the neighbourhood, so that you may be sufficiently recovered to attend at the Sessions, or purchase of some respectable druggist an abundance of Parr's Life Pills, or Morrison's, or those of some other eminent physician, and keep them in a box of magnesia, and take when required. Do not regard, either, the vulgar prejudice entertained by the ignorant against arsenic and prussic acid. They are as harmless in their effects as castor oil. I have known numerous instances of parties who have taken these invaluable remedies, and never required medicine again for the rest of their lives. Then take the advice of a friend, not merely a professional friend, taking a deep interest in your welfare. Procure an ounce of arsenic and an ounce of magnesia, dissolve each in a pint of hot water, warm tea or sherry, and drink while hot. Be careful to leave none; but after having swallowed the whole, take a lump of sugar to dispel the nauseous taste, and then placing your feet in hot water (as hot as you can endure it), and wrapping your head in a blanket, go to bed. Strictly follow this advice, and I have but one opinion as to the result. I have just seen my professional adviser, who says he will not stir in my case until he receives the four pounds. Please send the money as soon as possible to allow the man of law to prepare his brief. With many wishes for your welfare,

"Your's very truly,
"Henry Couch."

The trial took place, and the sentence was one year's imprisonment with hard labour. Throughout the proceedings, the demeanour of the accused was eccentric and defiant, and on the foreman of the jury returning the verdict of "guilty," the prisoner exclaimed, "Well, gentlemen of the jury, you have fallen six feet in my estimation within the last few seconds." On Sergeant Miller resuming his seat after closing the case for the prosecution, Couch leant over the dock, and touching him on the shoulder, said: "I say, lawyer, was that your first brief?" During his term of imprisonment, he was allowed to write an account of his proceedings, from the time he deserted from Canterbury, to the day of his apprehension at Skipton in Lincolnshire. In this remarkable record of a rogue's evil deeds, Couch gives a minute account of each day's proceedings, with the names and personal descriptions of the various people he cheated and deceived. Having provided himself with a forged furlough, he went from town to town, obtaining billets at the different public-houses, and on plea of being a soldier in distress, getting money from the magistrates whose residences he happened to come across on his road to London. He pursued the same tactics until he reached Thrapston, when, finding that he was under suspicion, he changed his mode of action and became a recruiting-serjeant, and possessing the "gift of the gab," and also the art of persuasion, many a yokel and young farmer, full of public-house beer and swagger, was induced to pocket the Queen's shilling, as he believed, and was afterwards bought off by reproachful and indignant relations. The sums demanded by the pseudo-serjeant for liberating his victims from their supposed enlistment, ranged from twenty to thirty shillings. Nemesis, in the guise of a Northampton county-policeman, put an end to the nefarious practices of this arch-rogue for some time: but the spirit of evil was too strong within him to allow of his becoming an honest citizen. Seven years after quitting Northampton gaol, he again found himself one of its inmates on the same description of charge as before, obtaining money under false pretences. On his way from Birmingham (where he had robbed his employer) to London, he entered a cottage in a village near Northampton, and told the good woman of the house that her son had just been apprehended on a charge of theft. After expressing his deep sympathy with her in her serious trouble, he informed her that he was a lawyer, and would take the delinquent's case in hand on a payment down of the customary legal fee of six and eightpence. After many protestations on the part of the unhappy mother as to her inability to pay such a sum, she contrived to raise it amongst her friends, and handing it over to her shameless impostor, she entreated him to enter at once upon her son's business. Very soon after his departure, the poor woman fell in with the rural policeman, and at once opened her heart on the subject of her sorrow. A few questions soon opened the eyes of the policeman to the real state of the case, and off he started in hot pursuit of the sham legal adviser. It was not long before he ran into his fox. The first public-house in the adjoining village was where he had gone to ground, and soon after the name of "Harry Couch" was on the list of prisoners awaiting trial at the ensuing Quarter Sessions for the county of Northampton. Greatly to the surprise and disappointment of a crowded court, the prisoner pleaded guilty, and he received the sharp, but not too severe sentence of "seven years transportation." But even at this apparently final stage in his career, the reader has not heard quite the last of him.

As one of the county-magistrates, it was the duty of the writer of this history, in company with a brother justice, to visit the convict in gaol, and to inform him that he would shortly be transferred to the government prison at Wakefield. Nothing occurred at the interview beyond the fact that the writer remonstrated with his companion on hearing him address the prisoner as "Mr. Couch." Not long after this the magisterial remonstrant received a letter bearing on the outside the official mark of "Wakefield Prison." On opening it, he proceeded to read as follows:—

"168 C. Register 5558.

"MY DEAR HARRY,—"I trust that you will not consider that my neglect in not writing to give you the opportunity of going to Northampton to take a farewell of me, involved a breach of that friendship which for the last six years existed between us. The fact is, that it was not until within two hours of the time that I found myself speeding away by express train that I knew that the hour of my departure was at hand. Had I, however, been aware of the fact in time to have written, I do not know that I could have done so, as from the strength of your affection, a personal interview might have led to a scene; and that, of all things, I mortally abhor. Let us then look forward, old boy, to our next merry meeting; and if it be true that absence makes the heart grow fonder, we shall neither of us regret our prolonged separation. Seven years, though, is beyond a joke, and it certainly was far more than I had bargained for; nor can I account for the severity of the sentence, except upon the presumption that the court must have seen something in my appearance that convinced them that it would be against the interests of the community that I should be at large. I had, however, taken every precaution to divest myself of all those indications by which your double-distilled, capped and jewelled rogue is usually known. I had been to a hatter and had the brims of my tile pressed down, and I had exchanged my doeskin gloves for black kid, but it all proved ineffectual. It can't be helped now, however; so we must each of us try to bear up against it. But to come to the more immediate purport of this letter. Our mutual friend, Hutton, as you know, has resigned the chaplaincy of the Northampton gaol. I verily believe that during the nine years that he has held the office, with singleness of heart he has endeavoured to do all the good in his power, and to discharge his duty with credit to himself, and satisfaction to all concerned. He deserves a testimonial, and ought to have one; and I ask you, my dear fellow, to set the thing a-going at once. Give him some such thing as a silver inkstand; and if it be said that this suggestion comes with a bad grace from one who sacrifices nothing but his time and trouble in making it, I authorize you to advance on my account the sum of two pounds. Preserve this letter as a proof of the debt, and I will either repay you when we meet, or you can deduct the amount when you make your will. In publishing the list of subscribers, I hope that the names will be printed alphabetically, so that 'Couch' will come in just after Barton and Bevan [two county magistrates]. It is very humiliating seeing one's name at the bottom of a list. I did not see you on Saturday last, [probably a visiting-day]. How was it? I was glad Barton didn't come either. His addressing me as 'Mister Couch!' Do you recollect it? As the virtuously-indignant Mrs. Gamp exclaimed, 'The hidear!' I felt truly grateful to you for checking him on that occasion. Well, I must now close."

[Here follows a picture of an imaginary domestic circle.]

"Remember me kindly to Margaret and Charlotte, and to the dear old lady, as well. I fancy I see her now, sitting in the chimney-corner with the cat in her lap. Good-bye, my dear Harry, and when you next hear me addressed as 'Mister Couch,' remind the person who thus forgets himself, that he compromises his dignity in so doing."

A letter written to the chaplain of the Northampton gaol, giving a description of Wakefield Prison and its management, is too graphic and amusing not to be given at length; after which this most remarkable example of abilities thrown away will disappear from view, his ultimate fate being unknown.

Wakefield Prison. Reg. 5558.

"Rev. and dear Sir,—My characteristic presumption leads me to imagine that I may confer a pleasure upon you by intimating that I am as comfortable here as the circumstances of my position will permit. This establishment is constructed on the same principle as that at Northampton, but it is far more extensive, affording accommodation for about four hundred government, and as many county prisoners. The former remain, as a general rule, subject to a different discipline, for about nine months; and after being carefully taught such lessons as are inculcated in the 1st Psalm, and 14th verse of Proverbs, chapter iv., are sent to associate with about one thousand others similarly prepared. I contemplate making an effort to remain in a state of separation, though I doubt not that I shall have to become honest by the ordinary routine of the "system," and so remain a rogue. The principal employments here appear to be tailoring and making shoes, and fancy and other sorts of mats. The establishment, so far as the convict department goes, must be little less than self-supporting; at any rate, all the labour is productive. There are none of your hand-labour mills here. Strange infatuation! miserable delusion! that idleness, the chief characteristic of criminals, is to be eradicated, and a love of industry acquired by compelling a man to turn three hundred revolutions per hour, for three hours in each day, of those diabolical machines which disgrace the gaol of Northampton. This, too, under the penalty of loss of food for non-performance of the task allotted out! The man sees that he is doing no good; that a complicated machine has been invented to torture his body, and he laughs at the idea of acquiring industrious habits by such means; habits formed by compulsion!! Compel a man to work, and his mind revolts from it; but lock him up for three or four days without work, then he will ask for work; which if it is not forced upon him as a punishment, he will gratefully accept as a boon. I am employed as a tailor. I am in a very comfortable cell, well supplied with books and writing materials. If sufficiently industrious I shall be credited with fourpence, sixpence, or eightpence a week out of my earnings; I do not know in what manner the remainder will be applied. I believe that the present amount of the National Debt is two hundred and eighty millions; but I have no doubt that the lesson taught by the affair of Paul, Strahan and Bates, will excite in the authorities a becoming caution as to how they invest it. The chapel holds about 1000 persons. There are two full services on Sundays; and one every day from ten to eleven. The manifestations of piety on the part of the congregation must be very edifying to observers possessed of sufficient charity to believe in their genuineness. The prisoners rise at six o'clock, and are supposed to work until half-past seven, when each is supplied with eight ounces of bread (baked about the time of the Norman Conquest), and half a pint of very apocryphal milk. I know nothing of the geological formation of this part of Yorkshire: about Scarborough there is a substratum of chalk. Dinner is served at one. This meal is superior in quality to anything to be found on the table of a working man, and of many an artisan. It is better than that allowed in any other of this sort of establishment, which, in general, is such as a Grosvenor or Belgrave Square cat, anxious to preserve caste among his peers, would not compromise his dignity by condescending to look at. At seven we drop work, and read until nine, when we go to bed. Some receive three or four hours' instruction in the course of the week, but for this privilege I am considered ineligible.

"Expressing my warmest and most grateful thanks for the kindness you showed me at Northampton,

"I am, dear and Rev. Sir,
"Yours very truly,
"H. COUCH."

Colonel W. Cartwright, to whom it fell, as Chairman of Quarter Sessions, to pass sentence on Couch at each of the trials at Northampton, about the same time received from another soldier a letter so opposite in its character to those given above, and yet so unique in its phraseology, that the reader of these pages must not be deprived of the benefit of it. An old serjeant in the Rifle Brigade, living at Weedon, wishing to fish in a small stream which ran through one or two meadows occupied by the gallant officer, thus addressed him :—

"Weedon Barracks, May 12th, 1856.

"HONOURABLE SIR,—A discharged serjeant of the Rifle Brigade, and one who had the honour of serving in the same company, and in more than one campaign under the command of the gallant and much lamented Captain Cartwright (killed in the Crimea), now makes bold to solicit of his honoured and bereaved parent a written permission to angle of an evening in that wealthy brook, which, pursuing its way by Divine Will through your honour's extensive domains, encourages and compensates the fertilizing efforts of your Honour's tenants, adds a cheerful vivacity to the face of nature, seasonably serene, and furnishes of its finny population many impressive convictions of the kind, unceasing regard of our great Creator in the various sustenance, delicate and invigorating, for the more worthy portion of His laborious creatures.

"Trusting, Sir, that indulgent time is reconciling you to the fate of my kind, deceased officer, your much-beloved and lamented son, and that your Honour will condescend to befriend the man whom that son so often befriended, I remain, Honourable Sir, with all due respect,

"Your Honour's most humble and devoted servant and faithful soldier,

"JOHN DUNT.

"War Department, Weedon Barracks."

It may be asserted, without fear of contradiction, that a parallel to the letter given above may be searched for in vain in any language. It is, moreover, a matter for wonder how a common-soldier's head could have contained such a wealth of imagery, and such a rich abundance of the gift of "high falutin'."

CHAPTER III.

Mr. John Chaworth Musters, *Master*, 1821.—Opinions on his hounds—Troublesome foxes—Attachment of his hounds—His qualifications for the Mastership—Mr. Osbaldeston, *Master*, 1827—His appearance, manners and abilities—Excellence of his hounds—The best riders at Melton, 1820-30—Osbaldeston's excellence as a steeplechase rider—Race on 'Grimaldi' against 'Moonraker'—Celebrity of his bitch-pack—Run from Misterton to Laughton Mills—Match to ride 200 miles in ten hours, with the horses used—Challenges all the world for 20,000*l.*—As a shot, a cricketer, a boxer, an M.P., and a Turfite—Mr. Wilkins, *Master*, 1834—Jack Stevens, huntsman; his early death—"Billy" Russell—Mr. George Payne, *Master*, 1835—The Earl of Chesterfield, *Master*, 1838—Lords Cardigan, Maidstone, and Macdonald—Old Times and Manners—Perfection of Lord Chesterfield's arrangements—His resignation in 1840—The Hon. Wilbraham Tollemache—"Ginger" Stubbs, and other hunters—Dick Christian and Matty Milton—Old horses not so safe as young ones—Daniel Lambert—Mr. T. Assheton Smith—Dick Christian and Bill Wright.

The modern history of the Pytchley Hunt may be said to commence in 1821, when Mr. John Chaworth Musters, of Colwick Hall, Notts, better known as "Jack Musters," moved with his own pack of hounds out of Nottinghamshire, to take the Mastership of the Pytchley country. The pleasant days and lively nights of the "old club" had now passed away; but, so far as hunting and convenience went, the removal of the hounds to a central point, and the abolition of what may be called the "alternate system," was greatly in favour of sport. To strangers the change was highly welcome; and Brixworth and Market Harbro' now became much frequented by hunting-visitors. The country at that time is described as being tremendously fenced, the posts and railing of other days having given way to hedges which never used to be cut. "Scarcely a horse," wrote "Acteon," "can go a season or so in this country without injury to, or partial loss of, sight; and the rider has so much to do to take care of his own eyes, that he cannot look out as he ought to do for those of his horse over these tremendously high and stiff quicks. Bullock-fences and all the variety necessary to keep in cattle, stiff stiles, locked gates, and wide brooks, bedeck the grass-country in great profusion."

Taking up his quarters at Pitsford Hall, recently vacated by Colonel Corbet of the Blues, a veteran sportsman, Mr. Musters entered upon his duties, which, according to "Nimrod," were scarcely equal to the nature of the country or the work expected of it. "Few packs of hounds will stand a close examination," says this great critic: "Mr. Musters certainly will not. The bitches are handsome, and of good stamp; but the dog-hounds are many of them past their prime, and as a lot, not so sightly as they should be. A liberal draught is wanted; and a large supply of three and four-year-old hounds is required."

About this time the country was unusually full of badgers, both in the woodlands and elsewhere; so much so, that while digging for a hunted fox in Brampton Wood, one day after a good run, five were found in the same drain. This very poor relation of the bear, so distant as scarcely to have the claim of kinship allowed by the latter, had grown so scarce in the Brocklesby country, that a member of the family was sent from the Kettering district into that part of Yorkshire to act as an "earth-maker" for the foxes. A great improvement on the artificial earth, which too frequently fails in its purpose.

Notwithstanding the depreciatory view taken by "Nimrod" of the hounds that had been brought out of Nottinghamshire, another writer in the "Sporting Magazine," speaking of Mr. Musters, says: "He remained in the Pytchley country four or five seasons, showing extraordinary sport, and convincing his numerous admirers that, not only was he the most skilful huntsman that had ever appeared in that country, [shade of Charles King! where were you, when this was penned!] but in any other." He goes on to say: "The stud-hounds of Mr. Musters were much sought after by the breeders of the day; and the blood of that excellent dog, 'Collier,' was second to none." The two great sporting critics of the day, "Nimrod" and "Acteon," do not seem by this to have taken at all the same view of the merits of a fox-hound in point of make and shape; and on many other points connected with hunting they appear to have walked on the lines of "two of a trade never agreeing."

A fox at Hunsbury Hill afforded some excellent runs at this time, and was so successful in evading his pursuers that he was known as the "Hunsbury Hill Devil." On the last occasion of his having been hunted by, and defeating the celebrated Jack Musters and his three merry men, Saddler, Derry, and Wood, he took his usual line through Wootton by Delapré, Brayfield Furze, and Yardley Chase, to near Olney Bridge, where he again succeeded in dodging the enemy, and sending them empty away. It was supposed, however, that on the following day the poor "demon," still aweary and stiff from his bucketting, fell a victim to George Carter and the Grafton hounds, who came across him before he was sufficiently recovered to find his way back to his "lares" at Hunsbury Hill. Another fox, always at home at Sulby Gorse when called upon, had often been "one too many" for Mr. Musters; and Mr. Osbaldeston, at that time Master of the Quorn, had frequently been treated in like manner by a "customer" at Gartree Hill. On the last day of the season, each master determined to finish up with a cut at his old foe, and Mr. Musters backed himself for five pounds to bring his fox to hand before the Squire had succeeded in catching his. No sooner had the former put his hounds into cover than an old hound challenged, and away went the "Flyer" pointing for Bosworth, and on past Theddingworth, to Laughton Hills. Here a man had been placed at the "earths," so he retraced his steps, running the same line back. Near Theddingworth, he was viewed in a large pasture, but Mr. Musters declined to lift his hounds a yard, saying that he would not take an unhandsome advantage of so good an animal. This over-chivalrous spirit lost him his fox, and his five pounds as well. A flock of sheep brought the hounds to a check, the scent suffered from a passing storm, and though he was spoken to on the Harbro' and Welford Road, nothing could be made of it; so that again the fortunate tenant of Sulby Gorse saved his brush, and lived to fight another day.

Amongst other qualifications rendering him pre-eminent

as a huntsman, Mr. Musters possessed, in no ordinary degree, that of attaching hounds to himself. In his "Notitia Venatica," Mr. Vyner tells a curious instance of this in the following interesting incident. When Mr. Musters hunted in Northamptonshire, the hounds, having to meet in that well-known cover, Badby Wood, were taken on the day previous by his first whip, Smith, to sleep at the "Bull's Head" at Weedon. On arriving at a place where the road from Northampton converges into that by which they were travelling, suddenly some of the most foremost of the hounds became restless, and by their manner Smith concluded that a travelling fox had passed near the spot. In a few moments, the whole pack, who had been fed, and were jogging listlessly along, seemed suddenly to be aroused from their torpor, and in another moment were out of hand. The Huntsman thought that the devil had seized them; the Whips rode after them and rated; but all to no purpose— to stop them was impossible. At last in turning a corner about a mile further on, who should appear in sight but Mr. Musters himself, who had come by a second road and was going quietly on his way, on the hack he usually rode to covert, to dine and sleep at a friend's house near the next day's meet. The delight of the pack at so unexpectedly coming across their beloved master was indescribable. One hound actually jumped upon the horse's quarters, and licked Mr. Musters's face, and it was so difficult a matter to call them off, that he was obliged to go out of his way to conduct them himself to the inn where they were to lodge for the night. A very spirited picture of this scene, with the hound leaping upon the horse's back, was drawn by the celebrated artist Alken, and decorates Mr. Vyner's book. Speaking of Mr. Musters, "Nimrod" goes on to say: "No man was ever better qualified by nature for a Master of hounds. His personal appearance and engaging manners could not fail to establish his popularity with all who hunted with him; and the practical science he displayed in the field delighted all true sportsmen. So complete a master was he of all athletic sports, that at one time of his life he would have leaped, hopped, ridden, run, fought, danced, fished, swum, shot, fenced, played cricket (a game in which he considered he greatly excelled), tennis, and skated, against any man in England!"

After remaining six years in Northamptonshire, and showing excellent sport, Mr. Musters returned to his own county, and the famous "Squire Osbaldeston," leaving the Quorn country which he had hunted for some years, became Master of the Pytchley in 1827. The prenomen of "Squire" by which he was better known in the sporting world than by his own patronymic, arose from the fact that out of the four packs of hounds hunting Leicestershire at that time, his was the only one not having a nobleman for its Master. Short in stature, not prepossessing in appearance even on horseback, rough of speech, and uncouth in manner, he excelled in every outdoor pursuit, and at a ball was fond of displaying his skill in dancing a reel. The chief event of the evening on the Race-Ball night at Northampton was when the "Squire," occupying the centre of the room, was the cynosure of all eyes as he danced, and excellently well too, a Highland reel. On these occasions, old Mr. Tattersall might be seen leaning against the wall with his lame leg slightly raised, watching the performance, while an amused and half-envious smile lit up his genial face.

Race "Ordinaries" were in vogue in those days, and the Squire not being a Rechabite, the dancing followed so immediately upon the dining that there was scarcely time to put on the armour of sobriety before the fiddles struck up. Take him altogether, it is probable that a better "all-round" man never lived, but in no one thing did he appear to have been superlatively good. In riding to hounds he had many superiors, as he also had in hunting them; at cricket he was not good enough to figure in the eleven of England; and as a shot he was not the equal of Captain Ross or of the Hon. G. Anson. Sprung from an old Yorkshire family, Mr. Osbaldeston had all the education and advantages which are the birthright of the children of wealthy parents, and was sent to Eton, and afterwards to Brazenose College; the latter, equally with the former, failing to elicit any sign of a predilection for classical learning. At the earliest possible moment he shook from his feet the dust of chapel and of lecture-room. Though not quick in mastering the secrets of the Latin tongue, nor in construing the metres of a Greek play, the Yorkshire squire was far from lacking in ability. With much natural acuteness, he speedily acquired a knowledge of anything upon which he cared to bestow his attention; and hounds and horses were the earliest objects of his interest. By strict adherence to the best principles in breeding, by selecting as sires the choicest blood of other kennels, and by rigidly rejecting every puppy that did not seem likely to reach his standard, he succeeded in possessing himself of a pack of hounds second to none in England. It was with such a pack as this that he commenced to hunt a country, about which he is reported to have said, " I have been in search of Paradise all my life, and have found it at last." Had they only been written at that time, he might well have quoted Whyte-Melville's lines :—

> " I will show you a country that none can surpass,
> For a flyer to cross like a bird on the wing,
> We have acres of woodland, and oceans of grass,
> We have game in the autumn, and cubs in the spring.
> We have scores of good fellows hang out in these shires,
> And the best of them all, are ' the Pytchley Hunt Squires.''

With such tackle, and with such excellent A.D.C.'s as Jack Stevens and Jem Shirley, the "Squire" was bound to show sport, which he undoubtedly did do ; but as Horseman or Huntsman, he at no time reached the same high standard as his predecessor, Mr. Musters. His nerve had been somewhat shaken by severe falls, and he always made it pretty hot for the man who did not give him plenty of room at a fence. One great drawback to Mr. Osbaldeston, as either Huntsman or Master, was that a natural love of gossip had grown into such an inveterate habit of chattering, that his tongue never seemed at rest ; and even in drawing a cover he would let the men do the work whilst he talked with some friend. In a book of Hunting-Songs collected by Mr. S. C. Musters, and published in 1883, a classified list of the best performers at Melton between 1820 and 1830, Osbaldeston is placed third in the second class. Given with all the formality of a University class list, the names stand as follows :—

First Class.	Second Class.	Third Class.
Tom Assheton Smith.	V. Maher.	Sir F. Burdett.
Lindon.	Maxse.	Chester.
Rolleston.	Osbaldeston.	F. Bentinck.
Lord Jersey.	Lord R. Manners.	M'Kenzie.
Chaworth (Musters).	Mills.	Lord Aylesford.
Cholmeley.	Pierrepoint.	Megler.
Hon. C. W. Forester.	Lucas.	Moore.
Sir Bellingham Graham.	F. Forrester.	Petre.
	Lord Dartmouth.	Napier.
Davy.	Bradshaw.	Walker.
White.	Barnett.	Drummond.
Ramsden.	Vane-Powlett.	Arnold.
Lowther.	Lord Tavistock.	Duke of Rutland.
Standish.	Lord C. Manners.	Lord Lonsdale.
Lord Plymouth.	Dottin.	
Rancliffe.	Christie.	
Lord Alvanley.		

In the above list the most notable in the first class are the names of the following, the first and foremost being that of Tom Assheton Smith, Master of the Quorn, and confessedly the straightest man across country that ever rode to hounds. He it was who said that on coming to a big fence, if a man only threw his heart over to the other side his horse was sure to follow; a dictum, the truth of which few will care to deny. Lord Jersey, father of the Hon. Frederick Villiers (himself a first-rate man to hounds, and twice Master of the Pytchley); Sir Bellingham Graham and Mr. Chaworth (Musters), both heads of the same establishment; Messrs. Davy and Ramsden, well-known with the Pytchley Hunt of that time; and of Lord Alvanley, Wit, and Welter weight. At the head of the third class appears the name of Sir Francis Burdett, in his early days the most outspoken of Radical politicians. A Radical of the Radicals, and an idol of the populace, for some time there was no measure which Sir Francis seemed incapable of digesting, or to be at variance with opinions which ultimately landed him a prisoner in the Tower. With advancing years, however, the political camera presented things in such a different aspect that the worthy baronet turned a complete "volteface," and ended his days in the full sanctity of Toryism. Two remarkable instances of a similar change of views came, on one occasion, to the notice of the writer of these lines. Dining at the table-d'hôte of an hotel in Florence, he found himself seated between two elderly gentlemen, one an Englishman, the other a native of the sister isle. In the course of conversation, the former stated that he had been the friend and principal coadjutor of the arch-chartist, Fergus O'Connor, whilst the other had been the lieutenant of Smith O'Brien, and had just missed being present at the capture of that patriot in the battle of the "Cabbage-garden." Each had lived sufficiently long to realize the fact that the colour of political views formed in hot youth will not always endure when exposed to the sunlight of time. The former adherent of the irrepressible "Fergus" had become a strong anti-O'Connorite, and the lieutenant of General Smith O'Brien had subsided into being a strong advocate of the English alliance.

Though not figuring in the first class as a rider to hounds, "Squire Osbaldeston" had few, if any, superiors in a steeple-chase, either among professionals or amateurs, his quick eye, powerful limbs, and undeniable nerve, when out of a crowd, being greatly in his favour where he had to steer a difficult mount; and his services in the capacity of a cross-country jockey were always greatly in request. The Harrovian of 1832 will not fail to recollect (especially if he shared the fate of the narrator of the event, and came in for "just a taste" of the birch for not being present at the four o'clock bill on that day) the great match for 1000 sovereigns between Mr. Elmore's "Moonraker" and Mr. Adams's "Grimaldi." The race, which excited extraordinary interest from the celebrity of the animals, and from the fact that a few days before, at St. Albans, the two horses had run within a head of each other for the steeple-chase at that place, came off over Mr. Elmore's farm near Harrow. Though "Grimaldi" had been defeated at St. Albans, Mr. Osbaldeston, who was the umpire on that occasion, was so impressed with his merit, that he gave the owner of "Moonraker" fifty pounds to run him for a thousand sovereigns, on condition that he himself should ride "Grimaldi." All London was emptied to witness the race, and it being a half-holiday, few indeed were the Harrow boys who did not prefer to risk a "swishing" to being absent from so great an event. Fate favoured the majority, but a few had to make acquaintance with the swing of Dr. Longley's arm for the breach of a fundamental law, and old "Custos," time-honoured birch-provider to the school, had a busy time in preparing the instruments of torture. The course selected was from a field close to the seventh milestone on the Edgware Road, and the winning-post was in a meadow near a farmhouse at Harrow Weald. The distance to be run was four miles, and the course, though heavy from recent rains, was all grass. "Grimaldi" started a good favourite, and won easily; thus confirming the good opinion his rider had formed of him at St. Albans.

There were giant chasers and giant riders in these days, and the former were mostly of a more genuine and hunter-like stamp than the turf-failures of modern times. The names of Lottery, Vivian, Seventy-four, Grimaldi, Discount, Cigar, Yellow Dwarf, the Chandler, and many another hippic hero, will come home to the memory of countless frosty-powed sportsmen of to-day. Great horses were each and all of these, but the greatest of all was Lottery. Jem Mason on Lottery, in a steeple-chase of forty years since, was what Archer on St. Gatien or Ormonde is at the present time.[1] No higher compliment was ever paid to a horse than when Lottery was barred out of a steeple-chase, open to all England, which came off at Wootton, near Northampton, in 1840, and which was won by Cigar, ridden by Allan McDonough.

No hounds in England had gained a greater celebrity than Mr. Osbaldeston's bitch-pack, one of their marked features of excellence being that they never lost their presence of mind when ridden over, or pressed upon by an overwhelming field; consequently their body never became broken up or detached. Proverbially fast, a more musical pack could scarcely be met with, which would seem to militate against the theory that "muteness" must needs accompany "fleetness." To the genuine lover of hunting, there could be no greater treat than to see these bitches swimming along the flat between Stanford Hall and Winwick Warren, so close together that the ground could scarcely be seen between them. Among innumerable good runs, the "Squire"

---

[1] Since this was penned, the famous jockey, like the author, has departed this life.—ED.

used to distinguish one at the end of March, 1830, from Misterton to the Laughton Hills, as one of the best he had ever seen. Though apparently making direct for the earths, the fox passed right over them, open as they were, and was killed within 200 yards of the shelter he had so unwisely rejected. One night after dinner at Pitsford Hall, some chaff having taken place as to the "Squire's" powers of endurance on horseback, he backed himself for 1000 guineas to ride 200 miles in ten hours—he to have as many horses as he pleased. The match was to come off on the round course at Newmarket, and thirty-two horses, chiefly the property of himself and friends, and all of the highest class, having been selected for the undertaking, Mr. Osbaldeston went into training for a week. During this time he took exercise of the severest description, and thought nothing of riding to Newmarket, sixty miles from Pitsford, after hunting on a Wednesday, and returning for the meet on the Friday following, after having galloped in turn (on the Thursday) the different horses he was going to ride in the match. In the accomplishment of his task, each horse was changed at the end of the four-mile circuit, some of them being ridden two and three times, and one, Tranby—well-known for his speed and lasting qualities—being pulled out a fourth time! In consequence of not being able to get several of the horses to approach a wooden horse-block turfed over and erected in front of the stand, the rider had to dismount on the completion of each round, which not only was a loss of time, but greatly increased the stress upon the muscles. In spite, however, of this drawback, the ill-temper shown by Ikey Solomon, and the ground not being in a favour-

[CHAP. III.] *Osbaldeston's Match against time.*

able condition, the distance was accomplished in eight hours and thirty-nine minutes.

The match, therefore, was won with an hour and twenty minutes to spare, without any apparent distress to the winner, who had ridden at the rate of twenty-five miles an hour for eight and a half successive hours. A list of the horses engaged in the undertaking, with the time occupied by each in accomplishing his four miles circuit, will show that Tranby was far the best, and Ikey Solomon far the worst of the party.

	M.	S.		M.	S.
Emma	9	0	Smolensko	8	52
Paradox	9	20	Tranby, 2nd time	8	0
Liberty	9	25	Skirmisher, 1st time	9	25
Coroner	9	15	Guildford	8	25
Oberon	9	40	Dolly	8	45
Don Juan	9	0	Ikey Solomon	12	0
Morgan Rattler	9	13	Tam O' Shanter	9	40
Paradox	9	6	El Dorado	9	2
Cannon Ball	9	23	Surprise	9	10
Clasher	9	25	Tranby, 3rd time	8	50
Ultima	9	10	Ipsala	9	0
Fairy	9	5	Streamlet	9	0
Coroner	8	40	Coventry	9	0
Liberty	9	0	Ringleader	8	42
Emma	9	21	Tranby, 4th time	8	15
Don Juan	9	8	Ipsala	8	20
Oberon	8	20	Skirmisher, 2nd time	8	15
Cannon Ball	9	45	Guildford	9	10
Ultima	9	0	Streamlet	8	50
Tranby, 1st time	8	10	Donegani	9	12
Fairy	8	8	Hassan	9	0
Morgan Rattler	9	28	Ringleader	9	30
Tramp	8	58	Coventry	9	30
Dolly	8	58	Donegani	10	15
Acorn	9	2	Skirmisher, 3rd time	9	40

From the above record it will be seen that Tranby performed his four circuits in 8.10, 8.0, 8.50, and 8.15 minutes respectively; that Skirmisher alone was used three times, occupying respectively 9.25, 8.15, and 9.40 minutes, and that Ikey Solomon occupied 12 minutes in completing his journey, and proved himself the black sheep of the lot. After the match, Mr. Osbaldeston gave a plate of fifty pounds to be competed for by the horses he had ridden, which was won by the Smolensko colt, Donegani being second. No sooner had the task been completed than people began to say any one could perform the same feat with the same horses. Nettled at this, the "Squire" wrote the following letter to the editor of *Bell's Life in London*:—

"Sir,—There are many men, I have no doubt, who can do the distance in the time I did it, who ride seven stone, if they are to be called men. Many foxhunters, and even jockeys, before the match thought it impossible to accomplish it in nine hours, who now say that any old woman could do it. It is the pace which a man is compelled to maintain, with such short intervals between every four miles, that distresses him, the muscles not having time to recover. I never was afraid of anything except sudden indisposition. Having been much chaffed about the match, and told that a jockey would do the distance in eight hours, I send the following challenge to the whole world, and I name a large sum, as I do not care to risk my health and stamina for a trifle. If no one takes me up, I hope that I shall no longer be bothered and told that 'any fool could do what I did.' A man of my years challenging all the world to bring a man of any age against me is unparalleled in the history of sporting, and scarcely to be believed. I now challenge any man in the world of any age, to ride from 200 to 500 miles, for 20,000*l.*; but if he will only ride 200 miles, I will stake 10,000*l.* Or, I will ride against a jockey of seven stone, 200 miles, receiving 30 minutes for the difference between seven and eleven stone odd; or I will take 10,000*l.* to 3000*l.* that I will ride 200 miles in eight hours, which would be a wonderful performance for one of my weight, and as I think, almost impossible. At all events the smallest accident would cast the match, and I should scarcely have time to mount and remount. I am always to be heard of at Pitsford, near Northampton. November 16th, 1832."

Great exaggerations prevailed as to the money won by the "Squire" over his match, some putting it at upwards of 30,000*l*., but the real amount netted by the winner after the payment of all expenses was 1800*l*.

As shots, Mr. Osbaldeston and Captain Ross—the latter the better man at cross-country—shared with the Hon. G. Anson, the honour of being the three "cracks of England." The three were constantly in competition, and it was hard to say which of the trio was the better man. In the match for 1000 sovereigns between Captain Ross and the "Squire," which came off at Battersea in the May of 1828, the latter suffered an easy defeat. Each was to shoot at 250 birds at a thirty yards' rise. Four days were taken up in completing the match, Ross killing 175 birds, and the "Squire" 164. On the first day the former missed only seven shots, on the second twenty-two, on the third eighteen, and on the last, when he was ill, twenty-eight. His opponent's misses, on each of the four days respectively, were twenty-three, twenty-five, twenty-three, and fifteen. In the November of the same year, a very interesting match took place between Captain Ross and the Hon. G. Anson, which should kill the most partridges, walking side by side, on a manor in Norfolk of Mr. Henry De Ros's. The amount of the wager was 500 guineas a side, shooting to commence at a quarter past eight a.m., and to close at a quarter past four p.m. Each party was to have three guns and as many loaders. The day proved to be foggy and therefore unfavourable, and the birds so wild, that at the end of the first hour only four birds had been bagged, of which Colonel Anson had secured three. Each shooter, hoping to fatigue the other, commenced walking at the rate of five miles an hour which they kept up for the two first hours. After that they dropped to a little more than four, and kept up that pace for the rest of the day, remaining all the time bare-headed. At three p.m. each had killed ten brace, and at four the number was still even. A quarter of an hour only now remained in which to decide the issue of the match. About thirty-five miles had been walked, mostly through heavy wet turnips, and Colonel Anson was beginning to fail in strength. At this juncture he killed a bird, which made him one ahead, but his walking power had ceased, whilst his adversary was striding away as fresh as ever. With a bird to the bad, and the time almost up, Captain Ross consented that the match should be considered a drawn one. The number of birds scored was twenty-three brace and a half, but many more were killed, the umpires (Mr. Osbaldeston being one) not being able to decide to which party they belonged. So fresh was Captain Ross at the close of the proceedings, that he offered to walk any of the party then present to London, for 500 guineas! As a cricketer the "Squire" was a good useful man; but here again he was not in the same flight with such men as Lord Frederick Beauclerk and Mr. Ward, and though he might have got a place amongst the eleven gentlemen of his day, he would not have figured, at any time, in the eleven of England. In the records of the matches kept in the pavilion at Lord's, good scores are often to be found attached to the name of "George Osbaldeston," Esq., but his fast under-hand bowling seems to have been his strong point. In the days when pads and gloves were only looming in the future, and cricket-grounds were not the billiard-tables they now are, the batsman might not be sure of a very rosy time who found himself confronted with Brown of

Brighton at one end, and the "Squire" at the other. In the Eton eleven, however, of 1835, was a bowler whose pace exceeded either of the above-named "rapid Jacks." Neither Harrovian nor Wykehamist who played against Eton in that year is likely to forget the Irish boy "Whacky" Kirwan, whose bowling or rather jerking created a perfect panic among his opponents. "Ducks" were the order of the day, and on one poor crest-fallen Harrow boy—Seeley by name—as he mounted the pavilion steps, remarking to old Mr. Aislabie that he "could not make that fellow Kirwan out," received the comforting reply: "No, sir, but he seems to have no difficulty in making you out." Fast underhand bowling was almost entirely superseded by the newly-invented round-arm of 1825 or thereabouts—Lillywhite, S. Broadbridge, and Bailey—three of the earliest professors of the new style, being all slow bowlers. Slow underhand bowling for a while went quite out of vogue, any muff being supposed to be able to knock it about, but at last a giant appeared in the form of "William Clerk" of Nottingham. So effective were his slows that he was little less dreaded than the best of the round-arm bowlers, the "Nonpareil" (Lillywhite) himself being at times less difficult to play. The style of his performance has been thus commemorated by some sympathetic and admiring rhymester:—

> "When old Will Clerk was in the flesh,
>   He used to trundle slows;
> Round bowling then was rather fresh,—
>   As every blockhead knows.
> He didn't bowl to break your leg,
>   Nor yet to smash your jaw,
> But dropped them dead on the middle peg,
>   Like Southerton or Shaw."

A devoted adherent of the "Prize Ring," few pugilistic encounters—which at that time were the alias for fights—of any moment took place without the patronage and support of the "Squire," who himself was a "customer" whose science and sledge-hammer blows were calculated to leave an impression both on body and mind of an adversary. Cast in a mould of iron, such were his powers of endurance that although he hunted his own hounds six days a week for several successive seasons, he never was heard to complain of fatigue. Born at Hutton Bushell, in Yorkshire, in 1787, he gave good proof of the strength of his constitution by enduring the changes and chances of a life of hazard and exertion for nearly eighty years, during a part of which he sat in parliament as M.P. for Retford. That any one with his tastes and mode of living should have cared for a seat in the House of Commons is somewhat surprising, but his attendance probably was very occasional, and the position was not one that he held long. Commencing life with a fortune sufficient to stand any ordinary wear and tear, the "animal," which from his earliest days was his chief pride and delight, ended by being his destruction socially and morally, as well as pecuniarily.

Shrewd, and well able to look after his own interests in most things, the "racehorse" was to him as it has been to myriads of others, moral and material ruin. Long before his career had come to a close, pecuniary difficulties overwhelmed him, and certain transactions on the turf caused him to retire from public life. For many years this one-time "hero of the sporting world," the companion of the highest in the land, lived in an obscure part of London, associating only with the stratum of "hangers-on of the turf," lowered to their level day by day; what was fine within him growing coarse to sympathize with clay; and he died unhonoured though not unsung in 1866. On resigning the Mastership of the Pytchley country in 1834, he sold his pack of hounds to Mr. Harvey Coombe for 2000*l.*, and never again undertook the duties of an M.F.H. His retirement was caused by a lack of support from the members of the Hunt, the subscriptions to which at that time did not reach 1600*l.* per annum. The price he obtained for his hounds was somewhat in excess of that which the famous Jack Mytton secured for a lot of his, which selling for about the value of their skins elicited from their Huntsman the remark that they "ought to have made more, for they were a capital lot of hounds and would hunt anythink, from a helephant to a hearwig."

When sold in lots at Tattersall's in 1840, Mr. Osbaldeston's hounds fetched 6440*l.*; five couple being sold to Mr. Barclay for 930*l.*

On the country becoming vacant in 1834, it was taken by Mr. Wilkins, M.P. for Radnorshire, a Welsh gentleman, who had hunted hounds in his own country, and was at that time living at the Rectory at Pitsford. To hounds of his own he added a quantity from the pack of Mr. Grantley Berkeley, who was supposed to have some share in the management, and who for some time took up his quarters at Brixworth. Mr. Wilkins took "Jack Stevens" for his Huntsman, and "Jack Goddard" as first Whip; but neither master, men, nor hounds could be said to be a success; and though the sport, consider-

H

ing all things, was better than might have been expected, the country again became vacant at the end of the same season.

Though Jack Stevens's acquirements in the science of hunting might have been said to touch the point of "unqualified nescience," he was an excellent first Whip, a brilliant rider, and much liked by everybody. The price given for the kennel-horses at that particular period of the P.H. annals, ranged between 25*l*. and 30*l*. Mounted one day on one of these costly animals, waiting for the hounds to emerge from their kennel, Jack Stevens said to a farmer near him, "They say that these horses can't jump, let's try this one;" and suiting the action to the word, he popped him over the five-barred gate leading into the little field adjoining the road, as if it had been nothing more formidable than a sheep-tray. In 1824, when first Whip to the Quorn Hunt, he broke a blood-vessel, but only laid by for a few days, saying "that it was no use living if he could not ride to hounds." Never really strong after this, he died at Brixworth in 1837 at the early age of forty-two. The *Northampton Herald* thus writes of him: "It has never been our lot to record the demise of a man more sincerely regretted than poor Stevens. He had numerous masters, and served them all faithfully and well. We have our doubts about his ever becoming a good Huntsman: as a Whipper-in he was first-rate, indeed stood unrivalled. He had a remarkably quick eye to hounds, and a fine hand and seat on his horse. It was delightful to see him cross the big grass-fields in the Harbro' country; and the ease with which he encountered the big fences that came in his way. But great as Jack's pace was, the unerring

hand of Time outrode him, and he is gone. May the turf which he adorned while living sit lightly over his head when dead!"

Pitsford Hall, usually the home of the Master of the hounds, was at this time occupied by "Billy Russell" of Brancepeth Castle, Durham, known to his friends from his property in coal-mines, and equally from his atro-rufous complexion, as the "Black Diamond." With "Ginger" Stubbs and Colonel Copeland as his guests, the horses in his stables, all of the highest class, did not stand idle. But he was not one of those who cared to forge ahead on his own account; and delicate health, attributable principally to a total indifference to dietary rules, soon led him to make his bow to the formidable fences of Northamptonshire. On the resignation of Mr. Wilkins, who afterwards assumed the name of "De Winton," there was some difficulty in finding a successor, but to the great delight, not only of his brother county-squires but of all sportsmen, the man best suited for the position in every way, George Payne of Sulby, consented to undertake the Mastership. As he will be spoken of at length at the time of his second assumption of the reins of government, it will be sufficient here to say that he held them for three years; when, in 1838, he made way for the Earl of Chesterfield. During this period—one in which hard riding was much the fashion—the three noble lords, Cardigan, Maidstone, and Macdonald (Lord of the Isles), were a trio hard to catch and bad to beat. The latter was only an occasional attendant at the Pytchley Meets; but, come when he might, he rarely failed to leave his mark; and a bottom under Great Harrowden, where his horse cleared thirty measured feet, is still shown as "the leap of the Lord of the Isles."

Lord Maidstone, hunting at that time as the guest of his brother-member of the northern division of the county, Colonel Maunsell of Thorpe Malsor, was a brilliant rider, and one who did not easily brook having to put up with a back seat in the hunting-field, or elsewhere. In the House of Commons, he undertook to "bell the wild Irish cat," Dan O'Connell, though it is doubtful if on that occasion his lordship had not the best of the encounter. Endowed with more than ordinary ability, boasting the possession of some poetical powers, a good classic, and not without statesmanlike instinct, few young men ever entered political life giving greater promise than this young lord. Changing the sex, it may truly be said on his career: "*Mulier formosa superne, desinit in piscem.*"

To the third noble lord, a true Northamptonshire worthy, further reference will be made when the "Woodlands" come for consideration. These were the days when the country squire, however innocent of racing proclivities, wore the coat known as a "Newmarket cutaway;" when sisters and mothers, and sometimes even wives, embroidered the silk or velvet waistcoat for their nearest and dearest. When the black satin "fall," set off with two costly linked pins, adorned the manly bosom of the dinner-swell, a blue coat with brass buttons and velvet collar (a far more seemly garment than the "clerowaiter" vestments that succeeded it) completed his evening "get-up." The schoolboy in those days returned to his books and his birch after the Christmas holidays on the outside of a coach, with no further protection from the cold than could be got from a coat of "pilot" cloth, and a little straw for his feet. Shortly prior to this, the "Growler" and the "Hansom" were alike unknown; and a "one-horse-shay" of any sort, when used by a gentleman, carried with it a taint of "infradigishness." The coach-stand in the street was occupied from end to end by dilapidated pair-horse vehicles; the "omnibus" system was just putting out its feelers; and the "Charleys" of old had only just made way for the "New Police." The telegraphic-wire was still among the hidden things of darkness, and letters from London to Northampton cost eightpence for postage. The railway-egg was only in course of incubation, and the London and Birmingham line had not yet burst its shell. Hunters for the distant Meets were sent on over-night, and there was no way of escaping the twenty mile homeward-ride with a tired horse. Such was the state of things when Lord Chesterfield became Master of one of the crack packs of hounds of England.

If a Hunt may be said to be at its zenith when outlay is the predominant feature of its establishment, it cannot be doubted that the P.H. touched that point during the reign of the magnificent Lord of Bretby. "Money no object" was the handwriting on every wall, and in every stall; and it is probable that a finer lot of horses were never got together than were to be found at Brixworth between the years 1838 and 1841. Himself the glass of fashion, if not quite the mould of form, the noble Master determined that everything should be carried out in accordance with the usual style of his expenditure at Bretby and elsewhere; and nothing was omitted to make the *entourage* perfect at every point.

Riding full sixteen stone, weight-carriers of the highest class formed the stud of the Master; and right well did he make his way across the big grass and through the stiff bullfinches of the Pytchley country.

One dry afternoon in March, the hounds ran fast from Langborough to Stoke Wood. Four men had the best of it throughout, Lord Chesterfield upon his favourite "Marmion" being one. Whilst "Derry" and "Ginger" Stubbs were struggling in the Loatland brook, Marmion was sailing away, and safely landed with his welter-weight on the other side; and when the fox was run into after a capital fifty minutes, the Master was there, but no Huntsmen. On another occasion, when riding Claxton, his sixteen stone did not prevent the Master being well up in a clipping forty minutes from Berrydale to Moulton. Running through Cottesbrooke "cow-pastures," leaving Spratton on the right and by "Merry Tom," the hounds quitted Pitsford on the left, crossed Boughton Green, and ran into their fox a little beyond Moulton village. In crossing Creaton brook, "Derry" left both his stirrups behind him, but was well up at the finish. Two unusually long runs at this time occurred with a fox from Long Hold, who, on the first occasion, beat his pursuers in the shades of evening at Earls Barton; and, on the second, fairly outran them at Kettering. Mr. Smith, Lord Chesterfield's successor, had a cut at the same gallant fox in the following season, but unsuccessfully, looking at it from *his* point of view. He fancied that he subsequently had the misfortune to chop him in the Lamport shrubberies.

The secret of Lord Chesterfield being able to live with his hounds (bought from Mr. Rowland Errington on giving up the Quorn) when they ran fast, consisted in his knowing how to gallop, a far more difficult thing to do than most people imagine. The general idea is that any fool can make his horse put his best leg first. Hear what "Nimrod" has to say on this point:—"I have known numbers of men," writes he, "who had plenty of nerve and who could ride well, who never saw a run when the pace was really fast. The reason of this was, that they were not quick themselves: they lost time at their fences, and seemed afraid to gallop. It requires more nerve and a finer finger to put a horse along at his best pace over rough ground and among grips, than to ride over big fences; but without doing this, no man will be able to ride up to hounds in a real good scent."

Like his predecessor, Jack Stevens, and many another brilliant first Whip, "Derry" lacked most of the essentials that go to constitute a Huntsman; and in an establishment where everything was splendid, he, to use the words of that excellent sportsman, Lord Charles Russell, was "the splendid failure." During his first season, Lord Chesterfield took up his quarters at the George Hotel at Northampton; after which he moved to Abington Abbey—the old-fashioned seat of a family who had long held an honoured name among the ancient Squirearchy. The hearty cordial manner and ringing laugh of Harvey, the last of the Thursby Squires, is still fondly remembered by a few surviving friends; as is that member of the family, who, as Rector of the parish, won the hearts of all by his good looks, winning address, love of sport, and attention to his duties.

Courteous and genial with all, Lord Chesterfield made

himself generally popular; but his Mastership was far from being a complete success. Surrounded by companions who delighted to turn night into day, and who neither in manners nor habits suited the idiosyncrasies of the country gentlemen, the hunting-atmosphere absorbed a taint which soon began to make itself felt. Late to bed meant "late to rise;" and so great was the unpunctuality at the Meets that a feeling of dissatisfaction grew to be universal. To be kept waiting upwards of an hour for the Master was not unprovocative of impatience, if not anger: but when the delay was caused by the non-arrival of one, who, though afterwards a lady of title, was at no time an ornament to the social *morale*, the burden was no longer to be endured.

At the close of the season of 1840, Lord Chesterfield shook from off his feet the dust of Pytchley entanglements, returning into his own county.

Noble as was the inheritance of the Lord of Bretby, the winnings of a "Priam" and a "Don John," an "Industry" and a "Lady Evelyn," did not suffice to fill the gaps made by rubbers and inordinate expenditure. The vampire "hazard" sucked the life-blood out of a princely estate, and 200,000*l.* disappeared within the precincts of a Gehenna of St. James's Street, known as Crockford's Club. The end was a mere matter of time. The usual Nemesis awaited the lordly punter; the wave of ruin swept over fair Bretby and all its pleasant associations; and after a while, an unpropertied title passed to a far distant kinsman. The Earl heading the illustrious "trio" will be referred to when the Woodland potentates come under review.

Another of the good riders of these days—perhaps the best of all—was the Hon. Wilbraham Tollemache, a member of Lord Chesterfield's suite, who could not find it in his heart to play second fiddle to any man when the most harmonious of all music was filling the air. Any one within hail of him had at all times the satisfaction of feeling that he was as near the hounds as he ought to be.

An individual much *en évidence* in a Pytchley field at this date was the well-known "Ginger Stubbs." In appearance, manner, and habits, no one ever earned the title of "sporting-looking cove" more than this somewhat notorious gentleman. Dapper and neat as a new pin from head to foot, always wearing a faultless white linen scarf, and with clothes fitting to perfection, he bore with him that *caveat emptor* air which seemed to say "beware." A good horseman with plenty of nerve, his chief delight in hunting seemed to consist in riding over big places in cold blood. What hounds were doing was to him a matter of comparative indifference, but a double post and rail or a wide piece of water were temptations not to be resisted with a "gallery" looking on. The vision of this gentleman riding at two rails with a young "quick" between, on a horse of his friend Billy Russell, comes before the writer as though it were yesterday. The fence was in one of the big grass-fields between Kelmarsh and Clipston, and though hounds were only on their way to draw, the wide place and the large field were impulses not to be withstood. The far rail brought horse and rider to grief; and though "the gallery" indulged in uncomplimentary remarks as to the folly of the "show-off," it was felt that the pluck of the attempt almost covered the amount of "swagger" that incited it. To the friend who mounted him he had a habit of saying, "I'll do your animal justice;" and accordingly taking for his motto, "*Fiat justitia, ruat Ginger*," he soon made it clear to himself and to others whether or no the horse of his friend was troubled with the "jumps." He rarely saw a run to its close, "grief" usually overtaking him long before the journey was completed. Living much in a society whose members did not on all occasions "take the first turn to the right and go straight on," he himself began to tread the tortuous pathways of the turf. A cloud arose under which this mighty "lepper" disappeared from view, and out of which he had not emerged, when his name appeared on the list of those who henceforth were to be sought for under, rather than above, the turf.

Amongst the county gentlemen hunting at this time were Messrs. Charles and Quintus Vivian, Mr. Bouverie, Mr. W. C. Nethercote (Royal Horse Guards), Sir Justinian Isham, Bart., Mr. Vere Isham, Mr. Harris of Wootton, Mr. Wood of Brixworth, Mr. T. Wood of Arthingworth, Mr. R. Knightley, Mr. G. Payne, Mr. Hungerford, Lord Cardigan, Mr. Tryon, Mr. W. Neville: the field being principally made up by strangers staying at Brixworth and Market Harborough.

Occasionally appearing at a Meet near the last-mentioned town was one who held the same high position among professional horsemen that Assheton Smith did among gentlemen-riders—Dick Christian.

Powerful in the saddle, perfectly fearless, and ready to undertake a mount which most men would decline *without* thanks, he was in constant request to act as schoolmaster to the young horses of the Meltonians, and also to ride steeple-chases. Talkative and fond of dilating, the "Druid" has filled half a volume with entertaining anecdotes of the exploits of himself and others of the same persuasion. One of Dick's earliest feats seems to have been to jump a flock of sheep. He thus describes it in his own words: "I once jumped a whole flock of sheep near Gadesby in Mr. Osbaldeston's time. I think we'd found at the Coplow. They had scuttled into a corner. Hounds were running like mad. I sends my horse at the rails and clears the sheep every one of 'em. My horse he hits the top of the rail and goes clear bang on his head. The shepherd he shouts, 'Now hang you, that just sarves you right.' I says, 'So it does, old fellow,' and I gathers myself up and kills our fox at Ragdale. Deary me! horses has rolled on me times and often; squeezed me, bones broke, and all that sort of thing. I was with Mat Milton for some time; got five guineas a week, and lived as he did—meat and drink best as was. He sold ninety-six horses to the gentlemen the season I was with him. Poor little Matty! I killed him. Old Matty would make him follow me. I well nigh drownded him two or three times. My reglar orders were 'to go and ketchem,' and the little chap (he was such a nice little boy!), only fourteen, was never to leave me. At those very owdacious places, poor little feller, he used to holler out, 'Dick, where are yer?' He couldn't spy me for them bullfinches, and didn't know if I were up or down. When I see those sort, I says, 'Matty, here's a rum un afore us, ketch hold, and don't fear nothing.'"

Poor little Matty! his experience of the "ups and downs" of life did not last long, and consumption all too soon distracted his attention from those *Christian* lessons which were ill-adapted to a weakly constitution. From the following incident it would seem that the worthy tutor of poor Matty was quite equal to a "plant," and by no means lived the "*nescia fallere vita.*" "I had a queer go near here one day when I was with Mat Milton. I had three horses out, all bays, and so like, you couldn't tell the three asunder. Two of 'em were placed for me. The first horse stood still with me going through those sheep-pens on the right yonder. The second was close by, and then I tires it. Two farmers, John Parker and Jack Perkins, them were two owdacious boys at that time of day—had been riding against me like fury, and never left me. I gets on to my third horse and rides him to the end of the run. The swells didn't know but what it was the same horse I had been riding all the time, and Mat sold him for three hundred guineas: he wasn't worth one hundred. He popped it on stiff; but the gentlemen then would just as soon give three hundred or two hundred as one. Blame me! the more you asked them the better they liked it."

In contravention of the prevailing idea, Christian did not look upon the "confidential mount" as an especially safe one. "Gentlemen," he used to say, "gets falls very bad; you see they're generally on old horses, and the old 'uns fall like a clot if they get into difficulties. Blame me! they won't try to get out; they haven't the animation of a young horse. Those young 'uns will try to struggle themselves right; and they'll not touch you if they can help it. I'll be bound I'd be safer riding twenty young horses than one old one." He also would declaim against what are well known in the horse-world as "great natural jumpers." "Great natural jumpers," Dick was wont to affirm, "are desperate dangerous—they won't collect themselves and get out of danger: if people get killed, a hundred to one them great natural jumpers does it. When they are a little pumped, down we comes with a smasher, and you gets killed or goes on by yourself into the next field." Dick was dead against "larking;" and vowed that many a good fencer had been disgusted by it and utterly ruined. Speaking of "Daniel Lambert," the celebrated welter-weight then living at Stamford, he says, "I knew Dan, and he knew me. He used to dress like a groom, and lived quite private. There wasn't then much more than forty stone of him, but he got to be fifty latterly. He could set a 'cock' uncommon well, for all he could hardly get near the table for his bulk. He was a cheery man in company, but shyish at being looked at." The too-solid flesh that would not melt from off poor Daniel's huge frame brought him to a comparatively early grave; but his clothes may still be inspected on payment of a trifling sum; and a painting of him as he appeared in the flesh decorates the sign-post of a small inn in his native town.

Christian's chief object of worship was Mr. Assheton Smith; and he used to say of him that "nothing ever turned him;" and he was fond of pointing out a big ravine near the "Coplow," jumped by his hero, which he described as "twelve feet perpendicular and twenty-one across." "He got a many falls, and always seemed to ride loose, and went slantways at his jumps. It's a capital plan; the horse gets his measure better. If you put his head quite straight, it's measured for him;

if you put him slantish, he measures it for himself. When Mr. A. Smith rode at timber, he always went slap at the post, because he said it made the horse fancy that he had more to do than he really had."

One of the most remarkable occurrences of this rough-and-ready horse-breaker's long life must have been the one described by himself as follows: "Yes, I remember Bill Wright of Uppingham. He was a good-hearted chap, but used such very vulgar language. Bill and me were partick'lar friends; boys together in the racing stable. We once quarrelled out hunting with Lord Lonsdale. If we didn't get to whipping each other! for three miles straight across country, cut for cut. All the gentlemen shouting, 'Well done, Dick! Well done, Bill!' It pleased them uncommon. We took our fences reg'lar. If he was first over, he waited for me. If I had fell, he'd have jumped on me, and blamed if I wouldn't have jumped smack on the top of him! We fought back-hand; any way we could cut. I was as strong as an elephant then. We pulled our horses slap bang against each other. He gives me such tinglers on the back and shoulders, but I fetches him a clip with the hook end of my whip on the side of the head, such a settler, and gives him a black eye. Then I says, 'Bill, will you have any more?' We were like brothers a'most after that. It was all a mistake. He thought I'd 'a-been crabbing a grey horse he wanted to sell. We were the biggest of friends after that, Bill and me."

It was not until after he had scored his eightieth year that this hero of a thousand falls was laid beneath the green grass over which he had galloped ten thousand thousand times, and though in "Cap" Tomline and the well-known Dick Webster he had worthy successors in his profession, never again can we expect to see a second Dick Christian. To the man of sporting proclivities troubled with *ennui*, to read the "Christian Lectures," compiled and arranged by the "Druid," will be a means of causing a heavy hour or two to pass more pleasantly than that adopted by the bed-ridden old woman, who, when asked how she contrived to get through the day, replied, "Well, you see, I prays a bit, and I coughs a bit, and I spits a bit, and it all helps to pass the time."

CHAPTER IV.

Mr. T. "Gentleman" Smith, *Master*, 1840—Sir Francis H. Goodricke, *Master*, 1842-44—The Brixworth Sporting-Pauper—Mr. George Payne, *Master*, 1844-48—Mr. Bouverie and Mr. C. C. F. Greville, his turf-confederates—"Alarm," "Speed the Plough," and "West Australian"—Whist-playing, 1836—Lord De Ros accused of cheating; and his action for slander—Mr. Payne a witness; his cross-examination—Sir W. Ingilby, a witness—Lord Alvanley's bon-mot—Mr. Payne's avidity for speculation; one in tallow—"Dirty Dick"—Fatal accidents in the hunting-field to Mr. Sawbridge and Lord Inverury—Mr. Payne, a good host—His iron constitution—Warm affection for his sisters and brother—Letter to Mr. Nethercote on the latter's death—A regular church-attendant—A good "whip"—Sam Daniel, J. Harris, J. Meecher, Davis, and Jem Pearson, popular coachmen, till ruined by railways—An inebriated horse—Mr. Payne and his brother, bad cricketers—Excellence of the Northamptonshire Cricket Club—Mr. Payne a skilful pugilist, and a patron of the P.R.—Presentation of a silver Epergne—Resigns the Mastership, 1848, and retires from the hunting-field—His death—Song in his honour by a Northamptonshire farmer.

After the resignation of Lord Chesterfield, the Pytchley country went a-begging for several months, and it was not until late in the season that Mr. T. "Gentleman" Smith of the Craven Hunt was induced by the liberality of Lord Cardigan to assume the Mastership. It was no light matter to follow such a prince as the Lord of Bretby in such a country as the Pytchley; but confident in his ability to show sport, Mr. Smith ventured upon the responsibility of getting an establishment together. The new chief was preceded by a great reputation acquired

in Berkshire and elsewhere, and in no way did he belie
it. A more thorough Master of the "noble science,"
or one whose thoughts were more completely engrossed
in the ways of "fox and hounds," probably never carried
a horn. Living *en garçon* in Brixworth, with the assistance of Jack Goddard as first, and Jones as second
whip, he contrived to get a deal of successful work out of
the worst lot of hounds and horses that had ever been
seen in the Pytchley country. The former were a part
of Lord Chesterfield's pack, purchased by the Hunt for
four hundred pounds after twenty couple had been
selected by Derry and sent to Lord Ducie, which it was
said were all hanged from being so incorrigibly wild!
With hounds such as these, and horses varying in value
from sixty to twenty pounds, there was an amount of
sport during these two seasons which had not been
approached during the splendour of the reign of Mr.
Smith's predecessor. A fine and powerful horseman,
the animal he rode, however valueless in appearance, was
bound to be pretty near hounds, "pace not fences"
being the only real difficulty. So delighted was Lord
Cardigan said to be at the close of an excellent run, that
he is reported to have fairly embraced the skilful huntsman who had been the means of causing him so much
pleasure. The subscriptions not being sufficient to
enable Mr. Smith to hunt four days a week, and meet
the difficulties of a weak establishment, at the close of his
second season he resigned office; and for the seventh
time in ten years, the Pytchley were seeking a new
Master.

Again Lord Cardigan came to the rescue with pecuniary aid, and Sir Francis Goodricke—brother-in-law to

Mr. George Payne—with "Smith" from the Brocklesby country as his huntsman, and Johnson and Ned Kingsbury for whips, assumed the direction of affairs. A more absolutely unsuccessful or unpopular huntsman than the one imported by Sir F. Goodricke never issued out of the Brixworth kennels; and the Master himself not having the knack of making himself liked, the new management only just outlasted two seasons.

At this particular period, dropping for a brief space like a meteor upon the Pytchley meets, appeared a figure which might truthfully be said to have been the cynosure of all eyes. Many a Hunt has had the honour of welcoming at its meet a mounted empress and a mounted prince, but to the P.H. alone has it been granted to number amongst its "field" a mounted pauper in the actual receipt of out-door relief from the Guardians of a County-Union!

Mounted on an aged and dilapidated-looking bay horse, how procured no one knew, and wearing on the place where his nose used to grow, a square of plaister, this sporting item of impecuniosity became the observed of all observers. The "get-up" of this attractive member of the field was strictly in accord with his social monetary position, and with the aspect and demeanour of his steed. Booted and breeched, it would have been difficult to assign a date for the original construction of either of these garments, but their antiquity did not exceed that of the tall and glistening hat. Literally as well as metaphorically, this was the crowning feature of the whole. To take a slight liberty with a popular song of the day, it may be said that—

> "A hat so grim was on his head,
>   Methinks I see it now;
> So wan and thin, with hue of lead,
>   And grease upon its brow."

However effective might have been the rest of the attire, the hat would have spoilt the lot; and is there any portion of a man's dress so potent in its effects as a "shocking bad hat"? The comeliest features and the most aristocratic bearing are alike at the mercy of a hat. The American poet, Oliver Wendell Holmes, formed his opinion of a bishop's character and fitness for his office on seeing him hand over his umbrella to a lady during a heavy shower, and walk off in a brand-new hat.

Having evidently formed a correct estimate of the importance of this covering, Mr. Wendell Holmes in one of his poems is found to say:—

> "Wear a good hat; the secret of your looks
> Rests with the beaver in Canadian brooks.
> Virtue may flourish in an old cravat,
> But man and nature scorn the 'shocking hat.'"

The Meets near home were naturally those which this unique specimen of the English citizen principally affected; but on one occasion "Ratepayer" (for by a fine irony, that must have been the old "crock's" name) was made to go as far as Misterton, some seventeen miles from his stable-door. The historian of these times tells us that after his long journey he looked sorry for himself and as if he would like to "lean against a wall, and think;" but a rally must have taken place, as we know that he joined in the chase for a while, and ultimately slept in his own stable. Hearing of this, his sixth or seventh day with the hounds, the Guardians seem to have arrived at the conclusion that in the matter of out-door relief a line should be drawn somewhere. A proposal made by the chairman of the board that it should be drawn at hunting, was put to the meeting and carried, nem. con. From that time, such hunting as fell to the lot of poor "Nosey" was done upon two legs instead of four, and he had to realize from experience the bitter fact that—

> "Them as is rich, they rides in chaises;
> Them as is poor must walk like blazes."

Hat, boots, and breeches, were still retained as an appropriate costume for such hunting as might be had on foot, but the gallant old "Ratepayer" was taken to the kennels and converted into a dainty dish to set before the hounds. Few will be found to deny that the remarkable individual just referred to successfully accomplished a feat without parallel in the history of his country. To hunt for ever so short a time at the expense of the payer of rates is an achievement of which any man may well be proud. This story may arouse the incredulity of some who read these pages, but fortunately for the narrator, many still survive who remember the noseless and impecunious sportsman, and can vouch for its accuracy.

Should it chance to meet the eye of the Rev. W. Bury, the present energetic Chairman of the Brixworth Board, or that of his "Fidus Achates," Mr. Albert Pell, they will wonder of what material Guardians could have been fashioned some five-and-forty years ago; taking comfort from the sure and certain feeling that in this our day the pauper is as likely to get relief on horseback as he is on foot, unless he walks into the "House."

Upon the relinquishment of the reins of office by Sir

F. Goodricke, a fine horseman, but at no time very popular as an individual, they fell into the hands of one, who not only was the idol of his county and of his neighbourhood, but also of society itself. For more than half a century "George Payne" has been a name to conjure with, not only in Northamptonshire, but in the wide sporting-world; and now that he has passed away for ever! its magic seems to have lost but little of its power. Other districts have had and still have their names to swear by. The West Riding of Yorkshire has its George Lane Fox, and Gloucestershire its Duke of Beaufort, but there never has been and never will be but one "George Payne." A stalwart form, handsome countenance, winning smile, and a charm of manner never equalled, took captive all who came within the circle of their attraction. It would scarcely be going too far to say that no man ever possessed in the same degree a similar gift of making himself acceptable to all sorts of persons. It seemed as though he could at all times reach the soft spot in any one's heart, be they of either sex, or in any condition of life. Heir to a fine place and a splendid fortune, and endowed with abilities of no common order, it is no wonder that he entered public life as a sort of "Prince Camaralzaman."

Oxford was not more successful than Eton in causing him to appreciate the beauties of Virgil or of Homer; and a Greek play was at no time "in it" with the *Racing Calendar* or the *Sporting Magazine*. Differing from the head of his college on matters touching its internal discipline, he was recommended to seek a more congenial sphere, and plunging forthwith into the ocean of temptation, he from that time commenced a career of unchecked extravagance and self-indulgence. Having lost his father before he had reached his seventh year, and with no one to look to for correction but a fond and too-indulgent mother, it is not to be wondered at that his early companions were not all that could be desired. Inheriting a love for gambling in all its phases, he put no sort of constraint upon the evil passion, and before he had attained his twenty-first year, cards, hazard, and the turf had begun to undermine his splendid patrimony.

It is recorded in the annals of the Doncaster St. Leger, that in the year in which Mr. Gascoigne's "Jerry" won that great race, Mr. Payne lost upwards of thirty thousand pounds, and that, before he had come of age. Undaunted by his ill-success in 1824, in the following year he followed the advice of Mr. Gully, and by backing "Memnon," for the same race, recouped himself for his previous losses.

Rarely fortunate with his own horses, considering the number he had in training, he occasionally won large sums backing those of his friends. When "Crucifix" won the Oaks, his own mare "Welfare" ran second. Her success which seemed imminent for a few seconds, would have cost him thousands, as he had backed Lord George Bentinck's famous mare for a large stake, not dreaming that his own had a shadow of a chance. His remarks upon his own feelings when it seemed as if he were going to have the honour of being enrolled upon the list of winners of the "Oaks," greatly amused those who heard them.

One of his earliest confederates upon the turf was Mr. Bouverie of Delapré Abbey, near Northampton, a country squire of the old school, who loved to see a thoroughbred mare with a foal at her side wandering under the elms which throw their shadows up to one of good Queen Eleanor's most lovely crosses. The colours of one of the partners being all black, and the other all white, it was agreed to mix the two, and hence the black and white stripe so familiar to the race-goer on the back of that excellent jockey "Flatman" (Nat the "incorruptible"). To the same origin may be ascribed the colours of the well-starched, twice-round linen tie, which invariably encircled the neck of Mr. Payne. Except with "Pyrrhus the First" and "War Eagle," the confederacy of these two Northamptonshire squires was not productive of very great results. The first, however, when the property of Mr. Gully, won the Derby of 1846, and the second carried off the Doncaster Cup of 1847, having previously nearly won the great Epsom event in the same year. As he ran by the side of his dam in Delapré Park, so greatly did he win the fancy of Mr. Spencer Lyttelton, that he immediately backed him to win the Derby, for which he was only defeated by a neck.

At another period of his turf career, Mr. Payne was the confederate of Mr. Charles Greville, Clerk of the Council, an ardent politician, and author of the most interesting "Memoirs of the Reign of Queen Victoria." By a noble lord, whose powers of satire were of no mean order, and who usually wrote with a pen sharply nibbed, Mr. Payne's ally was described in a "Society" poem of the day not only as

"Greville of a noble race,
With nose as long as Portland Place,"

but also as the possessor of qualities by no means of an

endearing nature. How two men so opposite in disposition could have worked together so amicably was a matter of surprise to the friends of each. One silent and morose, and constantly regretting that he did not " shake the straw of the racing-stable from off his feet, and turn his mind to more worthy objects;" the other always cheery, loving everything connected with the turf, and apparently perfectly satisfied with the course he was pursuing. The first the least, the second the most popular man in England; and yet they got on together as though they were made for each other. Mr. Greville owned many a good horse during his career; the best of which were " Pussy," winner in 1834 of the " Oaks," " Mango " of the " St. Leger," " Ariosto," " Muscovite," and " Alarm." Had the latter proved successful in the Derby of 1852, which he undoubtedly would have been had he not been kicked by another horse at the starting-post and rendered *hors-de-combat*, Mr. Payne would have been thirty thousand pounds richer than he was before the race. Undoubtedly the best horse of his year, " Alarm " afterwards won the " Cambridgeshire " under a heavy weight, thereby rendering the disappointment of the " Derby " all the keener. " Welfare," " Clementina," " Ascot," " Glauca," " The Trapper," " Glendower," all ran in the " black and white check " so familiar to the eye of turfites; and all lay claim to a certain amount of merit; but it was of the degree usually disastrous to owners—good enough to back, but not good enough to win when most wanted.

During an unusually long career on the turf, Mr. Payne cannot be said to have possessed one horse of first-rate powers, unless " Musket," a legacy from his friend Lord Glasgow, may lay claim to that distinction.

It is not a little singular that as with a filly of second-rate ability he seemed as though he were about to defeat the best mare probably that ever was foaled, so with a very inferior animal called "Speed the Plough" he accidentally beat "West Australian"—one of the greatest horses of the turf—for the "Criterion" of 1852. This astounding derangement of all racing form, arose from a mal-practice—to speak euphemistically—on the part of the jockey who rode him. Wishing another horse, "Sittingbourne," which was trained by his brother, to win the race, the favourite was deliberately "pulled," and "Speed the Plough" coming up with an unexpected rush, the mighty West had to lower his colours to an animal which two days afterwards he defeated out of sight for the Glasgow Plate.

A constant attendant at race-meetings, anywhere and everywhere, no form was more familiar at such places than that of the wearer of the black frock coat, and the black and white linen necktie. It used indeed to be said of George Payne, that if all the money he had spent in the hire of post-chaises in pre-railway days had been capitalized, the interest would have formed a fair income for a moderate man.

In addition to racing, cards and speculation of every description contributed to dissipate the originally splendid fortune of the owner of Sulby, Pytchley, and other Northamptonshire estates. At a time when whist took high rank as a science, though George Payne might have been included among the "wranglers" he could at no time have considered himself the equal of Lord Henry Bentinck, the

Hon. George Anson, Sir Rainald Knightley, or Mr. Clay. These too were not quite on the same level with three or four of the French division, who were considered to play a somewhat more scientific game than the Englishmen.

One of the most painful incidents in the life of the subject of this memoir was connected with the whist-table—an affair which for a time may be said to have fairly convulsed society. Amongst the most prominent members of "high life" at this time, 1836, and amongst the most assiduous devotees of whist was Henry, Lord De Ros, premier Baron of England. A long course of success both at that game and écarté, coupled with other circumstances, had brought the noble gamester under suspicion, and it was determined that he should be watched while playing at Graham's Club in St. James's Street. The first hint of foul play appeared in the *Satirist*, a slanderous and disreputable precursor of the society-papers of the present day. The allusion sufficiently denoting the party referred to, Lord De Ros directed proceedings to be taken against that journal for a libel. One of the members of the club, however—Mr. Cumming—undertook himself to "bell the cat," and justified the assertion that the noble lord had "played foully." Upon this Lord De Ros brought his action against Mr. Cumming instead of against the newspaper, and the trial came off before Lord Chief Justice Denman, Sir John Campbell being counsel for the complainant. There were two accusations against Sir John's client, one that he practised the trick called "sauter la coupe," i.e. changing the turn-up card, the other of marking the card so as to ensure an ace or king every time he dealt. Several witnesses testified to the latter fact, and Sir William Ingilby declared that he had seen the complainant do the "sauter la coupe," if not a hundred, more than fifty times. The jury found for the defendant, which virtually established the charge of cheating against the plaintiff. Mr. Payne being summoned for the defence, in cross-examination gave the following evidence:—

Counsel.—You have been a good deal connected with gambling transactions, I believe?

Witness.—Yes, I have.

Counsel.—You have lost a great deal of money on the race-course, and at cards?

Witness.—Yes, I have.

Counsel.—In the early part of your career you were very unfortunate?

Witness.—Very much so.

Counsel.—You lost, I believe, the whole of your patrimony?

Witness.—I lost a considerable portion of it.

Counsel.—You have been more fortunate latterly?

Witness.—No, my whole luck has continued pretty much the same throughout.

The Solicitor-General, replying upon the whole case, tried to make out that Mr. Payne had joined with Mr. Brooke Greville and others in a conspiracy against Lord De Ros, and stigmatized the former as a professional gambler unworthy of credit. He went so far as to say that the witness—Payne—having begun as a dupe, ere long crystallized into something worse. This, the last ounce of abuse, fairly broke the back of the calumniated "camel," and so exasperated him that he resolved to take personal vengeance upon his legal traducer.

For this purpose he waited two or three afternoons, armed with a horsewhip, in the neighbourhood of the law courts, but happily the opportunity he sought did not present itself; and after a while, through the good offices of Lord Althorp, peace was restored between the abuser and the abused.

Lord De Ros did not long survive the social ostracism consequent upon the verdict of the jury, and sank into an early and dishonoured grave. Lord Alvanley—the wit and bon-vivant of the day—on being asked if Lord De Ros had left a card upon him since the trial, replied, " Yes, and when I saw that it was not marked, I felt sure he did not mean it for an honour." He also concocted a mock epitaph for the peccant victim to cards, which he concluded with the words, " In patient expectation of the last trump."

A still more remarkable instance of cheating at cards was that of the famous Lord Barrymore, the first of the " Plungers," who whilst playing whist with C. J. Fox, took advantage of the large metal buttons on his opponent's coat to see what cards his hand was composed of! The career of this young nobleman, who was accidentally shot by his own servant in his twenty-fourth year, has never been equalled for recklessness, extravagance, and dissipation.

Ready to play for stakes of any amount—the higher the better—George Payne was of far too friendly a nature to refuse to take a hand at shilling-whist in a country house. On these occasions the interest he evinced in the game was much the same as if the points had been five pounds, and twenty-five the rub. It was a treat to hear him tell of how at one hotel at Hyères he once sat down with three Frenchmen after the table-d'hôte, and played for hours at "sou" points, and a franc the rub. But it was not by the turf, or "bits of pasteboard," or the "ivories" alone, that thousands melted from his grasp. There was nothing from the "Three per Cents" to Russian tallow in which he would not speculate. The investment he made in the latter, during the early days of the Crimean War, will not soon be forgotten by those who witnessed the delivery of the article. A few days subsequent to the completion of the purchase, while still in bed at Long's Hotel, he was awoke by the porter to be told "that the people had brought the tallow, and were waiting for orders." Hurrying down stairs he found to his dismay that Bond Street was so crowded with carts laden with tallow to be delivered at his address, that the street-traffic was seriously impeded. No one was more amused at the absurdity of his position than himself, and having extricated himself from it as quickly as he could, he vowed that that should be "his last speculation in that cursed stuff."

As Master of the Pytchley, George Payne was pre-eminently the right man in the right place. Devoted to hunting, and popular with all, the announcement that he was willing once more to be Master of the P.H. was received with general satisfaction. Sulby Hall having by this time passed into other hands, he made Pitsford Hall his head-quarters, and became his own Huntsman, taking Charles Payn and Ned Kingsbury ("Dirty Dick") for his first and second Whips. Ned, formerly rough-rider to Tilbury of Pinner, while acting strictly up to orders, did his master a bad turn on one occasion. Four kennel-horses having been bought of an M.F.H. selling off, for a hundred pounds, the worst of the lot, as far as appearance went, was handed over to the second whip. Falling in with a good thing, the despised one of the quartett acquitted himself so well, that the owner was asked whether he was disposed to sell? "Let us see him perform once more," was the reply, and when his turn came again, the orders his rider received were, "If they run, put him along, and get all out of him you can." They did run—he was put along—and all that was in him was got out of him, never to return, as he died soon after from being over-ridden.

Afraid of nothing, "Dirty Dick," civillest and most untidy of whips, had the ugliest seat on horseback that can well be imagined; but an animal, bad to ride, generally met his master when Ned Kingsbury had the handling of him. Ned was a useful servant, but sadly given to taking more than was good for him. One day, during early cub-hunting, he appeared at the meet, evidently "disguised in liquor." This so exasperated his master, that he not only gave him a sound thrashing there and then, but bade him "never more be officer of mine." The latter threat yielded to an earnest petition offered by the wife of "Ebriosus," that rather than quit Mr. Payne's service, he would prefer to remain as "boiler or anything."

Riding some fifteen stone, he required wellbred powerful horses, and in "Field Marshal," "John Bull," and the "Merry Shepherd," he obtained them. It is upon "Field Marshal," that he was mounted in Barraud's well-known picture of the "Meet at Crick," a somewhat ragged-

hipped grey, with great power, and a hunter all over.
A powerful and determined horseman, and knowing well
how to make the best of his way over ridge and furrow,
he rarely failed to be with his hounds at the right
moment. The tones of his voice being especially rich
and vocal, it was a treat to hear him encouraging hounds
in cover; and his cheer, when they set-to to run hard,
was a thing not easily to be forgotten. The echo of these
notes may still ring in the ears of a few who were present
at an unlooked-for gallop from Cottesbrooke to Harleston
Heath. The meet was at Stanford Hall, but the frost
was so severe that on arriving at Cold Ashby, where the
hounds were awaiting the Master, hunting was voted
impracticable. The second whip was sent on to proclaim
the fact of the return home of the hounds, and the
ground being less hard in the low parts about Stanford
Hall, the announcement was received with equal surprise
and disgust. Amongst those who rode homeward with
the hounds, were Lord Clifden, then living at Brixworth
Hall, Mr. Davenport Bromley, Lord Bateman, and Mr.
H. O. Nethercote. Before reaching Cottesbrooke a
marked change in the weather had taken place, and
riding seemed to have become practicable. Attempts were
made to induce the Master to try for a fox, which he
refused to do, urging the scolding he should get from all
those who had gone home under the belief that there was
to be no hunting. On approaching the Hall, Mr. Davenport Bromley again assailed Mr. Payne with a petition
for "just one try—only one—in that plantation opposite
the stables." Under the full belief that it did not hold
anything except a hare or a rabbit, the Master consented
to run the hounds through it. No sooner were they in

at one end than out went a noble-looking fox at the other, and Mr. Payne's cheer might have been heard at Brixworth. Passing the lodges and sinking the hill towards Hollowell, he bore to the left, and leaving Teeton and Holdenby behind him, just contrived to reach Harleston Heath, where he saved his brush by getting to ground. "A proper row you fellows have got me into," was the Master's remark upon receiving the congratulations of the half-dozen fortunate participants of the gallop. "It's all very well for you to call it a d—d good thing, but it's a d—d bad thing for me, and I shall never hear the end of it." Nor was he far wrong in feeling that his good-nature had got him into a scrape. For many a succeeding post he kept receiving outpourings of heart from those who had had to turn away from so favourite a meet as Stamford Hall; and on its becoming known that a capital run had taken place on that same day, a perfect storm of reproaches set in. They who were the cause of the offence did their "level best" to bear their share of the blame, and after a while another good run obliterated the recollection of the one that had been lost. During the whole of this time, the average sport was far superior to what it is now that surrounding circumstances are so different from what they were. A run from "Naseby Covert" or "Tally-ho" to the "Hermitage" or "Brampton Wood" was an event of no infrequent occurrence in those days, and from the stoutness of its foxes, Badby Wood became quite a favourite draw. For two or three seasons "Cank" rivalled "Crick" in popularity, and the Wednesday side was looked upon as safe to produce a good day's sport. The Badby foxes had acquired a habit, on being roused from their lair, of making hard all for the Bicester country, and on many a Saturday night, nine o'clock had struck before the wearied hounds had reached their kennels at Brixworth. "Crick Gorse," formed in 1817, and "Waterloo," which came into existence about the same time, have from their relative merits been the most popular of the Pytchley coverts; while in point of antiquity "Yelvertoft Fieldside" lays claims to precedence over all its fellows. For many a year, neither "Crick" nor "Waterloo" was in higher favour than "Misterton Gorse;" but latterly, either the virtue has gone out of the foxes that frequent these strongholds, or the enormous fields in the first part of the day prevent the possibility of sport. Amid many fine runs with George Payne, a fifty minutes from Crick Gorse to Naseby Reservoir sticks tenaciously to the memory of the writer; as does another, one dull November afternoon, from near Nobottle Wood to Cottesbrooke village. This run retains especial hold on the memory, from the fact that darkness having begun to cover the earth, it was necessary to call in the aid of a cottager's lantern to allow of the performance of the fox's obsequies. For some time before the end it had been a case of touch and go—and more of the first than the second—with the fences; and had it not been for the friendly light, hounds would have enacted this final operation, heard but unseen.

As Althorp House was passed, the present owner then ten years old, stood watching the scene, and can now tell from tradition every yard of the line.

Two unusually painful incidents occurred to leave their mark upon the second period of Mr. Payne's

K

Mastership—each ending in the death of a temporary member of the Hunt. A singular coincidence attending these melancholy occurrences, was that in either case the same fence, and a post and rail under Winwick Warren, brought about the fatal result. The first of the two victims to timber was a Mr. Sawbridge, an elderly gentleman hunting from the "Coach and Horses" at Brixworth. On a frosty morning, the meet being Chilcoats (a name unknown to the modern Pytchley Hunt), Mr. Sawbridge's horse slipped in the act of jumping a post and rail, and fell heavily upon his rider. Scarcely alive, the unfortunate gentleman was carried to Mr. Lovell's house at the Warren, where, without a hope of recovery, he lingered for some hours. Though a stranger, with the kindness so characteristic of himself, Mr. Payne remained at the bedside of the sufferer till all was over. Years after the sad occurrence, in reply to a question on the point, he said, "I asked the poor fellow if he would like to see a clergyman, and to my great surprise he replied, "No, thank you, there's no necessity, as I was at church last Sunday!"

The child who told the school-inspector that Adam and Eve were turned out of Paradise because they had displeased their parents and friends (!) showed little less ignorance than did this septuagenarian sportsman of the Christian scheme. That children, however, do not enjoy a monopoly of lack of accuracy in Scripture-teachings is clear from a letter of Canon Wilberforce, who writing from Ryde to a friend, says:—"A lady here—a mother of seven children, and a member of my Bible-instruction class—told me the other day that "Jonah was thrown out of the ark by Noah, and was snapped up by a whale passing by!"

T. Oliver, the celebrated steeple-chase rider, on his death-bed was invited to summon some clergyman to see him. "I only wish to see one," he replied, "Parson Russell, out of Devonshire." Mr. Russell was written to, and came immediately.

In the following season the same "post and rail," though not at the identical spot, caused the death of as fine a young officer as ever entered her Majesty's service. Lord Inverurie, heir to the earldom of Kintore, and a lieutenant in the 17th Lancers, had for some weeks in the season of 1843 been hunting from the "Coach and Horses" at Brixworth.

In a fast twenty minutes from Hemplow Hills, nobody had gone better than the young Scotch lord upon his favourite mare, "Quatre Ace." Patting her approvingly upon the neck when the gallop was over, he pronounced her to be "as good a bit of stuff as man ever rode." Within an hour after this expression, she had fallen upon him and killed him! Getting a bad start from the Yelvertoft cover, it was conjectured that he rode at the rails referred to in Mr. Sawbridge's case, when his mare, a famous timber-jumper, was somewhat "pumped." She caught the top rail, and fell a complete somersault upon her unfortunate rider. He gave one groan, threw his arms upwards, and never spoke again. He was carried to the house of Mr. Lovell, and Mr. Payne and the Duke of Montrose, residing at Sulby, remained with him till all was over!

On being referred to as to the disposal of the body, Lord Kintore's reply was, "Where the tree fell, let it lie," and a tablet in Brixworth church (*the oldest church in England*) records the simple fact of his lying near that spot. Rarely has a fatal accident in the hunting-field created a greater gloom than this. Beloved in his regiment—a universal favourite—a keen sportsman, and a bold rider, brightness followed him wherever he went. It was hard to realize the stern fact that such a one as he, in full fruition of health, youth, position and popularity, had passed from among us for ever. At Harrow with him, though much his senior, the narrator of this sad event well remembers the eagerness with which the juvenile sportsman sought to become a member of the " H.H." or " Harrow Hunt," for which his place in the school had rendered him for a time ineligible. The " H.H." here spoken of closely resembles a famous Hunt in one respect only, namely its initials; but it is doubtful if the young Harrovians did not derive as much pleasure in the illegitimate pursuit of the rarely-found hare, as did the older Hambledonians in that of Reynard himself. H. Royston, afterwards a well-known cricketer and bowler for the " M.C.C.," was Huntsman to the Harrow hounds; whilst to his unbounded delight, the young Scotch lord was appointed to the coveted office of first (and only) Whip. As the thoughts of the past arose before him, Charles Lamb's touching lines,—

> " My sprightly schoolmate gone before
> To that unknown and silent shore,
> Shall we not meet as heretofore,
>   Some summer morning?"

knocked loudly at the heart of the surviving Harrovian, who, by a few minutes only, escaped witnessing the death of his old schoolfellow.

As a host, George Payne had few or any equals. Neither witty nor particularly well-read, he knew everything that was going on, and had the happy knack of making each guest feel that he was an item of some importance in the party at which he was present. Full of anecdote and general information on the topics of the day, conversation could not flag, and the dinner ever seemed too short. Those dinners in the little Northamptonshire village, with George Payne at one end of the table, and " Billy " at the other, might well have been looked upon as *noctes cœnæque Deorum;* and that, in spite of an occasional going to bed a poorer, if not a wiser man. The three genii presiding over the little queer-shaped room into which the guests betook themselves after dinner, were whist, écarté, and vingt-et-un. The amount of the stakes was always tempered to the purse of the (so far) unshorn lamb; but a good many sovereigns were wont to change hands in the course of the evening. In reply to a query from the writer of this narrative to a noble lord who was a guest at Pitsford Hall, on one of these occasions, he thus writes:—
" Whist was not the game. We played vingt-et-un until a very late hour. The party consisted of George and Billy Payne, two Suttons, Bateman, F. Villiers, Rooper, and myself. F. V. lost two hundred and fifty in a very short time, went to his room, and brought down the money in new bank-notes, and retired from the contest. I happened to have thirty-three pounds in my pocket, my old bailiff having handed me thirty pounds (the produce of some trees sold), just as I was starting. I soon lost this and borrowed some more from G. P. I had a good deal of luck, and won a hundred; but the balance

gradually departed, and left me at the end of the evening with thirty pounds; therefore only three pounds to the bad."

To be obliged to decline a dinner at Pitsford Hall in those days must have caused much the same disappointment that Sydney Smith felt, when in refusing an invitation from a friend, he wrote, "Very sorry can't accept; got some first cousins. Wish they were once-removed!"

Possessed of an iron constitution, the Pytchley Master of 1844 knew not the meaning of the word fatigue, and he rarely cared to eat the sandwich he carried with him, the day of the small portmanteau (carried round the second horseman's waist) having then scarcely commenced. Quick and impetuous, of a naturally fine temper, the trials and aggravations of a huntsman's life rarely, if ever, elicited an unseemly outburst. In a time of strong words, of which it is not denied that he had a quiver-full, he rarely let out at individuals; and of the bitter sneer or sarcastic allusion, he absolutely knew nothing. The most frequent recipient of certain words that lurked on the other side of his tongue, was that neatest, nicest-looking, most respectable of grooms, John Cooper. Were he not at hand with the second horse at the right moment, John Cooper might look out for squalls, and mostly came in for one of more or less severity. Always ready to furl sail at any moment, no "old salt" cared less for a storm at sea, than did this faithful old servant for a land-breeze from his master's mouth. On being sympathized with one day by a strange groom, on having to put up with some expressions that were neither parliamentary nor complimentary, he only remarked, "Bless yer, he don't mean nothing by it; that's nothing to what I'm accustomed to."

The dispenser of these winged words is gone where silence is the only language, but he who bore the burden of them is still alive, and in the enjoyment of such a competence as is the fruit of long and faithful service.

One of the most marked characteristics of George Payne's disposition was his warm affection for his sisters, and his only brother—known to his intimates as "Billy Payne." So greatly did the two brothers differ in appearance, that nobody could have supposed them to be in any way related. Thick-set and dumpy in figure, so short was "brother Bill" in the leg, that after negotiating some fairly big fence, he would pat his right thigh, and laughingly say, "Well done, little 'un, you stuck to the pig's skin right well that time." To judge by his make and shape, few would have given him credit for great powers of endurance; but on more than one occasion when at college, he rode from Cambridge to Sulby to meet the hounds; hunted all day, and was back in his rooms before twelve at night. This is a feat which few would attempt to accomplish.

A college friend accompanied him on one occasion, but fatigue overcame him on the homeward ride, and he had to remain at Bedford for the night, leaving his companion to pursue his way alone. Subject to gout from his early days, the attacks of which he did not try to parry by any attention to dietetic rules, he ultimately fell a victim to it, and died at Pitsford Hall in the summer of 1848. The grief of the surviving brother for a time was piteous in the extreme. A letter to a neighbour one who truly lamented the loss of an old and kindly-hearted friend, will show the depth of the affection that existed between the brothers.

"My dear ——,—I am well aware how deeply you would all feel this awful visitation. I will not attempt to describe to you my misery, although I hope it may please God to mitigate the intense agony I now suffer. I have bid adieu to happiness in this world. The most affectionate and best of brothers, as well as the most amiable of human beings, has been snatched away. We were scarcely ever separate in life, and the future must be a blank to me."

Long after he had apparently recovered his spirits, he loved to recall some speech or act of poor dear "Bill." From his sisters, Mrs. T. Paris and Lady Goodricke—each holding strong views on religious matters—G. Payne imbibed a marked distaste to hearing sacred subjects treated with levity. Making a point of attending church once on a Sunday, few there were more attentive to what was going on, and an indifferent address from the pulpit was not unlikely on his homeward walk to be characterized as a d—d bad performance! Most truly might he be said to be one of the many

> "Who see and hail the better part,
> But fail to take it to the heart."

By no means the equal of Messrs. Musters and Osbaldeston in the number of his athletic successes, as a coachman or with "the gloves," he was something more than "bad to beat." At a day when "coaching" was at its zenith, and the names of Sir St. Vincent Cotton and Sir Henry Peyton were as household words, G. Payne took high rank as a "whip." To drive four-in-hand, town or country, was his great delight; and he doubtless would

have taken much the same view of the position as the
swell, who living in the West End, on being invited to
dine with a friend in Bloomsbury, as if there were no other
mode of getting there except with a coach and four, replied, " With pleasure, but where am I to change horses?"
Exceedingly powerful both in arms and shoulders, Mr.
Payne with his double thong could get the last ounce
out of the wheeler inclined to make his companion do
most of the work, and the point of his lash rarely failed
to reach a leader on the desired spot. Frequently on
the road between London and Northampton, when the
Sulby Squire was on the box of the Northampton coach,
both horses and passengers quickly discovered that some
other hands than those of the accustomed driver held the
reins. Sure but slow were John Harris—most civil—
and S. Daniel—smartest and most polite of Jehus; but
when the turn into the Angel-yard at Northampton was
made without any change of pace, it was clear to the
spectators that a pilot of a higher order than usual was at
the helm. Poor Sam Daniel! your good looks, engaging
manners, and fund of anecdote, sporting and otherwise,
made the journey by your side always a pleasant one.
The lad schoolward-bound, forgot for a while Virgilian
and Homeric horrors, as he listened to your pleasant talk;
and the glass of ale at Dunstable or Hockliffe looked all
the brighter and tasted all the sweeter for your words of
praise of it. The only act of yours, not quite to be forgiven, was, when you rode your inimitable little hack
against the "Telegraph" coach on the 17th October,
1837. To ask a horse to go sixty-six miles continuously
at the rate of ten miles an hour, seems to approach very
nearly the confines of cruelty; but both horse and rider,

if the reports of the time are to be believed, completed the task without suffering any serious fatigue. The match was made between the rider and Lieutenant Wellesley of the 12th Lancers, then quartered at Northampton. The coach and the horse quitted the Peacock, Islington, at a quarter before six, and Mr. Daniel arrived at Northampton, amid the acclamations of a large concourse of people, one minute and a half earlier than his competitor. The hero of this feat did not survive to share the fate that after the opening of the London and Birmingham railway awaited many of his brethren of the whip. "Ichabod" was indeed written on the brows of J. Harris of the Northampton coach, and J. Meecher of the "Nottingham Times," when each was reduced to driving a "one-horse bus" about the streets of the town through which for many a year they had tooled four well-shaped steeds. Nor could "Davis," driver of the "Manchester Telegraph"—the fastest coach out of London—entertain kindly thoughts of the advance of science, when he found himself a "walking postman" on certain remote highways and byways of Northamptonshire. It is scarcely a matter for surprise that, in common with many a brother of the craft of which he was so great a master, he strove to drown his cares in that usual refuge of the destitute—alcohol. Pindar, somewhat before the time of Sir W. Lawson, assured his friends that ἄριστον μὲν ὕδωρ, i.e. that water is the best of all good tipple; but the ex-coachman didn't seem to see it, and so hastened the end of a life out of which a great public benefit had filched all the brightness. Some of my readers will not fail to remember the sad end of Jem Pearson—the honest, burly, fiery-faced partner of J. Meecher—on the "Nottingham Times." Making his last journey on the day before the coach was to be taken off the road for good, a wheel came off, the vehicle was upset, and Jem's portly form and ruby-coloured visage were never seen again on that or any other stage. In numerous cases, well-conducted coachmen found comfortable berths on the new railways; but a hard fate awaited many a worthy man who, shutting his eyes to the inevitable, had failed to lay by for the rainy day.

A curious coaching-incident befell the Master of the P.H. during his residence at Pitsford Hall. Staying for a few days at Leamington he drove some friends to see a fight for the Championship of England, on a four-horse coach. On the return home, one of the leaders having knocked up, he was taken out of the coach, made to swallow a bottle of sherry, and left on the side of the road until further assistance could be sent. On nearing the town the noise of a horse trotting behind the coach was heard, and to the surprise and amusement of the party on the roof, the animal, revived by the wine, came up and took his place by the side of the single leader as if nothing had happened.

As a cricketer, the Sulby squire's pretensions were of the humblest order; but he was an ardent admirer of the game, and a liberal subscriber to a formidable-looking "red book," armed with which the Hon. Sec. of the "M.C.C." used to traverse "Lord's Ground," seeking whom he might induce to inscribe his name upon its pages. In the days of old, the expenses of the great matches played at Lord's were defrayed in part by the voluntary contributions of the wealthier members of the club, and the Hon. Sec.'s (Mr. Roger Kynaston) approach, armed with book and seductive smile, was a cause of frequent "shift of seat," and other mild tricks of evasion. In the days now referred to, when "Will Caldecourt," the well-known underhand bowler, was invited to give an opinion as to the powers of Mr. "So and So" as a cricketer, he would occasionally reply, " Well, sir, as you ask me, I should say that he could bat about as well as anybody's sister." This was about the form of the brothers "George and Billy" Payne, respectively; but it did not prevent the cricket ground at Sulby from being frequently enlightened with village matches. The one in which they themselves occasionally took part was the annual one between Sulby Hall and the " Town and County Club."

Always going in the two last wickets, the performance was a treat to see, and scarcely less to hear. If by some good chance the bat of either came in contact with the ball, go where it might, both set off to run, bound to score or die! A collision usually took place about midway between the wickets; whereupon expletives forcible and rapid were wont to fly from the elder brother, urging a hasty retreat on the part of his fellow-batsman. His legs being all too short for the emergency, he rarely got home in time, and then followed loud self-reproaches from the " not out " cause of the catastrophe. Should a catch be held or a good hit accidentally be stopped by either brother when out in the field, the congratulations from each to the other were highly diverting.

For the County Club, almost entirely composed of Northampton tradesmen, the match against Sulby was the event of the season. The eleven with whom it had to contend, though weakened by its tail, was by no means a bad one. Its strongest elements consisted of Charles Meyrick, a Wykehamist and college friend of W. Payne's—a beautiful bat and fieldsman; the Rev. W. Fox, rector of Cottesbach—a good bat and thorough cricketer, but unable to run the hits he made, from heart-complaint. It used to be said of this worthy parson, that like the cuckoo, he laid his own eggs, but could not hatch them, a view more in accordance with the eccentric habits of that bird than that taken by the schoolboy who, when asked by an examiner in what respect the cuckoo differed from other birds, replied "that he never laid his own eggs." Also two brothers from Leicester—W. and J. Davis—the one a superior batsman and good wicket-keeper, the other a fair left-hand round bowler; Sir St. Vincent Cotton, a well-known figure in sporting circles, who, if in practice, was likely by his hard-hitting to keep the fielders on the move; the Rev. R. Isham—a useful man all round; and two Pells from Clipston, William and Walton, with the two Paynes and members of the household, usually made up the eleven. In the Northampton team, Messrs. H. O. Nethercote, Jeffery, Shaw, Hewlett, Hollis, H. P. Markham, Emery, Wellneger-Davis, Dean, and "Jack" Smith—the latter a stalwart "lad o' wax," fully believing that there was nothing like leather; but preferring it in the form of a cricket ball. Unaccustomed to dining in marble halls, he on one of these occasions caused much amusement to his host by emptying the contents of a boat of lobster-sauce on to his cherry-tart!—a mixture that seemed to be highly palatable to the omnivorous son of St. Crispin. Not content with treating his opponents to a sumptuous repast in the house, "the Squire" would order out in the cool of the evening a lordly bowl of "bishop," a vinous compound almost unknown in these degenerate days. Placed on a side-table in the tent, the spiced mixture formed an eye-opener for those about to wield the willow, and a solace for those who had been constrained to lay it down.

Whether or no this old-fashioned mark of hospitality is more honoured in the breach than the observance is a matter of opinion, but it was much appreciated and never abused, and is much to be preferred to the detestable practice of treating professionals to champagne at the mid-day (or any) dinner.

Since these days the Northamptonshire Cricket Club has risen into a higher and more complete stage of existence, and can now hold its own *versus* the "M.C.C.," and counties of repute in the cricketing world. The Sulby Club, sharing the fate of its founder, has passed away—like himself ever to be remembered with emotions of pleasure, gratitude, and regret.

Falling in with the spirit of the day, the subject of this memoir by no means neglected the "science" of self-defence.

In the healthy and muscular country gentleman from the Midlands, the famous "Tom Spring" found a pupil of whom he might well be proud. His uninstructed arm, even in his Eton days, had been a formidable weapon of offence, but when science and strength came to act in combination, the "rough" who checked him on the race-course or in the street was pretty sure to come in for a bad quarter of an hour. One day at a cricket-dinner held in the Grand Stand at Northampton, having been informed that some "roughs" had got into a side-room and were making free with the provisions, he instantly took off his coat, and went for the lot. The appearance only of the stalwart cricketer was sufficient to scatter the thieves, and the captain of the Sulby side resumed his seat regretting that the "curs" would not stop to be thrashed.

The unaccountable "glamour" of the "P. R," has already been referred to, and in George Payne it found one of its most earnest advocates. An old sportsman living at Brixworth, and now approaching his seventy-eighth year, told the writer of these pages that he witnessed a great fight that came off near Towcester many years ago between two celebrated pugilists. Standing near him was a neighbouring Duke, and hard by were other county magnates and Justices of the Peace! The day was bitterly cold, but such was the excitement in seeing two men knock each other out of all shape, that the narrator never felt it for a moment, and described the spectacle as being "one of the most interesting and enjoyable he ever witnessed!" He added the following corollary to his proposition, namely, that on the same night three or four of the houses round about were broken into, and that the rioting and drunkenness that went on in Towcester were disgraceful in the extreme. Such was Mr. Payne's influence with the "P.R." and its associates, that when "Owen Swift" fought "Atkinson of Nottingham" near Horton, the contest was not allowed to commence until he appeared upon the ground.

During his second Mastership of the Pytchley hounds, ill-success upon the turf, and losses in other directions, had produced their usual results, and Sulby Hall with the property attached was doomed to pass into other hands. For two seasons it was hired by the Duke of Montrose, and was afterwards purchased by the Hon. Frederick and Lady Elizabeth Villiers, in whose possession it remained after the death of her husband. That Sulby should be connected with any other name than that of "Payne" did no little violence to the feelings of the many worshippers of the late owner, and the rough-handed villagers who had so joyfully picked up the almost red-hot shillings and half-crowns that were thrown about on the celebration of his "coming of age," could scarcely believe that the beloved squire had left his old home for good and all. The name of a contemporary, well known in the annals of the county's hunting and social life, "Mr. Hungerford," has likewise passed away, and the fine old Hall at Dingley, the one-time hunting-seat of James the First, no longer recognizes a Hungerford as its lord and master. Long connected by ties of the most intimate friendship, the owners of Sulby and Dingley were equally reckless in their expenditure, and in the end the same fate awaited either property. Happy is it for the interests of the "P.H." that the latter should have fallen into the hands of so excellent a sportsman, and so popular a nobleman, as Viscount Downe.

In the March of 1846, Mr. Payne was presented with a magnificent silver epergne, three feet six inches in height, and five hundred ounces in weight, upon the base of which he is portrayed under a tree, holding up over his hounds the fox which they had just run into. The following words were inscribed upon one of its sides: " Presented to George Payne, Esq., of Sulby Hall, by six hundred farmers, tradesmen and others, as a testimonial of their high esteem for him, and gratitude for his unceasing efforts to promote the manly and healthy sports of the county." The ceremonial of the presentation took place at the George Hotel at Northampton, where some hundreds sat down to dinner: the members of the hunt were in their red coats. The sun of the splendour of the popular idol had long begun to wane; but many of those present knew nothing of this, and looked upon the guest of the evening as the embodiment of sport, munificence, and pleasant manners. As, pushing back his chair, he arose to express his gratitude for the magnificent mark of the goodwill of those around him, he looked the model of a sportsman, and of an English country gentleman.

It was not without some difficulty that he repressed feelings, that, at first, seemed likely to overcome him; but warming to his work, his audience soon became aware that they were listening to a man gifted with oratorical powers of no common order. At political and other dinners he had previously given the public a taste of his quality as a speaker, but on this occasion his feelings gave such fire to his words, that the hearts of his hearers were deeply touched. On resuming his seat it seemed as though the roof of the old county ballroom must needs collapse with the loud, long-continued applause. It is sad to know that this splendid tribute of gratitude and esteem was never destined to decorate the table of him to whom it was presented. Too large for the dinner-table of the house in which Mr. Payne passed the latter years of his life, it remained under the care of the silversmiths (Messrs. Smith of Long Acre) in whose atelier it was produced. On the death of the owner it was bequeathed to Lord Spencer as an heirloom, on

L

condition that it never was allowed to leave the county, or pass into other hands than those of the Lords of Althorp.

To the great regret of all the county, and indeed, of all hunting-men, Mr. Payne resigned the Mastership of the "P.H." in 1848, and having done so was scarcely ever seen again at the cover-side. He would inquire how things were going on in the old county, and liked to hear of any notable run, but he never cared again to join in the sport.

One of the greatest of speculators, he never tried the grand speculation of all of entering a married life, and whether he took warning from the man who declared "that his wife had doubled the expenses of life, and halved the pleasures," or whether, like a Bishop Whately, he looked upon women as "interesting creatures who never reason, and poke the fire atop," it does not seem that at any time of his life he seriously contemplated matrimony.

What he might have become had he been suitably mated, who can tell? To those who knew him best there arise visions of a country gentleman, leader of society, Master of hounds, Chairman of Quarter Sessions, Member of Parliament, possessing everything that makes life desirable, including a popularity probably unequalled. But it was not so to be. Left to float alone on a sea never at rest; tossed hither and thither on the waves of never-ceasing excitement, he became a noble derelict, rescued by friendly salvors from utter shipwreck.

On the 10th of August, 1878, at Lewes Races, he was attacked by a paralytic seizure, from which he never recovered, and he died on September 2nd, in his house in Queen Street, May Fair, in his seventy-fifth year. In the book entitled "Famous Racing-Men," this event is thus spoken of: "Mr. Payne's death was sincerely felt and deplored by thousands, from the Queen herself to the humblest Northamptonshire tradesman; and the reason is not far to seek. G. Payne was a sterling English gentleman—sincere and unaffected in bearing—upright in his dealings—the soul of honour, and as one of his oldest friends said of him years ago, 'beloved by men, and idolized by women, children and dogs.'" In the volume "Racing" of the "Badminton Library"—one of the most delightful series of works on sporting subjects ever published—this eidolon, before which everybody seems to have bowed down, is thus referred to: "It mattered not to whom he was talking—the gravest statesman, the most matter-of-fact money-grubber, the shyest girl 'out' for the first time in her life—one and all, old and young, left him with the unalterable conviction that G. P. was the most delightful companion, he or she had ever come across; and this charm of manner never left him to the day of his death."

That the ex-Squire of Sulby must have been a man of more than ordinary mark is proved by the fact that on the occurrence of his death, though merely a "Prince of the Turf" and of the "Gaming Table," the obituary notices in all the leading journals were little less complimentary than if he had been a great statesman, a successful general, or an eminent divine. In his own county and neighbourhood, many a year will elapse ere in hall or under more humble roof, George Payne will cease to be a name regretted. A song composed by a Northamptonshire farmer in 1846, well shows the estimation in which the Master of the "P.H." was held:—

> "A tumbler of punch to the health of George Payne;
>   Come drink, my brave yeomen, the toast;
> We prefer it to Burgundy, claret, champagne,
>   For a man that's a whole county's boast!
> Here's a glass for the high, and a 'go' for the low,
>   Rich and poor will both bid him God speed;
> But we'll drink it in punch, for we very well know
>   Whose the foxhunter's friend at his need!
> There's no brook that's too wide, and no bullfinch too high
>   When he settles himself in his seat,
> As he cheers on his hounds in a scent, in full cry,
>   And for pace, Sir, he cannot be beat.
> When his musical notes through Vanderplank ring,
>   And Lilbourne resounds to his voice,
> I care not what rivals old England may bring,
>   George Payne is the winner for choice.
> In a county all grass, and where foxes abound,
>   And with farmers so fond of the sport,
> 'Twould be sad not to hear the blythe cry of a hound,
>   Or forget one of such a good sort.
> So we'll drink to the health of the man of first flight,
>   And the first in the flight is 'George Payne,'
> And when wanting a sportsman to do what is right,
>   We shall know where to find him again."

END OF THE HISTORY.

PART II.

OF THE

HISTORY OF THE PYTCHLEY HUNT,

IN

MEMOIRS OF THE MASTERS

AFTER THE RETIREMENT OF

MR. GEORGE PAYNE.

LORD ALFORD.
1848.

It was fortunate for the Pytchley Hunt and its members, that on the resignation of the Mastership of Mr. Payne, a suitable successor should have been on the spot, as it were, to fill the vacated situation. To follow such a man as the ex-Squire of Sulby greatly enhanced the responsibility attached to an office which of all others required to be burdened with no extra weight. The small boy who when desired by a school-inspector to give him his idea of the meaning of "responsibility" replied, "If I had only two buttons on my trousers, and one of them was to come off, the whole responsibility would rest on the other" must have been a lad "with all his buttons on;" no more just appreciation of the exact significance of a term can well be imagined. To come after a man like Mr. Payne, and to fail in any one of the points which had made him so popular would have exposed the new Master to those comparisons which do not assist in bearing a newly-undertaken burden. Happily in the case of the new "chef" there was no need for comparison. Half a county-man, from having married the eldest daughter of the Marquis of Northampton—residing at Harleston House—devoted to hunting, and a brilliant rider, it was not possible to find a man more acceptable to the farmers and landlords of the "P.H." than Viscount Alford, eldest son of Earl Brownlow. With charming manners and a remarkably aristocratic mien and appearance, the new Master speedily found himself enjoying a popularity which is only to be acquired by not allowing the wish to show sport to engender a harassing policy in the field. No greater mistake can be entertained by a master of hounds than to be constantly "nagging" at the horsemen who do not do everything exactly "according to Cocker." A strongly expressed monition, if hounds are being overridden or some neglect of the evident necessity of the moment is being put in practice, is always received as deserved and opportune. The writer, however, after an experience of more than half a century of Men and Masters is convinced that in the interests of sport, even the totally let-alone policy is preferable to the one of constant remonstrance. "Fussiness" in a Master produces irritation in those that hunt with him, and that begets a spirit of "you-be-hangedness" which should never exist between a M.F.H. and his field.

For some years, an over-keen Master (with a by no means over-good temper) of a neighbouring pack, robbed the day's hunting of more than half its enjoyment by his frequent interference with innocent offenders, and the surliness of his Huntsman did not detract from the general discomfort. There probably is no position in which tact and a knowledge of human nature are more necessary than that of a M.F.H., and woe betide both him and the county where these are greatly lacking. Lord Alford well knew when and to what extent the crack of his whip should be heard; but he never allowed it to get beyond the confines of courtesy or to excite ill-will.

Mr. Payne, who had bought fifteen couple of hounds at the sale of Mr. Green, when he gave up the Quorn county, had very few hounds, being unwilling to spare his best bitches, and the kennel was principally kept up by drafts from Lord Henry Bentinck. Lord Alford began with a large draft from the Belvoir kennel, since which time for some years, Charles Payn principally used the blood of Lord Fitzwilliam's and the Belvoir kennels.

If ever dog was the object of a man's idolatry, the Belvoir hound "Pillager" was the one before whom Charles Payn was ready at any time to fall down and worship. We read in the pages of "Silk and Scarlet" that this paragon of fox-hounds ran for six seasons without ever requiring a taste of the whip, and that in 1858 there were twenty couple of hounds—mostly tan—related to him. "Pliant," one of his daughters, seems to have distinguished herself in a run of thirty-five minutes from Lord Spencer's cover to Sulby reservoir. The fox after running along-side the reservoir for some distance, dashed in midway; the pack followed, and on reaching the middle cast themselves right and left, whereas Pliant went straight across and got half a mile beyond Sulby Hall before she was caught. The fox was so washed that the hounds never "enjoyed it" after emerging from the water, and made his escape. Pillager died somewhat suddenly of inflammation of the liver in his sixth season, to the great regret of his numerous admirers.

A case of wilful and genuine vulpecidism is usually looked upon in a hunting-country as an act so base that it never could have been perpetrated before. The offence, possibly, may be considered co-eval with "original sin"! At the time of which we are speaking a vulpecide—forgetful of the warning "be sure your sin will find you out"—attended a Meet two or three days after a well proven case of fox-murder. He had scarcely shown his face when an honest and indignant yeoman "went for him," and compelled him to hide his shame by a hasty and prudent retreat.

Hoping to improve the breed of foxes, the new Master turned down at Cottesbrooke six brace of the largest Scotch ones he could procure. For two seasons not one of these fresh importations was found, and Charles Payne could never come across or even hear of more than half of them. Nothing disappears more mysteriously, or in every way conduct themselves more disappointingly than foxes imported from other districts. Shortly before giving up the Pytchley country, Sir Bellingham Graham got a quantity of foxes from Herring in the New Road, and turned them down about Lamport, but they vanished to a fox, and not one of them was found during the short remainder of that season.

It was during the Mastership of Lord Alford, that Mr. H. Barraud painted the well-known and popular picture of the "Meet at Crick." Out of forty-three figures there represented ten only remain to tell the tale of a "Crick Meet" in the reign of John Hume, Viscount

Alford (b. 1812, d. 1851). These survivors are Lord Bateman, Lord Henley, Sir Rainald Knightley, Sir T. Steele, Messrs. Arkwright, H. O. Nethercote,[1] the present Sir F. Head, Mr. R. Lee Bevan, Charles Payne, and Ned Kingsbury.

Of the group there represented, apart from the Master himself, who, mounted on a beautiful chestnut, bought of Sam Pell of Ecton, is talking to his predecessor in office, Mr. George Payne, the names of Sir Francis Bond Head, General Sir Thomas Steele, Sir Rainald Knightley and Mr. Stirling Crawfurd are all more or less familiar to the sporting public. The welter weight on the ground, holding his horse in his left hand, talking to Charles Payn, is the one-time well known West of Dallington. A Northamptonshire yeoman of the grand old sort, to him hunting was the real enjoyment of life. Riding about seventeen stone, and usually having under him low thick horses, lacking alike in pace and quality, he possessed that within which enabled him to overcome the drawbacks of the bones being lined over-well, and the pocket too scantily. Occasional hints from a well-used pair of persuaders and vocal monitions from some point very low down in his "manly bosom," saw him safe through or over many a fence, which had been met with a "No, I thank you" from some better mounted men. A good farmer, he made an indifferent occupation carry him fairly well, ere prices began to wear a vanishing figure; but he had few equals in making an indifferent mount carry him across a country.

Being one who, as far as in him lay, was deter-

---

[1] Since the above was written, the author whose hand had traced it has also, alas! "joined the majority."—ED.

mined to keep on the line of the hounds, he was often heard to say that "he could not understand why people went out hunting if they did not mean to ride straight." Whilst enunciating this opinion, little did he remember that out of the many who in the winter-time choose to take their pleasuring in a hunting-country, not one in twenty-five cares for anything but the sociability—the spice of swagger—the air and exercise. Let a decree go forth that all the (hunting) world shall be taxed according to individual performance with hounds—that the "Customer" should pay lightly—and the "Funker" be mulcted in proportion to his funkiness, how many would remain to send in a return to the tax-collector? The now too-thickly frequented Meets would be shorn of three-fourths of their numbers, and the non-advertising experiment would give way to extra publicity. Happily it is given to few to believe that in their case "nerve" is an unknown quantity. They see very plainly that poor Shuffler is a terrible muff, and scarcely refrain from uncomplimentary criticisms on his style of riding; but they are more or less blind to the mote that is in their own eye. After dinner, such as these, on the third or fourth circular journey of the decanter of port or claret, almost persuade themselves that they "will have a cut at some big brook" on the morrow, and the feeling "crescit bibendo"—but on the morrow's advent the distant bridge is irresistible. The "P.H." has not been without some remarkable examples of members troubled with "jumpophobia." Many remember an ex-captain of a distinguished infantry regiment, who, hunting from Northampton for seven consecutive years, was never seen to jump but once. On this occasion a line of hurdles barred further progress, and no friendly rustic being near to remove one, there was nothing for it but "to do or die." The horse was willing, but the owner weak. The unwonted call upon his energies induced the surprised "quad" to rise higher than was anticipated, and the displaced rider found to his mortification that the saddle is not always one of those things which stick closer than a brother. The performance did not escape the kind observations of sundry onlookers, and "laughter rang around." It is not probable that the provider of the merriment just recorded ever persuaded himself that he would become a "hard man;" nor why should he? Let every man enjoy himself in the hunting-field or elsewhere as best suits his own idiosyncrasy. To do such violence to his own feelings as to cause his heart to leave its rightful spot and take up a position in the mouth is not required of any man. Upon such as these, however, the honest yeoman—a straight goer in the walks as well as rides of life—looked with pity, not unmingled with a spice of contempt. A true sportsman, cheery and respectful in manner, William West long enjoyed the goodwill and esteem of all his neighbours, but a cloud overshadowed him during the last few years of his life; but the hunting-days he loved to recall when all things else had well-nigh passed out of recollection.

A different stamp of horseman was Mr. Sam. Pell, a farmer well known in those days, who standing somewhat at the back in the Crick picture, seems to be looking at the rider of an animal which shortly before had occupied a stall in his own stable. The P.H. members of a quarter of a century ago will not soon forget the tell-tale visage—the hat with brims of dean-like curl—and the determined riding of another farmer of the Pytchley Hunt, Sam Pell of Ecton. To see him at the Meet, the men who knew him not would say that he was no strict observer of the formularies of the Rechabites and that it was evident that in his opinion it was not required of any man "always to come home to tea." The stranger who had gauged his habits thus, and a little later had seen him go to hounds, must have confessed that abstinence is not always the best policy, where nerve is required. No one liked a big place better or more quickly made up his mind where it was most negotiable; few farmers had a better class of horse or more completely repudiated the "lardy dardy" style of riding them: but his "form" across country was rather that of valour than of its better part—discretion. Of prudence he knew nothing or but very little, and before the end of "a real good thing" he had but too often come to grief over some all but impracticable place.

Bright and joyous in speech and manner, he ever seemed, when at the cover-side, as if he had not a care in the world; but "*post equitem sedet atra cura*," and it was not to be expected that even he had at all times the saddle all to himself. In spite of air, exercise and a healthful calling, when still in the prime of life he was fain to obey the irresistible summons, and the P.H. lost from amongst its followers one who was looked upon as a good specimen of the hard-riding Farmer.

Hugging themselves under the anticipation of a long continuance of a Mastership they thoroughly appreciated, the members of the Hunt were struck with dismay and regret when it became known that Lord Alford from delicacy of health had become necessitated to discontinue all active exercise, and he was compelled to resign a post the occupation of which he seemed thoroughly to enjoy.

THE HON. FREDERICK VILLIERS.

The difficulty of finding a successor to Lord Alford was soon happily overcome, the Hon. Frederick Villiers undertaking to fill the vacant office. The purchase of Sulby Hall and the estate from Mr. George Payne having given Mr. Villiers the position of a county proprietor, it would have been impossible to find a more suitable Master for the P.H. An elegant, though not powerful horseman like his father, Lord Jersey, Mr. Villiers rode well to hounds, and from invariably eschewing horses with no manners, he was certain to form one of the front rank during a good thing. Holding his field well in hand, he never failed to give the doer of mischief " a bit of his mind," but never exceeded the rights of his position, nor made a too constant remonstrance. An excellent man of business, the new owner of Sulby threw himself thoroughly into all county matters, and never permitted pleasure to take the precedence of duty. Two years, however, saw the completion of a first term of office as M.F.H.; and at the end of 1852, the P.H. was once more filling the *rôle* of " flock without a shepherd."

LORD HOPETOUN.

At a time when it seemed there would be some difficulty in procuring a successor to Mr. F. Villiers for the

"P.H." Mastership, a young Scotch Earl stepped in to fill the gap.

Having only recently left Oxford, where he may be said to have first acquired his hunting tastes, Lord Hopetoun found himself at a very early age without any experience of mankind or "dogkind," occupying the responsible post of a Master of Fox Hounds in a crack country. Naturally shy, and disliking any society except that of a few old college-friends, the position did not appear to be such an one as would adapt itself to the idiosyncrasies of the young Scotch nobleman; but he held it nevertheless for four seasons, much to the satisfaction of the members of the Hunt. Whether not being called upon for the usual subscription or not being called to order in the hunting-field for transgressions ever so great, in any way influenced the hearts and minds of those who hunted with him, it is certain that Lord Hopetoun earned for himself a popularity that any Master might covet. This is the more remarkable from his never laying himself out to please—from his marked coldness to strangers—and his dislike to making new acquaintances. That things went as well as they did may be attributed in a great measure to his having for his Huntsman a man so universally liked and esteemed as Charles Payn.

From him he gladly picked up the rudiments of hound-lore, and some knowledge of kennel-ways and necessities, and so became in a measure to feel himself at home in a position for which he was not naturally adapted by habits or disposition. A natural judge of a horse he required little assistance in the selection of his own animals or those for the kennels; and probably at no time have there been more good hunters in the Brixworth stables than during his Mastership.

Commencing apparently without any nerve or even desire for a forward place in a run, he gradually trained on into being an exceedingly hard man, and pretty sure to be found amongst the first flight. For the first season or two, his chief delight seemed to be to derive laughing material out of the falls and any ludicrous incident he chanced to witness during the day; any misadventure at water being a source of especial and unlimited delight. Naturally clever, and with a keen eye for the ridiculous, nothing escaped his observation or remark. Seeing a friend arrive at the Meet one day, riding a horse whose tail was nearly hairless and stuck almost straight up, he addressed him with: "Why, Vernon, what luck you were in to pick up such a horse as that; his tail will serve as a capital hat-peg when you don't want to hunt him." From that day to the last hour of his sojourn in Northamptonshire, the owner of the animal with the peculiar extremity was known as "Hat-peg Vernon," and is still spoken of as such when alluded to by any of the older members of the Hunt.

Pitsford Hall, as usual, was hired by the noble lord as his residence; thus becoming for the fifth time since 1821 the hunting abode of the Master of the "P.H."

That Lord Hopetoun took the rough with the smooth, and did not shirk the somewhat weary days in the Woodlands, is shown in the pages of "Silk and Scarlet," where we find that he and his friend Captain Newland remained with the hounds on one occasion from 5.15 a.m. to 3 p.m. It seems that the fox was found in a plantation close to the road between Kettering and Stam-

ford, soon after five on a morning early in August, 1853.
After being at it for three hours the hounds changed on
to a shabby little vixen, who slipped like a witch through
the briars and sedge, and fairly defied the dog-pack to
make her break. During the whole day they threw up
only twice, and for *four hours* expected to kill every
minute. At 3 p.m. Lord Hopetoun and Captain Newland, quite tired out, went home. A sort of cordon of
country-people was drawn up in one corner, but the
little vixen slipped through them over and over again,
and even when the second Whip had been sent to Brig-
stocke for four couple of the best bitches, and had tried
their best for another hour, she was as lively and
inexhaustible in her dodges as ever. Every hound was
stripped bare in his breast and forelegs, and some dropped
beaten on the road on their way home. To the
enthusiastic admirer of the working of hounds this may
have been a day of unmitigated delight and enjoyment,
but to any ordinary mortal the scene must have been one
of intolerable fatigue, weariness and monotony, and a
warning against a too frequent indulgence in the so-called
pleasures of hunting in the dog-days.

In the following season Lord Hopetoun had the good
fortune to be able to boast that his hounds had shown
the best run ever seen with the Pytchley up to that time,
and with which in the eyes of his huntsman, Charles
Payn, "the great Waterloo run" is in no way comparable. The details of this excellent day's sport were as
follows :—

On November 21st, 1854, a stormy morning which
cleared off into a lovely day, a large field met the
Pytchley at North Kilworth, and in a coppice under Mr.

Gough's (than whom no better preserver of foxes ever lived) house, a fox was found who went away by North Kilworth House through Caldecott Spinney, nearly to Misterton, where he turned to the left near Swinford, left Stanford Hall on the right, South Kilworth on the left, and crossing the Welland ran straight up to the Pond Close at Hemplow. Entering none of the covers, he made his way up to Welford toll-bar, the time up to this point being fifty minutes almost without a check, and the pace excellent. The hounds then swimming on by Naseby Woollies, skirted Sulby Gorse, Naseby covert and " Tally Ho," traversed Kelmarsh osier-bed and the Church Spinney, and crossing the Harboro' road, made for Johnson's Furze. Headed here, the fox made for Scotland Wood, but sticking to the siding he left it at the middle gate on the road to Hazelbeach, passed through Maidwell Dales, skirted Berrydale, and leaving Cottesbrooke on the right, also Creaton, Spratton and Chapel Brampton villages on the same quarter, he ran up to the Rev. G. Howard Vyse's garden at Boughton. Here the hounds nearly caught their fox, but he contrived to slip them, and making back through the osier-bed, he got to ground in the main earths in Boughton Clump, after running two hours and twenty-five minutes. It was nearly an eighteen miles point, and hounds must have run about twenty-six. Charles Payne, after the manner of all Huntsmen, was satisfied, by his peculiar mode of skirting all the covers, that it was the same fox throughout ; and if so, a stouter animal never lived before hounds. Out of a field of two hundred at starting, not more than five or six lived to see the end, amongst whom were Lord Hopetoun, who finished on his

M

hack, which he fortunately came up with on his way home, Colonel Shirley, Mr. Edmunds of Guilsboro', Mr. Elworthy of Brixworth, Charles Payne, and Jack Woodcock, first Whip.

Up to the Spratton road no one had gone better than Mr. Fred. Villiers; but at this point, with three shoes off, and a horse completely done up, he was fain to cry "hold, enough," and hope to hear of, if he could not witness, a kill. C. Payn was fortunate in having two of his best horses out, Nobbler and Firefly, and came across the second in the very nick of time. At the close of a career of fifty years with hounds he maintains that this was the finest run he ever saw, and that the "Waterloo day" is not to be mentioned with it in any way. To this statement, inasmuch as it was far the better scenting-day of the two—that during the two hours and twenty-five minutes occupied in accomplishing the twenty-six miles, there were two separate forty minutes of the highest character—that the country (except about Naseby) was mostly grass—and that the going was particularly sound and good—the writer, who was present on each occasion, gives his unqualified sanction.

Two years subsequently to this, a letter to the Editor of the *Northampton Herald* gives an admirable sketch of the "P.H." as it existed at that season—the last of Lord Hopetoun's Mastership. It ran as follows:—

"THE PYTCHLEY HOUNDS.

"MR. EDITOR,—Many a time during the present season have I found myself at the cover side with the above-named pack, an old and early love, to which I return with all the greater zest from the long interval that has

occurred between the days of my first courtship and the
current year. Alas!

> Many a lad I loved is dead,
> And many a lass grown old,

and the only men I recognized as representing the men
of old time were those of Knightley, Isted, Nethercote,
Isham and the young heir of Althorp. In vain did I ask
to be shown a Cooke, an Elwes, a Hanbury, a Payne, a
Hungerford—names that will stir the blood of many a
snowy head, and recall visions of the days from Dick
Knight to the 'Squire,' and his glorious bitch-pack. But
though these be gone, their places are not unworthily
filled.

"Messrs. Villiers, Cust, Sir G. Jenkinson, Clerk,
Bevan, Franklin (Hazelbeach) and last, that brave old
sportsman with hair of snow and heart of oak, Sir Francis
B. Head, satisfactorily make up the gap which time has
worked. Nor should a 'heavy weight' be passed over,
who, hailing from Kelmarsh, finds few to beat him across
the Waterloo or any other country, and seems only too
forgetful of the fact that the human frame is made up of
separate limbs, and that each limb is liable to fracture.
Charles Payne, the Huntsman, is as fine a rider as ever
steered a horse over a fence—is quick and cheery with
his hounds—most anxious to show sport—and from his
civility and excellent conduct is a favourite with everybody. One hint I would venture to offer him, namely,
that he should be more careful not to chop his foxes.
More than one have I seen this season snapped up for
lack of the awakening crack of the whip; and foxes here
are no longer plentiful as blackberries; indeed, in the

district about Overstone, a fox is nearly as rare an animal as a wolf. Though there has been no one run of especial brilliancy, the general sport has been above the average, and more foxes have been honestly killed after good hunting-runs than has been the case for some time.

"Badby Wood, Welton Place, Braunston, Vanderplanks, Buckby Folly; even Harleston Heath, Loatland Wood, Sulby Gorse, and Alford Thorns, have each contributed a quota to the general sport, and a forty-seven minutes from the first-mentioned place may perhaps be set down as the best thing of the season.

"I must not conclude these remarks without referring to the heavy blow the country has received in the retirement of the noble Master. The magnificent liberality displayed by the Earl during the four years of his Mastership, combined with his quiet and unaggressive conduct, will long be remembered with gratitude, and I doubt if the Hopetoun and Charles Payne epoch will not be looked back upon in after years as forming a very palmy period in the annals of the Pytchley Hunt."

After giving up the country, Lord Hopetoun purchased a small estate, Papillon Hall, near Lubenham, and hunted for several years with Mr. Tailby and his old pack which had fallen into the hands of Messrs. Villiers and Charles Cust, who shared the Mastership between them for a brief period.

In the spring of 1875 the sad news reached England that Lord Hopetoun had died suddenly at Florence of a virulent fever, the seeds of which had been sown at Rome or Naples. So universally known had the ex-Master of the "P.H." become amongst hunting-men, that the intelligence of his death in the very prime of life created a wide-spread feeling of sorrow and regret.

By nature clever enough to fill a position requiring abilities above the average, he had no taste for public life, and lacking ambition and habits of hard work, he took no part in politics, and rarely entered the House of Lords. Possessing a retentive memory, he delighted to recount the amusing things he had both seen and heard; and among those with whom he was intimate, he was ever a most entertaining companion. Few things used to amuse him more than the descriptions of runs given in local newspapers, the climax of his enjoyment having been reached when one day, during his Mastership of the "P.H.," in one of the Northampton papers he read an account of a Meet at Great Harrowden, ending with, "after waiting for a considerable time for his lordship's appearance, the horn of the Huntsman was heard, and the whole field was seen advancing to the place of meeting at full cry." He would greatly have enjoyed such deplorable announcements to sporting ears as are now to be seen in the sporting contributions to our county journals, where we read that "'a red un' was 'discovered' in Overstone Park, and that after a while the 'little beggar' seemed much 'fatigued.'" "That a fine 'redskin' left his 'city of refuge' and 'scampered up' the hill at a brisk pace before his pursuers. That 'puss rattled away' for a considerable distance. That Sywell Hayes was 'scrutinized' for a 'sly un,' but 'pug' was elsewhere." Such are a few of the "gems" of sporting contributions to country journals, whose hunting literature ought to be entirely free from such cockneyfied absurdities.

THE HON. F. VILLIERS AND THE HON. C. CUST.

In allying himself with Mr. Charles Cust in the Mastership of the P.H., which succeeded that of Lord Hopetoun in 1856, Mr. Villiers had for his partner one of those who by a natural geniality of disposition and winning manners and countenance, seem throughout their career to have at their command the wills and affections (especially the latter) of all men. Beloved by his school-fellows at Eton, as well as by his brother-officers in the Blues, he was no less popular with "all sorts and conditions of men" at his Northamptonshire home at Arthingworth, and his accession to even a moiety of the Mastership of the "P.H." was hailed with universal satisfaction. Ranking among the welter weights, and never riding horses of the very highest class, he nearly touched "customer" point, and when hounds were carrying ahead, never failed to occupy a forward place. Constitutionally delicate in health, he was compelled somewhat suddenly to decline hunting soon after assuming a share of the responsibilities of Mastership; and on Mr. Villiers objecting to continue in office by himself, the country once more was compelled to look about for a Master.

COL. ANSTRUTHER THOMSON.

When the Chelsea Seer declared that the population of England numbered 30,000,000 "mostly fools," he also divided them into two classes, natural fools, and d—d fools; the former being fools who are such by no fault of their own, fools congenital, so to say—the latter fools, in spite of knowing that they are such. To no one be-

longing to either of these sections of the human race is it possible to undertake the management of a pack of hounds with any hope of success.

A knowledge of mankind, womankind, and dogkind—command of temper—graciousness of speech—and a thorough knowledge of how to say "no;" coupled with a willingness to say "yes;"—ample means, united to a good acquaintance with economic principles, are only part of the qualifications necessary to form an ideal M.F.H. No wonder that many of this pattern are not to be found; but one such sat in his study one February morning of the year 1864, and perused the following letter from an old and dear friend.

"*Wootton Hall. Feb. 26th*, 1864.

"My dear Jack,—Under the influence of a ripping fifty minutes over grass, up wind, and all just as it ought to be, I write you a line as a feeler about our country. I have only just heard that you have really given up the 'Fife.' I know your habits so well that I am quite sure that you will not be happy without a pack of hounds; and indeed the longer I live the more cause I have to agree with Jorrocks, 'that all time is wasted that is not spent in hunting.' Now do you think that you would like this Pytchley country? We shall have no Master after this season, as Spencer has quite decided to give the hounds up. You know the 'pros' and the 'cons' of the Pytchley as well as I do. It has the best woodlands in the world. You can hunt from August to May, both inclusive as they say. The disadvantage is the crowd on a Wednesday, which you also know from your experience with the Atherstone does not do half the mischief it appears as if it ought to do. If there is a scent, it is soon disposed of;

if not, you have to feel your way. From what I see, I am sure that if you care to take our country you will be well supported. I am not, however, writing under authority; only between ourselves. We have a capital pack of hounds, although it is the fashion to abuse them. They can hunt as well as race. I think that you would enjoy riding over these grass fields, as much as the hunting in the deep Woodlands on the Kettering side.

"Don't tell Mrs. Thomson that I am trying to tempt you here, or I shall be in disgrace with her; and of course if you did come to us, no one in Fife would ever speak to me again. I should much like to see you here, but that of course is as much from private and 'mahogany' motives as from my good opinion of your ratcatching qualities. I should like it if it could come off.

"Ever, my dear Jack,
"Yours very truly,
"GEORGE WHYTE MELVILLE."

Anxious to secure the big fish that he knew to be lying in the Fifeshire waters, the angler threw his line with all the skill of which he was capable, and after awhile fairly landed the object of his desire. Well knowing his man, Whyte Melville felt assured that in his friend Jack Thomson, not only would the country have as its Master a gentleman to whom not only the science of hunting and the minutiæ of kennel-management were as familiar as his A. B. C., but also one who would reach the hearts of the Farmers almost as much as George Payne himself had done. An inexpressible charm of manner—a smile peculiarly winning in its brightness—and a seat in the saddle denoting the perfect horseman, almost immediately won for the new Master the goodwill of all his latest constituents.

With Charles Payne, Dick Roake, and Tom Firr, as assistants, the Pytchley team for 1864 presented a galaxy of hunting talent such as few countries could boast; and it was clear that if sport were lacking, the fault could only rest with absence of "scent."

Accustomed to large fields when Master of the Atherstone, Captain Thomson was little daunted by the Pytchley "Wednesdays," a drawback to which, as Whyte Melville shows in his letter, too much importance has ever been attributed as a sport-spoiler. Given a scent —a real run-any-way scent—and in four minutes or less after a fox has broken cover, five hundred horsemen will in no way affect the character of a run. With a bad scent or greatly-dodging fox, numbers undoubtedly tell injuriously. The less bold hounds are apt to get kicked or ridden over, and the field persist in creeping up to the Huntsman, and leave him little, if any, room for his cast on either side. With a scent such as here described, sport could not be expected, even if the Huntsman, Whips and Master were the only people out; and I still cling to the view that a large Field is no great misfortune so far as sport is concerned. The damage done is quite another matter; and so long as Thomas Carlyle's two descriptions of fools continue to infest the land, nothing will avail to prevent it.

The open secret of the Pytchley Wednesday Meets affects only the subscription-list, and a word of remonstrance from the Master or any well-known member of the Hunt, when injury is being committed unnecessarily, will be of more avail than any amount of non-publicity and of non-advertising.

The *entourage* of a Midland Wednesday at a crack

Meet must needs wear a more or less formidable aspect in the eyes of Master and Huntsman; but " nothing is so bad as it seems;" and it is to be doubted if an accurate return could be made of sport spoiled by the actual crowd on these occasions, whether it would not be a very humble one. To half a dozen irrepressible individuals, actuated partly by jealousy, partly by an insane desire to be almost on the backs of the hounds, is to be attributed all the harm that one hears so much of, as the consequence of " the enormous crowd—"

> " Vexation sore ofttimes he bore,
> Strong language was in vain,"

might be inscribed on the head-stone of many a defunct Huntsman; but after all, the sum total of what he " had to go through," in getting a living was a small matter compared to the heavy sloughs of trouble through which nine out of ten in the same situation of life probably had to struggle.

Occupying at first a temporary residence close to the kennels, Captain Thomson soon after moved to Pitsford Hall, the chosen abode, as has already appeared, of many a Pytchley Master. Afterwards returning to Brixworth, he made a home at the " Rookery," now tenanted by Captain Carden. For one season he contented himself with leaving the open country to be hunted by Charles Payne, whilst he himself undertook the Woodlands; but this arrangement not proving satisfactory, Payne accepted an offer to transfer his services to Sir Watkin W. Wynn, and his master alone carried the horn.

To hunt hounds and manage the Field at the same time in such a country as the Pytchley is by no means a task to be undertaken by the man of ordinary acquirements; nor should it, if possible, ever fall to the lot of one individual. At no time, however, did the task seem too much for Captain Thomson's shoulders, and by putting the same principle in practice in either case, that is to say letting alone as much as possible, he secured sport for his followers, and won the goodwill of all who hunted with him.

The average daily sport was probably never higher than during the first five seasons of Mr. Thomson's Mastership; but the great Waterloo run of February 2nd, 1866, so completely threw every other into the shade, that no other will be referred to in this brief memoir of the hero of a day which has earned for itself a reputation only to be equalled by that of the famous Billesden Coplow day.

The morning had been wet, and the wind was southwest, when a goodly field appeared at Arthingworth just as the weather began to improve and look well for scent. For an hour or so little was done with two or three short-running foxes in Loatland, and soon after two o'clock the word was given for Waterloo. With a word and a wave of the hand from the Captain, in went seventeen and a half couple of hounds, eager to find, and little dreaming of the day's work before them. It soon became clear that the animal was at home; but he lay so close in a heap of dead sticks that the hounds had to be taken all round the cover and back to the top before he could be persuaded to move. Old Morris, the second horseman, then "viewed" him away towards the tunnel; when swinging to the left he went over the brook and spinney at Arthingworth, and made for Langboro.

Quitting this on the opposite side, he crossed the Harboro' road, traversed Shipley Spinney, and on up the hill towards Clipston. Here the pace began greatly to improve, but Dick Roake, having viewed what he thought to be the hunted fox going another way, blew his horn, and for awhile some of the field were here thrown out. Two fields further on, Mr. Thomson fell at a bullfinch, and losing a spur, stopped to pick it up : this lost him a place which he did not recover for some time. Running on without a pause, the hounds passed the spinney between Oxenden and Clipston, leaving the former village on the right. A slight hesitation took place opposite Mr. Kirkman's house, but the scent was soon hit off, and crossing the bottom at Farndon, the hounds sank the hill towards Lubenham into the Harboro' road : they then raced down the big field, and crossed the Welland at the Harboro' corner. At the Harboro' and Lubenham road they turned their heads towards Bowden Inn, running hard, with the result that "grief was spread around." Birch Reynardson here fell at a nasty fence and was left in the ditch, and the Master was reduced to a trot. A whistle behind denoted the approach of Dick Roake, who, on coming up on " Usurper," said " Take my horse, Sir ; he has about ten minutes left ; " but a regular " buster " at the succeeding fence proved that his late rider had not laid his account with the difference of weight between himself and his Master. Mr. Thomson, however, caught the hounds again at Bowden Inn, where they paused for a bit on a ploughed field. The rail was crossed to the right of the Langton Road, and from thence the hounds made down for the brook, pointing to Langton Caudle. Custance, the jockey, who had had about the best of it throughout, got well over the brook, into which Mr. Frank Langham and several others fell. On the top of the next hill the fox was headed, and turning along the valley, crossed the road between Thorpe Langton and Great Bowden, quitting the Caudle on the left. Rising the hill, "Usurper" shot his last bolt, and Mr. Hay kindly lent his rider a brown thorough-bred horse to go on with, from whom two falls were obtained in pretty quick succession. He galloped so well, however, that Mr. Thomson did not lose his place, and was well with his hounds between Stanton Wyvill and Cranko. Carrying on well past Glooston village and through Glooston Wood, Mr. Hay's animal found that he had had enough, and Mr. Walter De Winton came to the rescue with a comparatively fresh second horse. Happily, when in difficulties with his fresh mount, "Rainbow" suddenly turned up, as if from the skies, and the Master now felt himself in paradise.

The Harboro' road had let in several horsemen who had borne little of the burden and heat of the day, and there was now little danger of the hounds being left to themselves. Reduced at this point to thirteen couples and a half, they ran through Keythorpe Wood towards Ram's Head, where there were two lines of scent. At this time it was about four o'clock, one hour and fifty minutes having elapsed, and eighteen miles of country having been crossed since leaving Waterloo Gorse. Getting a view, they ran on to Fallow Closes, past Mr. Stud's house down to Slawston Cover, and pressed on through the meadows to the Welland, the fox being one field before them. Here they turned along the bank of the river as far as the road leading to Medbourne Station, where the fox had been chased by a dog, and with a failing scent and light, at half-past five Mr. Thomson stopped further proceedings ; the last hound to own the scent, " Graceful," having been the first to speak to it in Waterloo Gorse. Thus ended, somewhat unsatisfactorily, one of the grandest runs ever recorded in the annals of foxhunting.

It was over the finest part of the Pytchley and Tailby countries, and for one hour and fifty minutes only three ploughed fields were crossed. For one hour and forty minutes Mr. Thomson was without a Whipper-in, nor once had the hounds turned to him. Assisted only by Captain Clerk, of Spratton, who, having lost the first, came in for the second part of the run on a comparatively fresh horse, he got the hounds safely home to Brixworth, a distance of eighteen or nineteen miles, about ten o'clock. At ten minutes to eleven he sat down to dinner, after which he drove eleven miles to the Hunt Ball at Harboro', where he received an ovation worthy of the day's performance. That this was a grand day's sport, no one who knows anything of hunting will deny ; that it " was the best ever known," as has been asserted, is simply claiming for it far more than its due. That a change of foxes must have taken place two or three times is evident, and only during the earlier portion of the run was the pace really severe. To Captain Thomson himself, the day must ever stand out by itself as the most remarkable one of a long and successful hunting-career.

To keep hounds on one line, if not always on the same fox, for three hours and a half, and half of that time unassisted by either Whip—to have ridden four or five different horses during the run—to have fallen several times—and yet never to be out of the way when required—is a feat which very few huntsmen are able to boast of having achieved. That the hounds should have shown no signs of especial fatigue, spoke well for the kennel management; and all the missing lot made their way home within twenty-four hours.

With a kill at Hallaton, or even a fair run to ground somewhere in the "Tailby" country, and the Waterloo run need have no fear of being eclipsed in all time to come.

It was on this day that Captain Thomson first discovered what a valuable horse he had got in his five-year-old "Rainbow;" an animal before whom the prize-winning "Iris" had afterwards to play second fiddle at Tattersall's rostrum. Though not his turn, on that famous Friday morning, after two hours' exercise and his water, Rainbow was unexpectedly called upon to take the place of a lame horse, and do the longest day he had ever known. Beginning upon his favourite mare "Valeria," from whom he changed to "Usurper," then to a horse of Mr. W. Hay's; and after him to an animal of Mr. De Winton's; it was not until Glooston Wood was reached that Rainbow appeared upon the scene. From that time until the close, i.e., for an hour and forty-five minutes, he did his work without making a mistake; and reached his stable at half-past ten, having been out about thirteen hours.

He was a rich dark brown, standing sixteen-two, very powerful, with fair pace, and most charming temper. Bold as a lion at a big place, he would either creep or jump as required, and could go on for ever and ever. Of the innumerable hunters that have necessarily passed through the hands of Colonel Anstruther Thomson, he would probably award the palm to Rainbow as the most accomplished animal of the lot. Many a "P.H." man of to-day, remembers the wall-eyed Iris—Valeria, most confidential of mounts—Borderer—Harold—Hypothec—Wanderer—Man of the Age—and Rainbow; but the greatest of these was Rainbow.

> . . . "every sportsman, they say,
> In his lifetime has one that outrivals the rest;
> So the pearl of my casket I've shown you to-day;
> The gentlest, the gamest, the boldest, the best."

His owner thought "Iris" badly sold at three hundred and seventy guineas, but he was not every man's horse out of the show-ring, and his purchaser, Mr. Padwick, soon found that in his latest acquisition to his hunting-stud he had furnished himself with a master and something to spare. When Iris again went to the hammer he fetched exactly the same sum as before, viz., 370 guineas; though at a later date he again became the property of his original owner at 500*l*. In point of money-value, no horse of Mr. Thomson's ever equalled his famous "Maximus," for whom, after his performance in the memorable run from Claydon Woods, Lord Stamford gave 680 guineas.. This took place during his Mastership of the Bicester Hounds, and was full sixteen miles from point to point over the heavy Marsh Gibbon country, up Brill Hill to "the Quarters" in Oxfordshire. The Master and five others saw the best of it, but no one was up at the finish.

Standing six feet three in his shoes, and riding rather over than under sixteen stone, Mr. Thomson found it expedient to crash through, rather than fly, the big

Northamptonshire fences; and though this took time, his hounds were seldom long without his assistance. His nerve in plunging into a brook, chancing the bottom, and struggling on to the opposite bank, was a sight to watch, rather than a tempting example to follow; but he never failed in surmounting the difficulty.

After five years' good service rendered to the "P.H." Mr. Thomson, to the great regret of both gentlemen and farmers of the Hunt, signified his intention of resigning the Mastership at the close of 1868-9. The reasons he assigned for taking this course were, a growing family all wanting to hunt—a balance at his banker's getting fine by degrees—and the illness of Mrs. Thomson.

A requisition numerously signed, urging him to revoke his determination, was of no avail; and the " P.H.' country again became in need of a Master. Mr. J. A. Craven, of Whilton Lodge, a keen sportsman, and devotedly fond of hunting, happily came to the rescue; so the Hunt was scarcely "off with the old love before it was on with a new." Before his horses were sent to Tattersall's, Mr. Thomson invited a large party of ladies, members of the hunt, farmers, and others, to a luncheon of inspection. A tent of considerable size was pitched in the little field opposite the Brixworth stables, and never was canvas more tastefully decorated with bits, bridles, brushes, whips, horns, and all the equipment of a hunting-establishment. At little tables scattered here and there, guests of high and low degree met with a hearty welcome from their hospitable host, and had no cause to find fault with a want of abundance in the provisions, or with the quality of the champagne. Rain somewhat marred the parade of the horses, but the entertainment gave unfeigned satisfaction, and forged another link of union between guest and parting host. So deeply indeed had the "Captain" made his way into the hearts of all connected with the "P.H.," that it was resolved as a parting gift to present him with his portrait, painted by Sir Francis Grant, the greatest artist of the day. On the completion of the picture, a work of art worthy of the painter, in which Captain Thomson is depicted on the back of "Iris," surrounded by five favourite hounds—all admirable likenesses—it was determined to follow the precedent of Mr. George Payne's ceremonial, and present it at a dinner to be held at the George Hotel. Colonel Loyd Lindsay (now Lord Wantage) presided, having on his right and left the late and present Master, whilst the vice-chair was occupied by Mr. Matthew Oldacre of Clipston.

Amongst a company too numerous to individualize, were the Earl of Rosslyn, the Hon. H. Liddell, the Right Hon. G. Ward Hunt, M.P., Mr. Sackville Stopford, M.P., Major Fairfax Cartwright, M.P., Albert Pell Esq., M.P., Major G. Whyte Melville, the Hon. Fitzpatrick Vernon, Sir F. Horn, Sir C. Isham, Bart., Sir Algernon Peyton, Bart., Messrs. R. Lee Bevan, H. O. Nethercote, A. A. Young, H. H. Hungerford, Col. Arthur, Col. Maddocks, W. G. Duncan, L. Thursby, John Oliver, J. Bennett, the Rev. C. F. Watkins, &c., &c. The latter, in virtue of his office as Vicar of Brixworth, returned thanks for the Bishop and Clergy of the diocese, and remarked that, "though no sportsman himself, he came there that evening, not only innocently but imperatively, as the clergyman of the parish in which the kennels were situated, to pay respect to the gentleman whom they had assembled to honour. The duty of a clergyman was not only not to sanction but to blame what was positively wrong; but at the same time not to be too severe with those things which had not been positively forbidden by Divine command. (*Cheers.*) He was about to say something which might create a smile, but he felt that there was a connection between Natural Theology and Fox-hunting. (*Laughter.*) Did they expect that certain instincts would be given to certain animals unless they were designed to be exercised? (*Laughter and cheers.*) For instance, there were the characteristics of the retriever, the pointer, the St. Bernard dog, and the foxhound, the latter of which brought to condign punishment master Reynard the thief, thereby giving them a lesson in retributive justice." (*Laughter.*) The remarks of the rev. gentleman, being somewhat "out of the common," caused considerable amusement.

In a speech full of pertinent remarks and happy allusions, the Chairman gave the health of the guest of the evening. Alluding to the picture, he said, "It is a time-tried tribute of respect, carrying with it the best wishes of no fewer than three hundred and seventy-five gentlemen, who have subscribed for it. It is a testimonial from neighbours and friends in return for unceasing efforts to promote the sport of fox-hunting, and it is as right for me to say, as it will be gratifying to the recipient to know, that the compliment originated among the large class of Farmers whom he has done so much to make his friends," &c. The picture, which had been veiled during dinner, was exposed at the appropriate moment during the Chairman's speech, and was received with loud and vehement cheering.

In a speech thoroughly characteristic of the speaker—manly—straightforward—and fairly free from the conventional platitudes, Mr. Thomson gave utterance to his gratitude for the high compliment that had just been conferred upon him—referred to the requisition that he had received requesting him to reconsider his determination—and expressed his deep regret that circumstances prevented him from complying with the flattering request. He also spoke of the many happy days he had spent with his Pytchley friends, and sat down amid tumultuous cheering.

In proposing the House of Lords, Mr. Young of Orlingbury pronounced Captain Thomson to be "one of the finest sportsmen—one of the most gallant horsemen—one of the most kind, urbane and courteous gentlemen that ever galloped over the grass fields of Northamptonshire." Tom Firr, late second Whip to the "P.H.," and at this time Huntsman to the North Warwickshire, sang an excellent song of his own composing, a poem upon Captain Thomson and Iris, to the tune of the "Fine old English Gentleman," which proved one of the features of the evening.

In response to the "Members for the County," Mr. George Ward Hunt, M.P., and Chancellor of the Exchequer—a keen lover of fox-hunting, but from a superabundant vitality requiring a dray-horse to carry him—made a very entertaining speech. "When I came here, to-night," he said, "I did not feel as if I were coming in my capacity as a member for the county, but as an admirer of the science of which our guest is so great a master. I was anxious to pay a tribute of respect to him for the sport he has given myself and my neighbours for the last five years. I have not, I regret to say, been able to appear personally in the hunting-field of late; that, however, is my misfortune rather than my fault, as it has been the pleasure of some part of this company to send me to a distant country, where I have been hunting with a very different pack from that of the Pytchley; and one which, to my feelings, is not nearly so pleasant a one. It is a stiff country though, and I have seen some very ugly falls in it. (*Laughter.*) It has some attractions, however, which no other pack can boast of. It never fails to meet, be the weather what it may, and there are never any blank days. (*Laughter.*) Like you, we too have lately had a change of Mastership; and we not only had a new Master, but an entirely new pack of hounds. (*Much laughter.*) You know that it is a very different thing taking up an old pack and getting a lot of old scratch-dogs together; and last season we had the pleasure of seeing at our first Meet a pack consisting of hounds of all sizes, and of all sorts of colours. (*Great laughter.*) In fact I heard some ill-natured people remark that a good many of the pack were pretty well used to the ratting-business; which didn't sound nice, at all events. (*Laughter.*) I, unfortunately, have got to such a weight [*the Right Hon. Gentleman rode about twenty-three stone*], that I ride to hunt, not hunt to ride; and I must say that I prefer the style of hunting in which the hounds and not the Huntsman hunt the fox. At the first Meet the other day of the St. Stephen's pack, I saw some new hounds, more extraordinary than any which appeared last season. They were importations from the Tipperary kennel (*great laughter*), which I don't think any Master of Hounds would like to see hunting;

but I hope that some of them will be drafted after a bit. I used to say that there was no ill of mind or body that a good gallop across country could not cure; but that was when I could get something to carry me. With the pack with which I shall have to hunt for the rest of the season, the hunting is of a kind that is apt to produce many ills both to body and mind; but I shall have pleasure in thinking that in pursuing the arduous labours of the hunting at St. Stephen's, I shall have the sympathy and good wishes of the Members of the Pytchley Hunt." (*Loud cheers.*)

Mr. H. O. Nethercote gave the health of the Chairman; and after speeches from Major Whyte Melville, Sir Charles Isham, the Hon. H. Liddell and others, a memorable evening came to a happy conclusion.

Thus was snapped, after five years of satisfactory wear, the last link that had united the Pytchley Hunt with the "long Scotch Gentleman," whom the Warwickshire yokel advised should be sent for again, when on one occasion a fox could not be persuaded to leave one of the Atherstone covers.

A writer in *Society* says, "No man ever crossed the formidably-fenced Pytchley pastures with more determination than Captain Thomson; and though hardly pretending, like Assheton Smith, always to be in the same field with the hounds, he rarely allowed them to get far away from him."

Aided rather than stopped by weight, he would make his horses crash through thick fences, and high timber that others could not get over, and he was therefore a very good man to follow, until a brook barred the way. Into that he would plunge boldly, trusting to chance for getting out on the far side ; so that those who had constitutional objections to a bath *al fresco*, seldom cared to accept his lead when they saw the gleam of water ahead. His wonderfully quick eye for a country, and his constant habit of taking advantage of every good bit of ground, enabled him to save his horse in a way that men of less bulk seldom think of. When there is time to draw rein he never remains a moment in the saddle. Dismounting quickly, he gives his horse all the relief possible, however brief the breathing-space may be. Few know how much is gained by a simple act of this kind, and very few of those who *do* know ever practise it.

For one winter after leaving Northamptonshire, 1870, Mr. Anstruther Thomson hunted the Atherstone, but the following season he was obliged to pass at Torquay, on account of the illness of his eldest son. In 1872 he again undertook the management of the Fife Hounds, and has continued to hunt them from that time to the present, this being the fortieth year he has occupied the position of a Master of Fox-hounds. Just at the close of Mr. Thomson's career with the Pytchley, an event occurred in the hunting-field of Yorkshire unparalleled in its tragical circumstances, and which cast a gloom throughout the breadth and length of the land.

The York and Ainsty hounds, whilst running between Copgrove and Newby Hall, crossed the River Ure, which was greatly swollen after the recent heavy rains. Several of the field attempted the ford, which was some distance up the stream ; but Sir Charles Slingsby and others made for the ferry, which is just opposite the Hall, and signalled for the boat to be sent across. The river was sweeping along, swollen and angry, with a strong, deep current, and much diverted from its usual channel. The stream was about sixty yards broad at this spot, and the ferry was under the charge of the Newby Hall gardener and his son. Sir Charles Slingsby was the first to enter, and was followed by fourteen or fifteen gentlemen with their horses, there being accommodation for only about half that number. Those in the boat were the Master, Sir C. Slingsby, Sir G. Wombwell, Ovis (the Whip), Captain Vyner, Mr. C. Vyner, Mr. Lloyd, Mr. Robinson, Major Mussenden (8th Hussars), Captain Molyneux, the Hon. H. Molyneux, and some other officers stationed at York. Lord Downe, Lord Lascelles, and others, not being able to find room in the boat, awaited its return on the bank. Ere one-third the distance had been traversed, the Master's horse became restive, and kicked the animal belonging to Sir G. Wombwell. The latter returned it, and a sort of panic set in amongst the horses. The boat swayed from side to side in a most alarming manner, and finally fairly turned bottom upwards. The scene that ensued is reported by a witness to have been heartrending in the extreme. Heads began to appear in different parts of the stream to sink again, and arms and hands were flung up in mute despair. Horses were seen to battle with the current, striking out with all their energy, but, unable to resist the impetuosity of the stream, they were carried away and sank. Lines formed of whips were tied together and thrown within reach of the drowning men, and several beams of wood were launched on the surface of the water. Captain Vyner saved himself by clinging to the upturned boat, and, reaching the top of it, was able to save Sir G. Wombwell, and afterwards one of the

York officers. Mr. White got ashore by means of the ferry-chain, and others were rescued from the banks. When all was over, and the roll was called, six were wanting; namely, Sir Charles Slingsby, Bart., of Scriven Park; Mr. E. Lloyd, of Lingcroft, near York; Mr. E. Robinson; William Ovis (first Whip); and the two gardeners at Newby Hall, the ferrymen. Such were some of the incidents of a catastrophe, the memory of which still hangs like a heavy cloud over the entire district in which the terrible tragedy was enacted.

Among the countless canine incidents which have crossed the path of Mr. Anstruther Thomson, not the least amusing must have been one which occurred in company with the present writer. Driving together near Buxton, they were encountered by the length and breadth of so unsavoury an odour as only to be attributed to horse-flesh slightly tainted. "Hounds, by Jove," exclaimed the ex-M.F.H. "Let us get out and have a look." No sooner said than done. Crossing an orchard, among the boughs of which were hung the joints which had so robbed the circumambient air of its natural sweetness, a kennel was soon espied.

Addressing a light, neat-looking man who was digging in his garden close to the kennel, he was asked whether we could be permitted to see the hounds? "Certainly, gentlemen," was the reply in rich Irish brogue. "I'm the Huntsman, and will show you them with pleasure." Laying down his spade and putting on his coat, he opened the kennel-door, and let out about as miscellaneous a looking lot of dwarf foxhounds as might be found in a long day's march. "You will be pleased to know," said I, "that you are showing your pack to the best judge of hounds in England—a gentleman of whom you have probably often heard—Colonel Anstruther Thomson."

"Oh, indeed have I," was the answer, "Colonel *Atherstone* Thomson! Why, of course I have, and being it's he, I don't mind telling him that he is now looking at the worst pack of hounds in England! They're called the Lyme harriers, and there's scarce a decent hound in the lot. When I take them out of a morning, they'll suddenly start off in full cry, and run for three or four miles after nothing at all."

Greatly amused at this candid confession of the shortcomings of his pack, one of the better-looking members was pointed out, and he was subjected to the question, "That's a good hound to judge by appearances. What about him, eh?"

"Well, gentlemen, I'll just tell you. He'll go ten times round the same field doing nothing; and then he'll stop and scratch, and the worst of it is, that some of the gentlemen who belong to the Hunt, though they're devils to ride, call it beautiful questing!"

"But why don't you get another situation?"

"Indeed, and I must, gentlemen, for I cannot stand it any longer; but a place is hard to find nowadays. I was some years Huntsman to a pack of hounds in County Carlow, but I can't go back there, for Ireland's a lost country. If you can help me in finding a new situation, I shall take it as a kindness." Promising to help if it were possible, we took leave of our ill-suited friend—as clean, nice, and well-mannered a servant as any Master of harriers might wish to have for a Huntsman.

MR. J. A. CRAVEN.

With Dick Roake for his Huntsman, Mr. J. A. Craven assumed the Mastership vacated by Colonel Anstruther Thomson, and straightway buckled into his new position as if he were to the manner born. An excellent judge of a horse, and sparing no expense in getting the right sort of animal, both master and men were mounted in a manner befitting the Hunt over which he presided. That he was himself capable of handling hounds at a pinch no one for a moment suspected, but on the occasion unexpectedly presenting itself, the new Master proved fully equal to it. An accident having incapacitated Roake, Mr. Craven at once assumed the horn, and for some time drove the coach with such success, that on giving the health of "the Master of the Pytchley hounds" on the presentation-night, Captain Thomson said, " Mr. Craven has many of the qualifications necessary for a Master of Hounds; keenness, determination, and a power of enduring fatigue such as he had rarely seen equalled. In punctuality he gave himself and other Masters a lesson they would do well to follow, for he well knew that they had often blessed him for keeping them waiting. Mr. Craven had been obliged to take the horn under very trying circumstances, and had acquitted himself exceedingly well. He had proved himself patient and steady, had shown some good sport, and with experience would undoubtedly take high rank as a huntsman."

Such words from such a judge could not but be pleasant to hear, and were some reward for undertaking an arduous and thankless duty at a critical moment. On the reappearance of Roake, which was not long delayed,

Mr. Craven again fell into the ranks, and in spite of the nine long miles between his own house and Brixworth, never failed in keeping time at the Meets or in attending to his duties at the kennels. After a while the distance from his work, the wear and tear of long rides to cover, and the longer journeys home, proved more than he cared to encounter; and after three years of office he signified his intention of giving up his post. Few persons in the course of three years, by unfailing courtesy to all, and a determination to carry out every arrangement in a spirit of thoroughness and liberality, had more raised himself in the good opinion of all hunting-men, and it was with no little regret that the news of his resignation was received.

LORD SPENCER.

On the Mastership of the Pytchley Hunt again becoming vacant, nothing could be more in accordance with the fitness of things, than that the post should be filled by a member of that noble house which had already occupied it three times, and whose name was sufficient to impart to it an *éclat* scarcely to be expected from any other quarter. "The hour" had arrived, and happily not without "the man." A fourth Lord Spencer was ready and willing to undertake an office which had been held by three of his ancestors, and which seemed as if it ought to constitute a part of the appanage of the Althorp establishment. Universal was the satisfaction caused by the announcement that Lord Spencer was willing to take

up the reins let drop by Mr. Naylor. Not the least among other advantages to be anticipated from his so doing was that it gave rise to a hope of that fixity and permanence which is one of the chief glories of an old-established pack of foxhounds; one which has been so marked a feature in the Badminton, the Grafton, the Berkeley, and the Fitzwilliam Hunts, and which has been so sadly lacking with two crack packs of England, the Pytchley and the Quorn. But as in the case of Man himself, a Hunt "never is but always to be blessed;" and it was decreed that the "P.H." was not to escape the common lot. After the lapse of three short years, Lord Spencer's constitution not fairly settled down in the saddle of endurance, had placed its veto upon further experiments with the physical power, and the edict went forth that there must be a cessation from anxiety and over-exertion, and that rest must be found in a more temperate climate than was to be met with during the trying months of an English winter.

Looking back upon the infantile days of the "P.H." Master of 1868, he who witnessed the blooding of "Master Jack Spencer" by Charles Payne in Harleston Park, little thought that the frightened shrinking child of four years old on the pony so carefully led by a groom, and sedulously watched by a governess, was to develop into the "Red Earl," one of Ireland's greatest Viceroys, and one of England's most determined riders. Six years after this, while standing near Althorp House on a November afternoon, "Master Jack" watched with no little excitement the hounds careering across the Park in the early part of a run memorable for its termination by candle-light. But it was not until he had left Harrow that the spirit of the old ancestral love of hunting began to move within him.

The small pony, the fourteen-hands cob, the dependable full-sized hunter, the three first rungs of the hunting-ladder were all mounted in turn; and then came the reaching of the top round. Every man has his own idiosyncrasies, hidden possibly from himself, but very apparent to those able to see the beams of light as well as the mote in their neighbour's eyes. Should the subject of this memoir not have escaped the fate of every public character—making enemies—his greatest opponent will be loth to deny that Thoroughness, Duty, and Justice, are the three principles by which he is governed in all his actions. To no one living are the words *fiat justitia, ruat cœlum*, more applicable. With him the best day's hunting has ever had to give way to a duty, however unpleasant, and easily to be shirked, and whatever he takes up is carried out with all the completeness that his strong and thoughtful mind enables him to bring to bear upon it.

The first of the above triplet of virtues was exemplified on each of the occasions upon which he became a "Master of Hounds," by the thoroughness with which he at once commenced various reforms in kennel and stables, not the least being the improvement of the hounds in every respect, and by the introduction of new blood. The importation of the Duhallow pack from Lord Doneraile's country, in 1874, did not prove altogether satisfactory; but on assuming the Mastership in that year, the hounds belonging to the "P.H." had reached so low an ebb, that fresh blood from any quarter was an object of the greatest importance. In the same spirit, the noble Master, to the injury of his health, spent many a laborious hour in the woodlands with the young hounds, returning to Althorp in the late evening, fairly exhausted with the day's work. A constitution not over strong for some time resisted the demands upon its powers, but the machinery gave way at last, and a warmer climate was called upon to undertake the repairs which could not have been looked for from an English winter. As in other things, the characteristic of "thoroughness" in Lord Spencer comes out strongly in the determination with which, from the very first day he commenced his hunting career, he has been accustomed to forge his way across a country. It is probable that except after a fall, nobody has ever seen him in the ruck when hounds are running, with or without a scent: his *sine quâ non* in hunting being, apparently, to keep at all times as close to the Huntsman as pace and propriety will permit.

The style in which the one object is carried out does not appear to be a matter for any consideration. The "big pill" in the shape of a hedge, with ditch on either side, which would be swallowed by a Foster or a Middleton at one gulp, the noble Lord is usually seen with the aid of spurs, heels, whip and words, to "do" at intervals. Nothing, however, is refused as being over-nasty; and be the obstacle what it may, the other side, sooner or later, is sure to be reached. The desire to ensure sport, and be thorough in doing this, carried the noble Lord at times too far—as he himself now admits—and he interfered with the movements of the Field more than they always liked. No regiment of dragoons was kept under stricter discipline than a Pytchley field at the time of which we are speaking. Woe betide the adventurous wight who risked a short cut to the next "draw," or in any way seemed out of the place which in the eyes of the Master was his proper one. Even the homeward-bound horseman, far on his road, met with a bad time if the fox, chancing to cross his path, altered his course, and caused a momentary check. Turning round upon one occasion in a Holdenby pasture to rebuke some horsemen, who, as he thought, were following too closely upon the hounds, the Master found himself reproaching a small band of shorthorn brothers, who, with whisk of tail and downward motion of the head, seemed to treat with defiance the half-uttered remark of the noble, but incensed huntsman.

An experience of fifty years with Masters of all sorts and conditions of temper, has taught the writer of these pages that nothing is more conducive to sport as well as to enjoyment in hunting than a thorough sympathy between a Master of Foxhounds and his Field. When in fault, the true sportsman, conscious of it, meekly accepts the mouthful of winged words—ἐπέων πτεροέντων —in a different sense from that used by Horne Tooke, from the privileged quarter; but the sneer and the scornful expression, when there is little occasion for them, rankle in the memory, and sow the seeds of a future collision.

Lord Spencer, in his eagerness to omit nothing to secure sport, may occasionally have said what some may have thought too much, but he studiously avoided the use of bad language, and would have felt the greatest regret if his words were unjustly applied, or if they rankled in any one's mind.

So much for the seamy side of the spirit of "thoroughness" which leaves no stone unturned to produce a desired result. It will not be denied by any one conversant with the habits and practice of Lord Spencer here being referred to, that "duty," the second on the list of attributes most justly apportioned to him in the commencing lines of this memoir, has ever been the guiding star of his life, and of his actions. To no one has it come more home that property has its duties as well as its privileges and it is asserted without fear of contradiction that no public man, statesman or otherwise, has more consistently acted upon this principle. Many a day's hunting has been sacrificed to the performance of some insignificant magisterial duty: many a horse posted in some likely spot, on the chance, after work was over, of coming in for the residuum of a run. But the spirits of "thoroughness" and "duty," conspicuous as they be as motive principles in the character of one of Ireland's most famous Lord-Lieutenants, scarcely hold their own with the third-named influence, "justice." Whether it be in governing a people, or in weighing the conduct, or deciding upon the treatment of an individual, the one and only goal arrived at by the representative of the great house of Spencer is "Justice." With that for a weapon, he believes that all the rugged places will be made smooth, and all difficulties overcome.

The following letter, written in the winter of December, 1869, is peculiarly interesting at the present time—the summer of 1886: "We are comparatively quiet just now. Irish affairs are undergoing a crisis, as must always be the case where great changes are taking place. They who are benefited are too accustomed to their old grievances to become champions of order, and the agitators do not distinguish between real and fictitious evils. I am satisfied, however, that patience and perseverance in doing justice and acting with impartiality will eventually bear their fruit. Those who have to deal with all this have their equanimity sorely tried, and must wear a thick skin." The writer then goes on to say: " I have had some gallops with the Ward Stag-hounds to keep me going. A sharp ride to covert and a good thirty minutes have saved me from collapsing. There is nothing like a good gallop across country, even to stag-hounds, to drive dull care away. Three hours' forgetfulness of a worry gives one a new start. We had a very good run two days ago, fifteen miles from start to take. I had the satisfaction of being in first; only five others up at all."

Here we see what hunting can effect for the care-worn and thoughtful statesman, and may learn to pity the Viceroy, to whom the pleasure and excitement of a gallop after hounds are unknown.

On a later occasion the Lord-Lieutenant was quite alone when the stag was captured after a good run. The Dublin journals loudly proclaim the feat of one man, and that man no other than the Viceroy himself, beating the whole Field, and that Field a " Ward Union " one. The news of this performance having elicited some inquiries from a Pytchley friend, Lord Spencer replied as follows: " My stag-hunting adventure was very funny. After carrying me well up to the hounds for about twelve minutes or so, my horse fell into a blind ditch attached to a fence, which would have staggered any field unaccustomed to Irish 'obstacles.' I lost a little time in getting my horse out, also my place among the first few. When I got up to the road where I lost sight of the leading men, I fell in with the Huntsman heading the second flight. He made me gallop a particular way, but finding that that was wrong, he turned back, knowing that it would be of no use. I persevered and made a dash down some lanes as a speculation. After going about twenty minutes I saw what is called 'the hunt,' and expected to catch it over a hill just in front of me. To my surprise, up came the stag right to me, and presently three couple of hounds, and then five couple more, but no one in sight. Of course I followed this lot, and had about three miles of splendid country all to myself. When the stag was taken not a soul was to be seen, nor did a horseman appear in sight until I had got to a road five fields off with the hounds, not one of whom knew me. Some labourers drove them to me; but when they disappeared, as they soon did, off went my reluctant followers. In about twenty minutes a stray man appeared, and ten minutes later the Whip, but not a soul beside. It was no great feat, but it was very amusing." Mr. Green, in page 78 of his very interesting volume, after describing an attack of a kestrel on a rook, goes on to say : "Another curious thing which I saw during my visit to Ireland, was a stag, hounds, and horses all run to a stand-still, or at least to such a state of exhaustion that none of them could move so fast as I could walk. I was sitting by myself one afternoon, when I heard the cry of hounds as if crossing the park. I ran out, came up with them, and had no difficulty in keeping up with them. Only five or six horsemen were near, and their animals looked as if they had not a leg to stand upon, and could scarcely raise a walk. We all went down to the river, and from one of its pools out jumped the stag, all amongst the hounds. He just managed to hobble along for a few yards up the slope of the green meadow with the dogs lopping along heavily beside him, and just behind, when he came to a few very low hurdles. He could only just get his fore-legs over them and then fell right among the leading hounds. He kicked out right and left with his hind-legs, scattered his pursuers, turned down again toward the river, tumbled over the hurdles once more, shook himself free from his enemies, and again sought the water. The hounds were now whipped off, and some rustics plunging into the water, the leg-weary animal was secured. Though quite unable to run, it was surprising to see the courage and strength he still retained. He fought and struggled with head and neck, and it required the efforts of some strong men to make him go in the direction they required. I was afterwards shown a place in the park where he had fallen through being unable to jump a ditch not above two or three feet wide, with a fence about a foot high. I never ascertained for certain what the length of the run had been, but though I had often been out hunting and greatly enjoyed it, it was very painful to me on that occasion to see all the animals so thoroughly exhausted. I suppose the hounds were the 'Ward Union' pack, and I was informed that the stag bore the euphonious name of the 'Devil.' This scene took place in the neighbourhood of Mullahuddart Bridge."

That the above narrative is absolutely a truthful one cannot be doubted; but after half a century's experience with foxhounds, the writer has not only never witnessed, but has never heard of a similar incident.

During the period of his first Viceroyalty, Lord Spencer was desirous that Mr. Craven, Master of the "P.H." at that time, should bring the Pytchley pack to Dublin for a few days' hunting in the Meath country. All was arranged for this sporting event to come off, but an accident to Dick Roake, the "P.H." huntsman, necessitated the giving up of the project. Determined, however, to introduce a hunting-element other than that by which he was surrounded, the Lord-Lieutenant invited six of his tenants from Northamptonshire and other counties to be his guests for a week's hunting, he undertaking to mount each of them twice, and to pay all expenses.

The following six gentlemen, tenant-farmers all, responded to the invitation, and passed such a time as has rarely fallen to the lot of the unfortunate agriculturist. Treated with a hospitality and a consideration which far exceeded all their preconceived ideas of what was likely to happen, it seemed as though Paradise had opened its portals to do them honour. From Northamptonshire came Messrs. Henry Sandars of Brampton, George Gee of Welford Lodge, W. Wykes, and F. Elliott of Brington. Hertfordshire sent Mr. L. Cox; Warwickshire, Mr. F. Fabling; and from out of Norfolk appeared that consummate horseman, Mr. Everett. Mounted on the picks of the basket in the Viceregal stable, each and all did credit to the different localities from which they came, and somewhat surprised the "bruisers" of Meath by the facility with which they found their way across an unaccustomed and difficult country. Messrs. Sandars and Cox alone came to grief, and all went merry as a marriage-bell from morn to night. Happy the tenant to have such a landlord; fortunate the country to have such a Viceroy!

Though something of a cricketer, and fond of shooting, it is horse and hound which really occupy the warm corners in the affections of the Pytchley Master of 1861 and 1874; and in no heart does the love of hunting burn more strongly. Be he where he may, abroad, in Ireland, or elsewhere, the thought of what he may be missing with the Pytchley is constantly present with him during the winter months. Making a personal friend of the horses who carry him well, to part with a favourite for any cause is a bereavement of no ordinary character. In a letter to a friend, bearing date February, 1858, he says: "I was out riding on Friday, and knew by old Sir George's excitement that hounds were near. I am glad to hear of the death of one of the many Nobottle foxes. The one you tell me of came, I presume, from Dodford Holt; if so, that is not a bad line if you keep the Weeden and Brington road sufficiently to the left, and so cross those fine grass meadows. I should indeed have enjoyed the Saturday gallop you speak of, with Wizard or Meteor in their old form.[1] I hope that the time may come when I shall drop in for a few such runs. I can count on my fingers every good day I have had with the Pytchley so far; so much have I been prevented by one cause or another from hunting regularly. I had a very sad parting with my dear old horses on Thursday last. I made up my mind to clear my stables, which were filled with a multitude of animals: many useless to me, and several nearly worn out. Reserving the two old favourites and my sister's horse, I sent eighteen to Tattersall's. I had no idea until the time arrived, how attached one can become to horses. I confess that I shed tears over Wizard and

[1] Both these horses returned to Althorp, and died there at a ripe old age.

one or two others that neighed whenever they heard my footsteps, and whose every movement I knew exactly. Poor things! I long to hear that they have fallen into good hands."

Three years after penning this epistle, the writer taking up the reins lately held by Messrs. Villiers and Cust, was Master of the Pytchley hounds, being, as has been stated elsewhere, the fourth member of his family who had filled that post. Though young and inexperienced, that aptitude for becoming master of any position taken up, which falls to the lot of a fortunate few, served him in good stead; and it quickly seemed as though he were "to the manner born." Few better proofs of the advantage of not feeling "squandered at a crucial moment," or in other words of being "master of the position," can be found than in the case of the Rev. Dr. Mountain, who, when consulted by Charles II. as to whom he should appoint to a vacant bishopric, replied: "If your Majesty had faith as a grain of mustard-seed, you would say to this Mountain, 'Be thou moved into that See.'" Filled with the aptness of this response, the king took the hint, and the Mountain forthwith was moved into the coveted position. That artists as well as clergy are occasionally, at all events, equal to the occasion, may be inferred from the following anecdote of Sir Francis Chantrey, the great sculptor. Whilst engaged on a bust of Lord Melbourne —eminent for his learning as well as for his statesmanship—the artist found himself getting somewhat out of his depth in discussing a scientific subject. Not willing to expose his lack of knowledge, he at once became master of the position by requesting his lordship, "to turn his head a little to the right, and *keep his mouth closed!*"

The then beardless face of the new chief betokened an

easy-going time for evil-doers with hounds as well as for "dodgers" and "short-cutters;" but all such rapidly discovered that they had reckoned without their host, or rather without their Master. Captain Bruiser was speedily admonished to modulate his bruising, and the sly shirker was warned of the possible consequences of his shirkiness. Whilst drawing a cover, the whole field was directed to be gathered together in one place, and few who hunted in those now distant days will forget the grip in the field under Yelvertoft Field-side, beyond which—no, not for the matter of an inch—was any horseman allowed to pass until the fox was away. Excellent in theory and full of promise was this edict of the grip, but it ever seemed to fail in its performance. A mistaken "view-holloa" or a false line out of cover at once scattered the impatient host of horsemen, and it was then useless to try and reform the line and bring it under subjection.

Having the great advantage of commencing his career as M.F.H. under the tuition of Charles Payn—the most pleasant and keenest of Huntsmen—Lord Spencer quickly mastered the details of kennel-management, and so prepared himself for his second term of office, when he found much that required undoing, and still more that wanted doing in the "P.H." surroundings. It was during the period of his first Mastership—in 1863—that Lord Spencer was honoured with a visit from his Royal Highness the Prince of Wales, who was pleased to seize an opportunity of proving that England's future King could hold his own after hounds over the big fences of the Pytchley country. That he was able to do so was shown in an afternoon gallop from Vanderplanks to

Purser's Hills, when, in spite of a pace that was not well adapted to a welter weight, H.R.H. occupied an excellent place until choked off by the hill leading from Blueberries up to Mr. Pell's house at Hazelbeach Hill, when he was fain to dismount, and like any ordinary mortal led his horse to the summit of the ascent. The hounds at this point being out of sight, H.R.H. seemed to think that next to being present at the kill, a "drop o' good beer" was the most desirable object at that moment, so pulling up at Mr. Pell's house, he quickly slaked a "hill-born" thirst in a flagon of Burton ale. A cigar about the size of a sausage-roll was quickly transferred to his lips, and the late formidable ascent soon formed the downward path on his road back to Althorp.

Few there present will forget the scene that offered itself when the Meet on the occasion of his Royal Highness's appearance for the first time with the Pytchley hounds was held at Holdenby House. The *cortège* of ladies and horsemen, headed by the Prince with Lady Spencer, was seen to issue from the lodge-gates at Althorp, and cross the pastures leading to this, one of the most interesting spots in English history. It seemed as though thousands had assembled to welcome the heir to the throne, the descendant of that king who had laid down his life on the scaffold, a victim to the unbridled hatred of his enemies.

On the following day, his Royal Highness being mounted on a clever dun-coloured horse—somewhat slow—from the Althorp stables, "Pale Ale" by name, a fox from Sandars Cover crossed the Spratton Brook, not far from "Merry Tom." Riding at the water "like a man," the Prince met with the sad experience that royalty does not always have it all its own way, and that when the ways of a horse and those of the first gentleman in the kingdom come into collision, it is not the former that usually has to give in. " Pale Ale" declined the brook, whip and spur notwithstanding, and the passage across the stream was finally effected by means of a friendly ford.

After the completion of a decade and a half from this time—namely in January, 1878,—another Royalty, different alike in sex, rank, and nationality, honoured the Pytchley Hunt during Lord Spencer's second Mastership.

Occupying the very highest rung on the social ladder, her lofty position did not prevent the Empress of Austria from freely indulging in her ruling passion, horses and hunting. At home, hours were spent in the riding-school, where she acquired a perfection of seat and hands, and a mastery over her animal which served her in good stead when a big fence intervened between herself and the hounds she was following. Attended by a suite bearing names illustrious in Austrian history, her Majesty took up her quarters in Cottesbrooke Park, where for six weeks she " witched the (Pytchley) world with noble horsemanship." *Sub duce* " Bay Middleton," the task she had set herself of seeing all that there was to be seen, was performed in a fashion that excited the admiration of a critical field, and aroused the envy of many a rival horsewoman. The custom of carrying a *fan* as well as a whip attracted much observation at first, but foreign ways are not always as English ways, and everything is good taste in an Empress. Courteous and affable, her Majesty was pleased to have any Members of the Hunt presented to her, and would converse freely on all topics connected with hunting. Selected for their powers rather than for their appearance, her horses all wore the hunting rather than the parky cut, and few of them looked worth the money that had been given for them. No sooner was it known that a horse was being looked at for the Empress, than up went its price, fifty per cent. if not more.

Not naturally of a robust constitution, her Majesty hoped to find in good English malt and hops an antidote to a feeling of exhaustion which at times sorely beset her. Calling at the house of the writer one evening on her way home from hunting, she smilingly rejected the proferred tea, saying, "Please let me have some beer, it will do me so much more good." It is to be hoped that the anticipated benefit followed upon the modicum of John Barleycorn absorbed on that occasion by her Imperial Majesty.

Few events in the annals of the "P.H." will stand out for all time to come in higher relief than the Empress's steeple-chase at Hopping Hill, which was got up by her own desire, and carried out entirely at her own expense, as a memento of her sojourn at Cottesbrooke.

This memorable event took place on the day of her Majesty's final departure from the neighbourhood, when she entertained at luncheon in a marquee erected on the crest of the hill a large number of royal and noble guests. Amongst the company there assembled were to be seen H.R.H. the Princess of Wales, H.R.H. the Duchess of Teck, the Duchess of Manchester, the Countess Spencer, the Countess M. Festetics, the Prince Imperial of Austria, Prince Lichtenstein, Earl Spencer, and many another bearing a name of European celebrity. Seated in her carriage, with the Princess of Wales on her left, and Lady Spencer opposite, she closely watched the competition for the prizes she had offered, and in one race, at least, had the satisfaction of seeing her pilot, Captain Middleton, arrive an easy winner. Before quitting for the railway station, she begged Lord Spencer to bring to the carriage any Member of the Hunt he could find, so that she might personally take leave of him—an act of royal courtesy and condescension that will not easily be forgotten by the recipients of the honour. The cheers that greeted her Majesty on leaving the field were loud and long, and seemed to afford her much gratification; and thus ended a memorable incident in the history of the Pytchley Hunt.

After an accident which occurred to Goodall early in 1877, Lord Spencer hunted the hounds himself, and continued to do so twice a week in the open; and was doing this during the Empress's visit. On many an occasion he had shown his aptitude for the difficult post, but on the day succeeding that of her Majesty's departure he hunted a fox from Naseby cover to Wilby, near Wellingborough, in a manner that would have done credit to "Gentleman" Smith himself. The distance from point to point cannot be less than fifteen miles; and the scent at no time being anything more than a "holding one," but for the exercise of great patience and perseverance, the run might have collapsed at any moment.

At another time, with a very catchy scent, Lord Spencer hunted a fox from Rockingham across the railway, twice, killing him in the open near Uppingham. On each of the occasions above referred to, his Lordship exhibited the true instincts of a huntsman, patience and self-possession, proving thereby that in the difficult art of hunting a fox, the amateur is not a whit behind the professional.

The dislike to the gentleman-Huntsman that prevailed so strongly for a while, seems to have yielded to the feeling that in the matter of handling hounds in the field he is little, if at all, inferior to the "regular dustman."

The main advantage that the Professional has over the Amateur, living as he often does away from the kennels, is his constant presence among the hounds. No skill will compensate for that lack of sympathy between a pack of hounds and their huntsman, which is the inevitable consequence of leaving them over-much to the care and society of some other person. An hour or so spent occasionally in the kennel will scarcely be sufficient to generate that passionate attachment which leads the hound to rejoice in his Master's scent and presence, and causes him to come at once to the sound of his voice or the blast of his horn. A fox is already half killed when his pursuers come quickly out of cover, and this is rarely the case unless the scent be good, and they be pretty close upon his back. The cracking thong and the "ger away to him" of the angry Whip, will have little effect if the scent be bad, and he who is "blowing away" outside the cover has failed to endear himself to his hounds by being constantly with and amongst them. On the other hand, a few words in the customary "*lingua canina*" from their own familiar friend, will cause every rightly-thinking hound to hurry to the well-known voice. In drawing a comparison between the amateur and the professional Huntsman, it would seem that if the former be willing to make a slave of himself and undertake the carrying out his duties in a similar manner to the latter, there is little to choose between them in the matter of proficiency in the field. That a Huntsman should always be with his hounds seems an indisputable axiom. It has been said that "mediocrity at the tail of the pack is infinitely to be preferred to the embodiment of science half a mile behind." To the Professional, want of nerve, save under peculiar circumstances, means loss of situation. To the Amateur much is forgiven in this respect if he be popular, and especially if he pays the piper. How Squire Lowndes and the late Lord Southampton, neither of whom ever "jumped," met with even the modicum of success they could fairly lay claim to as huntsmen, was a thing which "no feller could understand." Few who have ever carried the horn could compete with either of these well-known sportsmen in the art of "half-a-mile-behinding;" yet many a better man has been unable to show an equally favourable record of foxes killed.

The cuckoo-cry is often raised that "any fool can kill a fox with a scent;" the answer to which is "let the fool try." That he will not perform this much-desired feat without one is certain, but few take into consideration the "*aliquid amari*," "the always a something," that is pretty sure to turn up when least expected.

The old Scotch lady did not speak without an experience in disappointment, when in reply to a query from a friend, as to whether she might congratulate her on her daughter's approaching marriage, she said, " Oh, yes, I have nothing to say against it. It's true that Janie hates the man, but then there's always a something." So in hunting a fox, be the scent ever so good—the kill apparently ever so certain—the unexpected suddenly turns up in the form of a storm—a flock of sheep—a change in the atmosphere—a shepherd dog—or an unknown drain. In short "there's always a something;" and nowhere more than in the pursuit of the "wily animal."

It is a singular but indisputable fact, that however good a man may be as first or second Whip, he is by no means sure to succeed in the more important position of Huntsman.

Tom Rance, formerly with the Cheshire Hounds, feeling that he was in his right place as first Whip, always refused promotion; and the well-known Will Derry, huntsman to Lord Chesterfield, was little else than a brilliant failure.

Jack Stevens may be placed on the same list, as also many another, who so far as their reputation went would have been wise to have followed Tom Rance's example, and have remained content with the subordinate position. To him, skilled as he was in whipping in to hounds, the profession of stone-breaking would have been preferable to that of Huntsman, and this because he was conscious of lacking the necessary qualifications for the office.

Of all the pastimes common to Englishmen, to redress the balance of its manifold pleasures, there is none so fraught with disappointments as "the Chase." Be it stag, fox, or hare, everything hinges upon scent, and the number of really good scenting-days in a season may usually be reckoned on the fingers of either hand. In an able article on "Things pertaining to Sport" which appeared in a *Field* of January, 1886, it is maintained that a long course of weather, uniform in temperature, mild and equable, is favourable to sport. A fifty years' experience has taught the writer that in the Pytchley country, at all events, the truth is to be found in the converse of this proposition. There, a uniformly dry or mild winter is never productive of sport, and the cry of the Huntsman invariably is, "We mustn't look for any good scents until we have a change of weather."

In a letter from Lord Spencer, written long, long ago, and from a far distant spot, he says: "You must not expect many runs until you exchange your mild weather for some frost and snow to sweeten the ground;" and this used to be stoutly maintained by Charles Payne, as it still is by Will Goodall.

That "scent transcendeth all Huntsmen," and is as true now as it was when uttered by Edmund de Langley, one of the sons of Edward III., there is no disputing. But what is that "mystery of mysteries" which we call by the name of scent? Who can unravel the impalpable puzzle? Who interpret the riddle that has baffled generation after generation? "The world is growing old!" Those who know, or say they do, declare that it has long passed its six thousandth birthday, and yet neither physicists nor men of science have been able to tell whence it cometh or whither it goeth; or where or when it may be looked for. Things alike in their nature produce and destroy it—things totally dissimilar work with the same result.

One sporting rhymster tells us of a great run that came off when "the wind was north-east, forbiddingly-keen," whilst another bids us be of good cheer with a "Southerly wind and a cloudy sky, which proclaims a hunting morning." Some sporting pundits affirm that the rolling hound and the drop-laden hedge are each ominous of evil, and as regards the latter, all Huntsmen seem of one mind. No sooner, however, has the glistening liquid-atom been dissolved into thin air, than "Hope begins to tell its flattering tale," and a run is pronounced to be imminent by the sanguine believer in atmospheric effects. In hunting, however, nothing is sure, nothing is certain. Experience shows that over ground ever so parched or ever so sodden with wet, hounds will sometimes fly; others be scarcely able to own the line. Happily, however, for the sportsman, it may be said that the motto, *Nulla dies sine linea*—there is "no day without a line"—is strictly applicable to hunting, since no condition of soil or atmosphere can render scent absolutely non-existent. For lack of it the pace may be exasperatingly slow; but many a stout fox has been "walked" to death, and many a mile of grass, with fences to match, been crossed during the operation. As "half a loaf is better than no bread," so is a pottering run better than no sport. The evening before a frost is looked upon by many as a sure harbinger of good things to come; but it too often fails in performance to render the promise much to be depended upon. The same may be said of falling snow—a time of much hope with certain observers, and likewise of much disappointment. What is sauce on one day for the hunter, is poison on another; and the explanation thereof baffles the experienced sportsman, who learns to attach little credit to all outward and visible signs, be they of weather or aught else. Does the mystery lie in the wind, the state of the atmosphere, the nature of the soil, the hound, or in the fox himself? We know that scent consists of particles of extreme fineness, which when given off float lightly in the air for a time, and then vanish; whilst some coming in contact with the ground are united with the exhala-

P

tions left by the foot of the hunted animal, and exist for a longer period. These odorous particles are subject to the condition of the air, and ascend or descend according as it is light or heavy, dry or moist. When arrested a few inches above the soil, the scent is neither out of the reach of the hound, nor has he to stoop for it, whereby he "feels" it at the point most favourable to himself, and which is commonly known as "breast-high."

Scent also varies by difference of motion. The faster the animal goes the less of it he leaves behind; and if pursued by a dog not belonging to the pack, the chances are that every particle of it will have disappeared. Fogs are sometimes favourable for a run, whilst at others they seem to annihilate scent altogether. In like manner white frosts, influenced by some mysterious atmospheric law, on one day improve sport, on the next render it hopeless. A bright sun is usually fatal, but a warm morning without it is often productive of a red-letter day. It is said that scent lies best on the richest soils, and that good pastures are more retentive of effluvia than cold ones. On the other hand, the undrained lands of former days are said to have been in favour of sport; the lack of it, at the present time, being frequently attributed to the improvements in the science of farming. Be this as it may, it is certain that in some particular spots in every country, hounds cannot push a fox, even though the atmospheric conditions are all that can be desired.

In the Pytchley country, Harleston Heath may be said to be one of these ill-favoured spots. Be it the peaty soil or the withered "pins" of "Pinus" and of

"Picea," it is certain that a fox is "bad" to catch within the circuit of this well-known cover. As if aware of his comparative safety, Reynard is ever loth to quit this haven of security, and if he does so, is only too ready to return. He seems to think that a journey to the pheasantry or to Dallington village and back is as much as can be reasonably expected of him; and he moreover has become painfully aware that "to be or not to be" hinges upon his regaining the heath he left so imprudently. He well knows that there are others of the same complexion with himself, who should take their share of the danger impending over him, and he is also well aware that there is that within his ancient haunts which baffles his pursuers and impedes their course. But if on some March morning a stranger from a distant cover be disturbed in his love-making, and incontinently makes tracks for his far-off home, a gallop may be looked for with some degree of confidence. With one circuit round the bowers of bliss, he bids farewell to the abode of his lady-love and is off, maybe for Cottesbrooke, or for Sywell Wood. Better for him had he never forsaken the spot, where his footfall left little or no sign. With Brampton village well behind him, he stops for a moment to look and listen, and to catch his breath. He sees nothing but the flock of sheep, through which he had purposely passed, clustering under a hedge, and some white-faced bullocks excitedly cantering off in the same direction. All is silent for a brief while, and he begins to think that the danger is over. Suddenly the well-known sound of the horn again fills the air, and his heart seems to thump against his sides. He feels that at no great distance off his pursuers are thirsting for his blood, and that he must hurry on or leave his brush behind. Sandars Gorse—his usual "house of call"—is safely reached; but it is too hot to hold him; so skirting a familiar corner, he sinks the hill and pushes on, still hopeful of eluding his enemies. But the chorus of voices ceases not, and knowing that the soft grass, so pleasant to his feet, is adding to his peril, he turns upward to the ploughs, hoping thus to baffle his pursuers. Alas, for him! no rain has fallen to make the brown earth "carry," and plough and grass seem to have conspired together to take away his life. All too late he changes his intention, and makes for Boughton Clumps, but the earths are closed, and there is nothing for it but on, on, on, for Sywell Wood. A minute's rest in Moulton bushes gives him strength and hope, but the fatal clamour reaches his ear as he crouches in some dampish sedge, and he feels that the end is near. One more effort, but in vain. Another plough is crossed, but there is no escape. A single hound, "Changeling," child of "Changeful," coming out from among the pack, rolls him on the ground, and in another moment, the muffled growl is heard which speaks the knell of poor Reynard. Ill-luck has dogged his footsteps all the way, and he has fallen a victim to the impalpable essence called scent, which for once and away has remained constant over grass and plough without variableness or shadow of changing. On the morrow, over the same ground, with the wind in the same quarter, and the atmospheric conditions apparently in no way different, he might have left his pursuers far behind, and so deferred the fatal scrunch to a future day.

Such is scent! We all fancy that we know something about it and can give a pretty good guess as to what is, and what is not, a hunting morning; and so deceive ourselves. Captain Bruiser arrives at the Meet rejoicing in the southerly wind and the cloudy sky, or maybe in the clear but sunless surroundings of a December day. He at once jumps to the conclusion that a clinking scent is sure and certain; and he hails the presiding deity in cap and boots with "Morning, Will, sure to be a rattling scent to-day;" but the too sanguine Captain has missed the cobwebs in the hedge, and has looked upon the rolling of the hounds as possibly a happy thought for passing the time. Not so the Huntsman; nothing has escaped his vigilant eye, and he cautiously replies, "I hope so, sir, but I don't like saying much beforehand about good scents or bad scents: the more I see of hunting the less I know, it seems to me, about that article." Sensible huntsman! He has learnt the virtue of the Yankee advice, "Never prophesy unless yer know." A glance having passed between the Master and Huntsman, away trot the hounds, headed by the first Whip, rejoicing in the knowledge that their fun is soon to begin. In less than eighteen minutes every bush in the neighbouring gorse seems suddenly alive, and hound leaps over hound, jealous lest his brother of the kennel should be the first to fling his tongue. A ringing "view" proclaims the departure of the fox, and being close upon his back the pack have no difficulty in making him feel that he must put his best foot first. "Just as I thought," says Captain Bruiser to himself; "there's a rattling scent, and no mistake." But the words have scarcely escaped his lips when there is a sudden slackening in the pace, the leading hounds half-stopping throw themselves to right and left, whilst the duffers commence to stare about and look for the Huntsman's help. He casts round the field where the hounds have thrown up; then tries forward with a bold and increasing sweep, and then backward, and at last a well-known roadster "feathers" on the line. The chorus, but in greatly diminished volume, recommences, and hearts once more beat high. But though a mile or two are traversed, the pace never exceeds the conventional "donkey's-gallop;" and it becomes only too clear that the virtue has gone out of the whole thing. But why so? and for what reason was there this unlooked-for disappointment? Because the cobwebs and the rollers at the Meet were right after all, and there was that in the atmosphere—*nescio quid*—which prevented the scent from being at any time really a good one. So long as they were close at him, hounds could almost fly, but no sooner was he chivied by a shepherd's dog, than having shaken off this new enemy, he felt that he had done with the old ones; at least for the time being. Discontentedly riding home after a bad day, our friend "Bruiser" mournfully meditates over the uncertainty of things in general; but more especially of scent. Remembering his prophecy of the morning, he vows that never again will he venture to give an opinion on so ticklish a subject as a scenting day; and for a time keeps his word. But "guesses at truth" do not always tell against the question.

"Too blustering to draw the Gorse to-day," once said Mr. Langham to Will Goodall on one Wednesday morning, as each took shelter from a hurricane of wind under the lee of Crick Church. "Take the hounds home, and we will come to-morrow instead."

"Begging your pardon, sir," said Will, "we shall

disappoint a great many if we don't do something; and we shan't hurt the cover by running the hounds through it." "If we do find, they won't be able to run a yard," said the Master, "but I don't mind having a try, so move on at once." A fox was soon afoot and quickly "away," and such a forty minutes followed as will not soon be forgotten by those who saw it. The more it blew, the more hounds flew, and it seemed as if the scent could be almost cut with a knife. Of course it was "up wind," which points to the fact that foxes, like men, must, as Carlyle cynically declared of his own countrymen, be mostly fools! Tons of ink may be shed, reams of foolscap used in writing disquisitions upon scent; but the outcome of it all will be that "it is a thing that no fellow can understand."

With the single exception of Sir Francis Head, who will be spoken of at length elsewhere, and in whom the love of hunting continued in his eighty-fourth as strong as it was in his eighteenth year, it may be affirmed that no man has ever looked forward to the next day's hunting with greater eagerness than the noble Lord, who possibly will not care to deny that the most halcyon days of a somewhat troublous life have been connected with the chase. A series of beautiful pictures by Charlton serves to illustrate the period when, with his own pack, and Tom Goddard as first Whip, he thought it no drudgery to hunt the Woodland country. In an engraving from one of these, mounted on "Misrule," with Lady Spencer by his side, he is represented as surrounded by the pack just loosed from their Althorp kennels, and is passing the keeper's house on his way to rouse some too inactive cubs, and give his young hounds a lesson. The grey mare he is riding is not without her interest, though only a nominal one, at the particular date (July, 1886) at which these lines are being written. On seeing a friend upon her, soon after his first Viceroyalty, he inquired how she was bred; and on hearing that she was by " Irish Statesman," demanded her name. " Home Rule," was the owner's reply. " Not at all a good one, either," said Ireland's late Lord-Lieutenant: " no Irish Statesman would have anything to do with Home Rule." " I have changed the mare's name, as you didn't like the old one," said Mr. N. a little later on. " And what do you call her now ? " " Misrule " was the answer. " That is a much more appropriate title," was the remark of the ex-Viceroy. And soon after the animal passed into the Althorp stables, where she still is a standing memento how *tempora mutantur, nos et mutamur in illis*.

Most interesting some day will it be to read the letters of one of Ireland's most efficient Lord-Lieutenants, written in one of her most stormy periods. In an epistle bearing date October, 1882, the writer, referring to some gallops he has heard of with his old hounds, says, " Alas! those pleasant times seem past and gone, when a deep ride in Loatland Wood did not repress one's keen anticipation of a burst over those grass-fields alongside the brook. But they are pleasant to think and talk about, and will be so as long as one lives. We hope for a quiet winter, but I have plenty of trouble and worry still. The question among gentlemen now is " Will hunting be possible where it was stopped last winter ? It hangs in the balance, but I fancy that with judicious treatment the chase will win. It goes on capitally in Meath, and with the Ward Union, but I dare not go out, as they might, to spite me, make an effort to stop it."

In the year 1864, Lord Spencer completed his first term of service as Master of the P.H., to be succeeded by Captain Anstruther Thomson, whose reputation as a scientist in hunting-matters was at that time second to none. Compelled by warnings which brooked no delay, he successfully sought in Egypt the health which was denied him at home; the wear and tear connected with hounds having sapped a constitution at no time equal to continuous physical exertion. Always full of hunting thoughts, he thus writes from Suez in the spring of 1864: " Not having for some time received Charles Payne's reports, your hunting-news was most acceptable. The details you give of hunting-incidents and county-life made me somewhat sad and home-sick; but the sadness was only that which we all feel on hearing of things one loves so well, and which one hopes to see and enjoy again." A striking notice of the Suez Canal, at that time in its earliest stage of existence, then follows: " I have just completed one of the most instructive journeys I have ever made, having gone from Suez to Port Said by the far-famed French canal. I am immensely struck by the gigantic scale of the work, and by the marvellous energy and power shown by the French engineers. I travelled with the English Consul at Cairo and a party of scientifics and visitors for six days, and we ate and drank Suez Canal mentally and physically.

" The enthusiasm and energy of these men would alone convince any one that the work can be carried out, and money seems to be the only real difficulty. Where is this to come from? for the mere canal, as a commercial speculation, *can never pay the original outlay.* The whole place is a French colony. There are four or five villages, two of which are becoming towns rapidly, with fine houses, hotels, &c. This alone is marvellous, considering the whole isthmus is in mid-desert, without a drop of fresh water or blade of green grass near it. The administration is perfect, and made me admire the French immensely. It has become a question of the greatest international importance. The French are doing a world of good, but are they to remain? No politician outside France can allow that, but if they would hold and irrigate the desert they pass through, the speculation might eventually prove remunerative one. We sailed the whole way from Suez to the Mediterranean, a notable achievement in the teeth of the great Stephenson, who declared that it was an impossibility. The fresh-water canal, necessary for supplying the staff on the maritime one with drinkable water, and for the transport of materials, brings the Nile water to Ismaila in a stream six feet deep by twenty wide."

That the climate of Egypt did all that was expected of it for the ex-Master of the " P.H."—was proved by a P.S. to the above letter, which contains the statement: " We are all well; I never so strong since I remember anything." Ten years after this the writer of the above letter was again Master of the Pytchley Hounds; the interregnum of Mastership, 1864—1874, having been filled up by Messrs. A. Thomson, Craven, and Naylor, respectively. During this time, Lord Spencer had passed through the ordeal of an Irish Viceroyalty—a period during which, though the clouds were gathering which afterwards discharged themselves with such terrific force, the political atmosphere was comparatively serene and undisturbed.

In a letter from Zürich in the June of 1874, the writer says: "I am on my way to Ragatz, which I hope will strengthen the system, and enable me to carry out efficiently next winter my duties in county affairs, as well as those of M.F.H. I feel desperately eager to get back to superintend kennel-matters. The fact is that I have had to go into so many more details of management than I had when there was Charles Payne to lean upon, that I have got more interest, if more trouble, in my M.F.H duties. I like what I see of Goodall. He is keen as mustard, very active and sharp; and I breathe much more freely than when in the atmosphere of Squires, from whom breezes occasionally emanated other than those of milk, which was his usual outward and visible beverage. My regard for Tom Goddard made me very extravagant in my bid for "Newport;" but it is well perhaps that I missed him. I should have liked "Optimist" for Goodall, but I stopped after two hundred and thirty guineas. I hope that my purchase of the Duhallow Hounds will be useful. The dog-lot is rather too tall; but to my fancy they are very good-looking, and I have a wonderful report of them in the field. These and some Fitzwilliam reduced-establishment drafts, and the Holderness lot, ought to make our pack up to a state of efficiency."

During the four years that followed, there was nothing omitted by the noble Master to ensure that amount of sport which was the one great object of his desire, and which, more or less, occupied his thoughts by day and by night. The accident to his Huntsman having forced upon him the welcome necessity of carrying the horn, he increased the responsibility at the same time that he enhanced the enjoyment of his position; the only drawback to which was his too great anxiety to show sport. Never sparing himself, his horses or his hounds, he got into the habit of making longer days than was good for either, and the "one more draw," when it was really time to go home, eventually told its tale upon all three. Nor did long frosts and heavy snows serve to keep the establishment undisturbed. "Out you go!" was the cry on the slightest apparent change in the weather; and many an hour had been spent in Sywell Wood and Holcot Cover, in the vain hope of catching a fox in the snow, and of keeping the hounds in condition. The vision of a brave old Field-Marshal—one of England's most accomplished soldiers—now deceased, rises before the writer, as with the collar of his coat well up to his ears, and his thin grey silky hair peeping from under his hat, he beat his hands against his thighs and wished himself well out of the wood, and sitting over the fire, safe and snug, at Althorp.

Even under these depressing conditions, no "Mark Tapley" could look happier than the Master who carried the horn; the very fact of the difficulties seeming to inspire him with fresh energy. Besides the old warrior just referred to, Lord Granville—a genuine lover of sport in any shape—would occasionally appear at the Meet during Lord Spencer's Mastership; and one day falling in love with a slashing four-year-old of Mr. John Drage's —a regular Leicestershire galloper—made him his own at three hundred guineas, to ride with his harriers about the Dover cliffs. "Love at first sight," according to the Yankees, is "the greatest labour-saving machine in the world," but in this case it did not prove a *money*-saving one to the purchaser, inasmuch as it was not long before the animal in question found his way back into Northamptonshire—a present to Lord Spencer—his only fault being that he was "not weak enough for the place."

But a greater even than the noble Warden of the Cinque Ports gave by his presence quite a fillip to the Meet at Althorp, one fine spring morning. It was known that the "G.O.M." was staying in the house, and it was expected that he would appear—not exactly in scarlet and tops, but in "highlows" and jacket to match, just to say that he had been present at a Meet with the Pytchley. This did not, however, appear to be a great object of desire with the Premier of England.

Anticipating the irreverent sneers of Lord Randolph Churchill, he even then enacted the part of "an old man in a hurry," and after a brief survey of the scene, and without stopping to address the Field, the Huntsman, or even the second horseman, he hastily retreated to the more suitable surroundings of the famous Library. But his eyes were not closed during the few brief minutes of his attendance at the Meet. When invited by one of the guests after dinner to say how the farmers were to meet the distressful times which had then just commenced, the acute observer remarked, "They cannot be so badly off, or they would not ride such beautiful horses as I saw this morning;" adding—"And what do you think they really want?" "A slight duty on corn," was the reply. "They will never get it; and if they did, it would do them more harm than good," was the hopeful answer of the great Apostle of Free Trade; whilst a smile at the audacity of the suggestion played across his face.

"But can nothing be done by which landlord and tenant may each be saved?" was the next inquiry of the evidently interested interrogator. "Reduce the size of your holdings, and alter your system of farming," was the response of one, who without having closely studied the subject, saw where the weak points lay. Since then this advice has been acted upon to an immense extent, especially in the increased use of "silos" and "binders." But the black cloud still hovers over farming in all its branches; nor does even a glint of the sun peep out from the darkness to impart a ray of hope to the despairing agriculturist.

"Jam," for a time, was held out by the Prime Minister as a panacea for all rustic evils, but the remedy scarcely seemed suited to the complaint; and "Thou shalt be saved by jam," was never adopted as an article of belief into the creed of the British farmer.

At the close of his fourth season, Lord Spencer again becoming aware that his health was not equal to the wear and tear of the duties required of him, and also that he was neglecting the higher functions of political life, once more placed his name on the list of retired M.F.H's, and determined to pass the winter in the genial climate of Algiers.

Writing from "Mustapha Supérieur," in the autumn of 1879, he says, "Thanks for your account of the run from "Gib." How delighted Will Goodall must have been with it! It reminds me of one I had on the last day of the season of 1878. 'Valentia' was out. I rode

'Marvel' for the last time, and I am sorry to say that I lost my fox near Overstone. I love to hear of a good run; but as I ought to be curbing my hunting propensities, a slight pang will come across me when I feel that I ought not again to carry the horn or hunt as much as I have hitherto done. On reading an account like yours, I become conscious of the difficulty I shall have in breaking myself of the passion. If I could be satisfied with a moderate enjoyment of it, I might allow myself some rein; but I so easily become greedy for more, when once in the swing of it, that I scarcely know when to pull up."

Acting upon these feelings, and conscious that there was that within him which might be of more service to his country than the management of a pack of foxhounds, ever so distinguished, Lord Spencer now laid down the horn of the huntsman, and took up the portfolio of the statesman in its stead. As President of the Council, the new Highway Act and other important matters connected with county business came under his supervision. The same "thoroughness" which in all that he undertook seemed to be his moving principle, was brought to bear upon his new sphere of labour, with the result that the efficiency of his work has not been exceeded by that of many of his predecessors in office. Sore trouble awaited him in Ireland; but he met it in a spirit so gallant, and yet so gentle, that it may be said of him that in every Irish heart save that of the murderer and the dynamitard "*exegit monumentum œre perennius*."

As he has said in a letter quoted elsewhere, "many a time he was saved from collapsing by a gallop with the 'Meath' or the 'Ward Union' staghounds"—a hint that should not be lost upon future Irish Viceroys.

MR. HERBERT LANGHAM.

IN Mr. Herbert Langham of Cottesbrooke, the "P.H." were fortunate enough to find another country gentleman, the fourth in succession, ready to undertake the office of M.F.H. In social position, locality of residence, love of hunting, and general popularity, a more fitting successor could not have been found; and a liberal subscription enabled him to look forward to a happy and successful reign.

It was now arranged that the Woodland Country—a long-standing difficulty with the "P.H."—should, under the title of the "North Pytchley," be hunted by a separate pack of hounds and Master, thereby greatly lessening the labours of the establishment at Brixworth. Happily for the new experiment, Mr. Watson of Rockingham Castle—the keenest sportsman and the most popular man in the whole country-side—was willing to become Master of the "N.P.H.", and for two years contrived to instil life and animation into the proceedings; after which he retired into private life. Mr. Pennel Elmhirst succeeded Mr. Watson, himself carrying the horn; but being an entire stranger in the land, and unused to handling hounds in a strong country, the measure of his success was not very remarkable.

Lord Lonsdale next took up the running, or rather the hunting, and fairly astonished the land of Brigstock with the lavish munificence of his expenditure. Mounting his men as men never before were mounted; himself riding horses more fitted for the Waterloo than a Woodland country, and sparing no expense on either the kennel or stables, it seemed as though "Monte Cristo" himself was holding high jinks at the little hunting-centre known as "Brigstock."

A fine, powerful, fearless rider, his costly horses frequently had their jumping powers put to the test, the fences between the different woods being thick and hairy, and well furnished with strong posts and rails.

A "chestnutomania" having at one time got the better of the noble Lord, it was said that for a short period he had seventy horses of that colour standing in his stable. The craze, however, proving as extravagant as it was unwise, did not continue long, and the stud of one colour became, as of yore, one of infinite variety.

At the close of his third season, Lord Lonsdale transferred his establishment into Lincolnshire; and was succeeded in 1885 by Mr. M'Kenzie, late Master of the "old Berkeley" hounds, who by his unceasing endeavours to show sport in a district where few care to appear at the Meets and support him by their presence, has won the good opinion of the neighbourhood.

Succeeding to a somewhat masterful Mastership (1878), and having himself ofttimes had to suffer rebuke, Mr. Langham has gone on opposite lines to those of his predecessor in respect to the management of his Field; and, except in cases of flagrant misbehaviour, refrains from active interference. He has broken the custom that change of Masters is to take place every three or four years; and every one hopes that the Hounds will long remain under the guidance of the owner of Cottesbrooke.

Well mounted and always in a forward place when

hounds run, the Master is mostly at hand to restrain any "young man in a hurry;" and when necessary, can administer a suitable amount of verbal correction—always well received, from not being over-frequent.

In one of his letters, Lord Spencer speaks of the great comfort he experiences in having such a Huntsman as Charles Payne to "lean upon;" whereby he is saved much trouble and many anxieties. All who remember that accomplished horseman, great artist, and trusty servant, will be able to appreciate his lordship's feelings in this respect. To no one, however, will they come more home than to his successor, who in William Goodall possesses a Huntsman and servant who leaves nothing for a Master to require. Springing from a family to whom "hunting a pack of hounds" comes as naturally as finding game does to a setter, in him we have an instance of the brilliant Whip—losing none of his brilliancy when called on to carry the horn. The son of one who for nearly twenty years hunted the Belvoir hounds, and who met his death by falling upon his own horn, which he had thrust into the side-pocket of his coat, his first experience in stable-work was with Sir Thomas Whichcote, Bart., of Aswarby House, near Sleaford. He then "entered" to hounds as second Whip to Carter, who had succeeded to the post held by his (Goodall's) father, and for one year (1866) served with Roake and Firr, under Captain A. Thomson.

After a spell of four years with Lord Henry Bentinck, he returned to the "Belvoir," from whence he was selected by Lord Spencer, in 1874, to be Huntsman to the "P.H." Twelve years have elapsed since he first occupied the

Huntsman's cottage at Brixworth, and each succeeding year has afforded a fresh proof of the wisdom of Lord Spencer's choice. By the skill he has displayed in the exercise of his profession—by a trustworthiness never exceeded—by good conduct and a civility which have won the hearts of all, William Goodall has now earned for himself a place on the short list of those whose names have become household-words in the little world comprised in that part of the county of Northampton known as the "Pytchley country." With him on the list of Huntsman-worthies may be included those giants of old time, Dick Knight and Charles King; whilst in modern days we feel reluctant to add any other save that of Charles Payne "the inimitable."

In social life few things are more striking than the position occupied by a popular Huntsman. Belonging to a class from whence spring jockeys, professional cricketers, pedestrians, and such like, it is to their integrity, skill, good manners and conduct, that they are indebted for the consideration they meet with from their equals, and the almost familiarity with which they are treated by their superiors.

Look at the long roll of Jockeys from F. Archer downwards, and see how many there are, who for rectitude and honesty stand in the eyes of other men in the same light as do the well-known Northamptonshire Huntsmen, as Charles King, Charles Payne, William Goodall, Frank Beers, and old Tom Sebright. Honour to each and all respectively, at having attained by their own merits a position among their fellows of which they and their families may well be proud.

Neither time nor space would serve to narrate the

particulars of the many good runs that have taken place since the Whip from the "Belvoir" assumed the horn of the "P.H.;" but during that time none is more worthy of notice than one on the 12th of March, 1878, when a fox found at Vanderplanks, after crossing the cream of the country by Watford, Crick, Yelvertoft, Clay Coton, Swinford Cover, Stanford Hall, was finally run into at Clifton Mill, close to Rugby. Unpromising at its commencement, after leaving Crick village, the hounds began to run in earnest, and it seemed as though the fox was determined to make things pleasant all round by selecting the finest line in the Midlands to traverse.

Goodall, Major Curtis, the Hon. F. Henley, and Captain Soames went about the best; and the former still looks upon it as the crack run of his time. A run from Sywell Wood in 1877 to Whishton village was memorable from Goodall having swum the Nene just before killing his fox. Accoutred as he was, he plunged in, and bade bold riders follow; but these declining the invitation galloped right and left, determined to praise the bridge that carried them safely and quickly over.

Happily fortune in this case favoured the brave, and, instead of losing the fox, as usually happens after the performance of some notable feat by which an entire field is shaken off, the dripping fugitive from the depths of Sywell Wood was brought handsomely to hand. With a little whisky poured down his throat, and a larger supply into his boots (a hint for river-swimmers), Goodall escaped all cold, and had no reason to repent for self or horse their somewhat hazardous immersion.

Aged thirty-eight, and riding under twelve stone, bringing to bear upon his duties a zeal and conscientiousness that must needs have their reward, it is to be hoped that many a year may elapse before the "P.H." is divorced from its present Huntsman, and a stranger be seen in his place.

The same wish may well include Master as well as servant. The official life of the former has already exceeded the span allotted to the Masters of the "P.H." of modern days; and few will be found to deny that the path he has chosen to follow has been one of pleasantness to those who have hunted with him. On first trying his "prentis hand" at the duties entailed by ruling over a hunting-establishment, his knowledge of the kennel-part of it probably touched that point known as "unqualified nescience." Bringing natural aptitude to bear upon a determination to master a subject full of interest as well as of importance, he has now acquired the reputation of being one of the best "hound-men" of the present day. That this should be of great advantage to a Hunt need not be expatiated upon; the make, shape, blood, and quality of the constituents of a pack being nearly all that success requires.

For instance; to breed for speed alone would be to reduce the number of good days in a season to a very limited quantity. The fineness of limb and general formation necessary to produce extra swiftness would necessarily affect the parts where the scent-organs lie, and contract the space requisite for their full development. The familiar "howl" about each succeeding winter being the worst hunting-season on record may in a measure be laid at the door of the M.F.H. and Huntsman going in for galloping rather than scenting-power; a subject upon which Lord Charles Russell, in one of his admirable little brochures upon hunting-matters strongly animadverts. His lordship—prop and pillar of the Oakley Hunt through many a season—and now in his eighty-first year, both able and willing to give a lead at a " yawner," thus speaks of hound-breeding at the present day : " The modern system of farming, less rough country, fewer grass-baulks and headlands, fences neatly trimmed, early ploughing, steam-cultivation, artificial manures, and more stock— all tends to lessen the hold of scent. Game-preserving produces a quantity of bad fat foxes, and a fat bad fox is less easy to kill than a lean wild one. These new difficulties should be encountered by more hunting-power ; more attention should be paid to the faculty of scent. At Hound-Shows there are prizes for make and shape, but none for merit. No notice is taken of the all-important and indispensable nose. Everything is sacrificed to fashion and quality : only one type is recognized, and that the one best adapted to the small minority of hunting-countries—the flying grass ones. Any special provision for a class of hounds suitable for an enclosed, hilly, woodland, plough, or moorland country is not taken into consideration, everything being sacrificed to the craves for speed. 'Most haste, less speed.' The pack that stops the least goes the quickest ; and the one that carries most head and has the greatest number of line-hunters will be gaining on their fox; while the one that might shine for a short time in a catchy scent will be getting farther and farther behind, after the first check." Such are the words of one of the most acute, observant, and experienced judges of hunting now existing ; the moral of them being that the one thing needful in a hound is Nose.

Were it not for the "glorious uncertainty" of all things connected with the "Chase" as well as with the "Turf," the "P.H." might confidently look forward to a long continuance under its present Master, whose record already beats that of all his predecessors since 1818.

A few years ago, when the dire trouble of all connected with "dirty acres" first set in, it was prophesied that hunting was tottering to its fall, and had but a short time to live. It was said that one pack of hounds after another would die out for the lack of the necessary aliment, and that their place would know them no more. There is nothing, however, so safe to back as the unexpected. While these lines are being written, the number of packs in England and Scotland is much the same as it was in 1880. Captain ("Bobby") Soames, secretary to the "P.H.," and lord of the little paradise in the unelysianic village of Scaldwell, bad to beat when hounds run hard, and mounted as so good a sportsman should be, can testify that the financial position of the Pytchley never wore a more promising aspect than it does at the present moment (July, 1886).

How this is so, considering the portentous falling off in the amounts contributed by the old local Subscribers, it is hard to say; but the fact of its being so is a gleam of sunshine in the midst of the gloom surrounding many an old sportsman; a gloom through which he is unable to see his way to farther enjoyment of the sport which, through many a year, has formed the chief one of his life. Happily the prices given for yearlings, books, pictures, china, and bric-à-brac of all sorts, prove that there is plenty of money somewhere. The coffers of the "Beer-

Lord" and the "Share-Lord" still retain their rich linings of L.S.D.; and if the "Ploughshare-Lord" be constrained to turn a narrower furrow, capital will always be forthcoming to maintain and keep alive the "Sport of Kings."

The poet Campbell has sung the song of the "Last Man." If the "Last Hunt" is ever to be commemorated in verse, may it be the one whose history has been so imperfectly sketched in these pages.

PART III.
MEMOIRS OF MEMBERS.

MR. A. A. YOUNG.

ENTHUSIASM, even in a doubtful cause, has that within it which commands respect: how much more then will this be the case when the object is something more than praiseworthy? In the man fashioned in the ordinary mould the love of fox-hunting, however strong in the prime of life, will wax faint as years roll on, and his seventieth year will probably find him indifferent to his former love.

Fourscore years have passed over the head of Orlingbury's venerated "Squire;" but the passion for the chase that burned so strongly within him seems to have lost little of its intensity, though he can no longer gratify it as of yore. A fall from his horse, rather than lapse of time, brought about the result which compelled Mr. Young to follow hounds on wheels instead of in the saddle —a change deeply felt by the fine old sportsman. Accompanied by a lady whose love for everything connected with hunting fully equals that of her father, the old Squire never fails to appear in his little "Dagmar" when hounds are drawing Wilmer Park or any of the well-known covers round about. No sooner have the hounds given notice that a fox is a-foot, than the excitement of father, daughter, and cob (an animal of exceeding beauty) rises to summer-heat, and the latter can scarcely be restrained from following in hot pursuit where there is no "pathway of safety."

Should a fox not be "at home" in the Orlingbury plantations it will be no fault of the worthy Squire's, who will not have left a stone unturned, no dodge untried, to obviate such a result.

If a run worthy of the name takes place with an animal found in any of his covers, his heart is gladdened for many a day, and he never tires of going over the line and hearing of the incidents attending it. Then it is that the lady previously referred to recalls with a sigh the "Chestnut son of Thormanby," whom she rode so gallantly, in spite of a disinclination on his part to face the prickly fences that, sooner or later, he was forced to jump. With a lack of gallantry unbecoming a steed of such noble lineage, this child of a Derby-winner would think it no scorn to deposit his fair burden in a ditch, and to gallop off, apparently well satisfied with the performance—very unworthy of his illustrious sire.

Who is there that hunts with the Pytchley on the Monday-side of the country who is unacquainted with that " right little, tight little thicket," known as " Cock-a-roost"? Formed by Mr. Young some five-and-twenty years ago, by enclosing the patches of gorse growing naturally on the hillside opposite the Isham road, and scarcely exceeding an acre in extent, it has acquired a reputation that might be envied by many a more pretentious cover. Growing so thickly as to require two dismounted horsemen as well as the hounds to complete an effective draw, an hour is often cut to waste before a fox is induced to quit his snug surroundings. When well away, nothing but an absence of scent can prevent a gallop of more or less enjoyment, according to its pace and duration. To hear of a " forty minutes and a kill " from the "bantling" of his heart is gladdest of glad tidings in the ears of the worthy old Squire, of whom it is said in relation to this little spot of ground, that " after his death the word ' Cock-a-roost ' will be found imprinted on his heart."

With him time seems to deepen rather than to weaken recollections of old hunting-days. Speak to him of " Clarion " or " De Grey," and the glistening eye and reflective look speedily show into what region of the irrevocable past his thoughts are wandering. The last-named, bought as a four-year-old at Boughton Fair, occupies perhaps in the heart of his master a warmer place than any horse he ever possessed, but to him who was not " in the secret," the other appeared greatly the superior animal. Troubled with a bit of temper, the first was not always to be depended upon at his fences, and in the last stride would whip suddenly round; whereas the second was, if anything, in too great a hurry to arrive on the other side of the hedge and ditch. No man need wish to have two better hunters in his stable at the same time, but to the outsider, " Clarion " with his pace, quality, and jumping power, was the one to take for choice. Not given to award praise or blame in a niggardly fashion, it may be asserted without fear of contradiction that no two animals were ever made the subjects of so much laudation by an appreciative owner as these two.

Fond of seeing a mare and foal roaming within range of his study-window, Mr. Young ventured upon the experiment of breeding a few thoroughbreds, and many is the cigar that has been smoked whilst contemplating the beauties, imaginary or otherwise, of a placid-eyed mother and long-legged child. Commencing with selling a filly by "Fisherman" out of "Durbar" to Lord Stamford at a price something more than remunerative, it seemed to the fortunate vendor as if he had hit the secret of successful breeding at the first attempt. But fickle Fortune, content with bestowing a single favour on the hopeful country gentleman, soon shook her wings and fled. Each youngster after this that was born into the world seemed only a vehicle for fresh worries and mishaps, and it became evident to Mr. Young that he was not to escape the common lot of breeders of horses. Disappointment followed disappointment; but the "most unkindest cut of all" came one day, when on being asked by Mr. Bevan, what might be the price of a good-looking four-year-old then being ridden by Mr. Young, he replied, "Four hundred guineas." "Ah, I see," said the other, "a hundred a leg, and *three* of them very good ones!" It was only too true. The quick and practised eye had fallen upon a weak-looking spot, and a little work soon proved the truth of Mr. Bevan's discovery that all four legs were not equally good. Suffering a considerable shrinkage in value, the promising young one passed into other hands; and his late owner made no further experiments in the difficult science of breeding for profit.

In his sixtieth year a singular incident revealed to

Mr. Young the fact that his eyesight had undergone a sudden deterioration. In the full belief that it was impossible for him to mistake a hare for a fox under any circumstances, he one day "tallied" a hare crossing a ride in Sywell Wood. Chaffed by a friend upon his mistake, he offered to bet ten pounds that he had not been wrong. The bet was at once accepted, and the hounds were left to decide the issue. On being brought to the spot, not a hound spoke or showed any sign that a fox "had passed that way." The next morning's post brought to the winner of the wager a cheque for ten pounds, and on the following the loser received back his cheque torn into ten separate pieces. On a loose piece of paper was inscribed the legend, "Bets on certainties go for nothing."

The cause of the mistake in one hitherto peculiarly long-sighted now became apparent; a limited but unnoticed failure of vision had taken place, which from that time necessitated the use of glasses. Singular to relate, from that date, some thirty years ago, no further alteration of the eyesight has occurred; and the passage of poor puss across the ride still marks the moment when the discovery was made that time had robbed the optic of some of its power.

To such an extent did this true sportsman carry his love of hunting, that he was always delighted at seeing the remains of poultry in the neighbourhood of any of his covers. Turning over with his stick "disjecta membra" of some late inmate of his own poultry-house, he would say with a grin of satisfaction, "Well done, Charlie, my boy; you got hold of a fat one that time!"

In speaking of his old Northamptonshire days, Charles Payne still delights to tell how one afternoon, when hounds were running hard under Great Harrowden, he fell into a ditch, out of which he was with difficulty rescued by Mr. Young, who chanced to be near at hand, whilst his horse remained inextricably fixed between either bank. A boot, full to the brim of mud and water, came off in the struggle, "and there was I," says Payne, "with hounds running like mad, on the ground with no horse and only one boot." But the "Squire," as usual, was equal to the occasion. Whipping off one of his own boots he insisted upon its taking the place of the disabled one, and mounting the horseless Huntsman upon his own steed, he dismissed him in search of his hounds, by this time well out both of sight and hearing. "No man in England would have 'been and gone and done' such a thing as that except Mr. Young," is the no less grateful than truthful comment of the veteran who loves to narrate this sporting incident of the Squire of Orlingbury.

Another incident is still green in the memory of the ex-Pytchley huntsman; when in running a fox from "Long Hold," Mr. Young plunged into a canal, and emerging safely on the other side was followed by Sir G. Wombwell—afterwards so nearly drowned on the fatal day with the York and Ainsty, Dick Roake and "Cherry" Angel—the latter of whom contrived to turn over in mid-stream, and was with some difficulty rescued from a "false," if not dangerous position. The same keenness which induced a (by no means juvenile) sportsman to entrust himself to the cold embrace of the "Union Canal," led him into occasional developments of eagerness which were not without their amusing side. Colonel

Anstruther Thomson will not fail to remember how, when having brought a beaten fox into a field of high white turnips near Sywell Wood, the hounds threw up their heads and began to look about for assistance. Nor was it long in coming. With a full confidence in his olfactory organs, Mr. Young at once constituted himself a member of the pack, *dismounted from his horse*, and began sniffing about with all the intensity of an old hound. In a few moments up jumped the " missing one," and away went " bipeds " and " quadrupeds," to the great amusement of the Field, in hot pursuit of the doomed and leg-weary animal. Not a little elated at the success of his interpositions, Mr. Young's only reply to the " chaff " with which he was assailed was, " Well, never mind ; let those laugh that *find*." The ghost of poor Pug is said to be seen on winter nights, prowling round the precincts of Orlingbury village, bent upon avenging himself upon the cocks and hens of his destroyer.

For a friend to pass his door, homeward-bound, without looking in for a cut at the cold beef and ripe old " stilton " which are always awaiting the sportsman on hunting-days, is one of the things which would almost amount to an insult in the eyes of one, quick to take, if not to give offence. As in hunting, so in politics or aught beside, the worthy Squire is prone to express himself strongly, should the subject run counter to his own opinions. To mention the name, even, of a certain eminent statesman in his presence is not likely to increase the prevailing harmony; and to him who under his roof chanced to speak favourably of the " Pope," there will not be a very " gaudy time." Lord Byron, in his poetical creed, says,—

> "Thou shalt believe in Milton, Dryden, Pope,
>   Thou shalt not set up Coleridge, Wordsworth, Southey."

In his political belief our grand old sportsman will teach us that

> "Thou shalt believe in Dizzy, Cecil, Randy,
>   Thou shalt not set up Gladstone, Parnell, Morley;"

and long may he live to cling to his fine old-crusted opinions, and retain his love for the chase, and preserve foxes for the Hunt, his support of which for many a year past has been fully appreciated by every member of it. To him the words of Whyte Melville will some day be no less applicable than they are to the imaginary hero of his song :—

> "The labourer at work and the lord in his hall
>   Would smile when they spoke of his passion for sport ;
>   In ale or in claret he's toasted by all,
>   For they never expect to see more of the sort.
>   And long may it be e'er he's forced to retire,
>   For we breed very few like this worthy old Squire."

MR. GEORGE ASHBY ASHBY.

HARK! a holloa, away! Whose are the ringing tones proclaiming to all whom it may concern that the fox has quitted "the Woollies," and is making the best of his way for "Long Hold" or Naseby Cover? The voice is that of George Ashby Ashby, eke a captain in her Majesty's Eleventh Hussars, and now part proprietor of the well-known Lordship over whose surface swarmed, more than 240 years ago, the serried hosts of Royalist and Roundhead. Where Rupert vainly strove against forces still more determined than his own, and Cromwell's military genius made itself assured, is now to be found the peaceful "Naseby Thorns," the quiet home of many a gallant fox, the starting-point of many a noble run. Since the day of "Naseby Fight," no other cavalry save that attached to the Pytchley Hunt, or interloping Quorn, has galloped across the tenacious clay surrounding the above-named covert. No tones more warlike than a huntsman's horn has roused the cattle in the adjacent fields.

"Anything is fun in the country," said some one who evidently took the same view of rural, and possibly of matrimonial life, as that Duke of Buckingham, who, being bitten by a spaniel of King Charles's, exclaimed, in his wrath: "Oh! you little brute, I wish you were married and lived in the country," and who had assuredly never found himself in the middle of Naseby Field at the close of a November afternoon, a stranger, on a tired horse, and with the hounds fast disappearing from his view. Unconscious perhaps of his position, with little help to be got from his pocket-map, he would then realize the want of truth in the assertion above referred to. To the native sportsman the situation would not be nearly so depressing. With him would rest the sure and certain knowledge that behind that group of fir-trees, dimly looming through the fog, was to be found excellent accommodation for man and horse. Fortunate indeed is the belated and tired hunter, who on his homeward way has to pass those tall fir-trees! A turn to the right and a hearty welcome and good refreshment will not only rob the remainder of the journey of all its weariness, but will leave upon the mind of the recipient the feeling that the house he has just quitted is the very temple of hospitality. Than in its high priest it would be hard to find a more devoted worshipper at the shrine of "all sorts and descriptions of sport!" Bold as a lion across a country, the fence is hard to find at which the lord of the Woollies will not have "a cut;" and if pace is not his horse's forte he makes it up in jumping powers. With him, however, as with many a brother Squire, things are not as they used to be. Wheat at 30s. per quarter and New Zealand mutton mean "empty stalls and an absence from the covert side;" and on the principle of "eating a hair from the dog that bit you," the gallant Captain has substituted shorthorns with a pedigree, for hunters without one. Exchanging the Scylla of the chase for the Charybdis of the farm, Agriculture is not to be despaired of by this sanguine owner of many an acre of ungrateful clay; and taking for his motto "never say die," he vows that with the aid of the "midden" and the draining-pipe, he will force Madam Earth to repay some of the money that has been lavished upon her. Not being one of those who would try to "catch the wind in a net," or "empty the sea with a pie-dish," it may be looked upon as certain that he is not without good reason for the faith that is in him; and that he will eventually win for himself the proud distinction of being pointed out as "the pilot that has weathered the storm."

A keen and eager shooter, woe betide the "bunny" that crosses the ride within forty yards of the muzzle of his gun. In his eyes the rabbit has not the same fault that it possesses in those of Lord Granville and many another, namely, of being "a little too short." *Vide* Speech on "Hares and Rabbits Bill" at an agricultural dinner in the Isle of Thanet, on which occasion his lordship is reported to have said, "For my own part, I have nothing to complain of in the matter of rabbits, except that I frequently find them a little too short;" a remark that was followed by much laughter.

Accurate, however, as may be the aim of the gallant Captain of whom we are speaking, it can hardly exceed that of that other gallant officer, who in 1645 led the battue against the hosts of Fairfax and Cromwell. Standing in a garden at Stafford one day about this time, Prince Rupert, in the presence of Charles I, took a shot with his horse-pistol at the weathercock on the top of the church. The bullet pierced the tail of the gilded fowl, whereupon his Majesty pronounced the feat to be "casualty only," otherwise "nothing but a fluke." Aggrieved at this suggestion, the Prince, taking a second aim, again struck the bird, thereby causing Charles to recall the remark he had made on witnessing the success of the first attempt of his great cavalry-general. Proud of being able to affirm that a good round dozen of young people, two of whom have already done good service to their country, have the privilege of calling him "father," to the worthy parent there is no greater pleasure than to see any of these in the hunting-field. One fair member of the group, strong in the desire to be "well with hounds," never scruples to go whithersoever her father leads before; and it is a moot point with some whether she will come to an untimely end by attempting to follow her sire over some impracticable place, or if his hairs will be brought with sorrow to the grave by his daughter jumping upon his prostrate form. To Captain Ashby the village of Naseby is entirely indebted for the beautiful spire which now, with uplifted finger, marks the spot where was fought one of England's most memorable and bloody battles.

Begging with the pertinacity of a professional mendicant, and with an energy all his own, the Squire of the parish, like the leech's daughter, ceased not to cry "give, give," until he had carried the object so dear to his heart, and so desirable in every respect. Times may fail to improve; the cloud now overhanging the landed interest may grow darker and more dark; the old country Squire may go under socially and pecuniously, but the good that he has done will live after him. To the owner of "The Woollies," come what may, there will always be the comfort to take to heart, namely, that in all the changes of the mortal life of the little village of Naseby, the name of "Ashby" will ever be remembered and identified with that of its most kindly neighbour, friend, and benefactor.

MR. AMBROSE ISTED.

For upwards of sixty years few figures were better known at a Meet of the Pytchley Hounds than that of "Squire Isted" of Ecton. Possessing a striking presence and peculiarly pleasing and aristocratic features, few strangers would fail to inquire who the well-mounted man, 'all over a sportsman" and "every inch a gentleman," might be.

Born deaf and dumb, unable as he was wont to say of himself to hear the report of a cannon if let off close to his ear, so cheerful was he in manner and aspect, that none could tell how much or how little he was affected by loss of speech and hearing.

Twice happily married; possessed of a good estate,

fond of society, and noted for his beautiful dancing, also his clever drawing; few country squires had established for themselves a more distinguished position than this gentleman who could neither speak nor hear.

Though quite unable to catch a note of the music, he had few greater enjoyments than that of dancing; and so keen were his eye and sense of touch that if his partner chanced to get out of time he would almost make a grievance of it, and speedily show that he was aware of it. That partner, be she who she might, was never invited to dance with him a second time.

Considerable pains having been taken with his education, he was always well-informed on the current topics of the day. His skill in drawing was very remarkable. Rarely did he return from hunting without making sketches of some ludicrous or otherwise striking incidents that may have occurred during the day; and many a page is filled with valuable memorials of events which but for his graphic pencil would have passed into oblivion.

Mr. Isted's efforts at articulation were apparently painful to himself and not pleasant to hear, but to a great extent were intelligible to those with whom he was in constant intercourse.

By no means averse to exercising his speaking powers upon perfect strangers, it was amusing to observe the nervous effect his efforts at speech had upon these unfortunates. By nineteen out of twenty of those he addressed not one word was understood, and all that there was to fall back upon was a vacant smile and a nod of apparent comprehension. The usual resource of the nervous and uninitiated was to cry "yes" in a very loud voice, or to say something in broken English, but on one occasion a victim was heard to reply "oui, oui," as if that amount of a language other than English would meet the difficulty. In addition to the ready fingers, pencil and paper were always at hand to assist those who were not well instructed in finger-talking. So forgetful did nervousness make many people of the deficiencies of their lively neighbour, that they would write upon his tablets questions of the most absurd description. A lady whom he had taken in to dinner on one occasion at Overstone Hall confessed to having written " Have you heard Jenny Lind?" and received the harrowing reply, " I cannot hear anything at all." This was paralleled by a friend of Mr. Foljambe's of Osberton, who, long after he had lost his sight, offered him a candle on going to bed.

During all his early life it would have taken a very good man across country to beat the Ecton Squire. Between him and the parson of his village, the Rev. J. Whalley, there was not much to choose in this respect; and it was a moot point which was the better man of the two. The Squire, however, had always this advantage over the parson, that knowing he should not be wanted on the following Sunday, he had no fear of a congregation before his eyes. Always well mounted—on nothing did he go better than on a one-eyed grey horse, which he purchased from the well-known " Dick Garratt," of Great Harrowden.

His three "R's," "Reindeer," "Rejoicer," and "Reformer," all children of his favourite "Rosebud," are still green in the memory of some who love to think of hippic heroes of the past; and the "Maid of Orleans," bought from Lord William Compton on his quitting Harleston, still occupies a warm corner in the heart of the present Marquis of Northampton.

A great breeder of hunters, Mr. Isted was never so happy as when mounted on the produce of some valued mare, the last named being one of the most prolific of his much-cherished mothers. Inheriting sporting instincts from a long line of ancestors, no one more thoroughly enjoyed hunting with all its pleasant adjuncts. In all manly sports, however, he took great delight, and rare bird, beast, or plant never escaped his attention and remark.

The sporting magazines and the daily journals found in him a very constant reader; but the rare volumes with which the shelves of the Ecton Library are so abundantly stored had no especial charms in his eyes. Tailing off in his riding as he advanced in years (fences seem to grow less and less negotiable as the hair gets thinner), Mr. Isted began to give up the distant Meets, and to commence upon the "currant jelly" business, into which he entered with much spirit.

Getting together a tolerably level and useful-looking lot of small harriers, he assumed the horn himself, utilizing as his Whip his old keeper Daniel Tassell. The latter, a thorough original, did not at all appreciate his elevation to the pigskin, and for many a day would complain greatly of cuticular abrasion, and of his master's want of feeling in not supplying him with sticking-plaster, bees-wax, or some still more adhesive compound, for the more satisfactory performance of the fencing part of the business. Mr. Isted naturally had some difficulty in finding servants able and willing to adapt themselves to his condition. To him it was of great importance to have quick and intelligent second horsemen. In William Pridmore—now dead—and in the well-known Tom Jolly, still to be seen delicately handling an impulsive youngster of Mr. Earl of Earl's Barton, he found all that he could desire.

Many a time during the day's hunting would it devolve upon one of these to reduce into the vernacular the words issuing from his mouth, or to interpret the mysterious language of the fingers. Each, when accompanying his master in the hunting-field, formed a sort of " Refuge for strangers in distress," and was the means of relieving many a poor applicant for help. The survivor of these two much-valued and useful followers still is to be found at the Pytchley Monday Meets, and has no greater pleasure than in recalling the events of forty years of faithful service. He can tell of many a noble run of which he has himself been an eye-witness, and of others of which he has heard from his master's mouth. Of the latter none come up to a run with the Oakley in the time of Grantley Berkeley, when a fox, found in Odell Wood, was killed near Braybrooke, in the Market Harborough country.

Every Hunt rejoices in being able to record a run to which may fairly be attached the title of " historical," and the Oakley may well lay claim to that dignity for this performance.

The distance as the crow flies cannot be less than sixteen miles, the greater part of it being through a strange country and every hunting-man knows how greatly this adds to the enjoyment of a run.

It is often said that " the days of long-service are

things heard of but not seen in this our time." The forty years passed by Pridmore and Jolly in the stables of the Ecton Squire point to the fact that the race of attached followers is not altogether extinct. As confirmatory of this, a neighbouring squire, distant only a few miles, can boast of having eight servants in his establishment, who have lived with him on an average of thirty-four years each. This case is probably without parallel, and is a matter of unqualified pride alike to master and servant.

Dying at the ripe age of eighty-five years, Mr. Isted left no direct heir; and his successor not having assumed the name with the property, it has become extinct, save in the memory of the many friends who will ever hold it in esteem.

It may be truly said of this remarkable specimen of the "English country squire" that, "take him for all in all, we ne'er shall look upon his like again."

MR. R. LEE BEVAN.

IF jealous of the powers of an outsider, some resident member of the Hunt had been commissioned to "smash," "pulverize" (to use the phraseology of the Prime Minister), and lower the crest of the tenant of Kelmarsh, to no one could the feat have been confided with a greater likelihood of success than to Mr. R. L. Bevan of Brixworth Hall.

Born with a love for animals, and especially for horses, he took to hard riding as naturally as a duck takes to the water; and to give a lead to a semi-willing friend in cold blood over a stiff bit of country was a gratification he could never deny himself. However much importance he may have attached to the injunction " Thou shalt love thy neighbour as thyself," it is likely that he never felt so kindly disposed towards him as when he saw him declining to follow him over a big fence.

To pound any notable " customer " would have been to him a matter of much self-congratulation, but to have Mr. Angerstein taking " two bites at a cherry," which he himself had swallowed without difficulty, would have been an event in his life ever to be cherished with pride and satisfaction. The second son of the head of the eminent banking house, Barclay, Bevan and Co., the subject of this memoir never cared to throw in his lot with the money-changers. Hunting having greater charms in his eyes than banking, he quitted Lombard Street for Leicestershire, and reversed the well-known line :—

"He lived delights, and scorned laborious days."

To no class of those who come under the title of business men is hunting more indebted for support than to the lords of finance. The names of Glyn, Gosling, Lubbock, Hoare, Bevan, Robarts and Fuller, will ever mark the fact that the science of money-making and that of foxhunting may be successfully combined ; and the name of many a banker-prince is to be found on the list of Masters of Hounds. The present chief of the great house of Barclay, Bevan and Co., would probably doubt his own identity were he to be told that at one time there was no one except himself who could beat his brother " Dick " across Leicestershire or Northamptonshire. That it was so, however, no one is more willing to allow than the younger of the two brothers.

It is probable that few men now living have hunted a

greater number of times than Mr. R. Lee Bevan; have had horses of higher quality, or ridden them in a more workmanlike manner. Having studied the animal with an earnest desire of becoming acquainted with its structure and peculiarities of disposition, it would not be easy to find any non-professional with a better knowledge of what to look for in a hunter, and with a more assured feeling of the ease with which the most knowing are occasionally taken in. Possessed of perfect hands, abundant nerve, and a strong seat, until time and tumbles robbed him of it, he ever loved to school a "young one," and teach him such manners as are required in a hunter.

Combining persuasiveness with a modicum of coercion, the "four-year-old" in his hands was not long in finding out that refractory ways were not "those of pleasantness," nor led to the "paths of peace." Not greatly caring for an animal that required no riding, he at no time laid himself out for the purchase of a made hunter, and the hotter the mount, the more he seemed to relish his position.

For many a year, "Tomblin," the well-known dealer of Lye Lodge, near Oakham—the only horse-dealer who has ever filled the office of High Sheriff of a county—furnished Mr. Bevan with his entire stud. That a man occupying the position of Mr. Tomblin should have been required to undertake a duty of so much dignity and importance, points to the fact that Rutlandshire at that time must have been sadly deficient in gentlemen properly qualified for the office.

Although there are not many dealers of repute with whom Mr. Bevan has not had negotiatious since those days; with few exceptions, the horses from the Rutlandshire stables well maintained the credit of their vendor's reputation.

For many a year there might have been seen by the side of the Squire of Brixworth a lady, no less remarkable for her beauty than she was for her skill in the management of the animal she rode; one whose love for the chase equalled, if it did not exceed, that of her husband, and whose opinion of a horse was deferred to by him, as of almost unerring correctness. Twice a week, if not oftener during the winter months, two ladies in well-fitting habits and dress quite *en règle*, may be seen mounting their hunters at the steps of Brixworth Hall. Half way down the flight, watching the operation with an eye ready to detect anything that may not be quite as it should be, there stands one who betrays by every word and look that there is a warm corner in his heart for each fair huntress. There is many a little thing " to be set right "—a side-saddle is not in its right place, a curb has to be let down, and the groom is not unlikely to be inquired of whether there has not been a mistake, and if he is not the gardener? But at length all becomes ship-shape. " Pater Anchises " gets upon his horse, and the impatient steeds feel that the day's fun has commenced at last. Hands seat and nerve must all be brought into use before the highly-bred, amply-fed animals " settle down." But each of these requisites is ready on demand, and is used to reduce the too-excellent spirit into subjection.

In the eyes of either sister, " the young one that needs a little managing " is preferred to the more safe and " hum-drum " style of mount, and the horse that has had the teaching of either of these fair horsewomen is likely to be a quiet and pleasant hunter for some less courageous daughter of Nimrod. Though tempted at times to inquire of his groom whether or no the garden rather than the stable were not his more suitable vocation, Mr. Bevan little imagined that the smart-looking, oily-mannered individual he had just accepted as his stud-groom had recently been an officer in a crack infantry regiment! No less surprised at the small modicum of knowledge displayed by his new *chef* than by the courtesy of his demeanour, an inquiry into antecedents led to the disclosure of his having been a captain in H.M's —th regiment, reduced by circumstances over which he had no control to the position he then held. The relation between the ex-officer and his new master or rather employer having speedily suffered collapse, the former was invited to say what remuneration he would consider sufficient to repay him for his brief service? " Give me what you please," was the reply; " I shall return it you all again." After a lengthy and incoherent epistle to a member of the family other than its head, this somewhat singular incident terminated.

Though well on his way to the confines of octogenarianism, Mr. Bevan finds that the old love of a gallop after hounds is by no means extinct within him.

The flesh may denote its weakness by an early return to the comforts at home, but that the spirit is still willing is shown by an occasional display of the recklessness which marked his younger days. A promising four-year-old continues to be an almost irresistible attraction, and though the years of the purchased and the purchaser may not be quite in accord, the former is speedily made to learn that it is not he that is master of the situation.

A new generation springs up, and the heroes of old sooner or later pass out of remembrance. Many a summer and winter, however, must pass away ere it will be forgotten that among the hunting notables of a former day there were few more conspicuous names than that of " Richard Lee," otherwise " Dick, Bevan."

MR. WILLIAM ANGERSTEIN.

If any one hunting with the " P.H." some five-and-thirty years since had entertained a desire to dislocate a shoulder, fracture an arm, or suffer some still more serious bodily injury, he could scarcely have adopted a course more full of promise than by following over the " Waterloo country " a member of the Hunt who was in the habit of wearing in his button-hole a posy about the size of an ordinary dinner-plate. This was Mr. Angerstein, then residing at Kelmarsh Hall, the seat of the old county family of Hanbury, the head of which is now known under the title of Lord Bateman of Shobdon Court in the county of Hereford, an ancient possession of the family to which he belongs. Possessed of nerves in sufficient quantity for his own use as well as for that of any friend who had left his at home, Mr. Angerstein's chief delight was riding at formidable-looking places. The stiffer the rail, the thicker the bullfinch, and the wider the bit of water, the more it seemed to suit the taste of this reckless horseman. Never having taken to heart or appraised at its rightful value the old saying of "discretion being the better part of valour," danger when in the hunting-field seemed to be the element most courted by this somewhat eccentric Norfolk Squire. Not having occasion to deny himself the possession of any horse he fancied by the price demanded for him, he rode nothing but weight-carrying animals of high quality. Mostly a trifle " on the leg " (and none the worse for that), with a bit of temper of their own, they invariably were or became magnificent fencers, the result of the schooling they had to undergo. The soothing tones and endearing language in which Mr. Angerstein was wont to address a young one on approaching a fence, with a deep diapason and changed vocabulary which greeted the ears of the animal if he fell, were highly amusing, if not edifying. To the moralist it afforded food for reflection upon the imperfection of human nature, the outcome of the fall of man. Here, a Saint on one side of a " post and rail " became a Sinner on the other, and it was made painfully clear that the line dividing virtue from its opposite was no thicker than a slip of wood. In spite of constant apparent efforts to the contrary, the tenant of Kelmarsh Hall was only occasionally detained at home by accidents in the field, and " the arm in a sling " and the " bound-up shoulder," were far less frequent objects for sympathy than might have been expected.

On leaving Northamptonshire, the late member of the " P.H." established, on the principle probably of " half a loaf being better than no bread," a pack of stag-hounds in Norfolk; but he was not long in making the discovery that the pursuit of the deer in an essentially non-hunting country, and that of the fox over the big pastures in the neighbourhood of Crick or Market Harborough are enjoyments as distinct in their character as light from darkness.

Many years have come and gone since he of whom we have been speaking formed a no less conspicuous than popular member of a Pytchley Meet. It may, however, be confidently affirmed that neither time nor the cares and troubles of political struggles have erased from his memory the many happy hours that he has passed amid the broad acres of Northamptonshire and in the company of Charles Payn and his " famous little bitches."

CAPTAIN "BAY" MIDDLETON.

On five days out of six, weather permitting, there may be seen issuing from his enviable quarters at Hazelbeach on his way to the Meet, one of the most widely known of the hunting-heroes of the day. Whether Captain Middleton owes his sobriquet of " Bay " to the colouring assigned to him by nature, or to the celebrated Derby winner of 1836, is immaterial, but from either of these sources it may well derive its origin. A prominent member of the noble army of " bruisers," the subject of this memoir is not attached to the battalion which can see no good in fighting or hunting unless it be always carried on at " fever-heat." Thankful for all the plums that may fall in his path in the way of " brilliant " gallops, the day of small things is gratefully accepted by him for what it may be worth. Possessing the instincts of a true sportsman, to him the big fence and the " rattling " forty minutes are not all in all. Failing the quicker " mercy," the slow hunting-run is, in his estimation, by no means to be treated with contempt ; nor is a season stigmatized as " the worst ever known," because every day has not produced its clipping forty minutes. He may truthfully say of himself as regards runs with hounds, "*Video meliora proboque,*" but failing these, I am content "*Deteriora sequi.*" Owning a stud second to none—the result of much care in selection—and of great experience, be the country ever so big, or the pace ever so fast, bar the usual accidents of a hunting-field, he is sure to see the cream of every good thing.

Selected to "lead" the Empress of Austria during her six weeks' residence at Cottesbrooke, in the winter of 1878, no one could have performed a delicate and difficult duty more efficiently. To ensure her Majesty's seeing the sport without incurring unnecessary risk was a task requiring decision, nerve, and experience, and in each of these the "pilotage" of Captain Middleton was conspicuous. The history of England points to a day when one of her most famous kings, noted for his love of the chase, might have come to an untimely end by following out hunting an adherent of the monarch he had supplanted. One "Cherry," a famous rider, a loyal adherent of the exiled James II., one day when out with the stag-hounds, seeing that William III. followed him wherever he went, thought that by jumping down a steep bank into the Thames, he might perchance break the usurper's neck or drown him in the stream. The king, however, possibly "smelling a rat," turned away, and so escaped the trap into which the loyal but malevolent Cherry hoped to lead him. The beautiful lady who so gallantly followed the English officer across the fences of Northamptonshire, incurred no other dangers than those incident to every hunting-field, and even escaped these, thanks to the skill of her pilot, without mishap of any sort. Nor are the Chase and the Turf the only arenas upon which Captain

Middleton has distinguished himself. In the cricket-field his services with bat and ball alike are such as to be highly valued by the side on which he plays; and when " I Zingari " require a change of bowling, a " head " ball from his hand is more likely than not to fall into the grasp of some much expecting fieldsman, and so prove fatal to the batter. As a judge of the game, he has few superiors, and the management of a match could not well be placed in better hands.

On the list of its members the Pytchley Hunt may be well satisfied to see the name of so fine a rider and so good a sportsman as that of " Bay " Middleton, of whom it may truthfully be said,—

> " That the pace cannot stop, or the fences defeat
> This rum 'un to follow, this bad 'un to beat."

CAPTAIN MILDMAY CLERK.

We read in history of many a " man in a mask "—one worn compulsorily, and much to the moral and physical discomfort of the wearer. Rare, however, are the instances in which it has been assumed voluntarily, and for the sake of humouring a whim. Such, however, was the case when Captain Clerk of Spratton Hall, one of the kindest-hearted and most amiable of men, thought fit to hide his good qualities under a cloak of apparent moroseness and want of geniality. For twenty years or more, from 1847, no figure was more familiar, no name better known in mid-Northamptonshire than that of " Clerk of Spratton." The associations of a cavalry regiment having fostered a strong natural love for horses and everything connected with hunting, he no sooner obtained his troop than he severed the link which had united him to military life—drew a prize in the matrimonial lottery—bought a house and small property in a well-situated village near the Brixworth kennels—and mounted the white collar of the " P.H." The eccentricity which led him to conceal rather than expose his good qualities earned for him a sobriquet by which he became universally known, and by which he will ever be remembered, in spite of its being a libel on his true character. For this title he was indebted to a habit of estimating men and things at a considerably lower value than that at which they had been appraised by the parties themselves. In one respect, however, he greatly differed from his brother " crabbists," namely, that he was not a whit more merciful to things belonging to himself than he was to those of others.

His wine, for example, than which nobody had better, was dubbed by him " paraffin " or " petroleum ;"—his cook was bound to make those who had been so rash as to accept an invitation to dinner " ill for a week ;"—the horse upon which he, probably, had cut down a whole field, was only " an old screw ;"—a quick thirty minutes would be " about as fast as a cripple could kick his wide-awake ;"—and it was a fortunate hound which, according to him, possessed any of the qualifications requisite for an efficient member of a pack.

Possessed of too much amiability to give outward expression to his dislike of another, he would not lose an opportunity of indulging in a sly poke at any one who was not altogether to his fancy. Not being quite in accord with a Huntsman, who was nearly perfection in the eyes of every one else, he got his cut at him one day in the following manner. Taking a non-hunting friend to see the kennels at Brixworth, the hounds, as their manner is, began to fawn upon the stranger instead of on their Huntsman. Surprised at this, the unknowing friend sought an explanation, and inquired if the hounds did not like their Huntsman? "Like him?" was the reply, "Why they hate him!" Up to this moment the idea of hounds hating their Huntsman had probably never entered the mind of any man, and the spirit of fun, which was always strong within the utterer of this novel accusation, must have had a "high old time" as the words fell from his lips.

A friend having congratulated him upon the coming into his neighbourhood of a very pretty woman, his only comment was, "She'll be as ugly as the rest if she only lives a few years longer." At another time when authority rested with a Master who governed with a somewhat over-tight hand, Clerk was seen on a very cold morning, whilst hounds were drawing, to take up his position in the middle of a shallow pond.

"What are you doing that for?" asked an amused but puzzled friend.

"Trying not to head the fox," was the grave and caustic reply.

For the Christmas-holiday boy there was always a kind and encouraging word from the Spratton cynic. One, long since "married and done for," still recalls the pride he felt, when one day after a smart gallop, as he was washing his pony's mouth out with some water from a ditch, on hearing the words, "Well done, youngster, you've a better head on your shoulders than many an old one." Looking up, he saw that he was being addressed by a Member of the Hunt he had always held in a sort of awe, and liked him ever afterwards.

To a friend who, on his way home from hunting, had praised a glass of fine old Madeira brought to the door of his hospitable house, he sent on the following day six bottles of the same bin, with a card on which was the legend, "Petroleum for your hunting-flask."

Though it never lay in his power to give high prices for his horses, so complete a master was he of the art of getting across a country and of riding to hounds, that he never failed to hold a good place in any run; nor did he ever lose a start by giving way to the snare of "Coffee-housing." His motto was "*pauca verba ;*" and the man caught up by him on the way to cover, or on the return home after hunting, stood little chance of being "jawed to death."

Whatever else might have been laid to his charge, he never could have shared the fate of Miss Jex Blake, who, at the close of one of her somewhat tedious harangues, heard a wearied listener say, that he had long known that "*Lex*" was the Latin for "*Law*," but never knew till that moment that "*Jex*" was Latin for "*Jaw*."

Not strong constitutionally, he never cared to spare himself, and be the distance ever so far, or the weather ever so bad, the "uncheery one" never failed to be at the Meet on every hunting-day. Ill-health overtook him when little past his prime, and when he finally succumbed to an enemy, against whose attacks he had many a time unsuccessfully grappled, not only was the feeling that the Pytchley Hunt had lost a notable and much appreciated member generally recognized, but the regret was universal and profound.

COLONEL ARTHUR.

As surely as "every bean has its black, and every path its puddle," so certainly must members of a hunt, as of every other social circle, drop out of their places one by one, victims of time or else of circumstances. In these days of agricultural depression the latter has had more to do than the former in thinning out from the hunting-ranks the old County Squires, but the former still remains the greater and more inevitable evil of the two. From the clutches of time there is no real escape, though upon some favoured few he lays his hand so lightly that it would seem as though he had winked at being cheated of his rights. Though the capillary barometer may not indicate "much snow," and may have shown indeed for years past neither variableness nor shadow of turning, there is no escaping the ravages of Chronos. There is no rule, however, without its exception. Who that has hunted with the "P.H." any time during the last quarter of a century does not now still see at its Meets, on wheels instead of on horseback, a gallant Officer, the senior of most there present; in aspect the junior of half the field. Genial, courteous, gentlemanlike, his *raison d'être* in the hunting-field seemed to be to make things pleasant all round. To run the risk of imperilling his neck or fracturing a limb was with him at no time an object of ambition; but there was no one so ready to help in the capture of an escaped horse or to assist a brother-sportsman in distress. The very opposite of the other member of the hunt, whose taciturnity has been referred to elsewhere—the gallant Colonel here spoken of was the chief priest of that item of hunting-ordinances known as the "coffee-house department." By him nothing going on in the world, social or political, was unknown; nor did he think it a friendly or necessary act to keep his knowledge to himself. For some time in command of a distinguished cavalry regiment, he worked unremittingly and successfully to maintain its reputation for smartness, and under him the sloven soon learnt that it had become incumbent upon him to change his ways. Upon leaving the service the gallant Colonel changed his sword into a hunting-crop; and settling down in one of the best hunting-districts in England with one to whom "the pleasures of the chase" were as great as to himself, they together shared all the enjoyments of "a life in the Midlands."

That the familiar form of the kindly old Officer should no longer be seen at the cover-side, mounted as of yore, is a matter of no little regret to those who miss each dropped link of the chain uniting the present with the past; and the figure of the gallant occupant of Misterton and Desborough Halls must ever be connected with recollections of the pleasant Tailby and Pytchley Meets, when a neat-looking horse instead of a well-appointed trap was his mode of conveyance.

MAJOR WHYTE MELVILLE.

On the long list of those who have been members of the Pytchley Hunt, no name stands out in bolder relief than that of "George Whyte Melville," soldier, novelist, poet, and sportsman by birth and natural instincts. Son of a M.F.H., himself an "Admirable Crichton" in all things pertaining to sport, hunting came as naturally to the

future author of " Market Harborough " as his daily food.
A few years at Eton or Harrow, to be followed by a term
of service in some " crack " regiment is the usual lot of
the elder son, and the young Scotch scion of an ancient
race followed the routine chalked out for a majority of
those in the same position with himself. Entering the
Guards as soon as he quitted school, the ex-Etonian
evinced a more than ordinary aptitude for military life,
and devoted himself with ardour to his regimental
duties, as also to the attractions of a London life,
where he rapidly established a reputation for repartee
and conversational power, which caused the brilliancy
of his writings a little later on to be received by those
who knew him without any feelings of surprise.

Marrying the second daughter of Lord Bateman of
Kelmarsh Hall in the county of Northampton, he quitted
the army and settled down at Boughton, a little village
three miles from the Pytchley kennels, and about as
many from the county town. In the pages of "Holmby House," Boughton is often referred to as the
seat of Lord Strafford, to which Charles I. would frequently ride of an afternoon from Holdenby [*alias*
Holmby], stopping on his road to fish in the Nene at
Brampton; and it was here that the author drew his
inspiration for the various scenes and characters of the
most popular of all his novels.

The two great objects of his life at this time being as
he said of himself, "the pig-skin and the pen," his days
were devoted to hunting, and his evenings to literary
work. The evening's employment in no way interfered
with the full enjoyment of the sport to which he was so
ardently attached; though later on, after the " Argosy "

had come in, he made it a rule never to lay out upon his own personal gratification the money he earned by his pen. What he must have spent in his desire to benefit others may be inferred from the fact that a three-volume novel from him came to be worth fifteen hundred pounds. His gifts were ever of the most munificent description; the motto he adopted being, "Do the thing handsomely or let it alone."

One of the earliest uses to which he put a lately-inherited fortune was to establish a "Working-man's Club and Reading-Room" at Northampton, which he started with a present of five hundred pounds; a sum he supplemented with further gifts. Known as the "Melville Institute," after some infantile struggles it is now in a highly satisfactory condition, and is in every way worthy of its generous founder and benefactor. Not being in a position for some years after settling in Northamptonshire to ride horses of any great value, so long as he had quality all other requisites were a matter of secondary importance to a sportsman who knew that the impecunious had no right to be too particular. To him it mattered not whether his mount was easy or difficult to ride—whether it was good-looking or a bit three-cornered in appearance. So long as it could gallop and jump he ever went upon the old saw that "handsome is that handsome does." To Mr. John Clarke, the well-known fishmonger of Northampton—still to be seen in his seventy-fifth year at every near Meet on the back of a skybald cob—he was indebted for two or three excellent animals of an inexpensive sort, one of them a small, excitable, well-bred bay, being a hunter of unusual merit. A black mare of less pretensions that remained in the neighbourhood after her owner had quitted it, was long looked upon as an object of interest as having once belonged to the author of "General Bounce" and "Digby Grand." Many of his horses were not of the "confidential" sort; and if asked how many animals he was master of this season, a favourite reply with him was, "Not one; but I have four brutes in the stable that are masters of me."

With a fine temper, nice hands, and a sympathy between himself and his horse that rarely has been equalled, he never irritated the animal he was riding by jagging its mouth or knocking it about the head with his "crop," after the manner of some, but would coax it into more seemly behaviour by addressing it in terms on the lines of, "Are you not a horse and a brother?" Jealous with the jealousy of a wholesome ambition, he cared not to go where others had gone before, preferring a line of his own, and on being overtaken one day by a friend he hoped he had just pounded, he said with a beaming smile, "I thought I had you in that corner, old chap, but I see that I have no right to my *risus in angulo.*" Always quick to see the ludicrous side of anything, and full of anecdote, happy the man who had George Melville for his companion on the homeward ride after a day's hunting. It was easy to draw him out on the events of his bachelor-days, their vicissitudes, excitement, and extravagancies; and the usual moral he drew from his own experiences was, "What d—d fools men are." Scenes at Crockford's and other haunts of the gamblesome, card-loving club-man, coloured by his rich fancy, and told in words of the happiest choice, derived an interest which very few besides himself could have imparted to them. From out the great palace of iniquity in St. James's Street he had himself on more than one occasion retired a poorer if not a wiser man, a fellow-countryman and brother-sportsman having forwarded him sums to extricate him from difficulties that at the time seemed absolutely overwhelming. With him by your side, though it might be that

> "The way was long, the wind, too, cold,
> Your hunter both infirm and old,"

but you little recked of the gloom of a November afternoon, or of the "peck" of your wearied horse. "Another of those and down you come," was the usual encouraging comment on a step that had brought the heart into your mouth; and this would be followed by some amusing moralizing on the ups and downs of life. No one, however, met these with greater philosophy than himself; and on two of the most trying disasters that can happen to a hunting-man—one when his horse died in the field—and on another when a favourite mare was seriously injured by wire—he displayed a resignation to the inevitable which Socrates himself might have envied.

In his eyes the greatest evil in life, next to a failure of health, was Wire; and the greatest miscreant, the man who put it up. The spirited Ode he called "Ware Wire; a Protest," was breathed out from the very depths of his heart; and when he wrote the lines:—

> "And bitter the curses you launch in your ire,
> At the villain who fenced his enclosure with wire."

he gave utterance to emotions that nothing else could have aroused in his kindly nature. Whilst penning these lines, his feelings probably were of much the same sort as those of the woman, who, having brought a neighbour before the magistrates on a charge of assault, on failing in her case, addressed her enemy thus: "I'm a Christian woman and so bear no malice; I don't wish you no harm of any sort; but if any one was to tell me that you had got a wasp's nest inside your breeches, I should be very glad to hear it." A more suitable punishment for the merciless user of the wire-fence in a hunting country could scarcely be devised.

By no means given to the evil habit of punning, the opportunity of saying a smart thing was seldom thrown away. Hearing an artist-friend complain of his liver being out of order, he remarked, "Liver, my good fellow! Why I thought you painters never thought of anything but lights." And to a friend who on a hot dusty day had replied to his genial greeting of "How are you, old boy?" with "Oh, pretty tidy, thank you;" he laughingly said, "I'm glad you feel it, you don't look it." Unable to repress a little mild sarcasm, the writer will not easily forget the amused smile that lit up his face when, on being introduced one day as the author of "Holmby House" to Miss Strickland, the historian, she addressed him with the somewhat startling inquiry, "Did your publisher find that the work paid him?" "Alas, madam, he dates the commencement of his ruin from the hour that he undertook my unfortunate novel," was the prompt response to the unexpected query. The compiler of facts, incompetent to interpret the twinkle in the eye of the writer of fiction, accepted the statement with a conventional expression of regret, little thinking that not one of her own works had met with so many

readers as the novel, the very title of which she herself
was ignorant of up to that moment. To have heard
from the learned authoress of the " Queens of England "
that she knew nothing of a book bearing the title of
"Tilbury Nogo" would not have surprised any one; but
that the fame of "Holmby House" should not have
reached her ears argued on her part but little knowledge of what was going on in the world of light literature. The first-mentioned work—his earliest venture—at
once gained for Whyte Melville a foothold on the plat-
form of sporting novelists; but the reading public was
scarcely prepared for the advance to be met with in the
pages of "Holmby House"—a work that has taken its
place with the most popular historical romances in the
language. "Digby Grand" and "General Bounce"
confirmed the impression that in Whyte Melville, a
writer of no ordinary ability had appeared upon the
literary horizon—a rival, in his power of description and
his treatment of character, to the author of the great
"Jorrocks" himself. While some of his novels fell short
of the reputation he had so rapidly gained, "The Gladi-
ators," "The Interpreter," and "Katerfelto" raised him
to a level attained by very few of the writers of the
day, and caused his publications to be eagerly sought
for. That he was in any way really a rival of the
author of the inimitable "Jorrocks" and "Soapey
Sponge," cannot be asserted by any one conversant with
the styles of the respective authors. The one indulges
in broad farce—non-natural situations—and is always
treading outside the line of things as they are; the
other deals only with human nature in its more refined
phase—portrays character in its garment of every-day

wear—and never ventures upon caricature. As one could not have written " Good-bye," "The Place where the old Horse died," or the " Clipper that stands in the stall at the top," so the other could not have created " Jorrocks," a favourite equally with Mr. Pickwick himself in the affections of the hunting world. The " Handley Hunt " series will still be in demand when the " New Zealander " is contemplating the ruins of St. Paul's from London Bridge; but should the worthy Islander ask for a copy of " Market Harborough " he will probably be told that the name of such a book is quite unknown. Emanations of intellect, however telling at the time of their birth, should they be deficient in certain attributes, especially those of dramatic presentation, will needs be crowded out of immortality. It was an ill wind for the little Northamptonshire village that blew wealth into the lap of its most distinguished and popular resident. The little white hunting-box, upon the face of which is now engraved in deeply-cut letters " Melville House," became all too small for an increased power of expenditure; and a change was made to Wootton Hall.

After hunting for two or three seasons from here, Whyte Melville, to the sorrow of many a friend and neighbour, broke the link that had so long and so happily connected him with the " P.H." and took up his abode in London, from whence he got his two or three days a week with Mr. Selby Lowndes and the " Baron;" his chief friend and companion in his journeys to the Meet being the much lamented Hon. Robert Grimston. Upon the marriage of his daughter—his only child—Major Whyte Melville again moved into the country, and settled in the neighbourhood of Tetbury, in Gloucestershire. Here it was that while riding slowly along between cover and cover, a rabbit-hole caused thousands of the inhabitants of Great Britain, gentle and simple, to learn with sorrow and dismay that the popular and accomplished author of so many bewitching tales and poems had met his end in the hunting-field.

Not a hunting-man or woman in the United Kingdom was there, who was not more or less affected by the sad intelligence, and who did not look upon the death of Whyte Melville as a personal misfortune. It was universally felt that Society had suffered a loss which it was impossible to replace; such qualities as those which marked the individuality of the author of the " Queen's Maries," "The True Cross," and "The Galloping Squire," being rarely found in combination.

That "Good-bye" should have been written only shortly before the fatal event, almost apparently in anticipation of it, is an incident equally affecting and remarkable, and would seem to point to the fact that its author was in unconscious possession of his countrymen's uncanny attribute of "second sight."

Few authors whose names are attached to so much in Verse as well as in Prose can have the satisfaction of feeling that every book they have written has had for its aim some high moral object—fewer still, that not a line they have penned could offend the most fastidious.

Such, however, can be said of him of whom we are now speaking—one in whom power of description—quick appreciation of character—tenderness of feeling—the instincts of a true gentleman—humour and high moral tone, formed an amalgam that has been vouchsafed to few.

Of striking appearance, slight of frame and of gentle mien; with an eye that you felt gauged you at a glance, and a smile that at once restored your *amour-propre*, there was that in the countenance of Whyte Melville which denoted that his life was not without its "*aliquid amari*," and accounted for the tone of sadness that pervaded many of his writings.

Anxious to see something of the pomp and circumstances of war, Whyte Melville took service with the Turkish army during the Crimean expedition, and then it was that he laid the foundation for one of the most interesting of all his novels, "The Interpreter." Far more brilliant as a conversationalist than George Payne, quicker in reply, and of a more cultivated mind, he possessed many of his attractive qualities; and it would be hard to say which of the two was the most popular and admired member of Society—which the most lamented when death had removed him from it.

THE HON. H. LIDDELL (Lord Ravensworth).

THE tiny villa-like cottage at Boughton did not long remain unoccupied. A sportsman, embracing in his love of sport an area exceeding that of the author of "The Galloping Squire" himself—inasmuch as it included the pursuit of the "rat" in the old barn opposite, and the jack snipe on the banks of the Nene—now took up his residence in the little white-faced house of literary notoriety.

In the Hon. Henry Liddell—now Earl of Ravensworth—the love of outdoor life and of all things pertaining thereto, burned with a flame that has probably never waxed warmer in the breast of any man, though it was very clear that fox-hunting held the first place in his heart.

Not laying himself out for playing the part of Don Magnifico in anything, no man who hunted with the "Pytchley" or the "Grafton" Hunt saw more sport with a limited stud of no great pecuniary value.

Impatient of being anywhere except in the front rank, the horse that did not look, perhaps, as if he could "go and gallop and jump" with some that were to be seen at the cover-side, was usually to be found there or thereabouts when hounds were skimming over the big Faxton pastures, or the valley between Cottesbrooke and Lamport. Some may still remember the gallant but peppery little black mare, who carried her rider so well to the fore, and who was full up to the hilt of "notices to quit" in case any one approached Her Highness a little too nearly. Even on her road home after a hard day, she would give the unwary fully to understand that she brooked no familiarity, and that she always had a heel wherewith to mark her feelings on this subject. Fully recognizing the fact that amusement and self-indulgence are not the only objects for which we have been sent into "this wale of tears," the subject of this notice never allowed his love for the chase to interfere with his parliamentary duties. Sitting for many years as one of the representatives of his native county—Durham—the House of Commons had no more painstaking member; and his opinion upon any matter connected with the

Navy was looked upon by those connected with the
service, as of especial value. Family arrangements having
obliged him to quit his Northamptonshire home for one
in Hampshire, Mr. Liddell got his hunting for a few
seasons in the neighbourhood of Lyndhurst.

Although missing the big grass field and the flying
fences of the country he had quitted, there is a charm
about the New Forest which no other district can boast
—one too, which few were so well able to appreciate and
enjoy as this late member of the "P.H." On being
called to the Upper House, Lord Ravensworth retired to
his noble seat in the county of Durham, and now obtains
his hunting in a region about as opposite to those in
which he was wont to follow hounds in his earlier days,
as the parts about Sywell Wood differ from those in the
neighbourhood of Misterton or Crick.

THE REV. HENRY ROKEBY.

At the door of the picturesque old Manor House of
Arthingworth, dispensing hospitality to a bevy of horsemen on their way from Sunderland Wood to Kelmarsh,
stands the Lord of the Manor—the representative of
the ancient House of Rokeby. Combining in his own
person a double function, Mr. Rokeby occupies the
hybrid position so well known in country social life as
"Squarson," a compound of squire and of parson, smacking partly of the world, partly of the Church, and entail-
ing duties secular as well as clerical. To blend these so
discreetly as not to allow one in any way to interfere
with the other, has been the constant and successful

endeavour of one whose parishioners honour him alike for his admirable performance of either duty.

Suffering no parochial call to remain unheeded, this worthy chief of a country village is not blind to the fact that there is a world outside the limits of his own microcosm, wherein are to be found occupations and amusements which serve to relieve the monotony of the life of a rural rector. Born and bred in the creamy part of the finest hunting-country in England; nourished by the breezes that have scudded over Loatland and Sunderland Woods, Langborough and Waterloo Gorse, it is impossible that the subject of this memoir should not have been affected by their influence. To breathe such an atmosphere is to imbibe a love for the chase; and the squirearchical element in this case not having been lost in the clerical one, Mr. Rokeby has failed to perceive that when made subservient to duty, hunting is to be eliminated from the pleasures of parsonic life. Not claiming to be an hereditary sportsman, Mr. Rokeby is not indebted to any of his immediate predecessors for his love of horse and hound. One of these a gallant Colonel, the most popular but non-sport-loving of men, used to consider it his duty when the hounds met at Arthingworth to appear "outside a horse" to see the find. Being congratulated by a friend on one of these rare occasions on the hunter-like appearance of his steed, he remarked, "Oh, yes, he's a good-looking beast enough, but he has one fault about him that does not suit me at all." "What may that be, if I may venture to inquire?" asked the admirer of the unconscious animal. "Why he wants to jump, and I don't," was the honest and amusing answer of the gallant officer of Fencibles.

At the present time the occupant of the stall where once stood the unappreciated "Lepper" of Colonel Rokeby, has no reason to complain of not having his or her jumping proclivities put to their full test. If the good-looking black mare, whose pleasant duty it is to carry the "Squarson's" daughter as near the hounds as may be, fails in doing so, the fault will not lie with her fair burden; and the rail must be strong and high, and the bullfinch thick and thorny, that leaves her parent hesitating on the "take-off side."

A clear head for figures and an assiduous attention to his magisterial work have imposed upon Mr. Rokeby the difficult task of overlooking the county-accounts, and vouching for the accuracy of each county-rate—a duty that can only be satisfactorily performed by a thorough man of business.

A perfect acquaintance with the ways and feelings of his parishioners leads him to humour instead of running counter to their prejudices; nor by any unnecessary display of zeal will he subject himself to the reproach incurred by a brother-cleric, who had good reason to feel the impossibility of pleasing everybody. Solicited by one of the tenant-farmers of his parish to "pray for rain" during a period of drought, such a superabundance of the desired element followed that the occupant of the light-land farm at whose instance the petition was offered up, began to be looked upon as a public nuisance by the cultivators of the cold clays. Upon being remonstrated with as the author of all the mischief then going on, he remarked, "Well, I didn't want so much, but it's just like our parson, he always overdoes everything so." Nor is the Rector of Arthingworth himself, not unacquainted with the habits of stock, likely to make the mistake of a less well-informed clergyman, who, preaching upon the parable of the Prodigal Son, assured his hearers "that in the fulness of his joy the father killed the fatted calf that had been a favourite in the family for many years"!

Long may this model holder of a bi-fold office get his bi-weekly gallop with Quorn and Pytchley! May many a year pass away ere fresh experiences lead the inhabitants of Arthingworth to say, "Things aren't as they were in the good old Rector's time, when he or some of the family would come in and see that our fires weren't out for want of a bit o' coal, and that there was a bit o' summut in the cupboard for our supper."

MR. W. H. FOSTER.

In the adjoining parish of Spratton there lives, at Spratton Grange, Mr. W. H. Foster, late M.P. for Bridgenorth—a borough now sharing the fate of "old Sarum," but at one time so decided in its political bias as to have given rise to the saying, "All on one side, like the Bridgenorth election." The village is fortunate enough to have secured a "Squire," to whom the duties of his position are the paramount consideration, and after them the indulgence of his ruling passion—"fox-hunting."

It is easy to say that any one could ride such horses as those upon which Mr. Foster is seen, but if the heart be not in the right place the animal availeth little. Nor are his horses always of the most "confidential" sort. Many a "youngster" has to find out that there is "a man on his back" before he will attempt the still post and rail

in front of him; but finding that he is bound to go he is
pretty sure to land his rider among the favoured few who
have seen the brilliant thirty minutes. Those who really
stick to hounds when they run hard for any length of
time may usually be numbered on the fingers of one hand,
leaving out the little one, and perhaps the thumb also.
By the man who "means going" a back seat on these
occasions, however accidentally obtained, is a matter of
humiliation and probably of self-reproach also. A great
author tells us that "there is nothing impossible to conceal except love and a cough;" but the unfortunate above
referred to, in his desire to hide himself from second
horsemen and the joggers behind, will soon realize the
impossibility of concealment. Little dreamt of by the
utterer of the above apophthegm, though he feels disposed
to call upon the trees to fall upon him, and the mole-hills
to rise up and cover him, he will know for a surety that
until the moment of the much-desired check, he will be
exposed to the sneers of the grooms, and be set down by
the stranger as one of the "muffs" of the Pytchley Hunt.
To such an experience the owner of Spratton Grange
neither has been or is likely to be subject; and as there
is nothing that becomes a Master of hounds more than
brilliancy of performances across a country, it is much to
be hoped that in the event of the Pytchley country again
becoming vacant, its management will fall into the hands
of the subject of this brief and imperfect notice. (1886.)

MR. AND MRS. SIMSON.

From Broom Hill, nearly adjoining the Grange, on
three days if not four in each week of the hunting-

season, may be seen starting for the cover-side Mr. and Mrs. Simson—a husband and wife quite of one mind as to the pleasure to be derived from the chase, and fully bent upon seeing the end as well as the beginning of a day with hounds. Of a sportsman, to whom the excitement of fox-hunting must be as nothing compared with his experiences among the "big game" of India, it may truthfully be affirmed that the tiger of Bengal has had few more constant and determined enemies than the proprietor of the hunting-box so situate on Spratton Hill as to be under the influence of "'a' the airts the wind can blaw," and more to boot.

Deeply versed in the habits and peculiarities of the wild animals of the country in which he has passed so many years of his life, Mr. Simson has at this time on its way through the press a work which is likely to become the standard authority on the natural history of that part of India in which he has pursued his studies. Nor does he take less delight in finding out the ways of the winged and creeping creatures of his native land. An ornithologist of no ordinary acquirements, by him every bird he sees is recognizable by its flight, note, or plumage; and with its mode of nesting and general habits he is little less familiar than the accomplished Northamptonshire Nobleman, whose beautiful work on British Birds is now in course of publication.

With these tastes, and with a keen enjoyment of the ridiculous, to no one could the small boy's reply as to the peculiarities of the cuckoo have been more fittingly made. When asked in what respect this bird differed in its habits from others, he answered that "it was the only one that didn't lay its own eggs"—a display of ornithological knowledge about equal to that of the old woman, who, to confirm her assertion of having been present in church, declared to her clergyman that he *must* have seen her, as "she had sot right agin the turkey"—meaning, of course, the eagle forming the lectern.

An ardent and devoted floriculturist, the fair lady—who shares her husband's passion for hound and fox, and the pursuit of the latter by the former—yields to no one in the successful management of the garden. Choosing the rose and the carnation as the principal objects for culture, she is no less alive to the charms of every flower that can impart brightness to her borders. The frost may be long, the winter may be such as the never-to-be-forgotten one of 1886, but the spirit of *ennui* will fail to find an entrance into a household, where, like that of Broom Hill, the teachings of Mr. Jorrocks do not constitute the only philosophy deemed worthy of consideration.

CAPTAIN GIST[1]—MR. PENDER—MR. JAMESON.

In the stables of the house known as Spratton Hall—so long occupied by Captain Mildmay Clerk, spoken of elsewhere—Captain T. Gist can show three or four weight-carrying horses that would do credit to any stud where power is the one thing needful, and "place"—in a run—an object of some consideration.

Not far distant on the crest of the same hill, at

---

[1] Since the above was written, this gentleman, like the author, is numbered with the dead.—ED.

Thornby and Cold Ashby respectively, Messrs. Pender and Jameson have established homes for "P.H." purposes; and though comparisons are said to be odious, few will be found to deny that in point of "hardness," amongst his fellows the latter gentleman is beyond compare.

With a stud in no way fit to compete with many of those around him, the animal that Mr. Jameson has made his own is bound to go where even "good men" hesitate to try, and the "funker" feels that there must be an easier place elsewhere.

MR. HAZELHURST.

If there can be one greater certainty upon earth than another, it is that one if not more foxes will be "at home" in the Misterton osier-bed any day between November and April that the Pytchley hounds please to enter it. For this great blessing, all who from time to time meet Mr. Langham and his hounds at Misterton are indebted to Mr. Hazelhurst of the Hall. It is to his unceasing care, and determination to have foxes about his place, that the osiers have never been known to be drawn blank; and it is to be hoped that this fact is recognized with proportionate gratitude both by the Master and the Members of the Hunt. To have an indifferent or perhaps hostile resident at Misterton Hall would mean a loss to the "P.H." of its most important and popular district, and at once lower it to the level of a third-rate power. All honour then to him who saves it from such a fate.

MR. DANIEL.

To speak of Misterton and omit the name of "Daniel," would be equivalent to leaving out from a play one of its most conspicuous characters.

"Misterton" and "Daniel" run so much in couples in the thoughts of Pytchley-men, that to separate the two seems an impossibility, and it will be a bad day for hunting whenever the dissociation takes place. A yeoman of the good old school—from his youth a hunting-man—to few of the tenant-farmers of the district is the "P.H." more indebted for a constant and unswerving support.

"Daniel's Spinney" is a name little less familiar in the ear of the Wednesday follower of Will Goodall and his pack, than that of Misterton Gorse or Shawell Wood; and many is the gallant fox that has been found within its shelter.

With a keen eye for make and shape, and with much experience, there are not many better judges of a hunter than Mr. Daniel, and very few men better able to ride one.

MR. P. A. MUNTZ.

IN the same neighbourhood is to be found one of those stout-hearted sportsmen, to whom a superabundant vitality seems to be no detriment in the matter of getting across a country, and upon whom "pace and plough" seem to lose their hindering properties. Mounted upon cattle of great value, but in whom power is often more apparent than pedigree—horses of a different stamp from those ridden by those famous men of weight,

Messrs. Stirling Crawfurd and Little Gilmour—Mr. Muntz seems to form the exception to the rule that like pace "weight must tell." Be it in a point-to-point steeple-chase, or in a gallop from Lilbourne Gorse to Hemplow Hills, the broad shoulders of the honourable M.P. for South Warwickshire are sure to be seen well in front, thereby confirming the belief of many, that it is "the man that carries the horse, and not the horse the man."

Tom Assheton Smith was firm in his belief that where the heart was, there would horse and his rider be gathered together, the sympathy between the two being of so intimate a nature, that if the one "did not quite like it," the other was sure to be afraid. With all the disadvantages attendant upon the possession of a "too, too solid flesh," the man who has Mr. Muntz behind him in a run of note may go home pluming himself upon his own performance as well as on that of his horse. "The race is not always for the swift nor the battle for the strong," but the chase invariably preserves her plums for the stout-hearted.

LORD BRAYE.

There are more disagreeable ways of spending twelve or fifteen minutes any time between November and April, than in a gallop across the big grass-fields between Hemplow and Stanford Hall. Time was when hares so swarmed over this particular district that hounds were rarely able to cross it without several "hesitations," if not something worse. Happily, poor puss has had a bad time of late; and if only scent permit, so uninterrupted a "head" may now be carried between the respective points, that it takes a good man, and a good horse also, to keep well with the pack when once settled to its work.

On the long list of its fixtures the "P.H." has none more popular than that of Stanford Hall, the home since the days of Henry VIII. of the ancient family of Otway-Cave, now Barons Braye. In point of position, picturesqueness, and sporting-surroundings, this may well have earned the title of the "Pearl of the Pytchley Meets;" and he who has hunted from Stanford without sport feels as it were as if he had suffered a measure of wrong and robbery. From time immemorial have the owners of this favoured property been followers of the chase, the name of Otway-Cave being among the more prominent of the early members of the "P.H." The gallant officer—elder brother of the present noble owner of the Stanford Hall estate—who lost his life at the battle of Ulundi, fighting against the hosts of King Cetewayo, was famous for his bold and fearless riding; and his successor—though by no means a feather-weight—has no idea of being left behind if, like his neighbour, "pace and plough" do not put their veto upon his carrying out his intentions.

THE REV. J. TYRWHITT DRAKE.[1]

WITHIN a very circumscribed area of the surface of fair Northamptonshire there reside, for hunting's sake, eight

---

[1] This respected gentleman has, like several others mentioned in the work, departed this life since the Memoir was written.—ED.

worshippers of Nimrod, so devoted to their "cult," that if the assertion of a reverend Fortnightly Reviewer be founded on fact, any one of them would be prepared to pull down any cottage of his own, if in any way it could, did, or had interfered with the run of a fox. How it is likely that hereditaments of this nature—motionless, non-alarming—should work so serious a mischief, the essayist does not trouble himself to inquire; but with his pen in his hand and his hobby well by the head, a reviewer and *censor morum* is apt to ride at places where there is no taking off.

Amongst the devotees above referred to, not the least well-known is the rev. the Rector of Cottesbrooke, a village unequalled for its sporting associations, recollections, and situation; and also remarkable for the fact that the thirsty soul will hunt in vain for a public-house, be his sufferings ever so great.

An old proverb tells us—a proverb as defined by Earl Russell is the wit of one man and the experience of many —that "what is born in the bones is sure to come out in the flesh;" and in no family has the truth of this dictum been more exemplified than in that of the Rev. John Tyrwhitt Drake, Rector of Cottesbrooke near Northampton. Who that can remember "old Squire Drake," so long master of the Bicester hounds, and that great huntress, the Hon. Mrs. Drake, aunt to the present Lord Valentia, is surprised to know that no family in England could turn out four such sons to cross a country as their four? The same kind offices performed by a wolf for Romulus and Remus must have been undertaken by a fox for those rev. brothers, John and Edward Drake. What Graces, Lytteltons, and Studds have been between the wickets, the Drakes once were across the Midland fences and grasses; and if the Rector of Cottesbrooke may at no time have touched the same point of excellence as his rev. brother, the Rector of Amersham, few have better known how to persuade an ill-tempered one to try his best; or when and where to negotiate an uncomfortable-looking place.

Sent to Harrow in the heyday of boyhood, the near neighbourhood of the famous Tilbury, the dealer, and of his accomplished henchman, Jem Mason, the celebrated steeple-chase rider, it is not to be wondered at that the lessons taught at Pinner were more attractive than those inculcated in the Homer-haunted little village on the Hill. The question with the horsey spirits of the school, during the somewhat easy-going epoch of Dr. Longley, was not so much " to read or not to read " as " to ride or not to ride." The grand difficulty was " where to find a horse." Happily for those who boarded at the Rev. W. Oxenham's—afterwards second master, and most boy-bullied and forgiving of men—in one of the two stalls in the stable-yard stood a good-looking brown mare, who could both gallop and jump. Her Irish groom, Pat Barratt, was fond of his charge, and did well by her; but he was fonder still of a half-crown and the charms of the public-house. No palm was more easily greased than that unfaithful Irishman's, and William Oxenden Hammond, " Jemmy " Ingram, Tom and John Drake, and a few more—alas! that the name of " Bob " Grimston cannot now be here included—still survive to say how often they " passed his hand with a silver coin," and in exchange got a gallop out of that bonny brown mare. The only condition imposed by that most crafty of grooms

was that the ride should be an early one, so that no
suspicion might enter the breast of his unwary master.
"If you're waking call me early, call me early, Patrick,
dear," were the overnight instructions on one side; and
about four on many a fine spring and summer morning,
the pulling of a string attached to a sleeper's toe announced
the fact that the "hour and the man"—a horse—had
come. Then followed the rapture of the ride, probably
to Tilbury's farm, possibly elsewhere; but the bit of
timber by the road-side or the fence with all its leaves
was not omitted from the programme, and all was happiness unalloyed until a distant bell or a tell-tale watch,
pointed to the homeward road. I fancy if those who
have just been referred to chance to see these lines, will
they ask themselves, whether among their many happy
Harrovian days, they ever had such hours as those spent
upon the back of "Billy" Oxenham's mare?

The parents of the future Rector of Cottesbrooke did
not give Harrow the credit of being able to convert their
son into a depositary of classical lore, nor were they
disappointed. Though compelled to "enter" for the
quarterly examinations, "J. T. Drake junior" never went
into training for any of these events, with the common
result of not being able to live the course. Usually one
of the first in difficulties, on rising Euclid Hill he mostly
ceased to struggle, and rarely passed Judge Longley's
chair. Not finding that any of the Harrow "courses"
exactly suited his style of action, he changed his quarters
for Oxford, where he hoped that by a new system of
training he might win his way into the family Living of
Malpas, in Cheshire. Having successfully matriculated
at Brazen Nose, it seemed now as if the ex-Harrovian

might consider his path safe and easy, and that he might contemplate with some feeling of certainty the fruition of the good things looming in the future. But B.N.C. had its Phœnix Club; and in addition to lecture-rooms, literary societies, and debating clubs, Oxford at that time had its tandem-drivings, its professors of billiards, its hunting-stables. Between these J. T. D. seemed to get a little "mixed," and to have shared the view of the "coster," who when before the "beak" for an infraction of the liquor-law, thus philosophized over the matter. "The fact is, sir," said he, "there's such a lot of wisdom in the world now, that there don't seem no room for nothink else."

Newman, Gaisford, the Master of Balliol, Hawkins, were names to conjure with at Oxford, at that epoch; and so were those others—Quartermaine, Seckham, Symonds, Wheeler.

A Pindaric or Anacreontic ode were "nuts" to many a classic-minded wearer of cap and gown; but there were those also who saw more beauties in that old hippic song, in which the Oxford vendor of horses hopes to tempt the possible purchaser of an awful screw by affirming that—

> "If the Pope of Rome to England came
> To get an hoss to ride on,
> This bit o' blood's the werry quad
> I'd set his grace astride on."

Jealous of the progress made by their pupil in the unorthodox teachings of Messrs. Symonds and Co., the principal and tutors of Brazen Nose College shut their gates upon their too-sporting alumnus, and urged him to seek from the sister-University those honours denied to him at Oxford. Following this good advice, Mr. Drake proceeded to Cambridge forthwith; but the *bacilli* of learning and biblical lore could not have been in the air during his residence on the banks of the Cam. If they were, they did not care to enter either his rooms or his system; and again the vision of the Cheshire rectory seemed to grow more and more indistinct.

Happily, a road hitherto unthought of—a road by following which many a traveller in like condition with himself had found his way within the pale of the Establishment, was now pointed out. Pursuing this, it was not long before the village of Malpas found itself under the spiritual care of the Rev. John Tyrwhitt Drake, M.A. late of Oxford and Cambridge Universities. It is not expected of parishioners to be able to teach their ministers much, if anything; and the inhabitants of this Cheshire village soon discovered that while not at all to be despised in the wood, the new parson had nothing to learn from any one in those parts when once in "the open." By never neglecting the duties incident to a large country-parish, and by being a kind and generous friend to those who needed help, Malpas soon learned to like the new incumbent, who neither puzzled their heads by the too much learning, or aggravated their tempers by the too great length, of his discourses.

Speaking plainly, he never laid himself open to the snub received by one of London's most famous Bishops, who, when a curate, having preached upon the text, "The foolish body hath said in his heart, There is no God," was told by an old labourer afterwards, " Well, sir, you may say what you please, but I believe that there is a God all the same." In point of length too, he never forgot the merit that lies in a good fifteen minutes, nor the rebuke incurred by a brother parson, who, having preached for forty minutes, said to a friend on leaving church, "Having slept all the time, you can't know much of what my sermon was about." "Oh, yes, I do," was the reply, "it was about half an hour too long." It would seem as if the clergy were peculiarly liable to rebuffs—moral humiliations of the nature of those just described. One of London's most popular and distinguished preachers, an Hon. and Rev. gentleman, brother to a Cabinet Minister, on entering upon duties to which he had recently been appointed, made it known to his new parishioners that "he was at their service at any hour by night as well as by day," and that his only desire was that his own convenience should not be a matter for consideration. Summoned out of his bed at a late hour one winter night by an old member of his flock, well known to him as a very regular attendant at church, he was thus addressed: "I've sent for you, sir, as you desired, as for many nights I have been unable to close my eyes, and as I have often had some nice sleeps during your sermons, I thought that if you would be so kind as to read to me a bit, I might go off for an hour or so." This would seem to be a sufficient lowering of any little pulpit or other pride, but it scarcely can have touched the same point of humiliation as when after a peculiarly affecting sermon in a country church, the wife of the preacher, on seeing an old man remaining in his seat long after the congregation had gone, thus addressed the lingerer: "Well, John, I'm glad to see that instead of going out in a hurry with the rest of the congregation, you like to stop and think over the beautiful words you have heard in the sermon." "Yes, mum, they was beautiful; but it isn't exactly that, neither," was the reply; "the real matter is that I've bust my braces, and I'se sitting here to prevent my small-clothes coming down."

An incumbency in Lord Yarborough's country followed upon that which had bound Mr. Drake to Cheshire for some years, and then came the offer on the part of his brother-in-law, Mr. Herbert Langham, of the Living of Cottesbrooke. Here, naturally as it were, he fell into the office of Chaplain-General of the Pytchley forces, and has performed for many years the duties attached to that responsible position to the satisfaction of all concerned. For two or three seasons the worthy rector and Mrs. Drake—keen as his reverence in the pursuit of bold reynard—have been compelled to seek elsewhere that measure of health not to be found in Cottesbrooke's foggy vale; and it is to be feared that to the former, at all events, the pleasures of the saddle can only be looked upon amongst the enjoyments of life that have passed away.

LORD ERSKINE—MR. C. WROUGHTON—MR. F. AND MISS LANGHAM.

ALMOST within whisper's reach of the Rector of Cottesbrooke's boundary-fence is the hunting-abode of Lord Erskine, an acquisition to the "P.H." which it may well hope not to lose for many a year to come.

Hard by, in the little village of Creaton, may be found the fine and costly hunting-stud of Mr. C. Wroughton;

whilst Mr. F. Langham and Miss Langham, brother and sister to the Master,—devotees to all things pertaining to rural life, but more especially to hunting—have their home on the crest of the hill, masters of every tint of the setting sun, but slaves to each rough breath of the rude west wind.

It is not yesterday that Mr. F. Langham formed a conspicuous member of the "Eton Eleven," and helped to fight the annual battle against the hereditary enemy from Harrow on the Hill; but as he still takes a good deal of catching when hounds run; so with the cue and the tennis-bat there are few in his neighbourhood with whom he cannot successfully compete, without giving or receiving weight for age.

SIR RAINALD KNIGHTLEY.

To Sir Rainald Knightley, M.P. for the Southern division of the county, is to be assigned by virtue of a three months' priority of birth over Sir Charles Isham, of Lamport Hall, and Mr. Nethercote of Moulton Grange, the honour of being—in 1886—the senior member of the Pytchley Hunt.

All three are within easy, too easy, distance of the border-line which divides the sixties from the seventies, that doubtful decade of strength or infirmity preceding the record of four-score years, after which life is apt to become a *via dolorosa*, trodden with more or less painful and halting steps. Not that a man fourteen years on the right side of eighty has much reason to rejoice if that be true which was said in the hearing of the narrator of this story by a too close observer of statistics, to a fellow-sportsman who had just divulged that on that day he had reached his sixty-sixth birthday. "Sir," said the Jobean comforter, "I congratulate you, but I must tell you that sixty-six is a very ticklish age." He then pondered as if reckoning up tables, and continued: "It is a fact that there are more people die at sixty-six than at any other time of life." The haste with which the recipient of this encouraging and cheerful piece of intelligence made off may easily be imagined. His emotions on the occasion must have been much on a par with those of an old man in Northampton Street, who after placing his ear-trumpet so that he might hear a friend's remark, was told, "You are breaking very fast, John." Each of these speeches might serve to illustrate one of Mr. Punch's inimitable pictures of "things that a man had rather not have said."

A fifty years' experience in the hunting-field cannot fail to tame down that keenness for the sport which to many a young sportsman makes a high-day and holiday of every hunting-day. In his sixty-seventh year, Sir Rainald cannot be expected to evince the same enthusiasm in hunting as he did when it took a very good man to catch him or Mr. Frederick Villiers, in a sharp forty minutes from Braunston Gorse or Dodford Holt. He is still, however, to be seen at any Meet within reasonable distance of home; and from the class of horse he continues to possess, it is clear that he adheres to his old principle, that "no one should ride a brute but a beggar or a fool."

The stranger, whether attracted by a Meet of hounds or in search of the picturesque, who sees Fawsley for the first time, cannot but be impressed by the feeling that he is in the presence of one of the old historic mansions of England. Situated on a lawn of gentle elevation, it commands an extensive and beautiful prospect, and is surrounded by a park, which, inclusive of the well-known Badby Wood, extends over an area exceeding six hundred acres. For upwards of five centuries, Fawsley has belonged to the Knightleys: one Richard Knightley— the descendant of an old Staffordshire family deriving its name from the Manor of Knightley in that county— having purchased it in 1416.

During the great Civil War the owner of this fine property was a warm adherent of the Commonwealth; and, having married a daughter of Hampden, he became doubly bound to the party of the Protector. It was here that most of the measures were devised which chiefly affected the Royal prerogative, such, for instance, as depriving the Crown of the right of making peace or war—of the control of the militia—and of the disposal of places of trust and profit.

The old saying so constantly in use, of "sub rosâ"— "under the rose"—when there is a necessity for secrecy —is said to have derived its origin from the councils which were held here in the embrasure of an Oriel window, in one of the panes of which a Tudor rose was a conspicuous ornament. The Sir Richard Knightley who took so prominent a part in the politics of this disturbed period, did not in any way sanction the execution of Charles I.; and in 1660 was one of the Council of State who advocated the restoration of Charles II.

The old mansion having got into a somewhat dilapidated condition, was restored by the present Baronet in 1865 at a great cost, under the superintendence of Mr. Salvin, one of the most esteemed architects of the day. The magnificent Gothic Hall, as designed by him, is fifty-four feet long, forty-three feet high, and twenty-four feet in width. At the south end of it may be seen the family achievement, numbering no fewer than 343 quarterings.

No name—always excepting that of Spencer, which appears at least five times as Masters of the " P.H."—is more closely associated with the past days of the Pytchley, than that borne by the Lord of Fawsley. Sir Charles Knightley, spoken of elsewhere in these pages, was for many years the oldest member of the hunt, and was greatly distinguished for his fine riding and keen love for fox-hunting, and for a brief time was himself Master of the Hounds. Under his care Badby Wood became a stronghold for foxes; and without it and the adjoining covers, the Pytchley Saturdays would lose the better part of their attractions. Had Sir Rainald attained the same excellence in the saddle that he has done at the whist-table—for it would be an easy task to count those who would be considered his superiors at whist— there would have been very few able to beat him across a country in his younger days. Thirty years of parliamentary life—a period upon which, when he looks back, he may have the satisfaction of feeling that he has been throughout, like his father before him, a consistent Tory of the old school—have well entitled him to the respect of all. It is to be hoped that many a winter may come and go before he ceases altogether to appear at the cover-side, and relinquish a sport in which both he and his father have taken so conspicuous a part.

MR. DRURY WAKE.

THE eye scanning the constituents of a Pytchley field at the time of which we have been speaking, might have observed, mounted on a small brown horse, strong as a lion and active as a cat, a gentleman, who, recognized at that period by his college-intimates as "Whack" of Christ Church, is now more generally known as Mr. Drury Wake, of Pitsford House, near Northampton.

The third son of Sir Charles Wake of Courteen Hall, he was sent at the usual age to Rugby School, where, under his uncle, Dr. Tait—afterwards Archbishop of Canterbury—he in no way failed to make the most of such pleasures as are to be met with in public-school life; and suffered nothing in point of health by a too unremitting attention to classical and mathematical studies. Giving him credit for the possession of abilities, which under the forcing influences of perseverance and hard work might produce fruit of no ordinary character, Oxford was called upon by his relatives to bring about those results which Rugby had so signally failed in effecting. It was hoped that in the bosom of Alma Mater, and under the watchful eye of a college tutor, the spirit of application and a thirst for the acquisition of classical knowledge might take the place of an apparent indifference to the teachings of the philosophers of old. But parents are born to disappointment so surely as the sparks fly upwards, and to the old Rugbyan the system of "Figg-Tollitt" and Charles Symonds had more attraction than the less voluntary instruction to be had within the walls of a college. Under the new influences the hereditary love of horse and hound seemed to intensify rather than diminish; and it was not long before the whole University rang with the echoes of an equestrian feat to which there had hitherto been no parallel in its sporting annals. A member of Exeter College, having earned for himself a great deal of credit by riding to London and back in eight hours, it seemed to Mr. Wake as if "the cry" made over the performance was out of all proportion to "the wool" of which it was composed. The matter having come under discussion one evening at a wine-party, he offered to take two hundred pounds to fifty that he would ride the same distance in two hours less time. The bet being immediately snapped up, Tollitt—provider of horses—was invited to supply the necessary amount of hacks, for which he was to receive fifty pounds if the wager was won, nothing if it was lost. Without any sort of training, on a fine spring morning, the "hardy horseman" found himself in full career on his way to the Marble Arch, from which point the return journey was to commence. All things having gone favourably, and the various hacks, each and all, having done their work satisfactorily, Mr. Wake found himself back in Oxford with an hour to spare, the distance having been accomplished in a little over five hours, without any ill effect to horses or rider. As has been elsewhere recorded, Mr. Osbaldeston, in his famous ride at Newmarket, completed two hundred miles in eight hours and thirty nine minutes; but inasmuch as this took place on the springy, elastic turf of the Heath, with nearly thirty horses of the highest class, all ready to the moment, and Mr. Wake had eleven Oxford hacks—some not at hand when required, a hard turnpike road to gallop on, with a hill four miles in length to descend and to mount—the feat of the Oxonian shows well up when compared with that of the notable "Squire." To ride for five hours successively at the rate of twenty-two miles per hour on a hard macadamized road, argues the possession of remarkable powers of endurance, and of a cuticle something more than "pachydermatous." Greatly appreciated as was this arduous feat by the junior members of his college, the "Authorities" did not seem to see it in the same light; and the sporting member of Christ Church was ordered to retire into the country for twelve months, and so purge himself of the offence of having successfully accomplished a feat, which in the eyes of most Oxonians was a thing to be highly proud of.

This unlooked-for interruption to his studies, being not unlikely to excite the paternal indignation, the "hero of a hundred miles" was forced to bring the matter somewhat gingerly before the domestic Jove. The paternal ire, if aroused at all, seems—probably through the intervention of an ever-watchful allayer of storms—quickly to have subsided; and it was not long before the much-expecting son received the following communication:—

"DEAR DRUE,—You're a fool. Come home."

By those knowing the writer the above might have borne the following interpretation:—

"Am delighted: wish I ever could have done the same!"

In those, the palmy days of the Oxford stable-keepers, twenty hacks might have been seen in Oriel Lane on each hunting-morning, awaiting the completion of their hirers' breakfasts. So completely at that period did hunting seem to be looked on by the undergraduates as

a normal part of the collegiate course, that the
"intelligent foreigner" might have taken it for an item
of the regular curriculum of University education. Few
and far between, however, are the hacks that are now to
be seen pacing up and down outside "Canterbury Gate."
Increased demands upon the time of undergraduates, and
ever-recurring examinations, have proved insuperable
obstacles to enjoying the pleasures of the chase; and
"Ichabod" is written in full type on the stable doors of
many a once prosperous dealer in horses at the old
University town.

After a year's banishment, Mr. Wake returned to Christ
Church to pass his final examination, a feat he performed with as much in hand—and more in head—as
he had on crossing "Folly Bridge," at the close of his
famous ride. His tutor strongly urged him to read for
"honours;" pleading that another pupil of his, with
scarcely so good abilities, had by means of incessant
study and much self-denial greatly distinguished himself in the " Schools." "But what about his health
afterwards?" inquired Mr. Wake; "did he not utterly
break down; and has he not become a confirmed
invalid?" "I fear it was so" was the reply, "but his
case was an exceptional one." "Thank you, sir, but so
might mine be," was the rejoinder. "I have heard of
a Lady's maid who stated that in her opinion, 'Health
after personal appearance is the greatest blessing as is.'
I, sir, am disposed to put health before, not personal
appearance only, but also before classical distinction.
The last is a good dog, but the first is a better; and
therefore I mean to stick to the first." Thus the
interview ended; and the unambitious pupil was satis-

tied by the acquisition of a simple "pass," and the retention of unimpaired health.

With an eye, possibly, to the Judicial Bench, if not to the "Great Seal," Mr. Wake resolved to follow the Law as a profession; but before getting fairly into his wig and gown, a ride, far longer and more arduous than that which had made his name famous in Oxford annals, was looming in the future.

Happening to be at Constantinople on the eve of the Crimean War, Sir Hugh Rose—afterwards Lord Strathnairn—begged him to undertake the responsibility of conveying a despatch of the highest importance to London, and deliver it himself into the hands of the English Foreign Minister. Though very desirous to remain where he was at such an exciting moment, and watch the outcome of events—a time when men's hearts were failing them for fear of a great war, with all its attendant horrors and uncertain issues—Mr. Wake did not hesitate to undertake the momentous duty. It was enough for him to be told by Sir Hugh that there was no one else so well fitted as himself to be entrusted with the important document, and that upon his refusal or acceptance of the charge, hinged issues of the gravest importance. "No more important despatch," added the English Chargé d'Affaires, "ever quitted one country for another." Without any delay, with a tâtar to act as guide, and a led horse to carry provisions, on an April day of the memorable year 1854, the old Christ-Church man commenced his ride across the bleak and dreary Balkans for Belgrade. For seven days and nights—the road often a mere trackway, and the darkness so impenetrable as to render it highly dangerous to go beyond a foot's pace—with no rest obtainable, except such as might be risked in the saddle, or snatched during a change of horses—with no companion save a man of whose language he was almost entirely ignorant, and of whose probity he knew nothing—the rider pursued his lonely way. Happily without accident or misadventure, Mr. Wake arrived at Belgrade, and on proceeding to report himself to the "head swell" was informed that his Highness was in the arms of Morpheus, and that anybody who ventured to disturb him was not unlikely to have a "bad old time." The bearer of the despatch, taking a different view of the position, somewhat irreverently declared the sleepiness of his Excellency to be "all my eye;" and dwelling upon the importance of his mission, vowed that if the Mountain would not come to the Mouse, the Mouse must go to the Mountain, there and then. On receipt of this "protocol," the "Mountain" speedily "put in an appearance," in dressing-gown and slippers; and on learning the urgent state of affairs—Latin being the only medium of communication—immediately took the necessary steps for forwarding Sir Hugh Rose's messenger on his way to London. At the end of the eleventh day after leaving Stamboul, Mr. Wake entered the Foreign Office and delivered the important papers which had been confided to his care into the hands of Lord Clarendon, who was smoking his evening cigar, in his dressing-gown, over the fire. The Minister for Foreign Affairs read Sir Hugh Rose's despatch—urging him to call up the Fleet without any delay—apparently with much astonishment; and then turning to its bearer said, "What was the feeling as to Peace or War at Constantinople, when you left; and what is your own impression on the matter?" "That there will be immediate war, unless urgent measures are taken to prevent it." "Nonsense, young man, nonsense; there will be no war; we have Lord *Stratford de Redcliffe's* most certain assurance of peace; and he has but just left us." So Sir Hugh's despatch was quietly ignored, drowned in rivers of blood, not a drop of which probably would have been shed, had not its advice been totally disregarded. But are not all these things written in the Blue Books of that date?

In return for all the fatigue he had endured—the sleepless nights and intolerable weariness of the days—Mr. Wake received the same recompense as is awarded by my Lord Judge to a body of Jurymen on the completion of their duties: "Gentlemen, there is nothing further for you to do; you are discharged, and the country is obliged to you for your services." Too proud to solicit any more substantial reward for a service—worthy at least of the offer of governmental employment—Mr. Wake entered the Militia of his county, hoping thereby to obtain a commission in the Army. After serving with his regiment at Gibraltar and in Ireland, the " would if he could be " soldier was suddenly called upon by his father to lay aside his sword, and to exercise his brains and his legal knowledge in tripping up a recent Act of Parliament which was threatening a portion of the family-property which lay in and about Epping Forest. Having performed this duty satisfactorily, there was now nothing for it but to hoist the sign of the " Wig and Gown," and to seek for litigants on the look out for the best legal advice. Before, however, he had had time to get fairly fixed in his legal saddle, or to get a share of the briefs that were so surely awaiting him, it became evident that the long and weary ride with Sir Hugh Rose's despatch had found out a weak place in the spinal cord, and the hardy, healthy, untirable horseman, slowly settled down into a confirmed invalid. For five long years it seemed as though the most agile member of an active family was doomed to pass the rest of his days in a recumbent position. Happily the disease began to respond to the skilful and judicious treatment of Dr. Barr of Northampton, and at the end of the fifth year the invalid was occasionally seen at the Meets in a carriage constructed for the purpose. Driving with a courage apparently unaffected by years of confinement, the convalescent was determined, as of yore, not to be left out in the cold; and driving with some disregard for horse, carriage or self, contrived to see as much of the sport as many a mounted man.

After this, health soon came as a reward for patient endurance of a great calamity; and in the sixth year after his first absence, he, who had been so long and so sincerely missed by his hunting-friends, was once more to be seen at the cover-side.

An accident in the hunting-field some four years since, looked for a time as if it would entail a recurrence of the spinal evil. In riding at the Whilton Brook, Mr. Wake's horse swerved, and crossed that of Mr. Nethercote on the very brink of the stream. A collision followed, horses and riders fell into the water, and for a few moments the horsemen were having a bad time among the legs of the struggling and alarmed quadrupeds. Happily, neither of the former was struck; but on emerging from their perilous position, Mr. Wake, in addition to being contused about the head, had one of his ankles badly sprained. A ten-mile ride home in clothes thoroughly soaked did not serve to mend matters; and the fear arose, whether or not the so lately-recovered back might not have sustained fresh injury. Fortunately this did not prove to be the case; but it was six weeks before he was again seen in the hunting-field.

A curious fact attending this incident was that the collision was so sudden and unlooked for, that it was not until Mr. Nethercote had lifted his co-sufferer from beneath the water, that he was aware that it was his own son-in-law who was the cause of the misadventure.

Within a few yards to the left, the Viceroy of Ireland —Lord Spencer—was going through a single-handed aquatic performance, his horse having stopped to look, and then "plumped" ignominiously into the water!

Amongst the Christmas school-boys that go to swell a Pytchley field at that "halcyon" time for English lads, another Drury Wake may now be seen—keen as his father—full of ride for a youngster; and in every respect a "true chip of the old block."

MR. NETHERCOTE.

On the opposite side of the picture of the "Crick" Meet, next to Mr. Arkwright's, may be seen the figure of Mr. Nethercote of Moulton Grange, father of the writer of this volume, and the last surviving member of the old Pytchley Club. Of all those represented by the skilful brush of the painter, with him alone rested the recollections of the palmy days of the "P.H.," when the old

Club had on its list of Members some of the greatest names in the country, and to be one of the Associates of which was in itself a mark of distinction. The pages of the old *Sporting Magazine* have recorded that among the Members of the " P.H." Mr. Nethercote took high rank as a sportsman and as a rider to hounds; and such was his love of hunting that long after he had passed his eightieth year he would drive to every near Meet. Up to the day before his death, he begged to know the details of the day's sport, and faintly expressed his regret that it had not been a better one. So remarkable was this good old Country Squire for the geniality of his nature and his kindness of disposition, that one who lived with him for fifty years can conscientiously affirm that he never heard him speak ill-naturedly, scarcely even depreciatingly, of any one. Any decently clad pedestrian on his way to the county-town on market-day was sure to have the offer of a lift; and an almost imperturbable temper seemed proof against any annoyance save that of the " boozy " carrier on the wrong side of the road, on his homeward way from market.

A son may perhaps be pardoned for the assertion that there never lived a more complete embodiment of kind-heartedness and hospitality than the fine old English gentleman here spoken of; one upon whose death in his eighty-fourth year, the last link connecting the ancient and modern history of the Pytchley Hunt was severed for ever.

MAJOR NEWLAND.

FACING the spectator in the " Crick " picture is the then well-known form of Major Newland, formerly of

H.M.'s 5th Dragoon Guards, but at that time residing at Kingsthorpe, in the house now holding out the sign of the "Prince of Wales." Few men were better known, both in the Oakley and the Pytchley Hunts, than this cavalry-officer of the olden time. A thorough sportsman and true lover of hunting in early life, the Major—a heavy man—forged his way well across country; but latterly he had quite given up riding, and was satisfied to be beholden to the various means and appliances of seeing a run without incurring any obvious risk. He died still a young man, but those who love to recall the days and men of the Charles Payne era do not fail to connect with it the name of Bingham, commonly known as "Joe" Newland.

MR. STIRLING CRAWFURD.

In the extreme left corner of the "Crick" picture, addressing Mr. Gough of North Kilworth House—an old sportsman, and one of the "P.H.'s" staunchest friends and best preservers of foxes—sits Mr. Stirling Crawfurd of Langton Hall. From the days when he first dated his letters "Trinity College, Cambridge," to the hour that he passed away, the possessor of the finest stud of racehorses in the world, no name was more familiar in sporting circles than that of this Scotch gentleman.

Carrying in his mouth at the moment of his nativity that silver article by means of which the battle of life is fought most pleasantly and with the greatest success, Mr. Crawfurd had little opportunity of viewing existence on any other side save its sunny one. Indebted to things under the earth for the means of enjoying those above it, the gifts of "Mater Terra" were poured bounteously into the lap of her favoured son. As the blade of grass by evolutionary action becomes alternately developed into the priceless "shorthorn," so the insignificant-looking mineral by the process of exchange becomes converted into a "Thebais" or a "Sefton."

It may be safe to affirm that during a life extending to the confines of the conventional "threescore years and ten," no man ever owned so many good hunters and high-class race-horses. Though a heavy weight, members both of Quorn and Pytchley Hunts can testify that it took a good man and a good horse to cut down Mr. Crawfurd. During his tenancy of Langton Hall, near Market Harborough, he, with his brother-in-law, Mr. Harry Everard, seldom failed to meet the "P.H." at least twice a week. The very best of everything being "just good enough," it was a treat for a lover of horses merely to look over the two powerful, well-bred animals appointed to carry for that day the keen and joyous-looking sportsman from the other side of the banks of the Welland. Among a multitude of "first-raters," it is hard to select any one for special notice, but the beautiful form and grand performance of the kicking "Safety-Valve" must still fill the eye of the member of the "P.H." whose recollection carries him back to that day.

"Noli me tangere" would have been a more suitable name than "Safety-Valve" for this magnificent but dangerous animal, who would not brook the approach from behind of any other horse without fiercely lashing out. Inappropriate as this title may have been, Mr. Crawfurd succeeded in fairly puzzling all his friends by calling one of his racehorses "Semper Durus." Asked for an explanation of the name, one day at Newmarket by the writer of these pages, Mr. Crawfurd laughingly replied, "Why, don't you see, old fellow, I name him after my brother-in-law, Harry Everard." He was a bad horse, worthy of a name embodying so bad a joke. For the name of his famous mare "Thebais," Mr. Crawfurd was indebted to the well-stored intellect of his sister, wife of the gentleman whose name, rendered into Latin, became "Semper Durus." Requested by her brother to find a name for a filly by "Hermit" out of "Devotion," for many an hour, as she herself describes it, did she ponder over the task imposed upon her. Ideas in plenty sprang up suitable to the suggestive names of either parent, but to unite the two in a happy combination — *there* lay the difficulty. At length, early one morning—the time when the brain is clearest and at its best—the happy thought came across her of the desolate region on the banks of the Nile, where the Hermits of old used to eke out their miserable existence in holes in the rocks. This district, from being in the neighbourhood of the ancient city of Thebes, was known as "Thebais," or "the Thebaid." There it was! Hermit and Devotion—the aptest and most appropriate hit that could possibly be found. The elated inventor might well be pardoned for waking her partner with cries of "Eureka! Eureka!" and right good reason had she to be proud of her name and of the beautiful filly that bore it. The nomenclature of racehorses so as to bring the two parents into combination is no easy matter; but it is pitiable to see well-worn names used over and over again, denoting a poverty of invention on the part of the owners that is positively distressing. The thanks of all who appreciate a "happy thought" are due to the inventors of such combinations as :—

Name.	Sire.	Dam.
Canvas.	Rubens.	Vote.
Chameleon.	Camel.	Versatility.
Stray Shot.	Toxophilite.	Vaga.
Fast and Loose.	Cremorne.	Celerrima.
Roysterer.	,,	Caller on.
Scot Free.	Macgregor.	Celibacy.
Blubber.	Whalebone.	Tears.

But brightest of all thoughts was that which led the owner of a colt, the fatherhood of which lay between three sires, to call him "Trinidad." As a single side-name "Latchkey" by "Lothario" is worthy of all commendation; but the difficulty of making out a single and double acrostic, respectively, is not to be compared with that of discovering a name happily blending those of sire and dam. On the long list of horses owned by Mr. Crawfurd, no name can be found to equal that bestowed by his sister on that sweetest of fillies, "Thebais;" and probably none surpassed her in excellence as a racer.

During his long career on the turf, her owner picked all the principal plums out of the "racing-pudding;"—Sefton, Thebais, Craig Millar, Gang Forward having respectively inscribed his name among the winners of the Derby, Oaks, St. Leger, and Two Thousand Guineas. Though devoted to racing, and accustomed to stand a heavy stake when he fancied any particular horse—regardless also of the sum he gave for a fashionably-bred yearling, Mr. Crawfurd found no pleasure in the gaming-table. Living among "Punters," for him, happily, the "ivories" had no attraction; and to this may be attributed his escape from the sad fate of so many of his friends. For all things æsthetic, whether in art or literature, this Prince of the Turf had a true and deep admiration; and his rooms in "the Albany," as well as his house at Langton, were crammed with choice engravings, pictures, and valuable *objets-d'art*.

His death in 1882—long foreshadowed by a softening of the brain—deprived the Turf of one it ill could spare, and left a gap in the Jockey Club which will not easily be filled.

LORD HENLEY.

In point of resemblance, scarcely one of the forty figures in the "Crick" picture is more reminding of the original than that of Lord Henley, who, seated on his white-faced bay, seems to be considering the probability of a find in Watford cover, should the "Crick" draw fail. If the fox be at home and a good gallop follow, no one is more likely to see it than the noble owner of the picturesque mansion known as Watford Court, his riding-weight being no impediment to his getting over the big fences and many-acred grasses of the region round about. The educational advantages of Eton and Oxford not having been thrown away upon one who was intellectually capable of appreciating them, his County Town found in him a representative, able, moderate, industrious; with whom, for a time, it was well satisfied. Declining, however, to adopt the seven-leagued boots in which his constituency were striding towards the extremities of Radicalism, the city of "cordwainers" found in Mr. Bradlaugh a representative more to their mind; and so removed from the House of Commons one who was far from being the least useful of its Members. Occupying at the present time a seat in the House of Lords, as Baron Northington, he is again devoting his time and abilities to the service of his country; and it is to be hoped that his absence from the hunting-field, from a failure of health during the season of 1885-6, may be followed by the speedy resumption of a sport the charms of which he so thoroughly appreciates. Happily for the future prospects of the "P.H.," he, who in the course of nature should become Lord of Watford Gorse and the region round about, is a true son of his father, and considers that among the "gifts the gods provide us" not the least is the pleasure attendant upon the pursuit of the fox. Without the presence of the Hon. Frederick, alias "Freddy" Henley, on his customary days at a "P.H." Meet, it is felt by many there that something is lacking in the field. The "why and the wherefore" of his absence is made a subject of inquiry by many a friend, conscious, by the loss of his presence, that he is minus one item in the day's enjoyment.

Well-mounted, and bound to be pretty handy when genuine business is going on, should the great calamity of finding himself in the second or even the third flight overtake him, he will not yield to the temptation of immediate suicide. Even a heavier misfortune, if such is to be found among hunting-men, will not try the equanimity of an unusually even and charming temperament. If chaffed upon the "prominent position" he occupied in a rattling twenty minutes, he will own the soft impeachment, and laughingly allow "it was not jumping that post and rail at starting that did it."

Many may envy, but few can boast a popularity equal

to that of this young Member of the Pytchley Hunt—one who can "hold his own" in a gallop from Crick Gorse—between the wickets—on the lawn-tennis ground—behind the lights, and also at the whist-table.

MR. LOVELL.

AT the extreme end of the well-known picture, "The Crick Meet," behind Mr. Stirling Crawfurd, sits one of the few remaining members of the ancient family of Lovell of Winwick, one of a race remarkable for their comely looks, and at one time exalted position in the county. Mr. Lovell's appearance at the cover-side was attributable to the pleasure he felt in witnessing a "spectacle," rather than from any wish he had to distinguish himself as a Hunter. Such honour and glory as are to be derived from going well to hounds he left to a younger member of the house—one whose manly form and handsome countenance formed a pretty frequent item of a Pytchley field some five and twenty years ago. A thoroughly good judge of the sort of horse required to gallop over the splendid pastures he looked down upon from the elevation of his house, Lovell of Winwick Warren was a good man to follow, and could at all times hold his own in a run.

To him it befell, as has been elsewhere narrated, to experience the bitters as well as the sweets of foxhunting, as it was in his house that Mr. Sawbridge and Lord Inverury breathed their last (*temp.* Mr. George Payne), after falling over, in two consecutive years, a post and rail in one of the big grass-fields in the valley below.

Mr. Lovell himself fell a victim to decline in the very hey-day of life, and the Winwick property fell into the hands of Richard Ainsworth, Esq., who resides near Bolton. In the purchasing of this estate, the "Pytchley" have been very fortunate in finding a gentleman, who, though somewhat an absentee, does his best.

SIR FRANCIS BOND HEAD, BART.

In the popular biographical work entitled "Men of the Time," a considerable space is allotted to that one of the "P.H." representatives at the Crick Meet, who is wearing, as was his invariable custom, what were then known as "Napoleon" boots. Of the forty sportsmen assembled in front of the old village church, not one there was so much a "man of mark" as the keen-eyed, weather-beaten old soldier, whose experiences had led him to the conclusion that, in point of excitement, a good gallop with hounds was only second to that of a brush with the enemy. He of whom we are speaking was— for alas! he has long gone where the good soldiers go— the Rt. Hon. Sir Francis Head, Bart., the tenant for ten years of the house at Great Oxenden, now occupied by John Oliver, Esq.

After serving with the Royal Engineers at Waterloo, he fought under the Prussian General, Ziethen, at Fleurus, where he had two horses killed under him, but himself escaped unwounded. After quitting the army, in 1825 he undertook the superintendence of some gold and silver mines in Rio de la Plata, and in the course of his duties made a ride of 6000 miles, an account of which he published under the title of " Rough Notes taken during some rapid journeys across the Pampas and among the Andes." Upon his return to England he held the post of Assistant Poor-Law Commissioner in Kent, and in 1835 was sent at a moment's notice to Upper Canada to quell the formidable rebellion of the Frenchman, Papineau—the precursor of Louis Riel, so lately hanged for high treason against the government of the Dominion. This, with the aid of the Militia, and under the greatest difficulties, he not only accomplished, but he repelled the invasion of large bodies of sympathizers from the United States. For these services he received the thanks of the Legislatures of Nova Scotia, New Brunswick, and Upper Canada—was created a Baronet in 1838, and afterwards made a Privy Councillor. On retiring from public life, Sir Francis determined to devote some of the best of his remaining years to the enjoyment of a sport which was the one great passion of his life. To him the horse and hound were the noblest of animals—and after them the fox! "To the latter," he would often say laughingly, "he owed a debt of gratitude that nothing could repay!" He would then comment on the anomaly of taking a pleasure in trying to kill your best friend, and feeling a disappointment in failing to do so. Not one of the forty Pytchley men depicted in the "Meet at Crick" was so genuine a devotee to hunting as the old Officer of Engineers. Not, as was the case with Lord Althorp, for the sake of seeing hounds hunt, but from an innate passion for riding. There was no day in his life—until in his 82nd year he was compelled to lay by—Sundays included, upon which he did not take a ride if the ground permitted. Though not able to ride horses of any great value, nothing stopped him ; and being light of weight, he could always hold his own with "the swells." Neither distance nor weather, bar frost and snow, kept him at home; and the more it rained the higher his spirits rose, as he always looked for a scent on the wet days. The first at the Meet, he was always the last to go home; giving as an excuse for staying out on utterly hopeless days that "it might end in something, after all." Never so happy as when on horseback, to him hunting was an enjoyment almost without alloy. Like Lord Eldon, who used to affirm that there was no such thing as "bad" port-wine; there was "good" he used to say, and "better," but no "bad." So to Sir Francis no day with hounds could be a bad one: it was only "not so enjoyable as if it had been a better one." The air—the exercise—the excitement—the fence with the big ditch on the other side, were each and all distinct matters of enjoyment, but the working of hounds did not markedly catch his notice. Quick in making up his mind under all circumstances, the house at Oxenden in which he passed ten of the happiest years of his life—as he always maintained—was taken in the same time that most people would have occupied in looking over a four-stall stable. Meeting the hounds at Farndon, before Waterloo could be reached for the first draw, he trotted rapidly ahead to view "the house to let," which fortunately lay half-way between the two points. Thinking far more of the possibility of losing the find than of finding a house to suit his requirements, three minutes sufficed for the survey, and the friend who accompanied him was requested to take it for seven years; to which three more were added subsequently. "Happy's the wooing that's not long a'doing," was well exemplified in this instance, as the hasty proceeding never for a moment became anything but a subject for congratulation. Peculiar in many of his ways, and regardless of appearances, Sir Francis used to cause some amusement by the habit of taking his horse to cover tied to the back of the gig. This was done to save the weight of the groom, who, being a heavy man, was better in his master's trap than on the back of his master's hunter. The most marked characteristics of this fine old Officer of Engineers were hastiness of temper, combined with great amiability, and an extraordinary appreciation of the humorous. A Quarterly Reviewer and a somewhat voluminous writer, many of his works sparkle with fun, as will be attested by all who have read them; one, "Bubbles from the Brunnens of Nassau," a laughable description of "Life at the German Baths," especially so: also "Stokers and Pokers," an account of the working of a great Railway—the London and North-Western. Amongst others of his various writings may be mentioned "The Emigrant;" "A Narrative" (during his Governorship of Canada); "A Fortnight in Ireland," &c.

Devoted to children, nothing gave him greater pleasure than asking them questions, and listening to their replies; and any answer or remark denoting originality or a sense of fun gave him unfeigned satisfaction. Had he been the school-inspector, who, on asking a boy what the meaning of "responsibility" was, was told, "If I had only two buttons on my trousers, and one was to come off, the whole responsibility would rest with the other," he would not have ceased smiling for a week.

When engaged to be married, he was told that his *fiancée* might be obliged to have recourse to a medicine

—for she was much out of health—that would "ebonize" her complexion. "No matter," was the reply, "my affection is more than skin-deep;" and so it proved.

In a work he called "The Horse and his Rider," Sir Francis aired many of his crotchets on things equine, and on those pertaining to the saddle-room; and in it gives so lively and interesting a picture of a Meet at Arthingworth, as could scarcely have been excelled by Whyte Melville himself.

With the expiration of the lease of his house, this fine old sportsman, though full of vigour, determined that his "hunting lease" should simultaneously come to an end. To the great regret of every member of the Pytchley Hunt, Sir Francis Head quitted Northamptonshire and went to his old home in Surrey, taking with him the horses, without which life itself would be scarcely worth retaining. The fox now ceased to be an object of pursuit, but the animals that had so often conveyed their master across the green fields of Northamptonshire had now to carry him over the heaths and downs of Surrey, a duty in which there was no excitement. This was their daily duty until age, infirmities, and the doctor's mandate bade all riding cease. Forbidden to take horse-exercise, the wrecked old hunter caused a hammock to be rigged up in the boughs of a tree; and in this, for the sake of air, and of such exercise as it might give him, he was swung for three or four hours daily. Describing this contrivance in a letter to a friend, he says, with a spark of his old accustomed humour, "Though I am quite 'up a tree' for my daily ride, I do manage to get one; and my horse's name is Hammock. It isn't much like the real thing, but it is better than nothing." This condition of affairs did not continue long. The old coachman, whose duty it was to drive the Hammock, had scarcely got well into the swing of it ere he suddenly found his occupation gone. Calling to inquire one summer morning in 1875, a friend learnt to his sorrow that during the night the spirit of the gallant old soldier was gone.

His own pen will best portray the kindly nature, the keen sense of humour, and the unquenchable love of hunting of this one time highly honoured " Member of the Pytchley Hunt." Still writing from Surrey, in the January of 1870, he says, "I have, as you know, completely disconnected myself with the 'P.H.,' towards which, as long as I belonged to it, I endeavoured to 'do all that does become a man!' I greatly regret, however, the loss you have all sustained in the death of poor Jack Woodcock, as neat a rider, and as good a man in every way as ever whipped to a pack of fox-hounds. Your good father [the late Mr. John Nethercote] is a gallant old English Gentleman 'all of the olden time;' and I trust that he and his two nags will enjoy their full allowance of hunting this season. How I should like to be with you all at Waterloo to-morrow, if it were only to see you start away—a glorious sight."

CAPTAIN RIDDELL.

At Bragborough Hall, Captain Riddell maintains a stud, out of which any one in want of a thoroughly dependable Hunter is likely to be suited. Many years may have quenched, to a certain extent, in the gallant ex-Officer of Lancers, the old ardent desire to be first among the foremost; but they have not robbed him of either the hand or seat that proclaims the accomplished horseman.

MISS ALDERSON.

FEW more ardent followers of hounds and fox are to be found than the fair lady who has discovered that the best mode of recovering from the fatigues of a London season is a tri-weekly gallop with the "Pytchley" later on in the year. Winter, in short, is called on to restore the balance of health affected by the wear and tear of summer; and Brington Cottage is the chosen spot in which the recuperative process takes place. If the stranger imagines that the fair rider of the hunter-like brown horse is one whom he will not see again as soon as the fox has left the cover, it will be that he himself is in the background, whilst the lady herself is well in front. Quietly taking her fences as they come, Miss Alderson will be sure to hold her own in a run, and a note of her voice has more effect on the energies of her steed than the "flick" of her whip, or the "prick" of her spur. To mount a relation—a young lady to whom danger appears to be an "unknown quantity"—is another pleasure derived from hunting by the amiable tenant of Brington Cottage; one in no way lessened by her occasionally becoming aware of the fact that the lady going so gallantly ahead is her own niece mounted on a horse out of her own stable.

That a daughter and a granddaughter should be capable of taking rank among the more intrepid of the horsewomen of his country, would have been a matter of congratulation to Baron Alderson—a learned judge—who was not blind to the fact that the sports of the field have charms for either sex.

No one more than he—grave and learned lawyer that he was—would have appreciated the skill, daring, and grace of his fair descendants.

SIR CHARLES ISHAM, BART.

IF position in the county and the ownership of such covers as "Blueberry," "Clint Hill," and "Berrydale" may entitle a country gentleman to consideration as one of the mainstays of his Hunt, to few is this title more applicable than to Sir Charles Isham of Lamport Hall.

Without evincing that enthusiasm for hunting which has characterized other members of his family, Sir Charles has ever been amongst its most constant supporters, and in his younger days was often to be seen sufficiently close to hounds to keep up the credit of a name distinguished for its powers across a country.

That the "*animus venandi*" at no time raged furiously within his breast, is to be gathered from the fact, that the worthy Baronet was usually one of the first to turn his horse's head homeward, and leave others to participate in the good or evil that might be awaiting them after the first gallop. Pleased to hear of a good run, especially if from one of his own covers, the fact of having missed it by a too hasty retreat was never alluded to as a matter for regret or self-reproach; nor did the feeling of "better luck next time" seem at all to influence his future action. That he should of late entirely have withdrawn from the Hunting-field is a misfortune which may, however, be attributed to other causes than indifference to the charms of the chase.

That evil spirit "Agricultural Depression" has cleared out from many a stable the too costly luxury of a hunter, and in her flight across the broad acres of Northamptonshire it would seem as though she had laid her hand on the once well-filled boxes of the Lamport Hall stables. To share the blame with this "evil spirit" are the cold and damp of a Midland county winter,—evils which have necessitated for Lady Isham the formation of a home where a more kindly atmosphere gives hopes of an immunity from aches and pains.

To many, the loss of hunting and a forced absence from home would mean a serious diminution of life's enjoyments; to the owner of Lamport, however, occupation indoors and out is so continuous, that there is no time to find fault with "orders from above;" and whether in Wales or Northamptonshire, his only quarrel is with the rapid flight of time. To him every plant that grows, and every bird that flies, is an object of interest; and in his "ROCKERY," a home for Alpine Plants, unique in structure and appearance, he finds a never-failing source of amusement.

This remarkable adjunct to a lovely garden, placed stone by stone by his own hand, and tended by no other —lest some rare tenant suffer the fate of a common weed—forms an object of pilgrimage to many a lover of Horticulture. Rare and costly Plants from Alps, Apennines and Pyrenees meet the eye in every corner, in addition to which, "forest-trees" of Chinese minuteness

—vegetable dwarfs—grow between big boulders, which afford shelter to pigmy figures of weird and strange appearance. These are supposed to represent the "Gnomes" or "Little Men" that haunt the dark regions of the Black and other German forests, and give a quaintness and originality to the design which baffle description.

But by the *Amateur of Books*, as well as by the *Lover of Flowers*, a feast of good things may be had at Lamport Hall—a feast such as is only to be met with in a few others of the stately homes of England.

These literary treasures began to be accumulated, about the middle of the sixteenth Century, by JOHN—fourth son of EUSEBY ISHAM of PYTCHLEY—who founded the Lamport branch of the family. Having married a daughter of NICHOLAS BARKER—one of the members of the great and opulent family of that name, Printers to Queen Elizabeth—his descendants were thrown much into the literary society of the capital; and it is not improbable that to his son THOMAS, and his grandson JOHN, knighted by James the First, Lamport is indebted for the many rare and valuable volumes to be found upon the shelves of its library.

These may have been removed from town to the country for greater security from fire and from ill-usage during the Civil Wars—a period during which many a literary treasure was irretrievably lost. In the time of George I. SIR JUSTINIAN ISHAM, fifth Baronet, made great additions to the collection of books and altered the house to its present form. When the books became too numerous for the Library, the less valuable ones were removed to a garret, which for many years was kept carefully locked up, no one being allowed to enter it except Sir Justinian himself. After his death, in 1818, this room was constantly in use, though the books remained untouched. Here it was, that Mr. Charles Edmonds—representative at that time of the eminent firm of Sotheran & Co., of the Strand and Piccadilly—made the discovery of which for a while every book-lover in England, on the Continent, and in America, was talking. Commissioned by Sir Charles Isham in 1867 to arrange and report upon his library, Mr. Edmonds, having completed his work downstairs, was despatched to the realms above to look over the books that had been stowed away in the garret. Groping amongst the contents of the shelves—filled as was supposed with the poor relations of the great folk below-stairs—there came to light a small volume, wearing an outward covering of clean white vellum, the lettering of which had faded out through time. Little wotting of the value of the fish he had just hooked, he opened its title-page, and to his astonishment and delight became aware, at a glance, that he was the fortunate bringer to light of such a volume of gems as has seldom blessed the eyes of a Bibliomaniac. In front appeared a hitherto-unknown edition of Shakespeare's earliest work, *Venus and Adonis*, printed in 1599; secondly, the famous surreptitious collection of Sonnets entitled the *Passionate Pilgrime, by W. Shakespeare*, also printed in 1599, and of which the only other existing copy is preserved in Trinity College Library, Cambridge; and lastly, the notorious tract containing *Epigrammes and Elegies* by Sir John Davies and Kit Marlowe, all the copies of which were ordered by public authority to be burnt at Stationers' Hall in the aforesaid year of 1599. Very large sums were offered for this small volume—Mr. Edmonds being, before his public announcement of the astounding discovery, the bearer of a blank cheque from his principals. But Sir Charles was able to resist temptation, and the volume still holds its supremacy at Lamport, the chief attraction of a library replete with similar treasures, many of which were brought to light on the same auspicious day.

So great is the estimation in which this copy of the *Passionate Pilgrime* is held by members of the learned army of book-worms—on account of the remarkable history of its production, its excessive rarity, and fine condition, that though himself no very absorbed student of our great poet, its mere possession has caused Sir Charles to be known in literary circles as " Shakespeare Isham." What this diminutive gem might fetch under the hammer of the auctioneer, it would be difficult to say, but at a time when three early Bibles—one the famous *Mazarine* Bible—realize nearly ten thousand pounds, and a bookseller can see his way to giving four thousand nine hundred and fifty pounds for a book—Psalmorum Codex—printed in 1459, scarcely any sum would seem too extravagant for the acquisition of this great rarity. Nor was this the only " curio " that was dug out of these literary quarries. Upwards of a dozen other poetical tracts of the Elizabethan era, hitherto unrecorded and consequently unknown, were now brought to light, all in most beautiful and perfect condition, some bound in the fine vellum of the period, while others were *uncut*, just as they came from the printers.

In addition to rare plants and books, Lamport Hall is full of costly old Italian cabinets, Palissy ware, and other valuable china, fine pictures, and other "objets-d'art," worthy of a family whose progenitors were persons of distinction in Northamptonshire before the time of William the Conqueror.

That the ancestral love of the chase should be allowed to wax cold in such a family as this one—in whom to hunt is almost a case of "*noblesse oblige*"—is a misfortune which the "P.H." does not fail to recognize. It seems impossible to imagine that the brilliant Meets of old have passed away, under the influences respectively of bad times and an unkindly climate. Is not the space beneath the porch, with the formidable-looking "man-traps," on either side—innocent in their rustiness at this present, but wearing every appearance of having once been "ugly customers"—to be once more peopled with scarlet coats and well-fitting habits? Are smart carriages and "nobby"-looking dogcarts, no longer to stand waiting at the door, whilst their occupants are paying their respects to "my lady," or taking a nip of the "jumping powder" which presents itself in a variety of alluring forms to the chilled system? Are horses costly in price, with coats like satin, no more to be seen pacing up and down under the care of natty grooms, awaiting their rider's exit from the house; whilst Goodall, surrounded by his pack, is adding unconsciously to the picturesqueness of the scene? It cannot be that such mornings as these are to be consigned to the dark limbo of lost joys—bright moments never to return. No! they're over for a while, maybe—these hospitable ways—but "hope still lurks behind the cloud," and points to happier days.

At no time has the old adage of its being "a long lane that has no turning" been more necessary to be borne in mind than at this present hour; and well may be coupled with it the admonishment, " Hope on, hope ever." The motto " Ostendo, non ostento "—I show, I sham not —deeply imprinted on the walls of Lamport Hall, forms what is termed in heraldry " a punning motto," remarkably adapted to a family long notable for straightforwardness and sincerity.

MR. GILBERT.

IF whole-heartedness in fox-preserving can confer immortality upon any one, Mr. Thomas Gilbert of Swinford can show an unequalled claim to that distinction. Loving sport for its own sake, and bent upon using every endeavour to ensure the success of the pack to which he is chiefly attached, there is no one in the large Lutterworth area to whom the thanks of Pytchley as well as other sportsmen are more justly due than to Mr. Gilbert. To him, indeed, ought to have been dedicated the well-known lines composed by a Nottinghamshire sportsman, and entitled " The Whole Duty of Man."

> The lesson that I give,
> If any one holds cheap, he'll
> Find he cannot live,
> Or die with decent people.
> Your business all, if old,
> Young, or children in your frocks is,
> In one short precept told,
> Namely—*preserve the foxes.*
>
> If you this solemn claim
> Shall wickedly neglect, you
> Will hear the dogs bark, shame,
> And the puppies won't respect you.
> You may in woe find mirth,
> In pillory or stocks ease,
> But you won't find peace on earth,
> If you don't *preserve the foxes.*

You small boys in whose books
    Learning finds no lovers,
You may burn your books,
    If you preserve the *covers*.
And now, long live the Queen,
    And may no foe unnerve her;
That is, of course we mean,
    If she's a good *preserver*.

But Army, Church, and Crown,
    The Commons, Peers and Proxies,
Must certainly go down,
    If they don't *preserve the foxes*.
The way to cure all woe,
    And battle fortune's shocks is,
By singing " *Tally ho !* "
    AND PRESERVING OF THE FOXES.

MR. JOHN BENNETT.

No more familiar name with Pytchley, Quorn, or Atherstone Hunts is there than that of John Bennett of Marston. Now well past his seventieth year, the slim form, quick eye, and a gait smacking more of the rider than of the pedestrian, still proclaim the one-time elegant and determined horseman; and whether in a run or in a steeple chase, the man who was near John Bennett was pretty sure to be in a situation, where if he could not be first past the post, he would be likely to "run into a place." Beginning to hunt early in life, and a close observer of the ways of men as well as of hounds and horses, there is many a less pleasant way of passing a winter evening, than to recall, with a good bottle of old port, past times and old hunting heroes, with Mr. Bennett as your reminder-in-chief. Talk to him of "the Squire," Lord Chesterfield, George Payne, "Gentleman Smith," or Tailby, throwing in a few "asides" on racing matters;

and such a store of recollections will be aroused as will
last until the failing lights warn you that bed-time has
arrived. Like many another affected by Father Time—
and a time ruinous to agriculturists—his hunting-days
have well-nigh passed even the waning hour; but the
love for the sport burns no less brightly than of yore.
A brother, some years his senior, has long disappeared
from the cover side, but the genial hospitality that ever
awaited the hungry hunter at Marston Trussell Hall, will
be gratefully remembered by the older members of the
" P.H." As hounds hung about the Marston plantations
—puzzled by the " fur" that so plentifully prevailed—on
the welcome fact becoming known that a slice of ripe
Stilton, a glass of fine old brown sherry, and a beaker of
home-brewed, were awaiting any of Mr. Bennett's friends
and his friends' friend, the dining-room of the old Hall
soon became thronged with famished sportsmen, and
more than one good gallop has been missed by a too prolonged attention to the wants of the inner man under
that hospitable roof.

MR. MILLS.—MR. ENTWISLE.—THE LATE MR. GOUGH.

For many a year both Quorn and Pytchley have looked
to the owner of Welford House to see that the interests
of hunting suffer nothing for want of attention in those
parts which form his more immediate neighbourhood.
Nor has either been disappointed. The mere fact of the
properties at North Kilworth and Welford being owned
by such keen and excellent sportsmen as Messrs.

Entwisle and Mills, is a guarantee that hunting will abundantly flourish in the district which comes within the span of their influence. No member of a hunt ever had the preservation of foxes more at heart than Mr. Gough, the late owner of North Kilworth House; and it is pleasant to see the new proprietor following in the footsteps of his predecessor. May he have the satisfaction of witnessing from a cover of his own such a run as that which has been elsewhere described, commencing close to his own door and terminating at Boughton, three miles from Northampton.

A finer class of hunter than that which for many a year past has filled the stalls of Mr. Mills, it would take good judgment as well as a good balance at your bankers, to become possessed of; and rarely have horses been handled in a more workmanlike manner. If time may have run off with a portion of the old riding virtue, Mr. Mills has the satisfaction of feeling that it has only entered into the hearts of two gallant sons, either of whom will decline to be "pounded" by the hardest man out on the same day with himself.

NORTHAMPTON BRIGADE.

MR. WHITWORTH, SEN., AND DR. DODD.

From time immemorial, the County-Town has supplied its quota of followers of the Pytchley, Grafton, and Oakley Hounds, with the first for choice. Without going back to the days of old when the first Mr. Whitworth used to appear at the near home-meets, and trot about on his short-tailed horse, with three or four fellow-townsmen of the same age and habits as himself, we may mention, as amongst the most remarkable of Northampton sportsmen, that Dr. Dodd, whose ungainly form may still be remembered by some of the citizens of the ancient borough of St. Crispin. Long in face, long in back, and with lower extremities to match, this worthy son of Æsculapius was one of those who had few pleasures in life except hunting; and who, bidding defiance to the drawbacks of weight, and nags of inferior quality, always contrived to forge ahead during a run, and earned for himself the reputation of being a "wonderful man to hounds."

On a plain, light-ribbed, three-cornered chestnut mare, he was pretty sure to be in front of many a better mounted man; affording another proof that it is the "heart" and not the "horse" that is the "one thing needful" in making your way across country.

The Hon. C. Cust, thinking more of performance than

appearance, added the unattractive-looking chestnut to his stud; but the two did not look a match, nor ever seemed to be on thoroughly good terms with each other.

"LAWYER FLESHER."

The burly form of "Lawyer Flesher" might at this time be seen on every Monday and Friday, slowly wending his way to the cover-side ; a true love of hunting and of breeding hunters, being a marked characteristic of one, who, by nature, seemed most unfitted for the chase.

MR. HENRY HIGGINS.

"Coal and Corn-merchant Northampton" could boast a sportsman of the true and genuine type—one, who for many years devoted his leisure hours to fox-hunting; and, who, always riding horses of a superior stamp, could hold his own with the best-mounted man in the field.

THE THREE MESSRS. PHILLIPS.

The representatives of "Malt and Hops" have ever shown a leaning for all things connected with Fox and Hound. Of the three brothers Phillips—connected for some time with three important Breweries—it would be hard to say which were the "better man," no one of the trio having an advantage over the other in weight, keenness, or resolution.

MR. JOHN PHIPPS.

MR. JOHN PHIPPS, another malt-lord—now a "lost chord," with many a Northampton Institution—was rarely to be seen on a horse of inferior stamp; and gave many a proof of his right to be attached to the "not-afraid" division.

MESSRS. RATCLIFFE, EADY, AND HARRIS.

ONE of the partners—Mr. Ratcliffe—of the "Lion Brewery," by a pretty frequent attendance at the Pytchley Meets, still maintains the continuity of the sporting instincts of the "Guild;" and, by the excellence of the commodity in which he deals, does his best to uphold its reputation. To him the witticism will never be applicable, which a London brewer, famous for the weakness of his beer, was once made the victim of. Having unfortunately lost his life by tumbling into one of his own huge vats, Jekyll—one of the great wits of his time—upon hearing of the accident, remarked, "Oh, poor fellow! then he must be lying in his own watery bier!"

Neat as this may be, its utterer may well have envied the cooper's boy, who, when asked at a Board School examination to give a definition of "nothing," replied, "a bung-hole without a barrel round it!"

The Ram Hotel had for several years for its host a Sportsman—Mr. Eady—and the same spirit is still to be found in his representative of the present time—Mr. Harris—one to whom a day's hunting appears to be a class of enjoyment to which nothing else on earth is comparable.

FARMER MEMBERS.

MR. JAMES TOPHAM.

Looking down from the wind-blown heights of the fitly-named "Cold Ashby," the famous Hemplow Hills come into the full view of the spectator, a stronghold for foxes for many a mile around ; and in spite of its somewhat formidable ascent, dear to every Pytchley heart. Inseparably connected with it is the name of one, who, though he has now for some years quitted it for his native county, had so impressed his individuality upon it, that " Jem Topham " and " Hemplow Hills " seemed almost part and parcel of the same word.

A Lincolnshire yeoman, hailing from Lord Yarborough's country, where farming and hunting run in couples—a keen sportsman, and as good a judge of horse and hound as of sheep or shorthorn—it was a grand day for the " P.H." when the Hemplow property passed into hands determined to maintain its reputation as a great sporting centre.

In the whole area of the Pytchley Hunt, there is probably no more vital spot than that known as "the Hemplow."

Popular as a breeding-place, a year without four or five litters would be a phenomenon of more than ordinary evil omen, and would entail an inquiry of a most deep and searching character. As was said of the " Eternal City," " When falls the Colosseum, Rome shall fall," so it might be said of this important cover, " When fails the Hemplow, the ' P.H.' will fail."

From its lofty position it serves as a magnet to foxes from all parts of the adjacent country upon which it looks down; and " Lilbourne," " Crick " and " Hilmorton " Gorses, can tell of many a gallant fox, who, on being roused by the voice of his natural enemy from his cosy bed of sedge and bramble, has made the best of his way to the shelter of the hills. To stand upon the crest of these lofty heights, and look over the intervening grasses far away into the adjoining county, is a treat almost sufficient in itself, but to encompass any part of the same distance on a bold and accomplished hunter, after hounds running breast-high, is to the true sportsman, the skimming the cream of the highest enjoyment. The importance to a Hunt of a property so situated being in the hands of such a man as Mr. Topham—and happily this is no less applicable to its present owner, Mr. Simpson—one to whom the preservation of foxes was an object only second to a successful conversion of his clammy acres into loaves and fishes—is too manifest to need dwelling upon.

Some who read these pages will call to mind the interest with which the new Lord of the Hemplow was looked over on his first appearance with the " P.H." A glance was sufficient to show that the man must have been made for the place. Mounted on an animal—long, low, not particularly well-bred, but looking all over a hunter—there was no room for any mistake as to the new importation from the Brocklesby country being "every inch a sportsman," and an acquisition to any Hunt.

That he proved himself such for some eight or ten years, is in the grateful recollection of every Member of the Pytchley, as well as of many a stranger to the Hunt.

The odour of the Topham hospitality still hovers around the precincts of the famous cover; and many a hunting man remembers with gratitude the good cheer that at the end of a long day sent him on his homeward way rejoicing.

A sportsman of the old school, Mr. Topham never thought of joining the noble army of "thrusters," but was content to hold his own with the second flight, ever keeping his eye upon the leading hounds, and quick to make his point as they turned to right or left.

After eight or ten years of good service to the country of his adoption, the property again came into the market, and happily once more fell into the hands of a Sportsman, who, though somewhat of an absentee, in no way permits the reputation of the well-known cover to suffer an eclipse. During the last season, foxes ran about the hills like rabbits; and after three or four had been seen to follow in each other's tracks, the cry was "still they come."

Before quitting the neighbourhood, Mr. Topham received a compliment of which he may well have been proud—one accorded to such only, who, by some peculiar merit of their own, have won the esteem of those by whom worth is appreciated on its own account.

At a public dinner attended by a large number of hunting men, the late owner of the Hemplow was presented with a handsome mark of the esteem in which he was held by his friends and neighbours. From the kindly expressions made use of on that occasion, Mr. Topham had the gratification of feeling that his efforts to promote sport, and his wish to show hospitality to all during his sojourn in Northamptonshire had not been unappreciated. That he may long live to think of his pleasant days with the Pytchley, and of the friends he left behind him, is the sincere wish of many who still miss the stalwart form and hearty greeting of James Topham, one time owner of Hemplow Hills, and as good an example of the genuine English Fox-Hunter as ever followed hounds.

MR. ELWORTHY.

AMONGST the more familiar faces of those upon whom Time has served a notice to quit the farm and lands over which for many a year, without payment of rent or acknowledgment, without even a " by your leave or with your leave " to landlord or tenant, they've galloped as if they were their own, is William Elworthy, eke landlord of the " Ram Hotel " at Northampton, and for some years occupant of the farm at Brixworth, upon which stands the once well-known " Weston's Spinney."

There are those who appear at the Meets for many another reason than the love of hunting *pur et simple*, but from his earliest youth, to the fine old Sportsman of whom we are speaking, " the hound, the whole hound, and nothing but the hound," has been the motive principle of his constant attendance at the coverside.

Without pretence of doing more than what within him

lay, a thorough knowledge of country and a 'good eye to hounds, enabled the owner of the small but well-shaped hunter to see the choice bits of most of the good gallops of his time; and his name is to be seen amongst the few who were up at the end of the famous run from Kilworth to Boughton during the Mastership of Lord Hopetoun.

With a memory teeming with the recollection of events of former days, the student of the history of the Pytchley Hunt, of the great duels of the Prize-Ring, and of sundry incidents connected with the Turf, will find no better source to which he may apply for information. Speak to him of "Goody Levi," "Pickle Higgins," and the "top-booted old Yeoman of Sywell," and the whole drama of the "Running Rein Robbery" will be placed before you; whilst a still-smouldering admiration for the heroes of the "Lemon and the Sponge" will lead him on very slight provocation to dilate on the occurrences of certain—so-called—"Glorious Battles," of which he himself was an eye-witness.

Though no longer to be seen jogging alongside of the Huntsman to the Meet at Sywell Wood or Lamport Hall, his interest in the proceedings of the "P.H." in no way waxes faint; and it is to be hoped that many a year will elapse ere the respected subject of this brief memoir will cease to "babble o' green fields," grand runs, and Mr. George Payne.

MR. WILLIAM WIDDOWSON.

Though the name of William Widdowson of Great

Harrowden may be unknown to the present generation, and is associated with no great deeds of doughty horsemanship—though by him the "hog-backed stile" and the brook with rotten banks and muddy bottom were objects to be avoided rather than encountered—his memory as an old and honoured lover of the chase lingers kindly in the hearts of many an East-side follower of the "P.H." of a former day.

A tenant of the Hon. George Fitzwilliam, and occupant of a stretch of grass over which hounds are bound to run "hard, all," in spite of flocks and herds; to the worthy old Sportsman there was no pleasure in which he so much delighted as to watch hounds cross the valley between Harrowden Ness and Vivian's Cover.

By the non-adventurous the enlivening scene may be witnessed in safety from the heights above, an almost irresistible line of gates leading from and to the respective points, with a probable drawing of the rein for a few seconds at the interposing "Blackberry." For those who ride to, rather than from, hounds, the line is not without its perils—the intervening fences and a nasty bottom being objects requiring some negotiation, and not a little hardness of heart. At the time here referred to, it was as a "caretaker" rather than a "pursuer," that "old Bill Widdowson" took his place as a marked and well-known character in a Pytchley Field on the Monday side.

Of venerable aspect, with snow-white hair, and a long great-coat coming well over his knees, he bestrode a placid and sensible-looking old steed, which well matched the rider.

The two well-known covers, Blow Hill and Harrowden

Ness—the latter, alas! not even a shadow of its former self—were placed under his especial protection; and right well did he discharge a duty that he so much loved. The Ness was, from its position and sporting look, the peculiar object of his regard, and the trespasser in search of "fur" or "feather," was pretty sure to be made acquainted with the law affecting him who "shoots or snares what isn't his'n." When hounds were first put into cover, it was interesting to watch the alternations of hope and disappointment that played across the old man's face. As soon, however, as some deep and trusty tongue had proclaimed that a foxey smell had come betwixt the wind and his "caninity," a smile lit up the lately anxious face, and he would say to some one near, "I thought that they would find him in that bit of gorse by the brookside." On the disappearance of hounds and horsemen, the old horse received a reminder from the one spur of his well-satisfied rider, who no sooner reached his home than he proceeded to uncork a bottle of the old Port which was reserved for those red-letter days.

But there is no longer either Harrowden Ness to be looked after or old Bill Widdowson to look after it. Farewell, fine old Sportsman! Many a man of more importance has lost his billet without leaving so many pleasant memories behind him.

MR. MATTHEW OLDACRE.

In the noble army of Northamptonshire yeomen who go well with hounds, the foremost place may fairly be assigned to a heavy-weight who has no superior across a country. In Matthew Oldacre of Clipston, we have one of those exceptional organizations in whose hearts there seems to be no room for fear, and to whom the class of animal they ride seems to be a matter of no material consequence. Riding nearly seventeen stone, a "weight-carrier" was a necessity to Mr. Oldacre; and though he could not always command class as well as power, the runs were few and far between, the best part of which he could not dilate upon as "one who was there." The bigger the country, the more sure he was to be near hounds; the combination of weight and pluck serving him in good stead, when no one else saw a likelihood of arriving at the other side of an unyielding bullfinch.

Ill-health has for some time stood between him and a pursuit that in his eyes has no equal; but with only three score years and ten to grapple with, it is to be hoped the day is far distant when he will cease to appear, careering across the big grasses of Oxenden and Kelmarsh.

MR. CHARLES HEWETT.

WERE the name of Charles Hewett of Draughton to be omitted from the list of the hunting farmer-worthies of the "P.H.," the very hounds in their kennel would cry out. In early life a rider of no ordinary acquirements, his services in a steeplechase were in frequent demand by the owners of horses; but it was in pursuit of the fox that he was most at home.

Living in a position from which most of the Meets were easily accessible, in days gone by, the father and

two sons were constant members of a Pytchley field.
When death—striking from the suddenness of the blow—
removed the last of the well-known trio, it was generally
acknowledged that in the loss of Charles Hewett a gap
had been made in the farmer-clientèle of the "P.H."
which was not likely ever to be filled up.

MR. MATTHEW WARREN.

As every village boasts its "oldest inhabitant," so
every Hunt has its "oldest follower," and so far as the
"P.H." is concerned, that not-altogether-enviable distinction can be claimed in the person of Mr. Matthew
Warren of Boughton Mills, near Northampton.

Any one told off to find a finer specimen of the "genus
homo" at the age of ninety than this stalwart farmer
and miller—an honoured tenant of Mr. Howard Vyse—
might complain that he had had a task assigned to him
that it was impossible to perform.

In spite of all the long laborious days that go to make
up the sum of fourscore years and ten of a busy life,
early hours and regular habits seem so to have squared
matters with "Time, the Avenger," that the upright
form of the old Sportsman appears to have lost nothing
of its six-feet-two; and the stoop that is so often seen in
the bearer of sixty winters may be looked for in vain in
one who numbers half as many years again. "In every
life some rain must fall;" and doubtless this fine old
man has had his share of trouble and of sorrow, but of
gout and rheumatism he has known nothing, not even
for a day; and though he is constantly seen on and

about his farm, he smilingly says, "Ah, but I should be there oftener than I am, if I were not a little troubled with fever in the feet." With a memory for business and other matters quite unimpaired, he loves to talk of the many runs he has seen across the grass-fields around him, and will talk of the "P.H." days, from Lord Althorp up to the current year, as if they were events of yesterday. The general love and admiration for Mr. George Payne burn no less strongly within him than it did when he followed his hounds; and to any friend of that idol of the Northamptonshire farmer, it would not have been a little gratifying to have heard his aged admirer, when referring to him on a late occasion, emphatically exclaim, "Ah! that was a splendid man, indeed!"

For many a year, a near and kindly neighbour, Mr. Henry Philip Markham of Sedgebrook—himself a keen hunter in days gone by, and now represented by a son, who, lawyer as he be, takes "deeds, not words" for his motto when crossing a country—has sent his aged friend on each recurring birthday two bottles of the best wine his cellar holds, to drink the toast "Success to all my friends, and may they live as long as I, and know as little of sickness and ill-health." That this toast may often be repeated by the recipient of the friendly gift is the hearty wish of all who have the pleasure of knowing Mat Warren, the oldest follower of the "P.H."

MR. JOSEPH HUMPHREY.

Some may still remember the dark but not uncomely face of Joseph Humphrey, another Clipstonian, whose keenness for hunting has certainly never been exceeded. Riding cattle without quality or form, or anything for which they might be desired, he never failed to get fairly along; and at the end of the day could always give a pretty good account of what had occurred. Towards the end of his career, crippled by rheumatism, and unable to get into the saddle, he would not give up his favourite amusement, but turned his gig into a hunter, and followed over plough and ridge and furrow in a manner that must have been injurious alike to horse and vehicle.

With a farm-lad by his side to open the gates and "pick up the pieces" when he came to grief, Humphrey with his "flail"—a whip—and cobby chestnut dun, saw as much of the fun as many of the road-riding sportsmen; and proved that in the alternative of staying at home or hunting on wheels, he showed his good sense in choosing the latter; but why he would keep chained, in season and out of season, a gate leading out of the Clipston and Sibbertoft Lane direct to the "Windmill Meet," is "a thing that no fellow could understand" at the time, or does now.

With him has passed away another genuine lover of fox-hunting.

MR. AND MRS. SHARMAN.

In Mr. and Mrs. P. Sharman, constant attendants at the Pytchley Monday Meets, a family is represented from Wellingborough, certain members of which were famous through many a year for the boldness of their riding; and all who remember Mark Sharman, the father, and Edward, his son, will agree that few Hunts could boast two more determined horsemen, or more keen appreciators of the " Noble Science."

MR. WILLIAM DRAGE.

THE Sywell Wood, or as some deem it the " seamy side " of the Pytchley country, for seventy years numbered among its more sport-loving farmers, one who, though now in his eighty-seventh year, has still little need for the help of spectacles, and upon whose organs of hearing the assaults of Time seem to have had scarcely any effect.

The spare form and familiar features of William Drage of Holcot have not for many a year been seen at the old accustomed Meets; but his heart is still with "horse and hound," and he glories in the feeling that his two sons, John and Binyon, have long been amongst the more constant of the farmer devotees to the noble sport ; and that he has a grandson who is able to "hold his own" across a country with any of the followers of the " P.H."

MR. JOHN BARBER.

WITH the disappearance from the cover-side of John Barber of Hannington, another old friend to hunting seems to have left a gap in the yeoman-following of the " P.H.;" a vacuum created by the demon-touch of shrinkage in the value of agricultural produce, rather than by that of the arch-enemy, Time.

To the last hour of his life, will the occupant of the little red-brick house, standing apart in the big grass-field outside the village, have cause to remember, amongst other guests, the Empress of Austria, H.R.H the Princess of Wales, and H.R.H. Princess Mary of Teck, &c. &c.

The effacing fingers of " Free Trade " and " Science " sweep away one after another of those who looked to the land for a livelihood; and it would almost seem as if what used to be considered the backbone of hunting, must sooner or later cease to exist.

MESSRS. TOM TURNELL, LUCAS FORSTER, AND W. WHITEHEAD.

A SELECT and fortunate few may still be found to make up the thinned proportions of a Pytchley Monday Meet; and amongst these three wearers of the once highly-favoured cap are worthy representatives of a class, which from the earliest times occupied a peculiarly-honoured place in the social system.

To Oakley as well as to Pytchley men on the "seamy" side, the welter forms of Tom Turnell and of William Whitehead are scarcely less familiar than that of Sywell Wood itself; whilst the spare figure and sporting-look of Lucas Forster complete a trio remarkable in any Field. Upon each, Time has laid his finger with a more or less gentle pressure ; and if the first somewhat markedly holds out the sign of the " frosty pow," the other two have no great pull in the matter of years gone by.

With voice scarcely attuned to the softer measures of a
tenor-song, the vocal notes of Mr. Tom Turnell cannot be
accused of being deficient in far-reaching properties ; nor
is it the custom of its owner to deal in honied words.
For his use, plain old English terms and expressions are
quite good enough ; and in taking the occasion, he thus
retorted upon a noble M.F.H., who had just shown him
the rough side of his tongue. "My Lord ! I have
hunted with many Masters of Hounds, but as they have
all been Gentlemen and not Lords, I am not used to your
sort of language." With this flashing of his two-edged
sword the dispute happily terminated ; and " Lord " and
" Yeoman " drowned their difference in words of a more
kindly nature.

The prosperous Farmer has already become a " *rara
avis in terris:*" the whole race of Agriculturists—plus
Mr. Arch's " aristocratic goats," the Landlords—may
become as extinct as the " Dodo ;" but so long as we see
amongst us such excellent specimens of their cloth as the
triad of Sportsmen just referred to, we shall have the
satisfaction of knowing that Hunting has not quite
reached its bitter end.

MESSRS. J. AND G. GEE, AND MR. J. WOOD.

Two better " Gees " to hounds—John and George by
name—than those installed at Welford, it would not be
easy to find ; and in Mr. John Wood the same locality
can boast " a customer " whom only to keep in sight
during a run is to ensure being in a sufficiently good
place.

MESSRS. ATTERBURY AND JOHN COOPER.

The names of the two Messrs. Atterbury—good men and true when hunting, as well as when all other things are concerned—must not be omitted from this list of local farming-attachés of the "P.H.;" and as it would be hard to say where the name of John Cooper of East Haddon is unknown, it will suffice here to suggest that the anxious inquirer in search of a really good hunter will be out of luck if he fails to find it in the stables of this old "Pytchley-mentary hand."

MEMOIRS

OF

WOODLAND MEMBERS.

THE DUKE OF BUCCLEUCH.

In speaking of the different owners of that large tract of woodland country which reaches with intervals from Stamford to Kettering, the first and foremost place must be assigned to the Duke of Buccleuch, of Boughton House, —lord of thousands of broad acres, and sixty miles of avenue to boot. For this ornament to his property his Grace is indebted to an ancestor whose love of arboriculture earned for him the appropriate title of " John the Planter." The most noble of all butterflies, rarely to be seen, and frequenting only the tops of the loftiest oaks, is one known to lepidopterists as "the Emperor of the Woods.' No more suitable appellation could be found for the ducal proprietor of this vast estate, a large proportion of which consists of noble woodlands, than that of the stately "*papilio machaon*" just referred to. Rare visitants even of this lovely region, and frequenting only the topmost summits of the life allotted to them, " Emperor " Duke and " Emperor " Butterfly have much in common—much at which their less highly favoured neighbours have to gaze with envy and admiration.

Sportsmen by birth and inclination, the Dukes of

Buccleuch have ever been ardent followers of the chase, and though they seldom have listened to the sweet music of hound and horn in the Boughton Woods, it is that Scotland and the Roxburghe country have a prior claim upon their consideration.

Master of hounds for many a year in his own native land, the late Duke never failed to give ample support to the " P.H.," who, until within the last few years, only hunted this vast district for the purpose of breaking in its young hounds, and occupying a few weeks pleasantly in early spring, and again in early autumn. Thinking it hard that they should be expected to preserve foxes for the benefit of those who lived in other and remote parts of the " P.H." country, the cry for regular hunting and a separate establishment became too loud to be disregarded any longer, and arrangements were made which secured a pack with horses and men sufficient to afford two days a week exclusively in the Brigstock district. To this new disposition of things, the Duke of Buccleuch heartily lent himself; going so far as to make it the *sine quâ non* of his continued support.

A Meet at Boughton House forms a rendezvous for the entire neighbourhood; but despite its associations and the picturesqueness of the surroundings, there is an air of absenteeism about the old ducal mansion and grounds, which does not fail to strike the heart of every visitor, be he sportsman or otherwise. After having obtained the " Measure of Home-Rule " which gave them a separate establishment under the old imperial régime, things for a while went swimmingly with the " North Pytchley," and Castle (Rockingham) rule was voted the perfection of government; but after two years of office,

the Prime Minister resigned—a stranger filled his place
—times grew worse—and even the lavish expenditure
of a Sardanapalus—an hereditary legislator from the
north—failed to provoke attendances at the Meets.

Fine by degrees, and hideously less, on the fingers of
one hand may easily be counted the regular frequenters of
a Woodland Meet ; and amongst these there will not be a
single red coat, except those of the Master and his men.
Notwithstanding the wet blanket of a sparse attendance
at the cover side, the country continues to be well and
regularly hunted ; and though kills are not of frequent
occurrence, it must not be forgotten that no fox is so
difficult to bring to hand, as one born and bred in the
forest. As is said of the Gipsy race :—

"Try what you will ; do what you can :
Nothing will whiten the black Zincan."

The assertion that there is "no rule without an exception" in reference to the warning " Put not your trust in
keepers," has a brilliant example in the case of the
well-known family of " Fletcher," head-gamekeepers to
his Grace the Duke of Buccleuch at Boughton Park.
Familiar to all North Northamptonshire sportsmen is the
picturesque cottage standing at the junction of a group
of noble glades in the woods—the peaceful home for some
generations of the family here referred to. Keepers bred
and born—but with an instinctive love for the chase in
any form—in them " the fox " finds no relentless enemy
save when hounds are on his track ; and the burden of
their sporting creed is a belief in fox as well as pheasant.
In their ears the familiar bark of the evening prowler is
well-nigh as welcome as the crow of perching cock, and
the sound of hound and horn little less tuneful than

that of the deadly choke-bore. The lustrous skin of the old dog-fox—the duller coat of "my lady in the straw'—and the soft round form of the rolling cub—have beauties in their eyes, only exceeded by that of the broods of healthy chicks, picking and pecking in the adjacent pasture—" food for powder " in its early stage.

So much did the famous " Squire " value the services rendered to hunting by the Fletcher of his day, that he presented him with a favourite horn, as the best mark of his appreciation and esteem. Highly valuing the compliment, the worthy veteran was wont to carry it in the top of his right boot when hounds were in his beat, and posting himself at the corner of a ride, would sound upon it a sad imperfect note to proclaim that the fox had crossed. The " Squire" and his pack were quickly on the spot; and away rode the proud bearer of the horn, keen to render assistance in some other quarter of the wood.

That he set a due value upon the things coming more immediately within his own province, and that he was given to gauge the worth of his neighbour according to his skill with the gun, is amusingly exemplified by his comment upon hearing that Mr. Vernon Smith—proprietor of the adjoining woods—was about to be made a Peer. "Mr. Smith a Peer! What's the good of making him a Peer ? He can't shoot;" was the somewhat supercilious remark of the old and unerring gunner. To a member of this worthy family was it given to solve the problem—one which seems to have baffled many a " preserver's " brain—of " fox plus pheasant "—a discovery of far more importance to the " noble science " than " squaring the circle," or the discovery of " perpetual motion."

Valued by their ducal masters as old and faithful servants, esteemed by all who knew them, and held in especial honour by all North Pytchley men as model keepers; it may be said of them that their lot, unlike that of the policeman in the play, has been not only a happy one, but one offering an example to all similarly circumstanced with themselves. Happy, too, the Hunt, which, at a crucial point of its country, possesses such loyal friends and true.

THE EARL OF CARDIGAN.

NEXT in rank as a Woodland potentate and hunting-man,—whose name must for all time be associated with that memorable mistake the Balaclava Charge—comes James Thomas, seventh Earl of Cardigan.

Living at Deane Park, one of the most charming places in East Northamptonshire, Lord Brudenell entered early into the pursuits of country-life, especially those of hunting and shooting. A born soldier and officer of Cavalry, he entered the 8th Hussars, from which he, as years went on, was transferred as Lieutenant-Colonel to the 11th Hussars; which regiment he brought into a high state of efficiency and notoriety. The unfortunate " Black-bottled Reynolds" incident, the duel with Captain Tucker and the consequent trial, kept the noble lord's name full before the public; a phase of life which at no time was especially distasteful to him.

Having previously represented Marlborough and Fowey in Parliament, in 1831 he became one of the representatives for the north division of his native county in the Conservative interest, and retained the seat until 1837; when, succeeding to the title and estates, he became a peer of the realm. Passionately fond of hunting, there were few harder men across a country; and at a time when Quorn and Pytchley were well furnished with "bruisers," it was no easy matter for the best of them to get in front of the gallant Earl.

Taking a somewhat elevated view of his own social position, and of the deference that was due to an Earl of Cardigan, the Lord of Deane was wont to evince impatience when some low fellow chanced to come betwixt the wind and his nobility.

It was said of him that on one occasion, when in some danger of being drowned in a brook whilst hunting in Leicestershire, he was heard to exclaim, "Is there no one who will help to save the seventh and last Earl of Cardigan?"—a story which if not "vero" was certainly "ben trovato."

That he took an optimist view of his relations with his tenants is instanced by a characteristic incident which occurred in the presence of the writer. A fox having gone to ground in one of the Deane Woods, Charles Payn, contrary to Lord Cardigan's wish, commenced to dig for him.

"He has been killing some lambs, my Lord, and the tenants are complaining," urged the Huntsman to his lordship's remonstrance. "Tenants complaining!" exclaimed the noble and somewhat scandalized proprietor. "The land is mine; the woods are mine, and the tenants are mine; and my tenants are not in the habit of complaining about anything." Though somewhat over-proud of his birth, his position, his appearance, and his

military feats, when it became known one morning, in the
March of 1878, that Lord Cardigan had been killed by a
fall from his horse, the feeling was universal that in the
long-descended peer the county had lost one of its most
notable and distinguished characters. It is singular that
Mr. Tryon, of Bulwick Park, Lord Cardigan's old friend
and nearest neighbour, should not long after have met his
death by a similar accident.

MR. TRYON.

THERE was no more marked individuality in the Woodlands than the Squire of Bulwick Park. Tall, and of
Herculean frame, it was a sight to watch the stout-hearted
old squire—reckless of eyes and face—crashing through
the ash-plants and the binders of one of his own well-
nigh impenetrable woods.

A sportsman of the thorough-going type—equally good
behind a gun as in the saddle—attentive to his duties
as a county-magistrate—and a keen electioneerer on the
Tory side—a finer example of the ideal of the old English
Gentleman might have been looked for in vain. He lived
to be proud of a son who has won for himself an honoured
name amongst British sailors; and that son will never
cease to cherish the memory of a father who was respected and esteemed by all who knew him.

LORDS LILFORD AND LYVEDEN—MR. C. THORNHILL.

To Lord Lilford—most enthusiastic of Ornithologists,

and keenest of gunners—and to Lord Lyveden, of Farming Woods—shooter first and hunter afterwards—the "P.H." are indebted for an unfailing support; as it is also to Mr. Clarke Thornhill, of Rushton Hall—a gunner "pur et simple"—but one who would take to heart the knowledge that any keeper of his had done a fox unhandsomely to death.

APPENDIX.

1. HUNTING-SONG.

2. LETTER FROM A YOUNG LADY-NATURALIST.

3. LETTERS FROM SIR FRANCIS B. HEAD, BART.

    No.   Date.
1. February, 1862.
2. February, 1863.
3. Undated [1867].
4. November, 1869.
5. March, 1872.
6. Summer of 1873.
7. November, 1873.
8. January, 1874.
9. January 23, 1875.*

4. Finishing Remarks on the close of Sir Francis Head's Letters.

* The last letter ever written by Sir Francis Head.

"THE PYTCHLEY;"

A HUNTING-SONG.

Yes, Loatland! since first I stood under thy cover,
   When all nature looked young and old age seemed a crime,
Such an age has passed by, that I fail to discover
   The landmarks of life on the roadside of time.

So it *must* be; but oh! for one touch of the bridle,
   And oh! for the feel of a resolute horse,
When the darlings are racing away on the side-hill,
   And their heads set in earnest for Tally-ho Gorse.

How well I remember, we stood at the corner,
   The road choked and crammed in the orthodox way;
When whisking his brush at the sound of the horn, a
   Great grey-looking dog-fox broke boldly away.

Hold hard there! hold hard! (don't you pity the Master?)
   Pray! pray! give the time, you would anger a Saint!
He may well spare his breath, for the Field all the faster
   Breaks away out of hand and defies all restraint.

Along the brookside by the rush-covered meadows,
   Where bullfinch alternates with blackthorn and rail,
The rush passes on, till in sunlight and shadows
   Fair Arthingworth Church rises out of the Vale.

Ah! there are the willows; like ghosts you might fancy
   They wave their lean arms as they bid you beware;
And deep is the gulf, looking dark and unchancy,
   Where the rat finds his home, and the otter his lair.

Little Mayfly and Mermaid have taken the water,
   And the snipe rises wild as they enter the tide!
There's a turmoil of wave as the pack follows after,
   And a dripping of flanks as they gain the far side.

What a study the Field is! just see how the bold ones
    Sit down in their saddle and draw to the fore;
While the faint and false-hearted, the cowardly and cold ones,
    Vote discretion a virtue and valour a bore.

Look at Shirker! I own his get-up is perfection,
    And the tint of his leathers a triumph of art,
His boots, irreproachable, challenge correction;
    Superb, too, his pink, but how craven his heart!

Just watch him! He falters, inviting disaster,
    With the weakest of make-believes plain to the eye;
The chestnut has measured the length of his master,
    And with animal instinct, disdains to comply!

Forward, forward, they go; seven horses are over;
    There are two without riders, and four in the brook;
While the rest, taking warning, disperse to discover
    A ford, or a place with an easier look.

See Languish and Lucy—two comelier ladies
    The heart of an M.F.H. cannot desire;
And the Vanquisher puppy, well up at the head, is
    A model of form in the mould of his sire.

Who is that on a brute with an "oxer" before him?
    He means it, and sends him along like a man;
But the high-mettled heretic's temper comes o'er him,
    And he's bent upon shirking, if shirk it he can.

It's no use, he must have it; the man has the best of it,
    There's no bend in the blackthorn, no break in the ash;
He hesitates—jumps—you may guess at the rest of it,
    They are down in the ditch with a terrible crash!

There's a flash through the brain—there's a whirl of confusion—
    A struggling of hoofs—and a tangling of rein;
Gallant Jack's on his legs, with a trifling contusion;
    He is up on his horse, and they're at it again.

Under Sunderland Wood, and just threading the Spinney,
    And touching at Langboro' forward they go;
So sharp is the pace, you might venture a guinea,
    He will scarce save his brush on this side "Tally-ho

Tally-ho! What a title to welcome a stranger,
  Way-weary, distressed, in sore travail and pain;
Tally-ho! Every syllable echoing danger,
  Says, "Here is no rest:" so hark forward again!

Oh! could I apostrophize good Melibœus,
  Like the Mantuan Bard, I would say as we pass,
Surely man for his sins made the ploughshare, but "Deus
  Hæc otia fecit;" subaudi—the grass.

But look at those Herefords! all their white faces
  Amazed, in a stampede through mud to their hocks:
Can you be a colly, to cause such grimaces,
  As he steals through the bottom?—By Jove! it's the fox!

There are signs of distress; there is sobbing and sighing;
  There is crashing of timber, and plying of steel;
But still o'er the pastures the sirens keep flying;
  Crescendo the pace, for they're running to kill.

Holthorp Hills are in front: can he reach them? Ah, never!
  He hesitates—crawls through the "'meuse"—doubles back:
He has played his last card; and now gallant as ever,
  He turns on his foes, and he faces the pack!

Look! Firefly has got him! Whoohoop! It is over!
  There's a crash and a worrying, and muttering of sounds:
Will is up, and jumps off, just in time to recover
  A dark stiffened form from a tumult of hounds!

LETTER FROM A YOUNG LADY-NATURALIST.

THE following is a letter lately received by the author [1886] from a fair young Naturalist, whose chief enjoyment consists in watching all that goes on out of doors—one to whom a few hours only with hounds are placed on the list of joys unspeakable.

After informing her correspondent that she has had a present of a new pony—a real beauty—six years old—very fast and quiet—with a closely-hogged mane—and that with more respect to nationality than sex, it is called "Taffy"—lady though she be; she proceeds thus: "You would have laughed to have seen my sister Agnes and me the other day. We were out in the cart when we came across the hounds. We instantly joined the glad throng, and followed in spite of all obstacles—short of fences—much to the amusement of the lucky ones on horseback.

"We jerked bumpily across a very mole-hilly meadow—up a grass-hill about as straight as a wall—shaved through broken hurdles—laboured through a plough-field. I got out, and while I walked behind the cart, holding the reins, Agnes hung on to one of the shafts, and lent a hand to Taffy, who was pulling like a brick. We were rewarded for our toil by being well up with hounds for a long time, and saw all that there was to see—which was little enough. We were accompanied by a smart fox-terrier, who got immensely excited, and lifted up his harmonious voice in season and out of the same; so we worked to music—a great incentive, as you know.

"My birds are prospering fairly, but we have just been bereaved of a 'Shore-lark,' a 'Snow-bunting,' and a 'Bullfinch,' To all appearance they died content and happy; so I suppose that they had lived virtuous lives, and just closed their eyes for ever on this most delightful of all possible worlds. In their place I have got a pair of 'Cirl-buntings' and a 'Reed-sparrow' for my aviary.

"We are out every morning soon after six. I first let out Sir William and Lady Gull—two large seagulls—who skim over the wet grass, and go off in search of 'wums.' Then I let out the dogs—two Retrievers—mother and son—and two Fox-terriers—no relations. Then we go off for a walk, and tell each other we have the best of it over the people in bed. We watch the sun light up the sea, till it looks like a sheet of silver; then turn into a wood, and step quietly along, keeping eyes and ears well open as we go. A fat Wood-pigeon claps out of a big tree, and disappears somewhere in the shade; a brace of Partridges, in all the glory of their spring plumage, run along in front a little way, and then turn off into the wood—probably intent on the cares of setting-up house.

"A shrill yelping apprises us that the Terriers are hunting a too-inquisitive Rabbit: and they have to be called to order; while the young Retriever trembles with excitement—longing, but not daring—to join. He would, too, if I did not look very sharp after him. His fat old mother waddles along, and probably goes back to the time when she and other old dogs like her were having their day. And so we go on our way rejoicing; and return with an enormous appetite for breakfast."

In the above letter every word is alive with the spirit of "all out-of-doors," marking the true appreciator of the handiworks of the Almighty; and evincing an unaffected enjoyment of nature in all her moods.

LETTERS FROM SIR F. B. HEAD, BART.

1.

"February, 1862.

"I was glad to get your note, which made my fingers itch to shake the hand that wrote it. I always like to hear from you —but especially when you can feed me with a few dainty details of Northamptonshire Hunting. Indeed I can truly say that the hours I spent within the dominions of the 'Pytchley,' in riding and writing, formed the happiest ten years in my chequered life. On Saturdays I always read in the *Times* your Meets for the ensuing week; and think of them as I ride by myself over the Surrey Hills.

"I am very glad to learn that 'Waterloo' continues to do its duty. Ever since I put the sticks in it, it has 'honoured all the bills' Charles Payn has drawn upon it. The fences around it would now be a trifle too big for me; but anywhere else, I should greatly enjoy a gallop over the grass-fields. I am sorry that Bevan and Charles Cust are in hospital." &c., &c.

2.

"February, 1863.

"Do write me half a line, and tell me how the Prince of Wales went with the 'Pytchley.' How I should have enjoyed seeing you all assembled to meet him. Now that he has tasted the green fields of Northamptonshire, he will see what a mistake he has made in giving 240,000*l.* for an estate in the wrong county. The best thing he could do would be to sell it at once, and buy my little house at Oxenden; and if it gave him the health and happiness it gave me, it would be to him a capital purchase. There is nothing I am convinced so dangerous as not hunting. As a proof of this, on the day after Christmas, I had a worse fall than any I had during my ten years' hunting with the 'Pytchley.' I was galloping along over turf by myself, when my mare fell head over heels, and I lay on the ground insensible for fifteen minutes. I am getting over it, but being half-way between seventy and eighty, it is more easy to kill than to cure me." &c., &c.

3.

[1867]

In his seventy-eighth year, he thus writes to his friend :—

"Your welcome letter has set my whole mind and memory running riot. Its two pages are composed of a series of texts, upon every one of which I feel that I could write you a long sermon, except the one which says, 'And two good days in the woods.' I should have to scratch my head a long time before it would tell my pen how to connect together your adjective 'good' with your substantive 'wood,' which, although they rhyme very well together, I firmly believe them to be as dissimilar as the two words 'paradise' and 'purgatory.'

"The different runs you have detailed, I have gone over as carefully as a beagle picks out the trail of a jack-hare. I am very sorry that the one thing needful has so often been 'not at home.'

"The fable that tells us of 'the hare with many friends,' per contra, we now read all over England of the fox with many enemies. Though my hunting career has now ceased for some time, up to my seventy-sixth year I continued to amuse myself almost every day by riding over timber. I may add the same as before. In my seventy-seventh year, I found that I was always at every leap almost rocking off; and I then discovered that I had lost what Assheton Smith called the 'grip:' so, instead of giving up hunting in my seventy-eighth year, hunting gave me up.

"I continue, however, to ride sixteen or eighteen miles every day, clothing myself according to the weather. I can still go pretty fast, up or down-hill, and across rough ground; but over a fence as high as my knee. 'No.'

"My black boots, like a hatchment over a window in Grosvenor Square, stand in a row on the top of a mahogany wardrobe in my dressing-room. I sometimes give a very little short sigh when I look at them; but I had in them a good allowance of green fields, hedges, brooks, ditches, and dainty bits of timber, of all of which I occasionally enjoy a delightful dream.

"I very often think of the many happy days and jumps I had when at Oxenden; and heartily wish you all a long continuance of the sport I so much enjoyed." &c., &c.

4.

"November, 1869.

"In old times you used to cheer me up with one or two vivid descriptions of a good run; but when I tell you that in my last visit to Lord Hopetoun and the 'P.H.,' I rolled off, I thought you'd give me up, and I certainly am only deserving of the stereotyped motto of old age: '*Non sum qualis eram.*'

"I still continue, however, to read in the *Times* the Hunting Appointments; and see that the 'Pytchley Meet' to-morrow is Sywell Wood, which for years has been identified in my mind with the name, and what is more, with the appearance on his cob, of your worthy and excellent father; to say nothing of his cub!" &c., &c.

5.

"March 5th, 1872.

"I was delighted to learn from your note just received, that a horse, sent on trial to you, ran away with you from your very door—jumped a seven-barred gate—fell on his head, and 'only' sprained your ankle! I never think again of turtle-soup after it is swallowed; but I do ruminate with great pleasure, and I hope with becoming gratitude, on the escapes I have had;

and I always, as you know, enjoy a thing that 'ends'— as your scampavia did—in *something* that you will never forget!

"I greatly enjoy the 'bulletins' you send me of the sport. Yesterday, by chance, I happened to be in at the death of a Lawyer's 'Run,' which had lasted, with only two checks, for 102 days. I *never* go to London, but happening to be there yesterday, I strolled down to the Queen's Bench. Two fierce policemen, as I approached, said pompously, 'No room, Sir, of any sort or kind.' I insisted on sending in my card; and in less than two minutes I found myself sitting cheek by jowl with the Lord Chief Justice.

"Soon after, all hands were taken a-back by the Jury declaring that 'they did not want any more evidence.' I didn't holler [*sic.*] out 'whoo-hoop,' but I said it to myself." &c., &c.

6.

[Summer of 1873.]

The next letter to be quoted—written in the summer of 1873 —is, in its latter part, painfully touching in its description of the writer's physical condition. The passion strong in death as in life, being the burden of its song throughout.

" It was very kind of you to write to me so soon upon your return to Moulton Grange, after the brilliant run you had had across the most interesting part of Europe. The details, i.e. the jumps you took from capital to capital, will be 'oats, beans, and hay,' that will, I believe, cheer your mind as long as you have one. As regards myself, 'the least said, the soonest mended.' On the 23rd of September last, I mounted my horse for my daily canter across our open country—a hale, hearty, hardy, tough old fellow of eighty—impervious to rain, sleet, snow, fog, or cold of any sort. After my ordinary ride of over sixteen miles, I dismounted an invalid for life, as the old nurses say. I was immediately put to bed, where I remained for six weeks, to migrate for the same time to my sofa: I have lately been promoted from crutches to two sticks. While I was better, I tried to ride at a walk; but as I found it injurious, I am now finally divorced from the 'pig-skin.' Pray, however, do not think I contemplate the prospect before me in a gloomy spirit. The sunshine of the past years of my life brightens all that may be awaiting me. I very gratefully remember that for eighty years it has pleased God to grant me almost uninterrupted health. Instead, therefore, of allowing myself to reflect on the present, I derive constant enjoyment from the retrospect of the many happy days of 'auld lang syne.'

"I was deeply affected when I read in the *Times* the announcement of Lord Hopetoun's death. Few people know what a noble-minded, kind-hearted man he was. I never can forget the affectionate regard he always bestowed upon me.

"As it is always more delightful to buy than to sell horses, I am glad to hear that your stalls are empty. You will, I know, soon get some rushing, impetuous animals to fill them.

"As regards Women, it is said that 'if they deliberate, they are lost;' but your horses never allow you to deliberate; so, accordingly, you find yourself well over the rails before you had made up your mind to ride at them!"

7.

" November 5th, 1873.

"My spirit hovered over you all at your first Meet on Monday.

"I had always fancied that when the moment came to say Farewell to the pig-skin, I should be a most miserable creature; but as it pleases God to temper the wind to the shorn lamb, so I found, that without the slightest effort, I was able, when I sent my last horse out of my stable to put him simultaneously out of my mind; and I never think of future rides, though I do of past ones.

"On a German spring cushion, with an air one on the top of it, and with another at my back to recline on, I daily drive in an open carriage with my faithful old nurse—Lady Head—now in her eighty-second year—by my side. Besides this, I go through the fresh air at about twelve or fourteen miles an hour, in a swing on my lawn, that—by means of a transverse beam, a yard long, and two ropes—I can work myself, pulling alternately with each hand, about as hard as a good-mouthed snaffle-bridled horse.

"I was surprised to read an advertisement lately for a Huntsman for the Pytchley. I should have thought it impossible for any stranger to your brooks, rails, canals, &c., &c., to *lead* the Field to anything but grief!" &c. &c. &c.

8.

"January 28th, 1874.

"As my doctor has pulled me off my horse, and will not let me walk; having been accustomed all my life to rush through the air, I have set up a Swing on my lawn, which I work myself by hand-ropes. I send you a photo showing its construction; which I found admirably adapted for Gout, or any accident that confines the sufferer to a hot, fusty bed. In my Swing I enjoy both air and exercise; and really I look for it, as I used to look for my daily ride.

"I often think of you and the 'Firm of Sywell Wood & Co.' In the Saturday's advertisements in the *Times*, I have lately read the appointments of, apparently, two packs of Pytchley Hounds. What does it mean? Do you hunt on the same day with both?" &c., &c.

9.
[LAST LETTER, 1875.]

Here follows the last letter—written about five months before his death—which the author of this volume was privileged to receive from his kind and gallant old friend.

"January 23rd, 1875.

"Your kind note fed me with savoury dishes such as I like. As Rob Roy said to his old wife, Helen, 'The Heather we trod on when we were young, shall bloom over us when we are dead'—so although that whipper-in Time has driven me out of the hunting-field, it cheers the declining hours of my life to learn that 'the Pytchley were never in a more flourishing condition than in the Year of Grace 1875.'

"Your description of the efficient management of its Master (Lord Spencer), an English Nobleman and a noble Englishman, does not exceed what I expected; and I have often lately thought how greatly he must prefer tumbling over a bit of stiff timber, or going souse into a cold brook, to the warm adulation he justly received during his administration of Ireland.

"So far as my humble experience goes, there is no position in the pyramid of Society so barren and so cheerless as its apex. And if you would like to prove this; after a fast kill, just as Will Goodall, with uplifted arms, throws poor Foxy to the hounds, observe how suddenly you will blight the joy and happiness in your Master's countenance, if you suddenly call him—*hibernice*—'your Ixcellency.'

"The only twitch of pain that your picture of the 'P.H.' gave me was, that 'W. Goodall goes as straight as Charles Payne in his best day;' for as the latter is photographed in my mind as the *beau-ideal* of a bold, quick, beautiful horseman: like a good Catholic, I don't like to be told that another fellow's Saint goes as straight as the one he has always been worshipping.

"I was interested to read that at Harboro'—full of huntingmen—were four brothers Gosling; probably sons of a Gosling Banker—no goose—with whom I hunted, more than forty years ago, in Surrey.

"It seems, as the natural order of succession, that my old friends, Bevan, Hungerford, Clerk, Langham & Co., are now succeeded by their sons—and my dear kind friend, Charley Cust, by a joint-stock daughter and son.

"Of myself, I must tell you, instead of vainly saying, '*Ille ego qui quondam*,' it becomes me better to tell you as '*sed nunc*' that tho' I am knocked out of the saddle, I am now myself a quadruped, crawling along on two living legs and two wooden ones, i.e. sticks.

"I have every now and then a little pain to endure; but as soon as it passes away, thanks to my good, kind, faithful old Wife and Nurse—herself eighty-two—I am as happy as you could wish me to be. She, I am thankful to say, enjoys good health; reads to me, by dim candle-light, without spectacles; and with hair unchanged in colour, like my old friend Colonel Arthur's." &c.

FINISHING REMARKS ON THE CLOSE OF SIR FRANCIS HEAD'S LETTERS.

No apology is necessary to the readers of this volume for the insertion of these Letters, which are probably unique in style, geniality, pathos, and humour; and which evince a love of Hunting such as never can have existed to a greater degree in any man.

It will be observed that in these Letters—as in many others in the possession of him to whom they were addressed—there are no allusions to the past which would lead the reader to suppose that the writer of them had been at Waterloo—had quelled a serious rising in an important Colony—had been the Superintendent of a Gold-Mine—had ridden over six thousand miles of a Pampas, undermined with the holes of the "Prairie Dog" —was a "Quarterly Reviewer"—a popular author—a "Poor-Law Commissioner"—and a "Privy Councillor."—The contemplation of things as they existed about him, current events and the welfare of his friends, seem to have furnished sufficient occupation for his thoughts, and to have kept busy a pen rarely idle. As will be seen by his patient, and more, his cheerful endurance of the pains and penalties of old age, the old soldier was too much of a philosopher to "kick against the pricks," or complain of unavoidable misfortunes: he accepted, as they came, the good with gratitude, the evil of life with resignation. We know from himself that his *Horæ Pytchleyanæ* were the happiest hours of a life extending through eighty-five years; and long will his memory be dear to those Members of the Hunt, who can call to mind the decade, during which the thick, white, curly hair—the keen eye—and the comely countenance of the brave old Officer of Engineers, were to be seen at every Pytchley Meet. The only fault he ever found with the decade was that it was all too short.—But we know—

> "That Pleasure which the most enchants us,
> Seems the soonest done;
> What is Life—with all it grants us—
> But a Hunting Run?"

So determined was Sir Francis that, so far as in him lay, nothing should diminish his enjoyment of hunting, he laid down Rules of Diet for himself, and recommended others, who wished to preserve their health, to follow his example.

"A young Horseman," he says in one of his works, "who wishes to enjoy the greatest possible amount of Hunting, should ensure it by taking the greatest possible care—not of his neck, not even of his life—for, as has been shown, the less he interferes with his horse in jumping the better he will go—but of his Stomach, i.e. his Health. To attain this object he has no penance to undergo whatever; for as he is undergoing strong exercise, his system requires—is entitled to and ought to be allowed—ample support: say a capital Breakfast; a Crust of Bread in the middle of the day; and after Hunting is over, a glass of pure Water! to bring him home to a good wholesome Dinner, with three or four glasses of super-excellent Wine. Instead, however, of subsisting on the healthy diet just described, the ordinary practice of many Hunting-Men is to add the following ingredients:—

"(1) After breakfast, before mounting the spicey Cover-Hack—a *Cigar*.

"(2) On arriving at a hand-gallop at the Meet—a *Cigar*.

"(3) At two o'clock, some cold grouse—a long drain at a flat flask full of Sherry or Brandy and Water, and—a *Cigar*.

"(4) Refreshment at some road-side Inn for man and horse—a *Cigar*.

"(5) While riding home; per hour—a *Cigar*.

"(6) On reaching home; a heavy Dinner, Wine, &c., and—a *Cigar*.

"For a short time a stout system is exhilarated, and a strong stomach invigorated, by a series of gifts so munificently bestowed upon them by the right hand of their Lord and Master; but this slight constant Intoxication produced by Tobacco, Vinous and Spirituous Liquors, with a superabundance of ostrich-food, sooner or later, first weakens the Stomach, and then gradually debilitates the system of the strong man, as well as of the puny one. The first symptom of prominent decay is announced by "the nerves;" which, to the astonishment of the young Rider, sometimes fail so rapidly, that while the whole of the rest of his system appears to himself, and to others, as vigorous as ever, he is compelled to admit that "funking" has set in, and increases, do what he will. By giving the poor willing Stomach more food and liquor than it can conveniently take or digest, all sorts of unthought-of evils intervene. 'India, my boy,' said an Irishman to a friend on his arrival at Calcutta, 'is just the finest climate under the sun; but a pack of young fellows come out here, and they *ate* and they *ate*, and they drink and they drink, and they die; and then they write home to their friends, and they say, "it's the climate that has killed them."'

"The only sure and certain means by which a man can maintain his health is to adopt the system of the Scotchman, who, when asked by a friend why he invariably wore a *plaid waistcoat*, replied, 'Why? That I may always keep a *check* on my Stomach!'"

THE END.

INDEX.

A.

Ainsworth (Mr. Rd.), of Winwick Warren, 313.
Allix (Col. *Grenadier Guards*), one of "the three handsomest men in London," 15. 22.
Allix (Peter, M.P.), a daring rider; nicknamed "Scratchface," 22.
Alvanley (Lord), his Bon-mot on Lord De Ros, 124
Alwin, a Pytchley huntsman previous to William I., 3. 5.
Ambrose (Rector of Blisworth), a Sporting Parson, 3. 5.
Anderson (Mr., horse-dealer), his "Jerry" beats Lord Waterford's "Yellow Dwarf" at Little Houghton Steeplechase, 1838. 25.
Andrew (Mr.), of Harleston. 27.
Arundel (Lord) kept Fox-hounds in Wiltshire and Hampshire, 1670—1700, 5.
Austria (Empress of) hunts with the Pytchley in 1878. 202.—The Steeplechase got up at her expense at Hopping Hill, 203.
Austria (Prince Imperial of) hunts with the Pytchley, 203.

B.

Barratt (Pat), an Irish Groom at Harrow, 286.
Barrymore (Lord); his ingenious cheating of C. J. Fox at cards, 124.
Beaconsfield (Lord); his description of his run of thirty miles on an Arabian mare, and stopping at nothing, 2.
Beecher (Capt.) rides "Spicey" in a Steeplechase at Little Houghton, 1838. 25.
Beers (Frank), "an excellent and honest Northamptonshire Huntsman," 227.
Blunt (Capt.), of Crabbit Park, Sussex, 55.
Boughton; removal thither of the Pytchley Hounds, 10.
Bouverie (Col. of the *Blues*), an unrivalled gentleman-jockey, 23.
Bouverie (Squire), of Delapré Abbey, 23, 118.
Boxing; its support by people in high places, 34.

Bright (Right Hon. John), Pitchley or Pytchley? 1.
Brixworth: the Pytchley Kennels situated there, 47.
Brixworth Sporting-Pauper (the), 114.
Byron (Lord); his admiration of Jackson the Pugilist, 35.

C.

Caldecourt (Will), a famous under-hand Bowler, 140.
Chantrey (Sir F.) and Lord Melbourne's bust, 199.
Charlton (Mr.); Pictures of Lord Spencer's Woodland Pack, 215.
Childe (Capt.) wins the Steeplechase at Little Houghton on "Conrad," 25.
Christian (Dick), a famous horse-breaker, 106.
Clerk (Wm.), of Nottingham; a great under-hand Bowler, 95.
Cock-a-roost, a famous cover near Isham, 234.
Cook (Mr. John), of Hothorp, buys "Lancet" of Mr. Nethercote for £200, 15, 22.
Cooper (John); Mr. G. Payne's "most respectable of grooms," 134.
Cotton (Sir St. Vincent), a good whip, 136. —Member of the Sulby Cricket Club, 141.
Couch (Henry), Military deserter and felon; his singular career and remarkable Letters, 64.
Covers (Favourite), 30, 128, 129.
Cribb (Tom), the Pugilist, 36.
Cricket Match at Leicester between North and South of England, 1838, 44.
Cricket Match, Northampton v. Sulby Hall, 140.

D.

Daniel (Sam, *Coachman*); his match with Lieut. Wellesley: Coach v. Horse, 137.
Davis, Driver of the Manchester "Telegraph," 138.
Deaths of Sir Charles Slingsby and others, in the River Ure, 183.

Index. 373

Derry: First Whip under Lord Chesterfield, 103.
Dickens (Rev. Wm., of Woollaston); his smart sayings, 59.
Downe (Viscount) purchases Dingley Hall, 144.
Drake (Squire), Master of the Bicester Hounds, 285.
Drake (Rev. Edward), of Amersham, 285.
Drake (Hon. Mrs.), a great huntress, 285

E.

Edmonds (Mr. Charles): his remarkable discovery of precious Old Books at Lamport Hall, 323.
Elmore (Mr.); his famous horse "Lottery," 26.
Emery (John), the Actor, and Tom Cribb, the Pugilist, 36.
Everard (Mr. Harry), 307.

F.

Fawsley House, the seat of Sir Rainald Knightley, M.P.; its secret chamber: a Martin Marprelate tract printed there in 1588, 49, 294.
Flatman (Nat), Mr. Bouverie's incorruptible Jockey, 119.
Fletcher Family, Head Gamekeepers to the Duke of Buccleuch at Boughton, 350.
Fox (The); First notice of, temp. Richard II., 5
Fox-Hounds, First Pack of, 5; differences in their characters, 12; a "conceited" hound, 12; attachment of Mr. Musters's hounds to him, 82; the Breeding of Fox-hounds, 229.
Fox-Hunter; the Abbot of Peterborough, temp. Richard II., the first Fox-Hunter, 5.

G.

Gladstone (Rt. Hon. W. E.); his advice at an Althorp Meet to distressed Farmers riding beautiful horses, 221.
Goddard (Jack); First Whip under Mr. Wilkins's Mastership, 97.
Goodall (Will); his excellence as a Huntsman, 219, 226; his rectitude, 227; his bold swimming of the River Nene, and efficacy of whisky in the boots afterwards, 228.
Granville (Earl) hunts with the Pytchley Hounds, 230.
Greville (Mr. C. C. F., *Clerk of the Council*), a partner with G. Payne in racehorses, 119.
Grimston ("Bob"); his furtive rides at Harrow School, 286.
Gully (John), Pugilist and M.P.; his great Mill with "the Chicken," and Lord Althorp's delight thereat, 35.

H.

Hammond (Wm. Oxenden), his secret rides at Harrow School, 286.
Harris (John), Driver of the Northampton Coach, 137.
Harrow Hunt (the), 132.
Head (Sir F. B.): his Letters on Hunting Subjects, 362—371.
Humphrey (Rev. John Cave, of Laughton) and his hunting Niece, 60.
Hungerford (Mr., of Dingley Hall) runs "Brilliant" against "Billy" Russell's "Valentine," 24, 144.
Hunt (Rt. Hon. G. Warde, M.P.); his Speech at farewell dinner to Col Anstruther Thomson, 180
Hunting-Bankers, 256.
Hunting-Dandies, 20, 105.
Hunting-Song, "The Pytchley," 357.

I.

Ingram (Jemmy); his furtive rides at Harrow School, 286.
Inverurie (Lord); his melancholy death in the hunting-field, 131.
Ireland, Hunting in, 216.
Isham (Sir Justinian); his great run from Sywell Wood to Ashby by Welland, 30.
Isham (Sir Thomas): his Latin Diary, 9.
Isham (Rev. Vere, Rector of Lamport), 58.

J.

Jackson, the Pugilist, and Lord Byron, 35.
Jersey (Earl of), a first-rate rider to hounds, 23.
Jolly (Tom), Mr. Isted's excellent second horseman, 248.
Jumping and Jumpers, 154.

K.

King (Charles), Lord Althorp's famous Huntsman, 27; his Hunting Diary, 28; his rectitude, 227.
Kingsbury (Ned, nick-named Dirty Dick), Second Whip to Mr. G. Payne, 125.
Kingsthorpe, sinking for Coal at, 54
Kirwan ("Whacky"), the famous Eton Bowler, 95.
Knight (Dick), Earl Spencer's celebrated Huntsman, 1782, 7.

L.

Lambert (Daniel) and Dick Christian, 109.
Lamport Hall, near Northampton; its famous Rockery and rare Books, 321, 322.
"Lancet," sold by Mr. John Nethercote for 620*l*., 15.

Index.

Lane Family, Managers of the Pytchley Club for three generations, 10; Mr. Lane, the oldest Wantage tenant, 11.
Letter from a young Lady-Naturalist, 300.
Lonsdale (Earl of), Master of the North Pytchley Hounds, 225.

M.

Macdonald (Lord), Leap of thirty feet at Great Harrowden, 99.
Maidstone (Lord), a brilliant rider, 99.
Manchester (Duchess of) at the Empress of Austria's Steeplechase at Hopping Hill, 204.
Mason (Jem), a famous Steeplechase rider, 89.
MASTERS OF THE PYTCHLEY HUNT; its History under their management:—
ALFORD (LORD), 149.
ALTHORP (LORD THIRD EARL SPENCER), 13.
BULLER (MR.), 7.
CHESTERFIELD (EARL OF), 101.
CRAVEN (MR. J. A.), 187.
CUST (HON. C.), 166.
GOODRICKE (SIR F. H.), 113.
GRAHAM (SIR BELLINGHAM), 47.
HOPETOUN (EARL OF), 157.
KNIGHTLEY (SIR CHARLES), 45.
LANGHAM (MR. HERBERT), *present Master*, 224.
MUSTERS (MR. JOHN CHAWORTH), 77.
OSBALDESTON (MR. G.), 83.
PAYNE (MR. GEORGE), 4, 99.
PAYNE (MR. G.), *his second Mastership*, 117.
SMITH (MR. T.), 112.
SONDES (LORD), 15, 47.
SPENCER (FIRST EARL), 6.
——— (SECOND EARL), 6.
——— (PRESENT EARL), 188.
THOMSON (COL. ANSTRUTHER), 166.
VILLIERS (HON. FREDERICK), 157.
WARDE (MR. JOHN), 10.
WILKINS (MR.), M.P., 97.
Meecher (J.), Driver of the "Nottingham Times," 138.
"Meet at Crick;" Portraits in that picture by Barraud, 153.
Melton; best Performers at, between 1820 and 1830, 85.
MEMOIRS OF MEMBERS OF THE PYTCHLEY HUNT:—
ALDERSON (MISS), 319.
ANGERSTEIN (MR. WILLIAM), 254.
ARTHUR (COLONEL), 262.
ASHBY ASHBY (CAPT. G.), 240.
BENNETT (MR. JOHN), 327.
BEVAN (MR. RICHARD LEE), 249.
BRAYE (LORD), 283.
CLERK (CAPT. MILDMAY), 258.
CRAWFURD (MR. STIRLING), 306.
DANIEL (MR.), 254.

DRAKE (REV. J. TYRWHITT), 284.
ENTWISLE (MR. J.) 328.
ERSKINE (LORD), 291.
FOSTER (MR. W. H.), 277.
GILBERT (MR. J.), 326.
GIST (CAPTAIN), 280.
GOUGH (MR. J.), 329.
HAZELHURST (MR. H.), 281.
HEAD (SIR FRANCIS BOND), 313.
HENLEY (LORD), 310.
ISHAM (SIR CHARLES), 320.
ISTED (MR. AMBROSE), 244.
JAMESON (MR.), 280.
KNIGHTLEY (SIR CHARLES), 45.
KNIGHTLEY (SIR RAINALD), 292.
LANGHAM (MR. F.), 291.
LANGHAM (MISS), 291.
LIDDELL (HON. H., LORD RAVENSWORTH), 272.
LOVELL (MR. J.), 312.
MELVILLE (MAJOR WHYTE), 263.
MIDDLETON (CAPT. "BAY"), 256.
MILLS (MR. J.), 328.
MUNTZ (MR. P. A.), 282.
NETHERCOTE (MR. JOHN), 304.
NEWLAND (MAJOR), 305.
PENDER (MR.), 280.
RIDDELL (CAPT.), 318.
ROKEBY (REV. H.), 274.
SIMSON (MR. & MRS.), 278.
WAKE (MR. DRURY), 296.
WROUGHTON (MR. C.), 291.
YOUNG (MR. A. A.), 233.
MEMOIRS OF THE NORTHAMPTON BRIGADE:—
DR. DODD, 330—MR. EADY, 332—"LAWYER" FLESHER, 331—MR. HARRIS, 332—MR. HENRY HIGGINS, 331—MESSRS. PHILLIPS, 331—MR. JOHN PHIPS, 332—MR. RATCLIFFE, 332—MR. WHITWORTH, SEN., 330.
MEMOIRS OF FARMER MEMBERS:—
MESSRS ATTERBURY, 347—MR. JOHN BARBER, 344—MR. JOHN COOPER, 347—MR. W. DRAGE, 344—MR. ELWORTHY, 336—MR. LUCAS FORSTER, 345—MESSRS. J. & G. GEE, 346—MR. CHARLES HEWETT, 340—MR. JOSEPH HUMPHREY, 342—MR. MATTHEW OLDACRE, 339—MR. & MRS. SHARMAN, 345—MR. JOHN TOPHAM, 335—MR. TOM TURNELL, 345—MR. SAMUEL WARREN, 341—MR. W. WHITEHEAD, 345—MR. W. WIDDOWSON, 337—MR. J. WOOD, 346.
MEMOIRS OF WOODLAND MEMBERS:—
THE DUKE OF BUCCLEUCH, 348—THE EARL OF CARDIGAN, 352—LORD LILFORD, 354—LORD LYVEDEN, 354—MR. C. THORNHILL, 354.
Meynell (Hugo); his Pack at Quorndon, 1782, 6.
Murchison (Sir Roderick) as a Fox-Hunter, 53.

N.

Newspaper Accounts of Runs, 165.
Northampton Race-Course; the old and new Stands, 26, 27.
Northampton Cricket Club, 141.

O.

Oliver (T.), the celebrated Steeplechase rider, 131.
"Order of the White Collar:" The Costume of the Hunting Club formed at Old Pytchley Hall by John George, Earl Spencer, about 1752, was a scarlet coat, with white collar, and distinguishing buttons: the binding of the present work has reference to this costume, 6.
Oxenham (Rev. W.), Second Master at Harrow School, 286.
Oxford, Hunting at, in its palmy days, 293.

P.

Payn (Charles), First Whip under Mr. G. Payne, 125; his rectitude, 227.
Payne (" Billy "), Brother of Mr. G. Payne, 135.
Pearson ("Jem"), Driver of the "Nottingham Times," 138.
Pell (Admiral Sir Watkin), a bold hunter with a cork leg, 57.
Pell (Sam), a hard-riding farmer, 155.
Peyton (Sir Henry), a good Whip, 136.
Phillipson (Capt.), nicknamed "Handsome Jack," 25.
"Pillager," a Paragon of fox-hounds, 151.
Plymouth (Earl of), a first-rate rider to hounds, 22.
Pridmore (Wm.), Mr. Isted's second Horseman. 248.
Prize-fights: Gully and "the Chicken," 35; Owen Swift and Atkinson of Nottingham, 143; Great battle near Towcester, 143; Smith and Greenfield at Acheres, France, 38.
Prize-fighting, Downfall of, 37.
Pytchley Club Members in 1782, 1808, and 1838; 7, 15, 106.
Pytchley Hall (Old), built by Sir Euseby Isham, temp. Queen Elizabeth, 3: its successive owners, and demolition, 4.
Pytchley Hunt Races, 1838, 24.

R.

Racehorses, Nomenclature of; its difficulties. 308; its "happy hits," 309.
"Rainbow;" Col. Anstruther Thomson's best horse, 175.
Rance (Tom), First Whip under Lord Spencer's Mastership, 207.
"Rapping" at the Pytchley Club, 15.
Ravensworth (Earl of); see Liddell, 272.

Ros (Lord de) accused of foul play at cards, 122.
Rose (Tom), the Duke of Grafton's celebrated Huntsman, 11.
Royston (H.), Huntsman to the Harrow Hounds, and cricketer, 132.
Runs (Great) with Fox-hounds, 2, 13. 14, 19, 21, 30, 79, 90, 102, 127, 129, 160, 171, 228, 248.
Russell (" Billy ") at Pitsford Hall, 99.
Russell (Lord Charles), on the Breeding of Hounds, 230.

S.

"Safety-Valve;" one of Mr. Stirling Crawfurd's hunters, 307.
Sandars Gorse; a famous cover, 41.
Sawbridge (Mr.) killed in the hunting-field, 130.
Scent—What is it? 203.
Sebright (Tom), an able and upright Huntsman, 227.
"Semper Durus:" one of Mr. Stirling Crawfurd's hunters, 307.
Shirley (Jem), Whip to Mr. Osbaldeston, 85.
Shooting Match; interesting walking match between Capt. Ross and the Hon. G. Anson. 93.
Simpson (Mr.) of Hemplow, an excellent fox preserver, 334.
Smith (Mr. Assheton, Senr.) tries to cut down Dick Knight, 10.
Smith (T. Assheton); his big jump, 109.
Snow, Hunting in the, 21.
Soames (Capt.), a fine rider: his favourable report of the financial position of the P.H., 231.
Sound, instances of the power of, 9.
Spencer (Frederick, Earl), 40.
Spencer (Countess) at the Empress of Austria's Steeplechase at Hopping Hill, 203.
Steeplechases and Steeplechasers, 25, 87, 88, 89, 203.
Stevens (Jack), an unrivalled Whip, 97, 98; but a bad Huntsman, 207.
Stevenson (Mr. John) wins the Farmers' Cup with " True Blue," at the P.H. Races, 1838, 24.
Stubbs (" Ginger "), a hunting-dandy, 105.
Sulby Hall Cricketers, 141.

T.

Tassell (Dan), First Whip to Mr. Isted, 247.
Teck (Duchess of) attends the Empress of Austria's Steeplechase at Hopping Hill, 203.
Thursby (Harvey) of Abington Abbey, near Northampton, 103.
Tollemache (Hon. Wilbraham), a good rider, 105.
Tomblin (Mr.), Horse-dealer and High Sheriff, 251.
" True Blue," a famous Steeplechaser, 24.

Index.

U.

"Under the Rose;" origin of the phrase, 50.

V.

Vernon (Mr.), nicknamed "Hat-peg Vernon," 159.

W.

Wale (Mr. Drury): his unrivalled ride from Oxford to London and back in five hours, 29; his perilous ride from Constantinople to Belgrade, in 1854, with Government Despatches, 300; his immersion in Whilton Brook, 303.
Wales (H.R.H. the Prince of) hunts with the Pytchley; falls into Spratton Brook, 4 200.
Wales (H.R.H. the Princess of) attends the Empress of Austria's Steeplechase at Hopping Hill, 203.
Waterford (Marquis of) rides "Yellow Dwarf" at the Little Houghton Steeplechase, 1838, 25.
Watkins (Rev. C. F.): his speech at dinner to Col. Anstruther Thomson, 178.
Watson (Mr., of Rockingham Castle), Master of the North Pytchley Hounds, 224.
West (Mr., of Dallington), a Northamptonshire Hunting Yeoman, 153.
Whalley (Rev. John) at the P.H. Races, 1843, 25; his graceful riding, 59.
"Whole Duty of Man;" verses on Foxpreserving, 326.
William IV. (King): his horse "Hindoostan" beats Mr. Whitworth's "Peer." at Northampton Races, 26.
Wood (Jem). First Whip under Lord Althorp; a brilliant rider, 21.
Wood (Squire) of Brixworth Hall, 53.

A Catalogue of American and Foreign Books Published or Imported by MESSRS. SAMPSON LOW & CO. *can be had on application.*

St. Dunstan's House, Fetter Lane, Fleet Street, London,
April, 1888.

A Selection from the List of Books
PUBLISHED BY
SAMPSON LOW, MARSTON, SEARLE, & RIVINGTON,
LIMITED.

ALPHABETICAL LIST.

*A*BBOTT *(C. C.) Poaetquissings Chronicle: Upland and Meadow.* 10s. 6d.
——— *Waste Land Wanderings.* Crown 8vo, 7s. 6d.
Abney (W. de W.) and Cunningham. Pioneers of the Alps. With photogravure portraits of guides. Imp. 8vo, gilt top, 21s.
Adam (G. Mercer) and Wetherald. An Algonquin Maiden. Crown 8vo, 5s.
Adams (C. K.) Manual of Historical Literature. Cr. 8vo, 12s. 6d.
Agassiz (Alex.) Three Cruises of the Blake. With many Illustrations. 2 vols., 8vo,
Alcott. Works of the late Miss Louisa May Alcott :—
    Eight Cousins. Illustrated, 2s.; cloth gilt, 3s. 6d.
    Jack and Jill. Illustrated, 2s.; cloth gilt, 3s. 6d.
    Jo's Boys. 5s.
    Jimmy's Cruise in the Pinafore, &c. Illustrated, cloth, 2s.; gilt edges, 3s. 6d.
    Little Men. Double vol., 2s.; cloth, gilt edges, 3s. 6d.
    Little Women. 1s. } 1 vol., cloth, 2s. ; larger ed., gilt
    Little Women Wedded. 1s. }   edges, 3s. 6d.
    Old-fashioned Girl. 2s.; cloth, gilt edges, 3s. 6d.
    Rose in Bloom. 2s.; cloth gilt, 3s. 6d.
    Silver Pitchers. Cloth, gilt edges, 3s. 6d.
    Under the Lilacs. Illustrated, 2s ; cloth gilt, 5s.
    Work : a Story of Experience. 1s. } 1 vol., cloth, gilt
    ——— Its Sequel, "Beginning Again." 1s. }   edges, 3s. 6d.
Alden (W. L.) Adventures of Jimmy Brown, written by himself. Illustrated. Small crown 8vo, cloth, 2s.
Aldrich (T. B.) Friar Jerome's Beautiful Book, &c. Very choicely printed on hand-made paper, parchment cover, 3s. 6d.
Alford (Lady Marian) Needlework as Art. With over 100 Woodcuts, Photogravures, &c. Royal 8vo, 21s. ; large paper, 84s.

A

Amateur Angler's Days in Dove Dale : Three Weeks' Holiday in 1884. By E. M. 1s. 6d.; boards, 1s.; large paper, 5s.

Andersen. Fairy Tales. An entirely new Translation. With over 500 Illustrations by Scandinavian Artists. Small 4to, 6s.

Anderson (W.) Pictorial Arts of Japan. With 80 full-page and other Plates, 16 of them in Colours. Large imp. 4to, £8 8s. (in four folio parts, £2 2s. each); Artists' Proofs, £12 12s.

Angler's Strange Experiences (An). By COTSWOLD ISYS. With numerous Illustrations, 4to, 5s. New Edition, 3s. 6d.

Angling. See Amateur, "British," "Cutcliffe," "Fennell," "Halford," "Hamilton," "Martin," "Orvis," "Pennell," "Pritt," "Senior," "Stevens," "Theakston," "Walton," "Wells," and "Willis-Bund."

Annals of the Life of Shakespeare, from the most recent authorities. Fancy boards, 2s.

Annesley (Chas.) Standard Opera Glass. Plots of 80 *Operas,* with dates, 1s. 6d.

Annual American Catalogue, Books of 1886 and 1887. Each 10s. 6d.; bound, 14s.

Antipodean Notes, collected on a Nine Months' Tour round the World. By Wanderer, Author of "Fair Diana." Crown 8vo, 7s. 6d.

Appleton. European Guide. 2 Parts, 8vo, 10s. each.

Armytage (Hon. Mrs.) Wars of Victoria's Reign. 5s.

Art Education. See "Biographies," "D'Anvers," "Illustrated Text Books," "Mollett's Dictionary."

Attwell (Prof.) The Italian Masters. Crown 8vo, 3s. 6d.

Audsley (G. A.) Handbook of the Organ. Top edge gilt, 42s.; large paper, 84s.

—— *Ornamental Arts of Japan.* 90 Plates, 74 in Colours and Gold, with General and Descriptive Text. 2 vols., folio, £15 15s.; in specially designed leather, £23 2s.

—— *The Art of Chromo-Lithography.* Coloured Plates and Text. Folio, 63s.

—— *and Tomkinson. Ivory and Wood Carvings of Japan.* 84s. Artists' proofs (100), 168s.

Auerbach (B.) Brigitta. (B. Tauchnitz Collection.) 2s.

—— *On the Heights.* 3 vols., 6s.

—— *Spinoza.* 2 vols., 18mo, 4s.

BADDELEY (St. Clair) Tchay and Chianti. A Short Visit to Russia and Finland. Small post 8vo, 5s.

Baldwin (James) Story of Siegfried. 6s

Baldwin (James) Story of the Golden Age. Illustrated by HOWARD PYLE. Crown 8vo, 7s. 6d.
——— *Story of Roland.* Crown 8vo, 6s.
Bamford (A. J.) Turbans and Tails. Sketches in the Unromantic East. Crown 8vo
Barlow (Alfred) Weaving by Hand and by Power. With several hundred Illustrations. Third Edition, royal 8vo, £1 5s.
Barrow (J.) Mountain Ascents in Cumberland and Westmoreland. Crown 8vo, 7s. 6d.
Bassett (F. S.) Legends and Superstitions of the Sea and of Sailors. Crown 8vo, 7s. 6d.

THE BAYARD SERIES.

Edited by the late J. HAIN FRISWELL.

Comprising Pleasure Books of Literature produced in the Choicest Style.

"We can hardly imagine better books for boys to read or for men to ponder over."—*Times.*

Price 2s. 6d. *each Volume, complete in itself, flexible cloth extra, gilt edges, with silk Headbands and Registers.*

The Story of the Chevalier Bayard.
Joinville's St. Louis of France.
The Essays of Abraham Cowley.
Abdallah. By Edouard Laboullaye.
Napoleon, Table-Talk and Opinions.
Words of Wellington.
Johnson's Rasselas. With Notes.
Hazlitt's Round Table.
The Religio Medici, Hydriotaphia, &c. By Sir Thomas Browne, Knt.
Coleridge's Christabel, &c. With Preface by Algernon C. Swinburne.
Ballad Poetry of the Affections. By Robert Buchanan.
Lord Chesterfield's Letters, Sentences, and Maxims. With Essay by Sainte-Beuve.
The King and the Commons. Cavalier and Puritan Songs.
Vathek. By William Beckford.
Essays in Mosaic. By Ballantyne.
My Uncle Toby; his Story and his Friends. By P. Fitzgerald.
Reflections of Rochefoucauld.
Socrates: Memoirs for English Readers from Xenophon's Memorabilia. By Edw. Levien.
Prince Albert's Golden Precepts.

A Case containing 12 *Volumes, price* 31s. 6d.; *or the Case separately, price* 3s. 6d.

Baynes (Canon) Hymns and other Verses. Crown 8vo, sewed, 1s.; cloth, 1s. 6d.
Beecher (Henry Ward) Authentic Biography, and Diary. By his Son and Son-in-law. Illustrated, large 8vo. [*Preparing.*
Behnke and Browne. Child's Voice: its Treatment with regard to After Development. Small 8vo, 3s. 6d.
Beyschlag. Female Costume Figures of various Centuries. 12 reproductions of pastel designs in portfolio, imperial. 21s.
Bickersteth (Bishop E. H.) The Clergyman in his Home. Small post 8vo, 1s.

Bickersteth (Bishop E. H.) Evangelical Churchmanship and Evangelical Eclecticism. 8vo, 1s.
—— *From Year to Year: Original Poetical Pieces.* Small post 8vo, 3s. 6d. ; roan, 6s. and 5s.; calf or morocco, 10s. 6d.
—— *The Master's Home-Call; or, Brief Memorials of Alice* Frances Bickersteth. 20th Thousand. 32mo, cloth gilt, 1s.
—— *The Master's Will.* A Funeral Sermon preached on the Death of Mrs. S. Gurney Buxton. Sewn, 6d. ; cloth gilt, 1s.
—— *The Reef, and other Parables.* Crown 8vo, 2s. 6d.
—— *The Shadow of the Rock.* A Selection of Religious Poetry. 18mo, cloth extra, 2s. 6d.
—— *The Shadowed Home and the Light Beyond.* New Edition, crown 8vo, cloth extra, 5s.

Biographies of the Great Artists (*Illustrated*). Crown 8vo, emblematical binding, 3s. 6d. per volume, except where the price is given.

Claude le Lorrain, by Owen J. Dullea.
Correggio, by M. E. Heaton. 2s. 6d.
Della Robbia and Cellini. 2s. 6d.
Albrecht Dürer, by R. F. Heath.
Figure Painters of Holland.
Fra Angelico, Masaccio, and Botticelli.
Fra Bartolommeo, Albertinelli, and Andrea del Sarto.
Gainsborough and Constable.
Ghiberti and Donatello. 2s. 6d.
Giotto, by Harry Quilter.
Hans Holbein, by Joseph Cundall.
Hogarth, by Austin Dobson.
Landseer, by F. G. Stevens.
Lawrence and Romney, by Lord Ronald Gower. 2s. 6d.
Leonardo da Vinci.
Little Masters of Germany, by W. B. Scott.
Mantegna and Francia.
Meissonier, by J. W. Mollett. 2s. 6d.
Michelangelo Buonarotti, by Clément.
Murillo, by Ellen E. Minor. 2s. 6d.
Overbeck, by J. B. Atkinson.
Raphael, by N. D'Anvers.
Rembrandt, by J. W. Mollett.
Reynolds, by F. S. Pulling.
Rubens, by C. W. Kett.
Tintoretto, by W. R. Osler.
Titian, by R. F. Heath.
Turner, by Cosmo Monkhouse.
Vandyck and Hals, by P. R. Head.
Velasquez, by E. Stowe.
Vernet and Delaroche, by J. Rees.
Watteau, by J. W. Mollett. 2s. 6d.
Wilkie, by J. W. Mollett.

Bird (F. J.) American Practical Dyer's Companion. 8vo, 42s.
—— (*H. E.*) *Chess Practice.* 8vo, 2s. 6d.
Black (Robert) Horse Racing in France: a History. 8vo, 14s.
Black (Wm.) Novels. See "Low's Standard Library."
—— *Adventures of a House-Boat.* 3 vols., crown 8vo.
Blackburn (Charles F.) Hints on Catalogue Titles and Index Entries, with a Vocabulary of Terms and Abbreviations, chiefly from Foreign Catalogues. Royal 8vo, 14s.
Blackburn (Henry) Breton Folk. With 171 Illust. by RANDOLPH CALDECOTT. Imperial 8vo, gilt edges, 21s.; plainer binding, 10s. 6d.

Blackburn (Henry) Pyrenees. With 100 Illustrations by GUSTAVE DORÉ, corrected to 1881. Crown 8vo, 7s. 6d. See also CALDECOTT.
Blackmore (R. D.) Lorna Doone. Édition de luxe. Crown 4to, very numerous Illustrations, cloth, gilt edges, 31s. 6d.; parchment, uncut, top gilt, 35s.; new issue, plainer, 21s.; small post 8vo, 6s.
────── *Novels.* See "Low's Standard Library."
────── *Springhaven.* With 124 Illustrations by PARSONS and BARNARD, square 8vo, 12s.
Blaikie (William) How to get Strong and how to Stay so. Rational, Physical, Gymnastic, &c., Exercises. Illust., sm. post 8vo, 5s.
────── *Sound Bodies for our Boys and Girls.* 16mo, 2s. 6d.
Bonwick. British Colonies. Asia, 1s.; Africa, 1s.; America, 1s.; Australasia, 1s. One vol., cloth, 5s.
Bosanquet (Rev. C.) Blossoms from the King's Garden: Sermons for Children. 2nd Edition, small post 8vo, cloth extra, 6s.
────── *Jehoshaphat; or, Sunlight and Clouds.* 1s.
Boussenard (L.) Crusoes of Guiana. Illustrated. 5s.
────── *Gold-seekers.* A Sequel to the above. Illustrated. 16mo, 5s.
Boyesen (F.) Story of Norway. Illustrated, sm. 8vo, 7s. 6d.
Boyesen (H. H.) Modern Vikings: Stories of Life and Sport in Norseland. Cr. 8vo, 6s.
Boy's Froissart. King Arthur. Mabinogion. Percy. See LANIER.
Bradshaw (J.) New Zealand as it is. 8vo, 12s. 6d.
Brannt (W. T.) Animal and Vegetable Fats and Oils. 244 Illust., 8vo, 35s.
Bright (John) Public Letters. Crown 8vo, 7s. 6d.
Brisse (Baron) Ménus (366). A *ménu*, in French and English, for every Day in the Year. 2nd Edition. Crown 8vo, 5s.
British Fisheries Directory. Small 8vo, 2s. 6d.
Brittany. See BLACKBURN.
Browne (G. Lennox) Voice Use and Stimulants. Sm. 8vo, 3s. 6d.
────── *and Behnke (Emil) Voice, Song, and Speech.* Illustrated, 3rd Edition, medium 8vo, 15s.; Popular Edition, 5s.
Bryant (W. C.) and Gay (S. H.) History of the United States. 4 vols., royal 8vo, profusely Illustrated, 60s.
Bryce (Rev. Professor) Manitoba. Illust. Crown 8vo, 7s. 6d.
────── *Short History of the Canadian People.* 7s. 6d.
Burnaby (Capt.) On Horseback through Asia Minor. 2 vols., 8vo, 38s. Cheaper Edition, 1 vol., crown 8vo, 10s. 6d.

Burnaby (Mrs. F.) High Alps in Winter; or, Mountaineering in Search of Health. With Portrait of the Authoress, Map, and other Illustrations. Handsome cloth, 14s. See also MAIN.

Burnley (James) History of Wool and Woolcombing. Illustrated with mechanical Diagrams, 8vo, 21s.

Burton (Sir R. F.) Early, Public, and Private Life. Edited by F. HITCHMAN. 2 vols., 8vo, 36s.

Butler (Sir W. F.) Campaign of the Cataracts. Illustrated by Lady BUTLER. 8vo, 18s.

—— *Invasion of England, told twenty years after, by an* Old Soldier. Crown 8vo, 2s. 6d.

—— *Red Cloud; or, the Solitary Sioux.* Imperial 16mo, numerous illustrations, gilt edges, 3s. 6d.; plainer binding, 2s. 6d.

—— *The Great Lone Land; an Account of the Red River* Expedition, 1869-70. New Edition, crown 8vo, cloth extra, 7s. 6d.

—— *The Wild North Land; the Story of a Winter Journey* with Dogs across Northern North America. 8vo, 18s. Cr. 8vo, 7s. 6d.

CABLE (G. W.) Bonaventure: A Prose Pastoral of Acadian Louisiana. Sm. post 8vo, 5s.

Cadogan (Lady A.) Illustrated Games of Patience. Twenty-four Diagrams in Colours, with Text. Fcap. 4to, 12s. 6d.

—— *New Games of Patience.* Coloured Diagrams, 4to, 12s. 6d.

Caldecott (Randolph) Memoir. By HENRY BLACKBURN. With 170 Examples of the Artist's Work. 14s.; large paper, 21s.

California. See NORDHOFF.

Callan (H., M.A.) Wanderings on Wheel and on Foot through Europe. Crown 8vo, boards, 1s. 6d.

Campbell (Lady Colin) Book of the Running Brook: and of Still Waters. 5s.

Canadian People: Short History. Crown 8vo, 7s. 6d.

Carleton (Will) Farm Ballads, Farm Festivals, and Farm Legends. Paper boards, 1s. each; 1 vol., small post 8vo, 3s. 6d.

—— *City Ballads.* Illustrated, 12s. 6d.; paper boards, 1s.

—— See also " Rose Library."

Carnegie (A.) American Four-in-Hand in Britain. Small 4to, Illustrated, 10s. 6d. Popular Edition, paper, 1s.

—— *Round the World.* 8vo, 10s. 6d.

—— *Triumphant Democracy.* 6s.; also 1s. 6d. and 1s.

Chairman's Handbook. By R. F. D. PALGRAVE. 5th Edit., 2s.

Changed Cross, &c. Religious Poems. 16mo, 2s. 6d.; calf, 6s.

Chaplin (J. G.) Three Principles of Book-keeping. 2s. 6d.
Charities of London. See Low's.
Chattock (R. S.) Practical Notes on Etching. An entirely new Edition. 8vo, 10s. 6d.
Chess. See BIRD (H. E.).
Children's Praises. Hymns for Sunday-Schools and Services. Compiled by LOUISA H. H. TRISTRAM. 4d.
Choice Editions of Choice Books. 2s. 6d. each. Illustrated by C. W. COPE, R.A., T. CRESWICK, R.A., E. DUNCAN, BIRKET FOSTER, J. C. HORSLEY, A.R.A., G. HICKS, R. REDGRAVE, R.A., C. STONEHOUSE, F. TAYLER, G. THOMAS, H. J. TOWNSHEND, E. H. WEHNERT, HARRISON WEIR, &c.

Bloomfield's Farmer's Boy.	Milton's L'Allegro.
Campbell's Pleasures of Hope.	Poetry of Nature. Harrison Weir.
Coleridge's Ancient Mariner.	Rogers' (Sam.) Pleasures of Memory.
Goldsmith's Deserted Village.	Shakespeare's Songs and Sonnets.
Goldsmith's Vicar of Wakefield.	Tennyson's May Queen.
Gray's Elegy in a Churchyard.	Elizabethan Poets.
Keat's Eve of St. Agnes.	Wordsworth's Pastoral Poems.

"Such works are a glorious beatification for a poet."—*Athenæum.*

Christ in Song. By PHILIP SCHAFF. New Ed., gilt edges, 6s.
Chromo-Lithography. See AUDSLEY.
Cochran (W.) Pen and Pencil in Asia Minor. Illustrated from Water-colour Sketches. 8vo, 21s.
Collingwood (Harry) Under the Meteor Flag. The Log of a Midshipman. Illustrated, small post 8vo, gilt, 3s. 6d.; plainer, 2s. 6d.
—— *The Voyage of the "Aurora."* Illustrated, small post 8vo, gilt, 3s. 6d.; plainer, 2s. 6d.
Cook (Dutton) Book of the Play. New Edition. 1 vol., 3s. 6d.
—— *On the Stage: Studies.* 2 vols., 8vo, cloth, 24s.
Cowen (Jos., M.P.) Life and Speeches. 8vo, 14s.
Cowper (W.) Poetical Works: A Concordance. By JOHN NEVE. Royal 8vo, 21s.
Cozzens (F.) American Yachts. 27 Plates, 22 × 28 inches. Proofs, £21; Artist's Proofs, £31 10s.
Crew (Benjamin J.) Practical Treatise on Petroleum. Illustrated. 8vo, 28s.
Crouch (A. P.) On a Surf-bound Coast. Crown 8vo, 7s. 6d.
Crown Prince of Germany: a Diary. 2s. 6d.
Cumberland (Stuart) A Thought Reader's Thoughts. Cr. 8vo.
—— *Queen's Highway from Ocean to Ocean.* Collotype Illustrations. 8vo, 18s.

Cundall (*Joseph*) *Annals of the Life and Work of Shakespeare.*
With a List of Early Editions. 3*s*. 6*d*.; large paper, 5*s*.; also 2*s*.

Cushing (*W.*) *Initials and Pseudonyms: a Dictionary of Literary Disguises.* Large 8vo, top edge gilt, 21*s*.

Cutcliffe (*H. C.*) *Trout Fishing in Rapid Streams.* Cr. 8vo, 3*s*. 6*d*.

DALY (*Mrs. D.*) *Digging, Squatting, and Pioneering in Northern South Australia.* 8vo, 12*s*.

D'Anvers. *Elementary History of Art.* New ed., 360 illus., cr. 8vo, 2 vols. (5*s*. each) 10*s*. 6*d*.

—— *Elementary History of Music.* Crown 8vo, 2*s*. 6*d*.

—— *Handbooks of Elementary Art—Architecture; Sculpture; Old Masters; Modern Painting.* Crown 8vo, 3*s*. 6*d*. each.

Davis (*Clement*) *Modern Whist.* 4*s*.

Davis (*C. T.*) *Manufacture of Bricks, Tiles, Terra-Cotta, &c.* Illustrated. 8vo, 25*s*.

—— *Manufacture of Leather.* With many Illustrations. 52*s*. 6*d*.

—— *Manufacture of Paper.* 28*s*.

Davis (*G. B.*) *Outlines of International Law, Origin and Development.* 10*s*. 6*d*.

Dawidowsky. *Glue, Gelatine, Isinglass, Cements, &c.* 8vo, 12*s*. 6*d*.

Day of My Life (*A*); or, *Every-Day Experiences at Eton.* By an ETON BOY. 16mo, cloth extra, 2*s*. 6*d*.

Day's Collacon: *an Encyclopædia of Prose Quotations.* Imperial 8vo, cloth, 31*s*. 6*d*.

De Leon (*Edwin*) *Under the Stars and under the Crescent.* 2 vols., crown 8vo, 21*s*.

Dethroning Shakspere. *Letters to the Daily Telegraph; and Editorial Papers.* Crown 8vo, 2*s*. 6*d*.

Dictionary. See TOLHAUSEN, "Technological."

Diruf (*Oscar*) *Kissingen Baths and Mineral Springs.* Crown 8vo, 5*s*.; sewed, 3*s*. 6*d*.

Dogs in Disease. By ASHMONT. Crown 8vo, 7*s*. 6*d*.

Donnelly (*Ignatius*) *Atlantis; or, the Antediluvian World.* 7th Edition, crown 8vo, 12*s*. 6*d*.

—— *Ragnarok: The Age of Fire and Gravel.* Illustrated, crown 8vo, 12*s*. 6*d*.

—— *The Great Cryptogram: Francis Bacon's Cipher in the so-called Shakspere Plays.* With facsimiles. 2 vols., royal 8vo, 24*s*.

Doré (*Gustave*) *Life and Reminiscences.* By BLANCHE ROOSEVELT. Illust. from the Artist's Drawings. Medium 8vo, 24*s*.

Dougall (James Dalziel) Shooting: its Appliances, Practice,
and Purpose. New Edition, revised with additions. Crown 8vo, 7s. 6d.
"The book is admirable in every way. . . . . We wish it every success."—*Globe.*
"A very complete treatise. . . . Likely to take high rank as an authority on shooting."—*Daily News.*

Dupré (Giovanni). By H. S. FRIEZE. With Dialogues on Art by AUGUSTO CONTI. 7s. 6d.

EDUCATIONAL List and Directory for 1887-88. 5s.

Educational Works published in Great Britain. A Classified Catalogue. Third Edition, 8vo, cloth extra, 6s.

Egypt. See "Foreign Countries."

Eight Months on the Argentine Gran Chaco. 8vo, 8s. 6d.

Electricity. See GORDON.

Elliott (H. W.) An Arctic Province: Alaska and the Seal Islands. Illustrated from Drawings; also with Maps. 16s.

Emerson (Dr. P. H.) Pictures of East Anglian Life. Ordinary ed., leather back, 73s. 6d.; édit. de luxe, 17 × 13½, vellum, morocco back, 105s.

—— *and Goodall. Life and Landscape on the Norfolk* Broads. Plates 12 × 8 inches, 126s.; large paper, 210s.

English Catalogue of Books. Vol. III., 1872—1880. Royal 8vo, half-morocco, 42s. See also "Index."

English Etchings. A Periodical published Quarterly. 3s. 6d. Vol. VI., 25s.

English Philosophers. Edited by E. B. IVAN MÜLLER, M.A.
A series intended to give a concise view of the works and lives of English thinkers. Crown 8vo volumes of 180 or 200 pp., price 3s. 6d. each.

Francis Bacon, by Thomas Fowler. | Shaftesbury and Hutcheson.
Hamilton, by W. H. S. Monck. | Adam Smith, by J. A. Farrer.
Hartley and James Mill. |

Esmarch (F.) Handbook of Surgery. An entirely new Translation, from the last German Edition. With 647 new Illustrations. 8vo, leather, 24s.

Etching. See CHATTOCK, and ENGLISH ETCHINGS.

Etchings (Modern) of Celebrated Paintings. 4to, 31s. 6d.

Evans (E. A.) Songs of the Birds. New Ed. Illustrated, 6s.

Evelyn. Life of Mrs. Godolphin. By WILLIAM HARCOURT, of Nuncham. Steel Portrait. Extra binding, gilt top, 7s. 6d.

FARINI (G. A.) Through the Kalahari Desert. 8vo, 21s.

Farm Ballads, Festivals, and Legends. See CARLETON.

Fawcett (Edgar) A Gentleman of Leisure. 1s.
Fenn (G. Manville) Off to the Wilds: A Story for Boys.
Profusely Illustrated. Crown 8vo, gilt edges, 3s. 6d.; plainer, 2s. 6d.
—— *The Silver Cañon: a Tale of the Western Plains.*
Illustrated, small post 8vo, gilt edges, 3s. 6d.; plainer, 2s. 6d.
Fennell (Greville) Book of the Roach. New Edition, 12mo, 2s.
Ferns. See HEATH.
Field (H. M.) Greek Islands and Turkey after the War. 8s. 6d.
Field (Mrs. Horace) Anchorage. 2 vols., crown 8vo, 12s.
Fields (J. T.) Yesterdays with Authors. New Ed., 8vo, 10s. 6d.
Fitzgerald (Percy) Book Fancier: Romance of Book Collecting. Crown 8vo, 5s.; large paper, 12s. 6d.
Fleming (Sandford) England and Canada: a Tour. Cr. 8vo, 6s.
Florence. See YRIARTE.
Folkard (R., Jun.) Plant Lore, Legends, and Lyrics. 8vo, 16s.
Forbes (H. O.) Naturalist's Wanderings in the Eastern Archipelago. Illustrated, 8vo, 21s.
Foreign Countries and British Colonies. Cr. 8vo, 3s. 6d. each.

Australia, by J. F. Vesey Fitzgerald.
Austria, by D. Kay, F.R.G.S.
Denmark and Iceland, by E. C. Otté.
Egypt, by S. Lane Poole, B.A.
France, by Miss M. Roberts.
Germany, by S. Baring-Gould.
Greece, by L. Sergeant, B.A.
Japan, by S. Mossman.
Peru, by Clements R. Markham.
Russia, by W. R. Morfill, M.A.
Spain, by Rev. Wentworth Webster.
Sweden and Norway, by Woods.
West Indies, by C. H. Eden, F.R.G.S.

Foreign Etchings: from Paintings by Rembrandt, &c. 63s.; India proofs, 147s.
Fortunes made in Business. Vols. I., II., III. 16s. each.
Frampton (Mary) Journal, Letters, and Anecdotes. 8vo, 14s.
Franc (Maud Jeanne). Small post 8vo, uniform in cloth, gilt edges:—

Emily's Choice. 5s.
Hall's Vineyard. 4s.
John's Wife: A Story of Life in South Australia. 4s.
Marian; or, The Light of Some One's Home. 5s.
Silken Cords and Iron Fetters. 4s.
Into the Light. 4s.
Vermont Vale. 5s.
Minnie's Mission. 4s.
Little Mercy. 4s.
Beatrice Melton's Discipline. 4s.
No Longer a Child. 4s.
Golden Gifts. 4s.
Two Sides to Every Question. 4s.
Master of Ralston. 4s.

Also a Cheap Edition, in cloth extra, 2s. 6d. each.
Frank's Ranche; or, My Holiday in the Rockies. A Contribution to the Inquiry into What we are to Do with our Boys. 5s.

Freeman (J.) Lights and Shadows of Melbourne Life. Cr. 8vo, 6s.
French. See JULIEN.
Fresh Woods and Pastures New. By the Author of "An Angler's Days." 1s. 6d.; large paper, 5s.
Froissart. See LANIER.
Fuller (Edward) Fellow Travellers. 3s. 6d.

GANE (D. N.) New South Wales and Victoria in 1885. 5s.
Gasparin (Countess Agénor de) Sunny Fields and Shady Woods. Crown 8vo.
Geary (Grattan) Burma after the Conquest. 7s. 6d.
Gentle Life (Queen Edition). 2 vols. in 1, small 4to, 6s.

THE GENTLE LIFE SERIES.

Price 6s. each ; or in calf extra, price 10s. 6d. ; Smaller Edition, cloth extra, 2s. 6d., except where price is named.

The Gentle Life. Essays in aid of the Formation of Character.
About in the World. Essays by Author of "The Gentle Life."
Like unto Christ. A New Translation of Thomas à Kempis' "De Imitatione Christi."
Familiar Words. An Index Verborum, or Quotation Handbook. 6s.
Essays by Montaigne. Edited by the Author of "The Gentle Life."
The Gentle Life. 2nd Series.
The Silent Hour: Essays, Original and Selected.
Half-Length Portraits. Short Studies of Notable Persons. By J. HAIN FRISWELL.
Essays on English Writers, for Students in English Literature.
Other People's Windows. By J. HAIN FRISWELL. 6s.
A Man's Thoughts. By J. HAIN FRISWELL.
The Countess of Pembroke's Arcadia. By Sir PHILIP SIDNEY. New Edition, 6s.

Germany. By S. BARING-GOULD. Crown 8vo, 3s. 6d.
Gibbon (C.) Beyond Compare : a Story.
——— *Yarmouth Coast.*
Gisborne (W.) New Zealand Rulers and Statesmen. With Portraits. Crown 8vo, 7s. 6d.

Goldsmith. She Stoops to Conquer. Introduction by AUSTIN DOBSON ; the designs by E. A. ABBEY. Imperial 4to, 48s.

Gordon (J. E. H., B.A. Cantab.) Four Lectures on Electric Induction at the Royal Institution, 1878-9. Illust., square 16mo, 3s.

—— *Electric Lighting.* Illustrated, 8vo, 18s.

—— *Physical Treatise on Electricity and Magnetism.* 2nd Edition, enlarged, with coloured, full-page, &c., Illust. 2 vols., 8vo, 42s.

—— *Electricity for Schools.* Illustrated. Crown 8vo, 5s.

Gouffé (Jules) Royal Cookery Book. Translated and adapted for English use by ALPHONSE GOUFFÉ, Head Pastrycook to the Queen. New Edition, with plates in colours, Woodcuts, &c., 8vo, gilt edges, 42s.

—— Domestic Edition, half-bound, 10s. 6d.

Grant (General, U.S.) Personal Memoirs. With numerous Illustrations, Maps, &c. 2 vols., 8vo, 28s.

Great Artists. See "Biographies."

Great Musicians. Edited by F. HUEFFER. A Series of Biographies, crown 8vo, 3s. each :—

Bach.	Mendelssohn.	Schubert.
English Church Composers. By BARETT.	Mozart.	Schumann.
	Purcell.	Richard Wagner.
Handel.	Rossini.	Weber.
Haydn.		

Groves (J. Percy) Charmouth Grange: a Tale of the Seventeenth Century. Illustrated, small post 8vo, gilt, 5s.; plainer, 2s. 6d.

Guizot's History of France. Translated by ROBERT BLACK. Super-royal 8vo, very numerous Full-page and other Illustrations. In 8 vols., cloth extra, gilt, each 24s. This work is re-issued in cheaper binding, 8 vols., at 10s. 6d. each.

"It supplies a want which has long been felt, and ought to be in the hands of all students of history."—*Times.*

—————————— *Masson's School Edition.* Abridged from the Translation by Robert Black, with Chronological Index, Historical and Genealogical Tables, &c. By Professor GUSTAVE MASSON, B.A. With 24 full-page Portraits, and other Illustrations. 1 vol., 8vo, 600 pp., 10s. 6d.

Guyon (Mde.) Life. By UPHAM. 6th Edition, crown 8vo, 6s.

HALFORD (F. M.) Floating Flies, and how to Dress them. Coloured plates. 8vo, 15s.; large paper, 30s.

Hall (W. W.) How to Live Long; or, 1408 *Health Maxims, Physical Mental, and Moral.* 2nd Edition, small post 8vo, 2s.

Hamilton (E.) Recollections of Fly-fishing for Salmon, Trout,
and Grayling. With their Habits, Haunts, and History. Illustrated, small post 8vo, 6s.; large paper (100 numbered copies), 10s. 6d.

Hands (T.) Numerical Exercises in Chemistry. Cr. 8vo, 2s. 6d. and 2s.; Answers separately, 6d.

Hardy (Thomas). See LOW's STANDARD NOVELS.

Hare (J. S. Clark) Law of Contracts. 8vo, 26s.

Harley (T.) Southward Ho! to the State of Georgia. 5s.

Harper's Magazine. Published Monthly. 160 pages, fully Illustrated, 1s. Vols., half yearly, I.—XIV. (December, 1880, to November, 1887), super-royal 8vo, 8s. 6d. each.

"'Harper's Magazine' is so thickly sown with excellent illustrations that to count them would be a work of time; not that it is a picture magazine, for the engravings illustrate the text after the manner seen in some of our choicest *éditions de luxe*."—*St. James's Gazette.*

"It is so pretty, so big, and so cheap.... An extraordinary shillingsworth—160 large octavo pages, with over a score of articles, and more than three times as many illustrations."—*Edinburgh Daily Review.*

"An amazing shillingsworth ... combining choice literature of both nations."—*Nonconformist.*

Harper's Young People. Vols. I.-III., profusely Illustrated with woodcuts and coloured plates. Royal 4to, extra binding, each 7s. 6d.; gilt edges, 8s. Published Weekly, in wrapper, 1d.; Annual Subscription, post free, 6s. 6d.; Monthly, in wrapper, with coloured plate, 6d.; Annual Subscription, post free, 7s. 6d.

Harrison (Mary) Skilful Cook: a Practical Manual of Modern Experience. New edition, crown 8vo, 5s.

Hartshorne (H.) Household Medicine, Surgery, &c. Royal 8vo, 21s.

Hatton (Frank) North Borneo. With Biography by JOSEPH HATTON. New Map, and Illustrations, 18s.

Hatton (Joseph) Journalistic London: with Engravings and Portraits of Distinguished Writers of the Day. Fcap. 4to, 12s. 6d.

—— *Old House at Sandwich.* New Edition. Small post 8vo, 6s.

—— *Three Recruits, and the Girls they left behind them.* Small post 8vo, 6s.

"It hurries us along in unflagging excitement."—*Times.*

Hawthorne (Nathaniel) Life. By JOHN R. LOWELL. Small post 8vo, .

Heath (Francis George) Fern World. With Nature-printed Coloured Plates. Crown 8vo, gilt edges, 12s. 6d. Cheap Edition, 6s.

*Heath (Gertrude). Tell us Why? The Customs and Ceremo-*nies of the Church of England explained for Children. Cr. 8vo, 2s. 6d.

Heldmann (Bernard) Mutiny on Board the Ship " Leander."
Small post 8vo, gilt edges, numerous Illustrations, 3s. 6d.; plainer, 2s. 6d.
Henty (G. A.) Winning his Spurs. Illust. Cr. 8vo, 3s. 6d.; plainer, 2s. 6d.
—— *Cornet of Horse: A Story.* Illust. Cr. 8vo, 3s. 6d.; plainer, 2s. 6d.
—— *Jack Archer: Tale of the Crimea.* Illust., crown 8vo, 3s. 6d.; plainer, 2s. 6d.
Henty (Richmond) Australiana: My Early Life. 5s.
Herrick (Robert) Poetry. Preface by AUSTIN DOBSON. With numerous Illustrations by E. A. ABBEY. 4to, gilt edges, 42s.
Hetley (Mrs. E.) Native Flowers of New Zealand. Chromos from Drawings. Three Parts, to Subscribers, 63s.
Hicks (E. S.) Our Boys: How to Enter the Merchant Service. 5s.
—— *Yachts, Boats and Canoes.* Illustrated. 8vo, 10s. 6d.
Hitchman. Public Life of the Earl of Beaconsfield. 3s. 6d.
Hofmann. Scenes from the Life of our Saviour. 12 mounted plates, 12 × 9 inches, 21s.
Holder (C. F.) Marvels of Animal Life. Illustrated. 8s. 6d.
—— *Ivory King: the Elephant and its Allies.* Illustrated. 8s. 6d.
—— *Living Lights: Phosphorescent Animals and Vegetables.* Illustrated. 8vo, 8s. 6d.
Holmes (O. W.) Before the Curfew, &c. Occasional Poems. Crown 8vo, 5s.
—— *Last Leaf: a Holiday Volume.* 42s.
—— *Mortal Antipathy,* 8s. 6d.; also 2s.; paper, 1s.
—— *Our Hundred Days in Europe.* Small post 8vo, extra binding, top gilt, 6s. Special Large Paper Edition, 15s.
—— *Poetical Works.* 2 vols., 18mo, exquisitely printed, and chastely bound in limp cloth, gilt tops, 10s. 6d.
Homer, Iliad I.-XII., done into English Verse. By ARTHUR S. WAY. 9s.
—— *Odyssey.* Translated by A. S. WAY. Fcap. 4to, 7s. 6d.
Hopkins (Manley) Treatise on the Cardinal Numbers. 2s. 6d.
Hore (Mrs.) To Lake Tanganyika in a Bath Chair. Portraits and maps. Crown 8vo, 7s. 6d.
Howorth (H. H.) Mammoth and the Flood. 8vo, 18s.
Hundred Greatest Men (The). 8 portfolios, 21s. each, or 4 vols., half-morocco, gilt edges, 10 guineas. New Ed., 1 vol., royal 8vo, 21s.
Hutchinson (T.) Diary and Letters. Vol. I., 16s.; Vol. II., 16s.

Hygiene and Public Health. Edited by A. H. Buck, M.D.
  Illustrated. 2 vols., royal 8vo, 42s.
Hymnal Companion to the Book of Common Prayer. By
  Bishop Bickersteth. May be had in various styles and bindings
  from 1d. to 31s. 6d. *Price List and Prospectus will be forwarded on
  application.*
ILLUSTRATED Text-Books of Art-Education. Edited by
  Edward J. Poynter, R.A. Each Volume contains numerous Illustrations, and is strongly bound for Students, price 5s. Now ready:—
PAINTING.
  Classic and Italian. By Head. | French and Spanish.
  German, Flemish, and Dutch. | English and American.
ARCHITECTURE.
  Classic and Early Christian.
  Gothic and Renaissance. By T. Roger Smith.
SCULPTURE.
  Antique: Egyptian and Greek.
  Renaissance and Modern. By Leader Scott.
Index to the English Catalogue, Jan., 1874, *to Dec.,* 1880.
  Royal 8vo, half-morocco, 18s.
Inglis (Hon. James; "Maori") Our New Zealand Cousins.
  Small post 8vo, 6s.
—— *Tent Life in Tiger Land: Twelve Years a Pioneer
  Planter.* 8vo.
Irving (Henry) Impressions of America. By J. Hatton. 2
  vols., 21s.; New Edition, one vol., 6s.
Irving (Washington). Complete Library Edition of his Works
  in 27 Vols., Copyright, with the Author's Latest Revisions. "Geoffrey
  Crayon" Edition, handsomely printed in large square 8vo. 12s. 6d. per
  vol. *See also* "Little Britain."

JAMES (C.) Curiosities of Law and Lawyers. 8vo, 7s. 6d.
Japan. See Anderson, Audsley, also Morse.
Jefferies (Richard) Amaryllis at the Fair. Small 8vo, 7s. 6d.
Jerdon (Gertrude) Key-hole Country. Illustrated. Crown 8vo,
  cloth, 2s.
Johnston (H. H.) River Congo, from its Mouth to Bolobo.
  New Edition, 8vo, 21s.
Jones (Major) Heroes of Industry. Biographies with Portraits.
  7s. 6d.
—— *The Emigrants' Friend.* A Complete Guide to the
  United States. New Edition. 2s. 6d.
Julien (F.) English Student's French Examiner. 16mo, 2s.

Julien (F.) Conversational French Reader. 16mo, cloth, 2s. 6d.
—— *French at Home and at School.* Book I., Accidence, &c. Square crown 8vo, 2s.
—— *First Lessons in Conversational French Grammar.* 1s.
—— *Petites Leçons de Conversation et de Grammaire.* 3s.
—— *Phrases of Daily Use.* Limp cloth, 6d.
—— "*Petites Leçons*" and "*Phrases*" in one. 3s. 6d.

KARR (H. W. Seton) Shores and Alps of Alaska. Illustrations and Maps. 8vo, 16s.
Kempis (Thomas à) Daily Text-Book. Square 16mo, 2s. 6d.; interleaved as a Birthday Book, 3s. 6d.
Kent's Commentaries: an Abridgment for Students of American Law. By EDEN F. THOMPSON. 10s. 6d.
Kerr (W. M.) Far Interior: Cape of Good Hope, across the Zambesi, to the Lake Regions. Illustrated from Sketches, 2 vols. 8vo, 32s.
Kershaw (S. W.) Protestants from France in their English Home. Crown 8vo, 6s.
King (Henry) Savage London; Riverside Characters, &c. Crown 8vo, 6s.
Kingston (W. H. G.) Works. Illustrated, 16mo, gilt edges, 3s. 6d.; plainer binding, plain edges, 2s. 6d. each.

Captain Mugford, or, Our Salt and Fresh Water Tutors.
Dick Cheveley.
Heir of Kilfinnan.
Snow-Shoes and Canoes.
Two Supercargoes.
With Axe and Rifle.

Kingsley (Rose) Children of Westminster Abbey: Studies in English History. 5s.
Knight (E. J.) Cruise of the "Falcon." To South America in a 30-Ton Yacht. Illust. New Ed. Cr. 8vo, 7s. 6d.
Knox (Col. T. W.) Boy Travellers on the Congo. Illus. Crown 8vo, 7s. 6d.
Kunhardt (C. B.) Small Yachts: Design and Construction. 35s.
—— *Steam Yachts and Launches.* Illustrated. 4to, 16s.

LAMB (Charles) Essays of Elia. With over 100 designs by C. O. MURRAY. 6s.
Lanier's Works. Illustrated, crown 8vo, gilt edges, 7s. 6d. each.

Boy's King Arthur.
Boy's Froissart.
Boy's Mabinogion; Original Welsh Legends of King Arthur.
Boy's Percy: Ballads of Love and Adventure, selected from the "Reliques."

Lansdell (H.) Through Siberia. 2 vols., 8vo, 30s.; 1 vol., 10s. 6d.
—— *Russia in Central Asia.* Illustrated. 2 vols., 42s.
—— *Through Central Asia; Russo-Afghan Frontier, &c.* 8vo, 12s.
Larden (W.) School Course on Heat. Second Ed., Illust. 5s.
Layard (Mrs. Granville) Through the West Indies. Small post 8vo, 2s. 6d.
Leo XIII.: Life. By BERNARD O'REILLY. With Steel Portrait from Photograph, &c. Large 8vo, 18s.
Leonardo da Vinci's Literary Works. Edited by Dr. JEAN PAUL RICHTER. Containing his Writings on Painting, Sculpture, and Architecture, his Philosophical Maxims, Humorous Writings, and Miscellaneous Notes on Personal Events, on his Contemporaries, on Literature, &c.; published from Manuscripts. 2 vols., imperial 8vo, containing about 200 Drawings in Autotype Reproductions, and numerous other Illustrations. Twelve Guineas.
Library of Religious Poetry. Best Poems of all Ages. Edited by SCHAFF and GILMAN. Royal 8vo, 21s.; cheaper binding, 10s. 6d.
Lindsay (W. S.) History of Merchant Shipping. Over 150 Illustrations, Maps, and Charts. In 4 vols., demy 8vo, cloth extra. Vols. 1 and 2, 11s. each; vols. 3 and 4, 14s. each. 4 vols., 50s.
Little (Archibald J.) Through the Yang-tse Gorges: Trade and Travel in Western China. 8vo, 10s. 6d.
Little Britain, The Spectre Bridegroom, and *Legend of Sleepy Hollow.* By WASHINGTON IRVING. An entirely New *Edition de luxe.* Illustrated by 120 very fine Engravings on Wood, by Mr. J. D. COOPER. Designed by Mr. CHARLES O. MURRAY. Re-issue, square crown 8vo, cloth, 6s.
Longfellow. Maidenhood. With Coloured Plates. Oblong 4to, 2s. 6d.; gilt edges, 3s. 6d.
Lowell (J. R.) Vision of Sir Launfal. Illustrated, royal 4to, 63s.
—— *Life of Nathaniel Hawthorne.* Small post 8vo, .
Low's Standard Library of Travel and Adventure. Crown 8vo, uniform in cloth extra, 7s. 6d., except where price is given.
 1. **The Great Lone Land.** By Major W. F. BUTLER, C.B.
 2. **The Wild North Land.** By Major W. F. BUTLER, C.B.
 3. **How I found Livingstone.** By H. M. STANLEY.
 4. **Through the Dark Continent.** By H. M. STANLEY. 12s. 6d.
 5. **The Threshold of the Unknown Region.** By C. R. MARKHAM. (4th Edition, with Additional Chapters, 10s. 6d.)
 6. **Cruise of the Challenger.** By W. J. J. SPRY, R.N.
 7. **Burnaby's On Horseback through Asia Minor.** 10s. 6d.
 8. **Schweinfurth's Heart of Africa.** 2 vols., 15s.
 9. **Marshall's Through America.**

Low's Standard Library of Travel and Adventure—continued.
10. Lansdell's Through Siberia. Illust. and unabridged, 10s. 6d.
11. Hill's From Home to Home.
12. Knight's Cruise of the Falcon.
13. Thomson's Through Masai Land.

Low's Standard Novels. Small post 8vo, cloth extra, 6s. each, unless otherwise stated.
A Daughter of Heth. By W. BLACK.
In Silk Attire. By W. BLACK.
Kilmeny. A Novel. By W. BLACK.
Lady Silverdale's Sweetheart. By W. BLACK.
Sunrise. By W. BLACK.
Three Feathers. By WILLIAM BLACK.
Alice Lorraine. By R. D. BLACKMORE.
Christowell, a Dartmoor Tale. By R. D. BLACKMORE.
Clara Vaughan. By R. D. BLACKMORE.
Cradock Nowell. By R. D. BLACKMORE.
Cripps the Carrier. By R. D. BLACKMORE.
Erema; or, My Father's Sin. By R. D. BLACKMORE.
Lorna Doone. By R. D. BLACKMORE. 25th Edition.
Mary Anerley. By R. D. BLACKMORE.
Tommy Upmore. By R. D. BLACKMORE.
Bonaventure. By G. W. CABLE.
An English Squire. By Miss COLERIDGE.
Some One Else. By Mrs. B. M. CROKER.
A Story of the Dragonnades. By Rev. E. GILLIAT, M.A.
A Laodicean. By THOMAS HARDY.
Far from the Madding Crowd. By THOMAS HARDY.
Mayor of Casterbridge. By THOMAS HARDY.
Pair of Blue Eyes. By THOMAS HARDY.
Return of the Native. By THOMAS HARDY.
The Hand of Ethelberta. By THOMAS HARDY.
The Trumpet Major. By THOMAS HARDY.
Two on a Tower. By THOMAS HARDY.
Old House at Sandwich. By JOSEPH HATTON.
Three Recruits. By JOSEPH HATTON.
A Golden Sorrow. By Mrs. CASHEL HOEY. New Edition.
A Stern Chase. By Mrs. CASHEL HOEY.
Out of Court. By Mrs. CASHEL HOEY.
Don John. By JEAN INGELOW.
John Jerome. By JEAN INGELOW. 5s.
Sarah de Berenger. By JEAN INGELOW.
Adela Cathcart. By GEORGE MAC DONALD.
Guild Court. By GEORGE MAC DONALD.
Mary Marston. By GEORGE MAC DONALD.
Stephen Archer. New Ed. of "Gifts." By GEORGE MAC DONALD.
The Vicar's Daughter. By GEORGE MAC DONALD.

Low's Standard Novels—continued.
    Weighed and Wanting. By GEORGE MAC DONALD.
    Diane. By Mrs. MACQUOID.
    Elinor Dryden. By Mrs. MACQUOID.
    My Lady Greensleeves. By HELEN MATHERS.
    Alaric Spenceley. By Mrs. J. H. RIDDELL.
    Daisies and Buttercups. By Mrs. J. H. RIDDELL.
    The Senior Partner. By Mrs. J. H. RIDDELL.
    A Struggle for Fame. By Mrs. J. H. RIDDELL.
    Jack's Courtship. By W. CLARK RUSSELL.
    John Holdsworth. By W. CLARK RUSSELL.
    A Sailor's Sweetheart. By W. CLARK RUSSELL.
    Sea Queen. By W. CLARK RUSSELL.
    Watch Below. By W. CLARK RUSSELL.
    Strange Voyage. By W. CLARK RUSSELL.
    Wreck of the Grosvenor. By W. CLARK RUSSELL.
    The Lady Maud. By W. CLARK RUSSELL.
    Little Loo. By W. CLARK RUSSELL.
    The Late Mrs. Null. By FRANK R. STOCKTON.
    Hundredth Man. By FRANK R. STOCKTON.
    Old Town Folk.
    We and our Neighbours.
    Poganuc People, their Loves and Lives. By Mrs. B. STOWE.
    Ben Hur: a Tale of the Christ. By LEW. WALLACE.
    Anne. By CONSTANCE FENIMORE WOOLSON.
    East Angels. By CONSTANCE FENIMORE WOOLSON.
    For the Major. By CONSTANCE FENIMORE WOOLSON. 5s.
    French Heiress in her own Chateau.

Low's Series of Standard Books for Boys. With numerous Illustrations, 2s. 6d.; gilt edges, 3s. 6d. each.
    Dick Cheveley. By W. H. G. KINGSTON.
    Heir of Kilfinnan. By W. H. G. KINGSTON.
    Off to the Wilds. By G. MANVILLE FENN.
    The Two Supercargoes. By W. H. G. KINGSTON.
    The Silver Cañon. By G. MANVILLE FENN.
    Under the Meteor Flag. By HARRY COLLINGWOOD.
    Jack Archer: a Tale of the Crimea. By G. A. HENTY.
    The Mutiny on Board the Ship Leander. By B. HELDMANN.
    With Axe and Rifle on the Western Prairies. By W. H. G. KINGSTON.
    Red Cloud, the Solitary Sioux: a Tale of the Great Prairie. By Col. Sir WM. BUTLER, K.C.B.
    The Voyage of the Aurora. By HARRY COLLINGWOOD.
    Charmouth Grange: a Tale of the 17th Century. By J. PERCY GROVES.
    Snowshoes and Canoes. By W. H. G. KINGSTON.
    The Son of the Constable of France. By LOUIS ROUSSELET.

Low's Series of Standard Books for Boys—continued.
  Captain Langford; or, Our Salt and Fresh Water Tutors.
    Edited by W. H. G. KINGSTON.
  The Cornet of Horse, a Tale of Marlborough's Wars. By
    G. A. HENTY.
  The Adventures of Captain Mago. By LEON CAHUN.
  Noble Words and Noble Needs.
  The King of the Tigers. By ROUSSELET.
  Hans Brinker; or, The Silver Skates. By Mrs. DODGE.
  The Drummer-Boy, a Story of the time of Washington. By
    ROUSSELET.
  Adventures in New Guinea: The Narrative of Louis Tregance.
  The Crusoes of Guiana. By BOUSSENARD.
  The Gold Seekers. A Sequel to the Above. By BOUSSENARD.
  Winning His Spurs, a Tale of the Crusades. By G. A. HENTY.
  The Blue Banner. By LEON CAHUN.

Low's Pocket Encyclopædia: a Compendium of General Knowledge for Ready Reference. Upwards of 25,000 References, with Plates. Imp. 32mo, ornamental cloth, marble edges, 3s. 6d.; roan, 4s. 6d.

Low's Handbook to the Charities of London. Edited and revised to date. Yearly, cloth, 1s. 6d.; paper, 1s.

McCORMICK (R.). Voyages of Discovery in the Arctic and Antarctic Seas in the "Erebus" and "Terror," in Search of Sir John Franklin, &c. With Maps and Lithos. 2 vols., royal 8vo, 52s. 6d.

MacDonald (G.) Orts. Small post 8vo, 6s.
—— See also "Low's Standard Novels."

McGoun (G. D. A. and L.) Handbook of Commercial Correspondence. Crown 8vo, 5s.

Macgregor (John) "Rob Roy" on the Baltic. 3rd Edition, small post 8vo, 2s. 6d.; cloth, gilt edges, 3s. 6d.

—— *A Thousand Miles in the "Rob Roy" Canoe.* 11th Edition, small post 8vo, 2s. 6d.; cloth, gilt edges, 3s. 6d.

—— *Voyage Alone in the Yawl "Rob Roy."* New Edition, with additions, small post 8vo, 5s.; 3s. 6d. and 2s. 6d.

Mackay (Charles) New Glossary of Obscure Words in Shakespeare. 21s.

Mackenzie (John) Austral Africa: Losing it or Ruling it? Illustrations and Maps. 2 vols., 8vo, 32s.

McLellan's Own Story: The War for the Union. Illust. 18s.

McMurdo (Edward) History of Portugal. 8vo, 21s.

Macquoid (Mrs.). See LOW'S STANDARD NOVELS.

Magazine. See ENGLISH ETCHINGS, HARPER.
Maginn (W.) Miscellanies. Prose and Verse. With Memoir.
  2 vols., crown 8vo, 24s.
*Main (Mrs.; Mrs. Fred Burnaby) High Life and Towers of
  Silence.* Illustrated, square 8vo, 10s. 6d.
Manitoba. See BRYCE.
Manning (E. F.) Delightful Thames. Illustrated. 4to, fancy
  boards, 5s.
Markham (Clements R.) The Fighting Veres, Sir F. and Sir H.
  8vo, 18s.
—— *War between Peru and Chili*, 1879-1881. Third Ed.
  Crown 8vo, with Maps, 10s. 6d.
—— See also "Foreign Countries," MAURY, and VERES.
Marshall (W. G.) Through America. New Ed., cr. 8vo, 7s. 6d.
*Martin (F. W.) Float Fishing and Spinning in the Nottingham
  Style.* New Edition. Crown 8vo, 2s. 6d.
Matthews (J. W., M.D.) Incwadi Yami : 20 *years in S. Africa.*
  With many Engravings, royal 8vo, 14s.
*Maury (Commander) Physical Geography of the Sea, and its
  Meteorology.* New Edition, with Charts and Diagrams, cr. 8vo, 6s.
—— *Life.* By his Daughter. Edited by Mr. CLEMENTS R.
  MARKHAM. With Frontispiece, 8vo, 12s. 6d.
Men of Mark : Portraits of the most Eminent Men of the Day,
  specially taken. Complete in Seven Vols., 4to, handsomely bound,
  gilt edges, 25s. each.
Mendelssohn Family (The), 1729—1847. From Letters and
  Journals. Translated. New Edition, 2 vols., 8vo, 30s.
Mendelssohn. See also " Great Musicians."
Merrifield's Nautical Astronomy. Crown 8vo, 7s. 6d.
Merrylees (J.) Carlsbad and its Environs. 7s. 6d. ; roan, 9s.
Mitchell (D. G. ; Ik. Marvel) Works. Uniform Edition,
  small 8vo, 5s. each.

Bound together.	Reveries of a Bachelor.
Doctor Johns.	Seven Stories, Basement and Attic.
Dream Life.	Wet Days at Edgewood.
Out-of-Town Places.	

Mitford (Mary Russell) Our Village. With 12 full-page and 157
  smaller Cuts. Cr. 4to, cloth, gilt edges, 21s. ; cheaper binding, 10s. 6d.
Milford (P.) Ned Stafford's Experiences in the United States. 5s.
*Moffatt (W.) Land and Work ; Depression, Agricultural and
  Commercial.* Crown 8vo, 5s.
Mohammed Benani : A Story of To-day. 8vo, 10s. 6d.

Mollett (J. W.) Illustrated Dictionary of Words used in Art and Archæology. Terms in Architecture, Arms, Bronzes, Christian Art, Colour, Costume, Decoration, Devices, Emblems, Heraldry, Lace, Personal Ornaments, Pottery, Painting, Sculpture, &c. Small 4to, 15s.

Moloney (Governor) Forestry of West Africa. 10s. 6d.

Money (E.) The Truth about America. New Edition. 2s. 6d.

Morley (H.) English Literature in the Reign of Victoria. 2000th volume of the Tauchnitz Collection of Authors. 18mo, 2s. 6d.

Morse (E. S.) Japanese Homes and their Surroundings. With more than 300 Illustrations. Re-issue, 10s. 6d.

Morwood. Our Gipsies in City, Tent, and Van. 8vo, 18s.

Moxon (Walter) Pilocereus Senilis. Fcap. 8vo, gilt top, 3s. 6d.

Muller (E.) Noble Words and Noble Deeds. Illustrated, gilt edges, 3s. 6d.; plainer binding, 2s. 6d.

Murray (E. C. Grenville) Memoirs. By his widow. 2 vols.

Music. See "Great Musicians."

NAPOLEON and Marie Louise: Memoirs. By Madame DURAND. 7s. 6d.

Nethercote (C. B.) Pytchley Hunt. With Anecdotes and Authorised Portraits. New Edition, crown 8vo, 8s. 6d.

New Zealand. See BRADSHAW.

New Zealand Rulers and Statesmen. See GISBORNE.

Nicholls (J. H. Kerry) The King Country: Explorations in New Zealand. Many Illustrations and Map. New Edition, 8vo, 21s.

Nisbet (Hume) Life and Nature Studies. With Etching by C. O. MURRAY. Crown 8vo, 6s.

Nordhoff (C.) California, for Health, Pleasure, and Residence. New Edition, 8vo, with Maps and Illustrations, 12s. 6d.

Norman (C. B.) The Corsairs of France. With Portraits and Map. 8vo, 18s.

Northbrook Gallery. Edited by LORD RONALD GOWER. 36 Permanent Photographs. Imperial 4to, 63s.; large paper, 105s.

Nott (Major) Wild Animals Photographed and Described. 35s.

Nursery Playmates (Prince of). 217 Coloured Pictures for Children by eminent Artists. Folio, in coloured boards, 6s.

O'BRIEN (R. B.) Fifty Years of Concessions to Ireland. With a Portrait of T. Drummond. Vol. I., 16s., II., 16s.

Orient Line Guide Book. By W. J. LOFTIE. 5s.

Orvis (C. F.) Fishing with the Fly. Illustrated. 8vo, 12*s.* 6*d.*
Our Little Ones in Heaven. Edited by the Rev. H. ROBBINS.
With Frontispiece after Sir JOSHUA REYNOLDS. New Edition, 5*s.*
Owen (Douglas) Marine Insurance Notes and Clauses. New Edition, 14*s.*

PALLISER (Mrs.) A History of Lace. New Edition, with additional cuts and text. 8vo, 21*s.*
—— *The China Collector's Pocket Companion.* With upwards of 1000 Illustrations of Marks and Monograms. Small 8vo, 5*s.*
Parkin (J.) Antidotal Treatment of Epidemic Cholera. 3*s.* 6*d.*
—— *Epidemiology in the Animal and Vegetable Kingdom.* Part I., crown 8vo, 3*s.* 6*d.*; Part II., 3*s.* 6*d.*
—— *Volcanic Origin of Epidemics.* Popular Edition, crown 8vo, 2*s.*
Pascoe (C. E.) London of To-Day. New Edition for the 1888 season, with many Illustrations, crown 8vo, 3*s.* 6*d.*
Payne (T. O.) Solomon's Temple and Capitol, Ark of the Flood and Tabernacle (four sections at 24*s.*), extra binding, 105*s.*
Pennell (H. Cholmondeley) Sporting Fish of Great Britain. 15*s.*; large paper, 30*s.*
—— *Modern Improvements in Fishing-tackle.* Crown 8vo, 2*s.*
Perelaer (M. T. H.) Ran Away from the Dutch; Borneo, &c. Illustrated, square 8vo, 7*s.* 6*d.*
Pharmacopœia of the United States of America. 8vo, 21*s.*
Phelps (Elizabeth Stuart) Madonna of the Tubs. 3*s.* 6*d.*
Philpot (H. J.) Diabetes Mellitus. Crown 8vo, 5*s.*
—— *Diet System.* Tables. I. Dyspepsia; II. Gout; III. Diabetes; IV. Corpulence. In cases, 1*s.* each.
Plunkett (Major G. T.) Primer of Orthographic Projection. Elementary Solid Geometry. With Problems and Exercises. 2*s.* 6*d.*
Poe (E. A.) The Raven. Illustr. by DORÉ. Imperial folio, 63*s.*
Poems of the Inner Life. Chiefly Modern. Small 8vo, 5*s.*
Polar Expeditions. See MCCORMICK.
Porcher (A.) Juvenile French Plays. With Notes and a Vocabulary. 18mo, 1*s.*
Porter (Admiral David D.) Naval History of Civil War. Portraits, Plans, &c. 4to, 25*s.*
Porter (Noah) Elements of Moral Science. 10*s.* 6*d.*
Portraits of Celebrated Race-horses of the Past and Present Centuries, with Pedigrees and Performances. 4 vols., 4to, 42*s.* per vol.

Powles (*L. D.*) *Land of the Pink Pearl: Life in the Bahamas.*
8vo, 10s. 6d.
Poynter (*Edward J.*, *R.A.*). See " Illustrated Text-books."
Pritt (*T. E.*) *North Country Flies.* Illustrated from the
Author's Drawings. 10s. 6d.
Publishers' Circular (*The*), *and General Record of British and*
Foreign Literature. Published on the 1st and 15th of every Month, 3d.

RAMBAUD. History of Russia. New Edition, Illustrated.
3 vols., 8vo, 21s.
Reber. History of Mediæval Art. Translated by CLARKE.
422 Illustrations and Glossary. 8vo,
Redford (*G.*) *Ancient Sculpture.* New Ed. Crown 8vo, 10s. 6d.
Richards (*W.*) *Aluminium: its History, Occurrence, &c.*
Illustrated, crown 8vo, 12s. 6d.
Richter (*Dr. Jean Paul*) *Italian Art in the National Gallery.*
4to. Illustrated. Cloth gilt, £2 2s.; half-morocco, uncut, £2 12s. 6d.
—— See also LEONARDO DA VINCI.
Riddell (*Mrs. J. H.*) See LOW'S STANDARD NOVELS.
Robertson (*Anne J.*) *Myself and my Relatives.* New Edition,
crown 8vo, 5s.
Robin Hood; Merry Adventures of. Written and illustrated
by HOWARD PYLE. Imperial 8vo, 15s.
Robinson (*Phil.*) *In my Indian Garden.* New Edition, 16mo,
limp cloth, 2s.
—— *Noah's Ark. Unnatural History.* Sm. post 8vo, 12s. 6d.
—— *Sinners and Saints: a Tour across the United States of*
America, and Round them. Crown 8vo, 10s. 6d.
—— *Under the Punkah.* New Ed., cr. 8vo, limp cloth, 2s.
Rockstro (*W. S.*) *History of Music.* New Edition. 8vo, 14s.
Roland, The Story of. Crown 8vo, illustrated, 6s.
Rolfe (*Eustace Neville*) *Pompeii, Popular and Practical.* Cr.
8vo, 7s. 6d.
Rome and the Environs. 3s.
Rose (*J.*) *Complete Practical Machinist.* New Ed., 12mo, 12s. 6d.
—— *Key to Engines and Engine-running.* Crown 8vo, 8s. 6d.
—— *Mechanical Drawing.* Illustrated, small 4to, 16s.
—— *Modern Steam Engines.* Illustrated. 31s. 6d.
Rose Library. Each volume, 1s. Many are illustrated—
Little Women. By LOUISA M. ALCOTT.
Little Women Wedded. Forming a Sequel to " Little Women.

Rose Library (The)—continued.
    Little Women and Little Women Wedded. 1 vol., cloth gilt, 3s. 6d.
    Little Men. By L. M. ALCOTT. Double vol., 2s.; cloth gilt, 3s. 6d.
    An Old-Fashioned Girl. By LOUISA M. ALCOTT. 2s.; cloth, 3s. 6d.
    Work. A Story of Experience. By L. M. ALCOTT. 3s. 6d.; 2 vols., 1s. each.
    Stowe (Mrs. H. B.) The Pearl of Orr's Island.
    ——— **The Minister's Wooing.**
    ——— **We and our Neighbours.** 2s.; cloth gilt, 6s.
    ——— **My Wife and I.** 2s.
    Hans Brinker; or, the Silver Skates. By Mrs. DODGE. Also 5s.
    My Study Windows. By J. R. LOWELL.
    The Guardian Angel. By OLIVER WENDELL HOLMES.
    My Summer in a Garden. By C. D. WARNER.
    Dred. By Mrs. BEECHER STOWE. 2s.; cloth gilt, 3s. 6d.
    City Ballads. New Ed. 16mo. By WILL CARLETON.
    Farm Ballads. By WILL CARLETON.
    Farm Festivals. By WILL CARLETON.
    Farm Legends. By WILL CARLETON.
    Farm Ballads, Festivals, and Legends. One vol., cloth, 3s. 6d.
    The Rose in Bloom. By L. M. ALCOTT. 2s.; cloth gilt, 3s. 6d.
    Eight Cousins. By L. M. ALCOTT. 2s.; cloth gilt, 3s. 6d.
    Under the Lilacs. By L. M. ALCOTT. 2s.; also 3s. 6d.
    Baby Rue. By C. M. CLAY.
    Undiscovered Country. By W. D. HOWELLS.
    Clients of Dr. Bernagius. By L. BIART. 2 parts.
    Silver Pitchers. By LOUISA M. ALCOTT. Cloth, 3s. 6d.
    Jimmy's Cruise in the "Pinafore," and other Tales. By LOUISA M. ALCOTT. 2s.; cloth gilt, 3s. 6d.
    Jack and Jill. By LOUISA M. ALCOTT. 2s.; Illustrated, 5s.
    Hitherto. By the Author of the "Gayworthys." 2 vols., 1s. each; 1 vol., cloth gilt, 3s. 6d.
    A Gentleman of Leisure. A Novel. By EDGAR FAWCETT. 1s.

Ross (Mars) and Stonehewer Cooper. Highlands of Cantabria; or, Three Days from England. Illustrations and Map, 8vo, 21s.

Rothschilds, the Financial Rulers of Nations. By JOHN REEVES. Crown 8vo, 7s. 6d.

Rousselet (Louis) Son of the Constable of France. Small post 8vo, numerous Illustrations, gilt edges, 3s. 6d.; plainer, 2s. 6d.

——— *King of the Tigers: a Story of Central India.* Illustrated. Small post 8vo, gilt, 3s. 6d.; plainer, 2s. 6d.

——— *Drummer Boy.* Illustrated. Small post 8vo, gilt edges, 3s. 6d.; plainer, 2s. 6d.

Russell (W. Clark) Jack's Courtship. New Ed., small post 8vo, 6s.

Russell (W. Clark) English Channel Ports and the Estate of the East and West India Dock Company. Crown 8vo, 1s.
——— *Frozen Pirate.* New Ed., Illust., 8vo, 6s.
——— *Sailor's Language.* Illustrated. Crown 8vo, 3s. 6d.
——— *Sea Queen.* New Ed., small post 8vo, 6s.
——— *Strange Voyage.* New Ed., small post 8vo, 6s.
——— *The Lady Maud.* New Ed., small post 8vo, 6s.
——— *Wreck of the Grosvenor.* Small post 8vo, 6s.; 4to, sewed, 6d.

SAINTS and their Symbols: A Companion in the Churches and Picture Galleries of Europe. Illustrated. Royal 16mo, 3s. 6d.
Samuels (Capt. J. S.) From Forecastle to Cabin : Autobiography. Illustrated. Crown 8vo, 8s. 6d.; also with fewer Illustrations, cloth, 2s.; paper, 1s.
Sanalands (J. P.) How to Develop Vocal Power. 1s.
Saunders (A.) Our Domestic Birds: Poultry in England and New Zealand. Crown 8vo, 6s.
——— *Our Horses : the Best Muscles controlled by the Best* Brains. 6s.
Scherr (Prof. F.) History of English Literature. Cr. 8vo, 8s. 6d.
Schley. Rescue of Greely. Maps and Illustrations, 8vo, 12s. 6d.
Schuyler (Eugène) American Diplomacy and the Furtherance of Commerce. 12s. 6d.
——— *The Life of Peter the Great.* 2 vols., 8vo, 32s.
Schweinfurth (Georg) Heart of Africa. 2 vols., crown 8vo, 15s.
Scott (Leader) Renaissance of Art in Italy. 4to, 31s. 6d.
——— *Sculpture, Renaissance and Modern.* 5s.
Semmes (Adm. Raphael) Service Afloat : The "Sumter" and the "Alabama." Illustrated. Royal 8vo, 16s.
Senior (W.) Near and Far : an Angler's Sketches of Home Sport and Colonial Life. Crown 8vo, 6s.
——— *Waterside Sketches.* Imp. 32mo, 1s. 6d.; boards, 1s.
Shakespeare. Edited by R. GRANT WHITE. 3 vols., crown 8vo, gilt top, 36s.; *édition de luxe*, 6 vols., 8vo, cloth extra, 63s.
Shakespeare's Heroines : Studies by Living English Painters. 105s.; artists' proofs, 630s.
Shakespeare. See also CUNDALL, DETHRONING, DONNELLY, MACKAY, and WHITE (R. GRANT).
Sharpe (R. Bowdler) Birds in Nature. 40 coloured plates and text. 4to. In preparation.

Sidney (Sir Philip) Arcadia. New Edition, 6s.
Siegfried, The Story of. Illustrated, crown 8vo, cloth, 6s.
Simon. China: its Social Life. Crown 8vo, 6s.
Simson (A.) Wilds of Ecuador and Exploration of the Putumayor River. Crown 8vo, 8s. 6d.
Sinclair (Mrs.) Indigenous Flowers of the Hawaiian Islands. 44 Plates in Colour. Imp. folio, extra binding, gilt edges, 31s. 6d.
Sloane (T. O.) Home Experiments in Science for Old and Young. Crown 8vo, 6s.
Smith (G.) Assyrian Explorations. Illust. New Ed., 8vo, 18s.
—————— *The Chaldean Account of Genesis.* With many Illustrations. 16s. New Ed. By Professor Sayce. 8vo, 18s.
Smith (G. Barnett) William I. and the German Empire. New Ed., 8vo, 3s. 6d.
Smith (J. Moyr) Wooing of Æthra. Illustrated. 32mo, 1s.
Smith (Sydney) Life and Times. By Stuart J. Reid. Illustrated. 8vo, 21s.
Smith (W. R.) Laws concerning Public Health. 8vo, 31s. 6d.
Spiers' French Dictionary. 29th Edition, remodelled. 2 vols., 8vo, 18s.; half bound, 21s.
Spry (W. J. J., R.N., F.R.G.S.) Cruise of H.M.S. "Challenger." With Illustrations. 8vo, 18s. Cheap Edit., crown 8vo, 7s. 6d.
Spyri (Joh.) Heidi's Early Experiences: a Story for Children and those who love Children. Illustrated, small post 8vo, 4s. 6d.
—————— *Heidi's Further Experiences.* Illust., sm. post 8vo, 4s. 6d
Start (J. W. K.) Junior Mensuration Exercises. 8d.
Stanley (H. M.) Congo, and Founding its Free State. Illustrated, 2 vols., 8vo, 42s.; re-issue, 2 vols. 8vo, 21s.
—————— *How I Found Livingstone.* 8vo, 10s. 6d.; cr. 8vo, 7s. 6d.
—————— *Through the Dark Continent.* Crown 8vo, 12s. 6d.
Stenhouse (Mrs.) An Englishwoman in Utah. Crown 8vo, 2s. 6d.
Sterry (J. Ashby) Cucumber Chronicles. 5s.
Stevens (E. W.) Fly-Fishing in Maine Lakes. 8s. 6d.
Stevens (T.) Around the World on a Bicycle. Over 100 Illustrations. 8vo, 16s. Vol. II. in preparation.
Stockton (Frank R.) Rudder Grange. 3s. 6d.
—————— *The Casting Away of Mrs. Lecks and Mrs. Aleshine.* 1s.
—————— *The Dusantes.* Sequel to the above. Sewed, 1s.; this and the preceding book in one volume, cloth, 2s. 6d.
—————— *The Hundredth Man.* Small post 8vo, 6s.
—————— *The Late Mrs. Null.* Small post 8vo, 6s.

Stockton (Frank R.) The Story of Viteau. Illust. Cr. 8vo, 5s.
—— See also LOW'S STANDARD NOVELS.
Stoker (Bram) Under the Sunset. Crown 8vo, 6s.
Storer (Professor F. H.) Agriculture in its Relations to Chemistry. 2 vols., 8vo, 25s.
Stowe (Mrs. Beecher) Dred. Cloth, gilt edges, 3s. 6d.; boards, 2s.
—— *Little Foxes.* Cheap Ed., 1s.; Library Edition, 4s. 6d.
—— *Old Town Folk.* 6s.
—— *Old Town Fireside Stories.* Cloth extra, 3s. 6d.
—— *We and our Neighbours.* 6s.
—— *Poganuc People.* 6s.
—— *Chimney Corner.* 1s.; cloth, 1s. 6d.
—— See also ROSE LIBRARY.
Stuttfield (Hugh E. M.) El Maghreb: 1200 Miles' Ride through Marocco. 8s. 6d.
Sullivan (A. M.) Nutshell History of Ireland. Paper boards, 6d.

TAINE (H. A.) " Origines." Translated by JOHN DURAND.
    I. **The Ancient Regime.** Demy 8vo, cloth, 16s.
    II. **The French Revolution.** Vol. 1.   do.
    III. **Do.**   do.   Vol. 2.   do.
    IV. **Do.**   do.   Vol. 3.   do.
Talbot (Hon. E.) A Letter on Emigration. 1s.
Tauchnitz's English Editions of German Authors. Each volume, cloth flexible, 2s.; or sewed, 1s. 6d. (Catalogues post free.)
Tauchnitz (B.) German Dictionary. 2s.; paper, 1s. 6d.; roan, 2s. 6d.
—— *French Dictionary.* 2s.; paper, 1s. 6d.; roan, 2s. 6d.
—— *Italian Dictionary.* 2s.; paper, 1s. 6d.; roan, 2s. 6d.
—— *Latin Dictionary.* 2s.; paper, 1s. 6d.; roan, 2s. 6d.
—— *Spanish and English.* 2s.; paper, 1s. 6d.; roan, 2s. 6d.
—— *Spanish and French.* 2s.; paper, 1s. 6d.; roan, 2s. 6d.
Taylor (R. L.) Chemical Analysis Tables. 1s.
—— *Chemistry for Beginners.* Small 8vo, 1s. 6d.
Taylor (W. M.) Elijah. Crown 8vo, 6s.
—— *Moses the Lawgiver.* Crown 8vo, 7s. 6d.
—— *Joseph the Prime Minister.* 6s.
—— *Paul the Missionary.* Crown 8vo, 7s. 6d.
Techno-Chemical Receipt Book. With additions by BRANNT and WAHL. 10s. 6d.

Technological Dictionary. See TOLHAUSEN.
Thausing (Prof.) Malt and the Fabrication of Beer. 8vo, 45s.
Theakston (M.) British Angling Flies. Illustrated. Cr. 8vo, 5s.
Thomson (Jos.) Central African Lakes. New edition, 2 vols. in one, crown 8vo, 7s. 6d.
—— *Through Masai Land.* Illust. 21s.; new edition, 7s. 6d.
——— *and Harris-Smith. Ulu: an African Romance.* 2 vols., crown 8vo, 12s.
Thomson (W.) Algebra for Colleges and Schools. With Answers, 5s.; without, 4s. 6d.; Answers separate, 1s. 6d.
Tolhausen. Technological German, English, and French Dictionary. Vols. I., II., with Supplement, 12s. 6d. each; III., 9s.; Supplement, cr. 8vo, 3s. 6d.
Trollope (Anthony) Thompson Hall. 1s.
Tromholt (S.) Under the Rays of the Aurora Borealis. By C. SIEWERS. Photographs and Portraits. 2 vols., 8vo, 30s.
Tucker (W. J.) Life and Society in Eastern Europe. 15s.
Tupper (Martin Farquhar) My Life as an Author. 14s.
Turner (Edward) Studies in Russian Literature. Cr. 8vo, 8s. 6d.
Twenty Original Etchings by French, &c., Artists. Edited by S. R. KÖHLER. 147s. and 63s.

UPTON (H.) Manual of Practical Dairy Farming. Cr. 8vo, 2s.

VALLANCE (Lucy) Paul's Birthday. 3s. 6d.; also 1s.

Van Dam. Land of Rubens; a companion for visitors to Belgium. Crown 8vo.
Van Kampen (S. R.) Nicholas Godfried Van Kampen: a Biographical Sketch. By SAMUEL R. VAN CAMPEN.
Variations of Fortune. Sketches of some of the Old Towns of Italy. 3s. 6d.
Veres. Biography of Sir Francis Vere and Lord Vere, leading Generals in the Netherlands. By CLEMENTS R. MARKHAM. 8vo, 18s.
Victoria (Queen) Life of. By GRACE GREENWOOD. Illust. 6s.
Vincent (Mrs. Howard) Forty Thousand Miles over Land and Water. With Illustrations. New Edit., 3s. 6d.
Viollet-le-Duc (E.) Lectures on Architecture. Translated by BENJAMIN BUCKNALL, Architect. 2 vols., super-royal 8vo, £3 3s.

BOOKS BY JULES VERNE.

WORKS.	Large Crown 8vo. Containing 350 to 600 pp. and from 50 to 100 full-page illustrations.		Containing the whole of the text with some illustrations.	
	In very handsome cloth binding, gilt edges.	In plainer binding, plain edges.	In cloth binding, gilt edges, smaller type.	Coloured boards.
	s. d.	s. d.	s. d.	
20,000 Leagues under the Sea. Parts I. and II.	10 6	5 0	3 6	2 vols., 1s. each.
Hector Servadac	10 6	5 0	3 6	2 vols., 1s. each.
The Fur Country	10 6	5 0	3 6	2 vols., 1s. each.
The Earth to the Moon and a Trip round it	10 6	5 0	2 vols., 2s. ca.	2 vols., 1s. each.
Michael Strogoff	10 6	5 0	3 6	2 vols., 1s. each.
Dick Sands, the Boy Captain	10 6	5 0	3 6	2 vols., 1s. each.
Five Weeks in a Balloon	7 6	3 6	2 0	1s. 0d.
Adventures of Three Englishmen and Three Russians	7 6	3 6	2 0	1 0
Round the World in Eighty Days	7 6	3 6	2 0	1 0
A Floating City	7 6	3 6	2 0	1 0
The Blockade Runners			2 0	1 0
Dr. Ox's Experiment	—	—	2 0	1 0
A Winter amid the Ice	—	—	2 0	1 0
Survivors of the "Chancellor"	7 6	3 6	3 6	2 vols., 1s. each.
Martin Paz			2 0	1s. 0d.
The Mysterious Island, 3 vols.:—	22 6	10 6	6 0	3 0
I. Dropped from the Clouds	7 6	3 6	2 0	1 0
II. Abandoned	7 6	3 6	2 0	1 0
III. Secret of the Island	7 6	3 6	2 0	1 0
The Child of the Cavern	7 6	3 6	2 0	1 0
The Begum's Fortune	7 6	3 6	2 0	1 0
The Tribulations of a Chinaman	7 6	3 6	2 0	1 0
The Steam House, 2 vols.:—				
I. Demon of Cawnpore	7 6	3 6	2 0	1 0
II. Tigers and Traitors	7 6	3 6	2 0	1 0
The Giant Raft, 2 vols.:—				
I. 800 Leagues on the Amazon	7 6	3 6	2 0	1 0
II. The Cryptogram	7 6	3 6	2 0	1 0
The Green Ray	6 0	5 0	—	1 0
Godfrey Morgan	7 6	3 6	2 0	1 0
Kéraban the Inflexible:—				
I. Captain of the "Guidara"	7 6	3 6	2 0	1 0
II. Scarpante the Spy	7 6	3 6	2 0	1 0
The Archipelago on Fire	7 6	3 6	2 0	1 0
The Vanished Diamond	7 6	3 6	2 0	1 0
Mathias Sandorf	10 6			
The Lottery Ticket	7 6			
Clipper of the Clouds	7 6			
North against South	7 6			

CELEBRATED TRAVELS AND TRAVELLERS. 3 vols. 8vo, 600 pp., 100 full-page illustrations, 12s. 6d., gilt edges, 14s. each:—(1) THE EXPLORATION OF THE WORLD. (2) THE GREAT NAVIGATORS OF THE EIGHTEENTH CENTURY. (3) THE GREAT EXPLORERS OF THE NINETEENTH CENTURY.

WAKEFIELD. *Aix-les-Bains: Bathing and Attractions.* 2s. 6d.
Wallace (L.) Ben Hur: A Tale of the Christ. New Edition, crown 8vo, 6s.
Waller (Rev. C. H.) The Names on the Gates of Pearl, and other Studies. New Edition. Crown 8vo, cloth extra, 3s. 6d.
—— *Words in the Greek Testament.* Part I. Grammar. Small post 8vo, cloth, 2s. 6d. Part II. Vocabulary, 2s. 6d.
—— *Adoption and the Covenant.* On Confirmation. 2s. 6d.
—— *Silver Sockets; and other Shadows of Redemption.* Sermons at Christ Church, Hampstead. Small post 8vo, 6s.
Walsh (A. S.) Mary, Queen of the House of David. 8vo, 3s. 6d.
Walton (Iz.) Wallet Book, CIƆIƆLXXXV. Crown 8vo, half vellum, 21s.; large paper, 42s.
—— *Compleat Angler.* Lea and Dove Edition. Ed. by R. B. MARSTON. With full-page Photogravures on India paper, and the Woodcuts on India paper from blocks. 4to, half-morocco, 105s.; large paper, royal 4to, full dark green morocco, gilt top, 210s.
Walton (T. H.) Coal Mining. With Illustrations. 4to, 25s.
Warner (C. D.) My Summer in a Garden. Boards, 1s.; leatherette, 1s. 6d.; cloth, 2s.
—— *Their Pilgrimage.* Illustrated by C. S. REINHART. 8vo, 7s. 6d.
Warren (W. F.) Paradise Found; the North Pole the Cradle of the Human Race. Illustrated. Crown 8vo, 12s. 6d.
Washington Irving's Little Britain. Square crown 8vo, 6s.
Wells (H. P.) American Salmon Fisherman. 6s.
—— *Fly Rods and Fly Tackle.* Illustrated. 10s. 6d.
Wells (J. W.) Three Thousand Miles through Brazil. Illustrated from Original Sketches. 2 vols. 8vo, 32s.
Wenzel (O.) Directory of Chemical Products of the German Empire, 21s.
White (R. Grant) England Without and Within. Crown 8vo, 10s. 6d.
—— *Every-day English.* 10s. 6d.
—— *Fate of Mansfield Humphreys, &c.* Crown 8vo, 6s.
—— *Studies in Shakespeare.* 10s. 6d.
—— *Words and their Uses.* New Edit., crown 8vo, 5s.

Whittier (J. G.) The King's Missive, and later Poems. 18mo, choice parchment cover, 3s. 6d.

―――― *St. Gregory's Guest, &c.* Recent Poems. 5s.

William I. and the German Empire. By G. BARNETT SMITH. New Edition, 3s. 6d.

Willis-Bund (J.) Salmon Problems. 3s. 6d.; boards, 2s. 6d.

Wills (Dr. C. J.) Persia as it is. Crown 8vo, 8s. 6d.

Wills, A Few Hints on Proving, without Professional Assistance. By a PROBATE COURT OFFICIAL. 8th Edition, revised, with Forms of Wills, Residuary Accounts, &c. Fcap. 8vo, cloth limp, 1s.

Wilmot (A.) Poetry of South Africa. Collected and arranged. 8vo, 6s.

Wilson (Dr. Andrew) Health for the People. Cr. 8vo, 7s. 6d.

Winsor (Justin) Narrative and Critical History of America. 8 vols., 30s. each; large paper, per vol., 63s. (Vols. I. to VI. are ready).

Woolsey. Introduction to International Law. 5th Ed., 18s.

Woolson (Constance F.) See " Low's Standard Novels."

Wright (H.) Friendship of God. Portrait, &c. Crown 8vo, 6s.

Wright (T.) Town of Cowper, Olney, &c. 6s.

Written to Order; the Journeyings of an Irresponsible Egotist. By the Author of "A Day of my Life at Eton." Crown 8vo, 6s.

YRIARTE (Charles) Florence: its History. Translated by C. B. PITMAN. Illustrated with 500 Engravings. Large imperial 4to, extra binding, gilt edges, 63s.; or 12 Parts, 5s. each.

History; the Medici; the Humanists; letters; arts; the Renaissance; illustrious Florentines; Etruscan art; monuments; sculpture; painting.

London:

SAMPSON LOW, MARSTON, SEARLE, & RIVINGTON, LD.,

St. Dunstan's House,

FETTER LANE, FLEET STREET, E.C.

www.ingramcontent.com/pod-product-compliance
Lightning Source LLC
Chambersburg PA
CBHW051739300426
44115CB00007B/624